D1522917

Hollywood Presents
# JULES VERNE

# JULES VERNE

## The Father of
## Science Fiction
## on Screen

### BRIAN TAVES

UNIVERSITY PRESS OF KENTUCKY

Copyright © 2015 by The University Press of Kentucky

Scholarly publisher for the Commonwealth,
serving Bellarmine University, Berea College, Centre College of Kentucky,
Eastern Kentucky University, The Filson Historical Society, Georgetown
College, Kentucky Historical Society, Kentucky State University, Morehead
State University, Murray State University,
Northern Kentucky University, Transylvania University, University of
Kentucky, University of Louisville, and Western Kentucky University.
All rights reserved.

*Editorial and Sales Offices:* The University Press of Kentucky
663 South Limestone Street, Lexington, Kentucky 40508-4008
www.kentuckypress.com

Cataloging-in-Publication data is available from the Library of Congress.

ISBN 978-0-8131-6112-9 (hardcover : alk. paper)
ISBN 978-0-8131-6114-3 (pdf)
ISBN 978-0-8131-6113-6 (epub)

This book is printed on acid-free paper meeting
the requirements of the American National Standard
for Permanence in Paper for Printed Library Materials.

Manufactured in the United States of America.

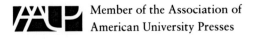 Member of the Association of
American University Presses

For the memory of Larry Graber—cousin, mentor, inspiration

# Contents

# How a French Author Met Hollywood

From the outset of his career as a novelist in the 1860s, Jules Verne was an author who broke the rules. He not only defined a new genre, science fiction, but also appealed to a wide audience—readers of all ages around the world. Now, going on 150 years later, his novels continue to sell in all languages as well as in condensations for children and comic books.

In the 1870s, Verne's stories became stage blockbusters, and they remain staples of the theater. By the beginning of the twentieth century, his tales emerged as mainstays of the screen. From trick films to the introduction of special effects, color, widescreen, and three-dimensional filming, and in television specials, series, and miniseries, whether live action or animation, Verne has conquered every screen form. In these pages, I discuss all of these forms, and the reader will learn how Verne films have also resonated in theme parks and video games.

Just as Verne's writing broke the rules, so too do the screen adaptations. There is no one-to-one correspondence between a novel and a film; Verne's stories have given rise to multiple versions, adjusted for various mediums, produced for all audiences. To understand Verne films involves not only discussing famous titles, spectacles that have triumphed over the movie screen and echo on television and video release, but also analyzing others that, although less recognized, are no less deserving of attention.

Few writers have enjoyed such enduring screen success as Verne in so many forms. In these pages, there has been no need to reach for or suggest abstract influences or tenuous links between these films and the author: they all are squarely rooted in his writing. Such films nearly always advertise their source; the phrase "based on Verne" presells a film and is a form of box office insurance no less than a big-name star. At the same time, Verne films reveal a historical development, an intertextuality, as they interact with the influences of previous versions, screen technologies, and publishers' treatments of the author. Verne films continue to evolve today in ever more complex recognition of the fact that when we are speaking of Verne, the text of his writing essentially now includes an awareness of his screen adaptations.

If you pronounce Jules Verne's name with the proper French lilt, outside of some academic circles you'll receive only bewildered stares. When his works were presented in 1970 to my sixth-grade class through Scholastic Book Services, school chums called him "Julius" Verne; Isaac Asimov recounted how he thought the name was "Jewels Voine."[1] Whatever the pronunciation of Jules Verne's name, he has long been the best-loved French author among English speakers, who have adopted him as one of their own—and screen adaptations have played a major role in public understanding of his work.

Even for those few who have not read Jules Verne (1828–1905), the author's very name conjures a submarine traveling twenty thousand leagues under the sea, a tour against the clock around the world in eighty days, a trip from the earth to the moon, and a journey to the center of the earth. Verne's name is synonymous with scientific progress and the challenges, glories, and disasters it has brought. More than simply an author, Verne is a phenomenon of the scientific age; in him we see both a reflection of our advances and the perils they have engendered.

Despite Verne's adoption of a nineteenth-century romantic sensibility, his enthusiasm for the idea of "progress" was tempered from the time of his earliest stories, whether by the insanity of the Arctic explorer in *Journeys and Adventures of Captain Hatteras* (1866) or by Captain Nemo's use of the *Nautilus* as a warship in *Twenty Thousand Leagues under the Seas* (1870). Verne's publisher rejected his 1863 novel *Paris in the 20th Century* as too downbeat, and it was not published until some 130 years later to recognition as a pioneering dystopia. Verne introduced not only science into the novel but also the attendant social concerns, revealing technology's effect on humankind. He never concentrated purely on gadgets or machines but rather on their effect and context, regarding science, society, and politics as intertwined.[2] He was one of the first authors to study the relationship between humanity and nature, noting his heroes' practical dependence on the environment in a global perspective. Verne's works are shaped by conditions around the world, and Vernian characters' motivations are less personal than the result of political, colonial, and economic forces, such as Nemo's battle against British imperialism or the struggle for Hungarian nationalism in *Mathias Sandorf* (1885).

The nineteenth- and early-twentieth-century conceptions of Verne as a prophet of the future have been increasingly supplanted by recognition of his status as a literary figure. On the European continent, Verne has been revived and esteemed since the 1950s, studied from a variety of ideological and methodological viewpoints, and utilized by many of the most prominent figures in contemporary theory and criticism. Structuralists and post-structuralists as well as critics from the Marxist to the psychoanalytic schools have found the Verne canon especially amenable to their endeavors.

Growing up in the seaport hub of Nantes familiarized the young Jules with the lure of distant horizons. A contradictory influence emanated from Verne's father, a lawyer who enforced a strict, by-the-clock life on his family, tendencies that Verne would later mock in his characterization of the human machine, Phileas Fogg, in *Around the World in Eighty Days* (1873). Resolving the conflicting influences of rationality and imagination resulted in a duality that would form the foundation of Verne's fiction; he found his creative métier by combining scientific background and adventurous incident through science fiction.[3]

In 1886, Verne was shot by his brother's son, Gaston, who had become mentally unbalanced; the bullets left Verne walking with a cane, and Gaston was sent to an asylum. Yet Verne rebounded by becoming a member of the town council of his adopted city of Amiens; he concealed conflicts in his life and writing under a conventional, respectable surface, which Jean Chesneaux calls the "bourgeois facade."[4] His radical, unconventional inclinations were exposed only in his fiction, Walter

James Miller argues, confronting the reader with rebels and dissidents "who have rejected all shackles of society and convention," such outcasts as Hatteras, Nemo, and Robur, "the master of the world" in the 1904 novel of that title.[5] Indeed, Verne's own grandson regarded him as an undercover revolutionary with the temperament of an anarchist.[6] Yet only his Bohemian life in Paris while he tried to become a playwright at the end of the 1840s and the early 1850s was in any way unusual, and even that period fell along familiar, accepted lines for a struggling artist. Verne disdained Rousseau, opposed the Paris "commune," and was antifeminist and anti-Dreyfus.

One of the most vital aspects of Verne's novels is their underlying psychological power, with a combination of idealism, disillusionment, and a streak of misanthropy projected onto many of his characters.[7] These characters are often mythic types, larger than life, epitomizing tendencies, emotions, and ideologies that become their dominant traits; Verne was more interested in exploring these extremes than in creating three-dimensional human beings. His oeuvre is filled with obsessed individuals, often hostile or indifferent to the people around them and to the mores they impact, although these individuals are not simplistic "mad scientist"–style caricatures. Hatteras is attracted like a magnet to the pole; Robur to the air; Nemo to the sea; the Baltimore Gun Club to artillery that can provide travel to the moon or change Earth's axis (as in *From the Earth to the Moon,* 1865; *Around the Moon,* 1869; *Topsy-turvy,* 1889); Godfrey Morgan to imitating Robinson Crusoe (*The School for Robinsons,* 1882); Palmyrin Rosette to his comet (*Hector Servadac,* 1877); Lidenbrock to the center of the earth; Fogg to speed and Fix to pursuing Fogg (*Around the World in Eighty Days*).[8]

These characters hardly seem the type to become favorites among American readers, yet they did. This popularity was in part a result of Verne's fascination with the United States, which in the nineteenth century was still part of the new world and a nation symbolizing hope and the future. More than a third of Verne's novels feature the nation, its citizens, or the American continent. The United States was the land of Yankee ingenuity, inventiveness, and industrialization, part of the technological wave that formed the undercurrent for his series "Extraordinary Journeys." The prototype of such a practical American is found in the characterization of Captain Cyrus Smith in *The Mysterious Island* (1875). Despite the lack of tools and supplies, Smith transforms the castaways' deserted Lincoln Island into a metaphor of the Industrial Revolution through his knowledgeable use of raw materials.

However, Verne also saw the United States as full of cranks, frauds, and schemers for whom no undertaking was too audacious or extravagant and who often were possessed by the hubris of self-destructive greed: science creates a doomed millionaire's city in *Propeller Island* (1895); the nation is transfixed by the competition engendered in *The Will of an Eccentric* (1899); Virginia astronomers claim priority over discovering gold from outer space in *The Hunt for the Meteor* (1908).[9] New York is the location of the Barnum-type huckster who claims to have unearthed the skeleton of a 120-foot-tall prehistoric man in "The Humbug" (1910). To Verne, the United States was a center of mechanical engineering, whether the hot-air balloons of the Weldon Society in *Robur the Conqueror* (1886) or the exploits of the Baltimore Gun Club. In proclaiming himself "master of the world," an even more dangerous engineer, Robur, centers his exploits in North America, revealing an unexplained affinity that obliges him to exhibit his final vehicle, the *Terror*, nowhere else.

The sincerity of Verne's interest in the United States is demonstrated by the fact that he had already used this country as a setting for *From the Earth to the Moon* and *The Blockade Runners* (1865) before his books were discovered in America through English-language translation. Verne made his only journey to the United States in the spring of 1867, a time when he was virtually unknown in the English-speaking world, although his books were already best sellers in France. The highlight of his trip was a visit to Niagara Falls, the memory of which proved so durable that more than two decades later he laid pivotal episodes of several subsequent novels there and recounted his journey in *A Floating City* (1871). Verne hoped to return someday, until advancing age and ill health finally made such a trip impossible.

English readers caught up with their French brethren during the 1870s and literally could not get enough of Verne for the next twenty-five years. His works began their regular serial and book publication, and every new story was eagerly awaited as the product of a reliably exciting and imaginative author. He was in the unusual and enviable position of writing books that appealed in their totality to adults but were still accessible to young people, and this ability to write on multiple levels was one of his outstanding talents.[10] Like his predecessor and model Edgar Allan Poe, Verne offered thrilling surfaces but also deep literary subtexts. In France, Verne's books were awarded as school prizes, and around the world his volumes became a typical holiday gift for adolescent readers, a status they still retain.[11]

His popularity may have been due in part not only to his frequent use of American settings and characters but also to his use of familiar generic traditions—historical adventure, the Robinsonade, the Poe-style fantasy—that were internationally recognized. In the first flush of enthusiasm for Verne, critics hailed his writing as a new form of entertainment. There had been no predecessor by which to judge his work, and not until the advent of H. G. Wells (1866–1946) was there a literary yardstick by which Verne could be compared.

By the late 1880s, imitators appeared in many countries who often outsold Verne's later works. Many readers, however, did not know of the literary damage committed by the poor translations that were often rushed into publication for the mass market of the day. In rendering Verne's French to English, translators felt free to omit or alter sections, and they mangled technical passages. Characterization and complexity were habitually diluted, distorting motivations, shifting personalities and even names and nationalities. One-fifth of the text of *Twenty Thousand Leagues under the Seas* simply disappeared in the Lewis Mercier edition of 1873; two decades later such habits remained with the 1895 British publication of a Verne novel about Ireland, *Foundling Mick*.[12]

Translators even added passages that they felt Verne neglected to include. The notorious Edward Roth, who also rewrote *Hector Servadac* and *Around the Moon*, proudly announced in the preface to his version of *From the Earth to the Moon* that he had probably improved on the original.[13] More than incompetence or commercial deception was operating here. Censorship of Verne became the norm as translators routinely deleted passages judged to be potentially offensive to conservative political and religious sensibilities. For instance, in deference to nineteenth-century British imperial sensibilities, W. H. G. Kingston reversed

the motivation Verne gave Captain Nemo as he explains his early life in
*The Mysterious Island*. In the original French version, Verne has Nemo
reveal that, prior to his nautical exile, he was the prince Dakkar and
had absorbed the teaching of the West in order to overthrow England's
rule of his native India. In Kingston's version, however, Dakkar went
to the West to learn to better his primitive people. Even in a more pro-
empire Verne story of India, *The Steam House* (1881), a typical footnote
appears in both British and American editions when Verne's chapter on
the 1857 rebellion mentions British atrocities: "The translators beg to
say that they are not responsible for any of the facts or sentiments contained in this account of the mutiny."[14] The situation did not improve
eight decades later; a 1959 edition of *The Steam House* simply deleted
the chapter in its entirety.[15]

Political questions became the deciding factor in whether the latest
Verne books would be published in English. One or more Verne titles
continued to be published annually in France until 1910, but after 1898
only two of these books appeared simultaneously in English. The reason
was not commercial: in England and the United States, new editions were
issued of even such minor novels as *Claudius Bombarnac* (1892) into the
1920s. The portrayal of colonial depredations had become more embedded in Verne's later works, and other issues emerged that Anglo-American
publishers of the time were unprepared to present. For instance, *The
Aerial Village* (1901) told of a "missing link," an African creature more
manlike than ape, and *The Kip Brothers* (1902) was sympathetic toward
the struggle of Irish Catholics for independence from Britain.

Although Verne died at age seventy-seven in 1905, more than a century ago, a selection of his works are commonly available in even the
smallest bookshops throughout the Western world. His popularity is
global; UNESCO surveys consistently reveal that he is one of the most
widely translated authors of all time. Today "Verne" is a name that continues to face us not only from near-permanent best sellers but also from
adaptations in children's editions, comic books, postage stamps, and,
perhaps most prominently, movies and television.

Before his death, Verne had seen some of his dreams come true.
The Wright Brothers had flown the first heavier-than-air machine, but
perhaps just as important was the development of modern sound and

motion picture technology to record and replay events, as suggested in his 1892 novel *The Castle in the Carpathians*. Here, Verne wrote of a baron who can listen to recordings of his love, a deceased opera singer, as well as project a ghostly, chimerical image of her.[16] Verne was probably aware even before his death that his stories were an active source of inspiration for the new medium of motion pictures; several adaptations had already appeared in France before 1905. After beginning his writing career with farces and musical comedies for the French theater, from 1874 to 1883 Verne wrote (usually in collaboration) spectacular stage versions of his novels *Around the World in 80 Days* (1874), *The Children of Captain Grant* (1878), *Michael Strogoff* (1880), and *Keraban the Inflexible* (1883). Because his publisher encouraged only science fiction with an earthbound, contemporary, and pedagogical bent, Verne also wrote an original play, *Journey through the Impossible* (1882), that used many characters from his novels and had them traveling from the depths of the sea to a distant planet.

Hence, spectacles that could draw huge audiences were a major part of Verne's career, and understanding his legacy always required going beyond the printed page. Even in his own time, readers enjoyed his stories while simultaneously seeing theatrical presentations. In the twentieth century, the Vernian book and stage text would expand because of a new medium, with the accumulation of impressions gained through many screen versions. For the generation of Baby Boomers and those following them, film adaptations have been a defining element in the discovery of this author. Verne has been brought to the screen not only in the United States but also around the globe, in most of the European countries and from Mexico to Russia to Japan.

For instance, when I first encountered Verne as a ten-year-old in 1969, many movie adaptations were already showing on television, and since then such visual renderings have continued to be produced for both the large and small screen. As with so many other future Verne enthusiasts, films led to seeking his books; viewing and reading became unavoidably intertwined.

Verne on screen encompasses every form, from early movie shorts and serials to feature films, all types of television, animated and live action, for both education and entertainment—not to mention hundreds of audio versions and radio broadcasts. A study of Verne in film is necessarily distant from the tradition of adaptation studies, which is usually ahistorical—with the typical formulation of a canonical author (from Jane Austen to Ernest Hemingway) and a given novel compared to a live-action feature.

Verne's influence has led to more than three hundred film and television versions of his stories around the globe (and another hundred films have told of his life in documentary form or as a biographical reenactment).[17] This number of Verne adaptations is second only to screen versions of the plays of William Shakespeare or the stories of Edgar Allan Poe, Arthur Conan Doyle, Charles Dickens, and Edgar Rice Burroughs. No less than Shakespeare, Poe, Doyle, Dickens, and Burroughs, Verne was a major box office name; like Poe, he could rival many performers as a "star" and thus as security to finance a production. However, whereas the Doyle, Dickens, and Burroughs adaptations have centered largely around three mythic characters—Sherlock Holmes, Ebenezer Scrooge, and Tarzan, respectively—Verne's Captain Nemo and Phileas Fogg are not the sort of titans around whom Verne films must be organized in the way required for an examination of Dickens, Doyle, or Burroughs. In Verne's case, it has not simply been individual stories or characters that have appealed to filmmakers, but a substantial portion of his oeuvre. Nearly half of his sixty-eight novels have been brought to the screen; in the Anglophone world, some twenty different stories, along with his biography, have been adapted into approximately ninety films and television productions, Hollywood setting the tone and standard in the best-known adaptations. (I use the name "Hollywood" in its widest context, not simply for those productions filmed or shot within the city's geographical locality, but to indicate the industry's commercial influence in the Anglo-American world; financing of British or Australian films typically includes some American funding or distribution guarantees.) Given this formidable number of films to cover, spanning more than a century, in this book I discuss only Verne films either made or coproduced in the English language, whether live action in movies and television or animation. This is not to denigrate other nations' Verne films; far from it—I have analyzed many of these non-English adaptations in articles and hope to continue to do so in the years to come.[18]

At the same time, it is important to concentrate specifically on those films derived from Verne—although some films do not openly credit him, and others that do acknowledge him nevertheless have little or no resemblance to his narratives. Hence, I have examined films that are either sold as based on Verne or, lacking that label, have nonetheless clearly adapted his narratives. Equally significant in my study has been the publicity surrounding these films, especially in pressbooks revealing the use of the Verne connection. By contrast, to loosely trace off-shoots or the influence of Verne on cinema generally results in a spiral that quickly encompasses generic motifs and films derived from other authors' ideas.[19] For instance, the broad range of "center of the earth" stories is virtually its own subgenre, with Edgar Rice Burroughs's Pellucidar saga an equal if not greater inspiration. Some movies as disparate as *Rodan* (1956, imported from Japan) and *Death Race 2000* (1975) have used the Verne name in advertising slogans, but their content has nothing in common with anything conceived by the writer.

In this review of more than a century of Verne on the English-language screen, I analyze each film in critical terms as well as in relation to the original work, and in discussing the first adaptation of a work, I describe the source itself. All theatrical film releases are included in the review, along with those broadcast on television and given mainstream commercial video release; I have neglected only a smattering of educational films for classroom consumption that had ephemeral distribution and miniscule viewership. The approach to each film depends in part on its importance, although in a few instances commentary is briefer because the film apparently does not survive or has been impossible to locate. To fully reflect Hollywood's ongoing fascination with Verne as well as its peaks and valleys, I also note those occasions when a foreign production received domestic distribution, whether on the big screen or television. This has happened periodically since the beginning of Verne filmmaking, although by contrast Hollywood's saturation of overseas markets—in the theater and on the small screen—remains unabated.

I examine Verne films that were box office hits in their time and that remain cinematic landmarks as well as others that were produced on a lower budget but are no less significant and have largely been forgotten.[20] Many of these films are accessible on television, and their availability has increased on video since the late 1980s; Verne enthusiasts will be able to retrace my research path and see many of these films for themselves.

It would be possible to analyze all of these films encyclopedically or to arrange them by source, but doing so would lose crucial elements highlighted through a chronological approach that takes into account the intertwined industries of filmmaking and publishing.[21] A chronology also reveals the intertextuality as various versions of different stories were produced simultaneously and successively. There have been "cycles" of Verne filmmaking in both live action and animation, and through this historical approach I am able to reveal the degree to which a film of one story often impacted not only a remake but also a film of another story. Simultaneous, related currents have also run in Verne publishing; filmmaking hardly occurred in a vacuum, and numerous exchanges have been made between the visual media and the appearances of Verne books, comic books, biographies, and children's editions. Such trends as the emergence of Verne animation and film pastiches clearly echo the developments in the print media. So, too, the more Verne titles in print, the more often filmmakers turn to a variety of stories, and the opposite trend occurs when the number of stories available to readers becomes limited.

To understand the screen incarnations of Verne works (such as *Journey to the Center of the Earth* [1864]) requires an understanding of versions over the years; these films look back not only at the author's words but also at the previous adaptations. This proclivity is not limited specifically to a given story, but also to characterizations, most notably Phileas Fogg and Captain Nemo, both also frequently offered in original screen pastiches. Design elements may relate to preceding formations; for example, the screen configurations of Captain Nemo's *Nautilus* sometimes emulate predecessors but also sometimes strive to distinguish themselves.

Several recurring topics appear in the analysis of these films. Do they retain Verne's original characters with the same traits? How does the enactment impact characterization, and is the dialogue commensurate with the setting or a more modern vernacular? Are the themes the same ones that Verne addressed, or are they expanded, or are others substituted in their place? Is the ending to the story the one provided in the source, or is it modified or altered completely? What myths about the author does this alteration create? Is the period the one intended by Verne, or is it shifted to another time or updated in other ways—for instance, by adding advanced technology not foreseen by the author (such as atomic power)? How do such technical aspects as color, widescreen, special effects, and three-dimensional filming contribute to visualizing Verne's imagination? How has the mimetic tradition of Verne filmmaking been enriched by the constant contrast and exchange with that which is more representational and experimental, especially the animated offerings?

Here then is an exploration of a specific industry's treatment of an author over more than a hundred years. It reveals the degree to which his name provides a presold product to audiences and producers. At the same time, the fluctuating popularity of the novels impacts the making of Verne films, which in turn shapes perceptions of the author. It will become clear that fully understanding the Anglophone reception of Verne in the twentieth and twenty-first centuries requires knowing how Hollywood has brought the author to the screen. Verne and the film industry have become inseparable, and the Hollywood treatment of Verne in turn has had global ramifications and influence, shaping his reputation and the way he is read.

# 1

# The Silents

To early filmmakers, Jules Verne was not only a legend but also a contemporary author of international repute, and his global reputation was still at its peak. One or two new books had been published annually since 1863, and even after his death in 1905 his works continued to appear regularly, with the last original book published in 1919. Verne's tales were already regarded as classics that appealed to every audience and geographical locale; there was scarcely a language into which his works had not been translated.

Short films inspired by his ideas and predictions abounded in Europe and America, and countless movies during the first decades of science fiction filmmaking incorporated one or more Vernian concepts. Typical notions shown were aerial and space flight, submarines, diamond manufacturing, underwater tunnels, wireless communication, pseudo-scientific organizations, comets colliding with Earth, polar expeditions, invisibility, and technically advanced cities. However, only a few films tried to adapt Verne's stories.

The most influential that did do so were the lively creations by Georges Méliès, who earned a reputation as "the Jules Verne of the cinema."[1] Others of the time also drew on Verne for inspiration, such as Segundo de Chomon, again using the aesthetic of trick films. As live-action features began to emerge in 1913, among those setting the pattern was the author's son, Michel Verne. During the latter years of his father's life, Michel was a trusted collaborator who saw many of Jules's last works through to posthumous publication between 1905 and 1914, although altering them in both minor and major ways. He simultaneously turned his attention to "Les Films Jules-Verne," supervising the first production, *Les Enfants du Capitaine Grant,* which was imported into the United States as *In Search of the Castaways* (1914). Michel wrote and directed four adaptations before serving as a producer on the 1920 nine-part French serial of *Mathias Sandorf,* which was also released in a feature version, shown in the United States as *The Isle of Zorda* in 1921.[2]

Jules Verne's own stage versions of *Around the World in Eighty Days, The Children of Captain Grant* (1868), and *Michael Strogoff* (1876) had been immediately translated for the English-language theater, and *Around the World in 80 Days* and *Michael Strogoff* ran for decades throughout the United States and Europe.[3] Meanwhile, an assortment of other playwrights composed their own unauthorized versions. Hence, Verne was an author familiar to both readers and theater-going audiences, and the first films made from his stories drew heavily on their respective stage background.

The first Hollywood Verne films were not science fiction; they exemplified the genre to which more than half of his novels belong: adventure. He was indebted to the classical forms of his predecessors Daniel Defoe, Sir Walter Scott, and Alexandre Dumas *père,* and their formulas allowed Verne to keep up his astonishing output of one or two novels annually. The adventure tradition celebrated the era's rise of individual freedom and self-determination, usually in a nationalistic context, and heralded exploration and the establishment of overseas empires—an inherently contradictory mix that facilitated portraying European encounters with peoples of distant lands. Unlike most adventure writers of the day, however, Verne had sympathy with colonial struggles for liberation, and his viewpoint was far in advance of the predominating "white man's burden" ideology. Adventure themes would also influence Verne's science fiction; for instance, in *Twenty Thousand Leagues under the Seas,* Captain Nemo both explores the earth's remote regions and uses his science against a colonial oppressor.

For Verne, *Michael Strogoff* (1876) was his supreme adventure novel. All of his most notable previous works involved science in one way or another; even *Around the World in Eighty Days* relied on various mechanical forms of transportation to take the hero on his journey. By contrast, Strogoff has nothing but his own physical resources as he begins an epic journey from Moscow to Irkutsk to deliver a vital message from the czar to the grand duke. Along the way, Strogoff falls in love with Nadia, is captured by rebelling Tartars, and is apparently blinded with a hot sword placed before his eyes—although it turns out that his vision is saved by the tears he was shedding at that very moment for his mother, Marfa, and he survives to save Russia by killing the traitor Ivan Ogareff.

In the United States, *Michael Strogoff* remained a regular part of the repertoire of touring theatrical companies through the first decades of the twentieth century. As *Variety* reported, *Michael Strogoff* was still a popular theatrical production: "a standard melodrama in the one-night stands . . . one of the annual events in the small towns. Those who never saw it at least heard of it."[4] Early American film versions were derived not so much from the novel as from various stage renditions, relying on audience recognition of their incidents and tableaux, a fact that reviewers noted in anticipating audience reaction. In 1908, the Essanay film company produced *Michael Strogoff,* starring Gilbert "Broncho Billy" Anderson and lasting one reel (one thousand feet), about twelve minutes. The 1910 Edison remake, adapted and directed by J. Searle Dawley, starred Charles Ogle in the title role, Mary Fuller as Nadia, and Marc McDermott as Ogareff; it was the same length as the 1908 version and was billed as "A Superb Motion Picture of Jules Verne's Famous Story."[5]

The first feature-length production of *Michael Strogoff* was made in 1914 by Popular Plays and Players at the Lubin studio in Philadelphia. Lloyd B. Carleton directed a scenario by Benjamin S. Kotlowsky, and the picture ran five reels, 249 scenes, or roughly one hour. The cast of two hundred included director Carleton as the grand duke, Daniel Makarenko as Ogareff, Eleanor Barry as Marfa, Rosetta Brice as Sangarre, Ormi Hawley as Nadia, and George Trimble as Feofar-Khan. In the opening credits, *Michael Strogoff* pretentiously gives the eminent sixty-year-old romantic stage actor Jacob P. Adler the lead above the title, followed by brief scenes of Adler in the makeup and costumes from some of his other famous characterizations. This was Adler's cinema debut; although reviews were unkind in commenting on his per-

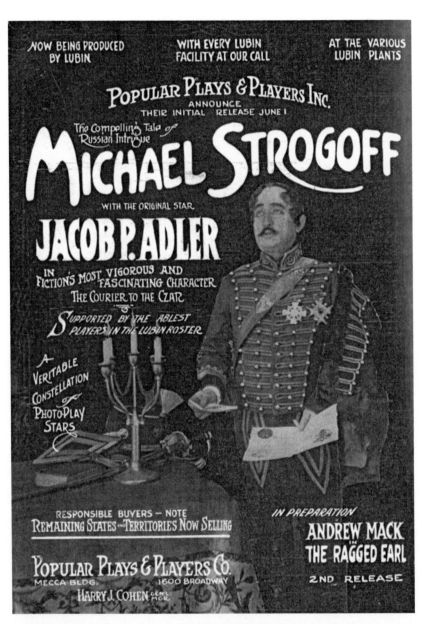

A trade advertisement for *Michael Strogoff* (1914), emphasizing the star.

formance, from today's viewpoint his acting seems sedate in relation to that of his costars, with Carleton's own grand duke the most unabashedly hammy.

The 1914 *Michael Strogoff* is very much of its time and belongs to the stereotypes of the early cinema. Camerawork is nearly always stationary; compositions tend to be long shots. Only rarely is the resulting tedium broken by intercutting two parallel actions (although some of the editing rhythms have been lost in the surviving copy, which is decomposed and has much footage missing[6]). However, the numerous and acceptably varied exteriors diminish the tendency toward staginess.

The picture opens with the release of the traitor Ivan Ogareff from prison through the trickery of a guard, and he obtains a special passport from the governor, an episode included in several stage versions. Strogoff is introduced as the most popular man at the palace ball, when he is summoned by the grand duke and given a message to deliver, with dialogue provided through a sequence of intertitles containing the exchange of words by both characters. His message reads, "Impossible to send troops before two weeks. Resist Tartars at all costs until that time." Strogoff is told to put on a disguise, and we see him add a wig and beard in a clear homage to the opening shots of Adler's ability to transform himself for various roles.

Along the Siberian border, Strogoff meets Nadia, who is searching for her father, held by the Tartars. Ogareff, meanwhile, is behind Russian lines in the guise of a Cossack. The portrayal of Ogareff here is considerably more vital and likeable than in many other renditions, and there is frequent and honest affection with his lover, Sangarre. A key episode in the novel and the play is Strogoff's unintentional encounter with his mother, Marfa, along the journey; to preserve his disguise, he must publicly deny that he is her son, who is known to be a courier. In this film version, Sangarre seeks vengeance on Marfa, who was instrumental in having her publicly whipped as a spy. This leads to the second key episode in Verne's narrative: when Marfa is found and flogged, Strogoff grabs the whip and strikes Ogareff in the face. His cover exposed, a passage from the Koran is shown decreeing Strogoff's punishment. He is apparently blinded when a heated sword is drawn directly over his nose and eyes, a grueling, direct shot seldom shown on screen in later versions.

Strogoff staggers away, supported by Marfa and Nadia, but after soldiers mock him at the roadside, he reveals the truth to his two companions. He tells his mother, "When I thought I was looking on you for the last time, my eyes were so deluged with tears that the heated blade did but dry them without destroying the sight." To isolate the grand duke, Ogareff orders oil emptied into the river, but Strogoff has already navigated it in a raft. Strogoff tears off the wig and beard and announces his true identity, while simultaneously on the right side of the screen an image appears of an earlier, indecisive confrontation, when Strogoff sacrificed his pride not to risk a duel with Ogareff. Ogareff now draws his sword on Strogoff, who kills the traitor with a knife after a fight. The grand duke, learning all, decorates Strogoff on the spot. Stock-style footage of buildings aflame follows as an intertitle relates that the fire has spread to Moscow; the whole film has tended to confuse the novel's geographic direction and minimize the duration of the journey. The sun rises over the smoke as Marfa, Strogoff, and Nadia walk in front of the scene, with a final iris-out on Strogoff.

Although Strogoff is certainly a hero, he is not a dominant, overwhelming one; the adventure elements are present, but action is treated in a theatrical fashion. The film makes a few novel twists, but the narrative is clearly told with the expectation of some audience familiarity with the story. The Russian milieu from the opening ball to the emir's camp is depicted in a sympathetic fashion as simply another historical European locale.

The next American Verne film utilized the theme of travel combined with humor, which was the centerpiece not only of *Around the World in Eighty Days* but also of other novels that tried to recapture its success: *Keraban the Inflexible* (1883), *Clovis Dardentor* (1896), *The Will of an Eccentric*, and, in particular, *The Tribulations of a Chinese in China* (1879). The amusement these stories provide is dependent in part on such bizarre characters as Phileas Fogg, the Turk Keraban, and Kin-Fo in China. Following *Around the World in Eighty Days* by only six years, *The Tribulations of a Chinese in China* emulated its mix of travel, a race against time, encounters with new cultures, and a hero who begins as wealthy and insular but learns the value of life and love. It shares the distinction of serving as a source for numerous cinematic adaptations, perhaps because it utilizes a well-recognized narrative with a unique twist: the story of a man who decides to commit suicide but then changes his mind after he has already set his plans in motion.

Focusing on a Chinese hero in his native land (as the title almost redundantly notes), Verne was able to explore a new region but also capitalize on the tropes of the "celestial" empire that so obsessed the Western mind. His China is a land of junks, long pigtails, tea drinking, and pagodas, opening with a discussion of the meaning of existence among several men of the country. Protagonist Kin-Fo, born to wealth, has never had to overcome adversity, which has left him apathetic, disengaged, following an unalterable routine—no less than the Englishman Phileas Fogg. When Kin-Fo receives word that his California bank has collapsed, he takes out a life insurance policy, naming the widow La-oo, whom he loves, as beneficiary, along with Wang, a longtime family servant who has been Kin-Fo's adviser since the death of his parents—but who also has connections in the rebel underworld. Because the policy covers suicide, the company details two men to guarantee Kin-Fo's safety. Kin-Fo asks Wang to arrange his death.

After Wang disappears to accomplish his mission, word arrives that the bank failure was merely a device to devalue its loans, but now Kin-Fo cannot inform Wang that, as rich as ever, he has changed his mind. As Kin-Fo searches for Wang throughout China, Wang has arranged for Kin-Fo to have the adventurous experience that will change his whole outlook on life, no less than happened to Phileas Fogg. Not until Kin-Fo has known trouble and anxiety can he find true happiness, and just as Fogg falls in love with Aouda, Kin-Fo's tribulations will lead to a happy life with La-oo.

Stories using an arranged suicide form a small genre of their own; this plot device certainly predates the Verne novel, giving the latter a wider range of connections with a number of other works. The particular nuance that Verne brought to the formula was of a wealthy man who loses his fortune and decides to arrange his death so that the benefits will go to his loved ones, only to find himself wealthy again, while the man he has asked to murder him has disappeared and passed on the task to a professional killer. Many adaptations dropped the Chinese setting but retained the plot or its basic devices; in fact, Verne first intended his hero to be an American but changed his mind because suicide did not seem part of the American character.

The suspenseful farce *After Five,* a play by William C. DeMille and Cecil B. DeMille, produced by Wagenhals & Kemper in 1913, was credited to "one of the earlier stories of Jules Verne." The play opens with bachelor Ted Ewing bankrupt after having invested his own fortune and that of his ward, Nora Hildreth, whom he loves. He believes that the only way he can repay her is to insure his life, name her as beneficiary, and then meet with an accident. He is run over by a car without enduring so much as a scratch. A German blackmailer, Bruno Schwartz, from the Black Hand society, has been threatening to kill Ted, so Ted asks Schwartz to arrange his death after 5:00 p.m., with his servant holding the final payment of $1,500 for this service.

The second and third acts are set at a camp in the Maine woods where Nora and her aunt live, to which Ted and his servant flee, with Schwartz lurking nearby. Ted feigns illness to avoid going out, and when the women summon a doctor for him, it is Schwartz in disguise. An echo of Verne's original Asian setting occurs in the Japanese nationality of the servant, Oki, evoking a bit of the novel's exoticism for its Western readers, although not departing from the comfort of a typical American setting. Oki's inflexible sense of honor binds him to an ancestral oath that forbids him from turning over the $1,500 for any other purpose than that for which it was intended. A telegram arrives revealing that the speculation in fact has doubled Ted's fortune, and Ted is able to pay Schwartz and set his romantic life on the right course. Critical reaction was generally negative, finding the same fault as in *The Tribulations of a Chinese in China* itself: there was not enough wit to develop the premise beyond its tritest aspects.

A year later, Cecil B. DeMille left for Hollywood, and after initial success with other projects in 1915, *After Five* was filmed at Paramount as a five-reel Jesse Lasky production. William de Mille rearranged some of the play's incidents for the screen, with direction by Oscar Apfel, and reviewers praised the scenes of Big Bear Lake Valley as the Maine exteriors. Edward Abeles was Ted, and Nora was played by Betty Shade, with Jane Darwell as Aunt Diddy. As the antagonists, Theodore Roberts played Schwartz, and Sessue Hayakawa, Hollywood's most prominent

Ted (Edward Abeles) arranges his death with Schwartz (Theodore Roberts) in *After Five* (1915); Sessue Hayakawa as Oki is in the background.

Asian actor of the time, portrayed Oki (played previously on stage by an Anglo actor).[7]

Although the screen adaptations of *Michael Strogoff* and *The Tribulations of a Chinese in China* were influenced largely by their stage sources, the remaining Verne silent movies were conceived to use special effects. Verne was fascinated by one of the new technologies of his time, submarines, and around 1860 penned the short story "San Carlos," named for a person, not a place—a smuggler who is able to flee the law in a vehicle beneath the waves. Curiously, this superb short story was never published during Verne's lifetime, probably because the author regarded it as a sketch for a longer work. A submarine would be the centerpiece of his 1896 novel *Facing the Flag*, in which it becomes part of a pirate's arsenal, and vessels engage in deadly combat beneath the waves. Verne recognized that the future of submarines would be for warfare, as he discussed in an article that appeared in the June 1904 issue of *Popular Mechanics*.[8]

It was in 1870 that the best known of Verne's undersea novels was published, his literary masterpiece *Twenty Thousand Leagues under the Seas,* unique for having as one of its protagonists the *Nautilus.*[9] Far in advance of the primitive submersibles then in use, operated by electricity, and 230 feet long by 26 feet wide, this submarine could dive to great depths, with a propeller giving a speed of fifty knots. In a manner characteristic of the time, Verne also made the *Nautilus* a model of luxury; a salon offers a twelve-thousand-volume library, an art collection, a museum of marine life, and an elegant fountain. Yet the vessel is also a warship, for Captain Nemo uses it to sink ships at sea.

In the enigmatic Captain Nemo, Verne offered one of his finest characterizations, an embittered but brilliant and cultured superman. Having adopted a name that is Latin for "no one," Nemo nurses an unexplained desire for revenge. He is, however, not a misanthrope, but an implacable rebel, the avenger of society's victims who salvages sunken gold to finance revolts against oppression. He is also a reflective, contemplative man, enamored of the isolation and beauty offered by the sea. The novel is ultimately open-ended, the *Nautilus* drawn into a maelstrom in which it disappears, and Nemo's identity remains unknown.

In *The Mysterious Island,* published five years after *Twenty Thousand Leagues,* Verne finally clarifies the secret of Nemo's life. He is actually Dakkar, the Hindu prince of an independent state in India who joined the Sepoy Rebellion of 1857. As a result, his family was massacred, and he escaped with a few loyal followers to build the *Nautilus* and hurl his submarine as a ram on the warships of the hated British. However, although this clarification is an adequate explanation for Nemo's desire for vengeance (albeit one whose timeline is incompatible), by making Nemo's background concrete, it robs him of the ambiguity and universality of his characterization in *Twenty Thousand Leagues under the Seas.*

Beyond Nemo, however, *The Mysterious Island* belongs to a different genre entirely, reflecting Verne's strongest literary influence, the Robinsonade, as pioneered by Daniel Defoe's novel *Robinson Crusoe* (1719) and Johann Wyss's 1812 follow-up featuring the shipwrecked Swiss family. The themes of survival under adverse circumstances in strange lands and the re-creation of civilized forms of living made an imperishable impression on Verne's mind.[10] Augmenting Verne's childhood reading was the experience of growing up in a seaport, Nantes, where the Île Feydeau was completely surrounded by the river Loire. At school, Jules listened eagerly to the tale of one of his teachers, Madame Sambain, whose sailor husband had shipped out shortly after their marriage, never to be heard from again; she imagined him stranded on a desert island—a situation Verne would re-create and resolve when he wrote *Mistress Branican* (1891).

Verne carried the Robinsonade to its extreme in *The Mysterious Island,* with five Union soldiers escaping from a Confederate prisoner-of-war camp in an observation balloon, only to be caught in a storm that carries them to an uncharted Pacific island.[11] Whereas Defoe's and Wyss's shipwrecks offer bounteous supplies, Verne strands his castaways with nothing more than the contents of their pockets and minds.[12] Over a four-year period, the Civil War refugees progress from primitivism to industrialism, developing most of the necessities of life and eventually its luxuries as well. The leader is a Renaissance man whose mind is a repository of all practical human learning, the engineer Cyrus Smith; on the occasions when they are in danger, Captain Nemo, "the secret of the island," intervenes and assumes providential dimensions before he is revealed.[13]

These two novels composing the saga of Captain Nemo are combined in the  movie *Twenty Thousand Leagues under the Sea* (1916), not as sequential, separate narratives, but as a single tale that jumps back and forth between the *Nautilus* and the island. Writer-director Stuart Paton also added new elements that are wholly incompatible with the sources, including several romantic subplots. The result was a bizarre script; S. J. Perelman, screenwriter of a later Verne spectacular, *Around the World in 80 Days* (1956), remarked that this *Twenty Thousand Leagues under the Sea* unintentionally borders on surrealism, and the director could have made "a cryptogram out of Mother Goose."[14]

The opening is more or less from Verne. Professor Pierre Aronnax (Dan Hanlon) and his daughter (Edna Pendleton)—substituting for Aronnax's servant, Conseil, in the novel—join the warship *Abraham Lincoln*'s search for a sea monster during the Civil War. Before the two vessels meet, Captain Nemo (Allen Holubar) is introduced as he grieves over unavenged wrongs. He pledges that he will die without revealing his secrets unless his purpose is accomplished; already the audience knows more than Aronnax and the others. The *Nautilus* circles the *Abraham Lincoln,* but the latter's gunfire and the harpoons thrown by Ned Land (Curtis Benton) have no effect on the submarine. After the ships collide, Nemo rescues Ned, Aronnax, and Aronnax's daughter.

In the next segment of the movie, five Union prisoners of war in America escape via balloon across the Pacific to Mysterious Island, where Nemo helps them to survive. Neither the group of prisoners nor Nemo yet realizes that the island is already inhabited by a daughter of nature, a previous castaway who substitutes for the novel's Ayrton. Lieutenant Bond (Matt Moore), replacing Verne's Gideon Spilett, rescues her from the menacing sailor Pencroft (Wallace Clark), who subsequently becomes an outcast. Some of the narrative lapses and disunity may have resulted from editing because what was originally a ten- to eleven-reel feature was cut to eight reels for general release on a state rights basis, a system that allowed various distributors to modify the film in any way they wanted because they controlled all rights over its sale in their own region.

After Nemo, the castaways, and the daughter of nature, a distinctly non-Vernian fourth character enters the plot. Wealthy Charles Denver (William Welch) is losing his sanity because of his memories of trying to force himself on Princess Daaker (the film's spelling of "Dakkar"), who stabbed herself to death rather than submit. He then abducted her daughter (June Gail plays both roles). The remorseful, gesticulating Denver returns in his yacht to Mysterious Island, searching where the daughter had been abandoned years earlier. Pencroft, meanwhile, has conspired with Denver's rebellious crew to seize the yacht and abduct the girl. Just as the Denver yacht is torpedoed by Nemo, she escapes with Bond.

When Nemo and his daughter meet, they instantly recognize one another, and he exclaims, "Allah be praised!" Nemo tells the story of his past: once the happy Prince Daaker in a far-off Eastern kingdom, he had become friends with Denver, only to be betrayed by Denver's lust for his wife. Because of Denver, Daaker was also held responsible for a native revolt he deplored: "My native land was made a place of death and deso-

The Indian prince Daaker who becomes Captain Nemo in *Twenty Thousand Leagues under the Sea* (1916).

lation." When his vengeance is finally satisfied, Nemo abruptly dies and is buried in a coral cemetery in a brief undersea funeral. Without further explanation, an intertitle then states that the crew has disbanded and the castaways have returned home, as the submarine is sunk without "The Great Commander" to direct her. As in the 1954 remake, in the 1916 movie the submarine is identified with its designer, linking the life and death of both Nemo and *Nautilus*.

The film's plot is simultaneously a travesty of the two novels and an attempt to be faithful within melodramatic conventions. From the outset of the adaptation, Nemo weakens in the resolve to remain isolated from his fellow men, and no explanation is provided for why or how the *Nautilus* came to be built or its scientific achievement. The motivation provided makes Nemo closer to Alexandre Dumas's Count of Monte Cristo, a man seeking private revenge, not the revolutionary Verne imagined. Although all the various strands in the plot are finally woven together, the result remains incredible both from a dramatic standpoint and within the generic context of science fiction.

In other ways, the movie dispatched unfortunate and incorrect per-

Captain Nemo (Allen Holubar) as commander of the *Nautilus*, costumed akin to Verne's description, in *Twenty Thousand Leagues under the Sea* (1916).

ceptions of Verne. Nemo's Indian heritage, although based on details from *The Mysterious Island*, is announced as a story not told by Jules Verne, and reviewers assumed it was the filmmakers' invention. There is no sense of Daaker's having any relationship to his people, and he is certainly no leader to the Indians; he is changed from Hindu to Moslem. Indeed, the British seem to be defending his palace and preserving his authority. With the exception of Daaker, the Indians are presented as eccentrics in an overdrawn, unsympathetic portrayal. Equally egregious is the opening intertitle, claiming Verne died a broken man because he was fifty years ahead of his time and the world did not take him seriously. However, Nemo's physicality is among the most faithful ever achieved, with his non-European ancestry clear in the narrative as well as in makeup, costume, and decor. Holubar's Nemo is the best player in a weak ensemble, featured in many dramatic close-ups, his dark complexion highlighted against his flowing white beard. The rest of the crew, by contrast, are very light-skinned. Nemo dresses exotically in boots, a turban, and cummerbund, not in the modern, occidental naval-style costumes that would be adopted by most of his successors in the role, even in animation.

The design of the *Nautilus* is compatible with Verne's vision, and appropriate decor echoes Nemo's ethnic background. The diving suits and submarine merge Verne's ideas with the expectations of 1916—for instance, adding a modern periscope and torpedoes. The exterior of the *Nautilus* has fins, propeller, rudder, and a small control tower, and the preparations it makes to attack a ship are just as Verne described. Yet underwater views show the submarine to be fat and wobbly, unconvincing even though an authentic submarine was used, not a model.

Despite its narrative dissonances, *Twenty Thousand Leagues under the Sea* was a major if not overwhelming box office success. The overall theme was enhanced by the public concern over submarine warfare in the Atlantic during World War I, and on the day the movie opened, a German U-boat appeared unexpectedly in New York harbor. Some four hundred thousand people saw the movie in the New York first run, and audiences in other major cities were large before the state rights release in outlying territories. The novelty of underwater photography attracted new audiences to the cinema. Profits more than covered the $500,000 cost, with shooting taking place at Universal City in Hollywood (where a vast Hindu city was constructed), at Universal's eastern studio in Leonia, New Jersey, and in Nassau in the Bahamas.[15]

Many of the aspects of the film adaptation that seem so hokey today were recognized as such even at the time, and several satirical shorts were made in 1917. Universal, the company behind *Twenty Thousand Leagues under the Sea,* produced a Pat Sullivan–animated one reeler, *20,000 Laughs under the Sea,* in which Captain Nemo takes Professor Punk to the bottom of the sea in his "scrubmarine." The company also produced *The Cross-Eyed Submarine,* a three-reel featurette written by Jack Cunningham and directed by W. W. Beaudine as a direct, live-action lampoon of the original feature.

THE MOST WONDERFUL AND MARVELOUS PICTURE THAT WE HAVE EVER BEEN ABLE TO SHOW
TO THE PATRONS OF OUR THEATER

# NOTHING LIKE IT ON EARTH

This picture shows a hunting trip on the bottom of the ocean. A pearldiver making a dive from his boat is seen under the water going to the bottom of the ocean, where he is caught by a devilfish. Seen by Capt. Nemo from his submarine and rescued. And many more marvelous secnes of the bottom of the ocean.

ADMISSION: MATINEE AND EVENING 15c          CHILDREN 5c

In 1916, the movie *Twenty Thousand Leagues under the Sea* was considered an extraordinary achievement.

In *The Cross-Eyed Submarine,* Captain Nemo (William Franey) builds a submarine, but his supposed friend Denver (Milburn Morante), in love with Nemo's wife (Gail Henry), arranges to have him arrested. This arrest provokes a revolution during which Denver's attempt to force himself on the wife causes her suicide, and in revenge he steals her seven-year-old daughter (Lillian Peacock). When Nemo finds his wife, she stubbornly claims she is alive, although the movie script indicates she must be dead. Nemo roves the sea in his submarine, training frankfurters to behave like torpedoes. Denver is haunted by what he believes to be a ghost but is in fact the real physical presence of Nemo's wife, and to flee he takes a rowboat to an island where he has left the daughter. Meanwhile, she has grown up and has encountered some soldiers who escaped from prison via a toy balloon, and she falls in love with the oldest of the men. Nemo locates Denver, and they again become sudden friends until they quarrel while diving with mermaids. Nemo's wife mistakes her daughter for one of his girlfriends, but he seems to recognize his wife and after consulting the script places her where her portrait should be, bringing her back to life.

Verne was the object of other cinematic lampoons at the time; an earlier example was 'Round the World in 80 Days, the title given in the United States to a feature imported from Germany in 1914. As indicated by the original title, Die Jagd Nach der Hundertpfundnote Oder die Reise um die Welt (The hunt for the hundred pound note or the trip around the world), this version lacked the elements that would be associated with later versions of the novel, resembling instead subsequent pastiches. The trend went as far back as 1879 and Albert Robida's epic novel that included Nemo, Phileas Fogg, and many other Verne characters: Voyage tres extraordinaires de Saturnin Farandoul dans les cinq ou six parties du monde et dans touts les pays connus et meme inconnus de M. Jules Verne (Extraordinary journeys of Saturnin Farandoul in five or six countries of the world and in all the countries known and unknown of Monsieur Jules Verne).[16] Filmmakers were familiar with such literature; a portion of Robida's satire was filmed in Italy in 1913 as Le Aventure di Saturnino Farandola: Farandola contro Fileas-Fogg. This was one of many subsequent "Phileades"—additional races around the world by Fogg's fictional descendants or actual chronicled attempts to replicate Fogg's trip from Nellie Bly in 1889 to Michael Palin a hundred years later.

In March 1922, a musical "Phileade" of Fogg's nephew making the journey, Round in Fifty, had opened at the London Hippodrome.[17] Given the theatrical as well as the filmic precedents, Hollywood adopted the "Phileade" approach in its first cinematic treatment. Around the World in 18 Days, a 1922–1923 Universal serial, was directed by B. Reeves Eason and Robert F. Hill from a script by George Bronson Howard and Frank Clark, with the story supplied by Robert Dillon after Verne. The twelve episodes, each about twenty minutes in length, were titled successively "The Wager," "Wanted by the Police," "Apaches of Paris," "The Man Who Broke the Bank at Monte Carlo," "Sands of Doom," "The Living Sacrifice," "The Dragon's Claws," "A Nation's Peril," "Trapped

A trade advertisement for the serial *Around the World in 18 Days* (1922–1923).

in the Clouds," "The Brink of Eternity," "The Path of Peril," and "The Last Race." William Desmond starred as Phileas Fogg Jr., with Alfred Hollingsworth as his father; Laura LaPlante played the leading lady, Madge.

In the serial, Verne's novel was updated from 1872 to contemporary times, using all the latest inventions, from airplanes to speedboats and submarines, each somewhat more advanced than current technology. Fogg Jr. must travel the globe to visit the widely scattered stockholders of a company and obtain their proxies to support the development of a synthetic fuel for the benefit of the poor. Madge's father is owner of the company, and she provides inspiration for the journey and accompanies Fogg. The proxies must be obtained in a mere eighteen days, providing young Fogg with the impetus to best his father's record; there is also a $100,000 wager with the adversaries. Attempting to stop Fogg as he races around the globe are thugs hired by his business antagonist, but Fogg narrowly escapes their traps each time.

Verne filmmaking during the silent era encompassed the author's most famous novels, *Twenty Thousand Leagues under the Seas, The Mysterious Island,* and *Around the World in Eighty Days,* but also novels best known because of their stage presentations, *Michael Strogoff* and *The Tribulations of a Chinese in China.* Hollywood's interest in Verne did not wane, and in the mid-1920s Metro-Goldwyn-Mayer (MGM) began the biggest production yet, a movie to be shot in Technicolor and using the undersea photography that had been such a sensation with audiences for *Twenty Thousand Leagues under the Sea.* Exhibitors eagerly booked the new film, to be titled *The Mysterious Island*—and then waited an astounding four years as the production of the planned silent spectacular dragged on so long that it became an early talkie.

**2**

# Searching for a Popular Approach, 1925–1945

The 1916 silent film *Twenty Thousand Leagues under the Sea* had been recognized during its time as a milestone for presenting an elaborate production of a Verne science fiction novel. The absurdity of many of its plot elements did not diminish audiences' fascination when movie cameras descended beneath the waves to tell a blockbuster fictional story.[1] The interest in this camerawork as a scientific advance, culturally as well as cinematically, was evidenced by Grosset & Dunlap issuing a "Special Submarine Edition" of the novel illustrated with scenes from the movie and containing a special foreword; some copies showed a roly-poly submarine on the cover. Variations of this publication, with scenes from the movie on the dust jacket, continued to be published well into the 1930s, nearly two decades after *Twenty Thousand Leagues under the Sea* was produced—indicating the depth of its impression on public consciousness.[2]

The process of underwater photography had been developed by two brothers, George Williamson and John Ernest Williamson, retooling an invention of their sea captain father, Charles Williamson: the deep-sea tube. This tube was composed of concentric, interlocking iron rings that stretched, flattened, and swayed like an accordion, suspended from a specially outfitted ship, allowing easy communication and plentiful air, whose pressure could be equalized through pumps. At the bottom of the tube was a five-foot spherical observation chamber, the photosphere, with the whole mechanism raised or lowered by chains attached to the ship.

In 1912, J. E. Williamson realized that the mechanism could be used not only for salvage, but also for photography. Depending on depth and location, a special light could be suspended from the mother ship, sufficiently illuminating the area. After newspapers published their photographs of the depths of Hampton Roads, Virginia, Williamson relocated to the Bahamas, where the clearer waters would suit motion pictures. The result was *Thirty Leagues under the Sea* in 1914, climaxed by J. E.'s fight with a shark, which he killed with a knife while remaining within the camera's range. The brothers quickly realized that fictional films could be an even more popular and lucrative outlet for their endeavors, and as Verne enthusiasts, they took the next obvious step; two years later *Twenty Thousand Leagues under the Sea* would be completed in partnership with Universal.

Undersea action was staged in front of the photosphere's window, allowing scenes of pictorial beauty ranging from coral to a hunting expedition to a battle with an artificial octopus. However, a heavy sea rocking the barge from which the tube was suspended would make photography impossible, and nearby barracudas menaced the divers pretending to encounter sharks and other monsters of the deep. Submarines were impossible to obtain during wartime, so J. E. built a full-size facsimile of the *Nautilus* and piloted it; it carried actors, had an underwater airlock, and could submerge to a depth of thirty feet and surface again.

After *Twenty Thousand Leagues under the Sea*, J. E. Williamson carried on his undersea filmmaking, usually from his own scenarios, refining his techniques and beginning to film in color. In 1925, these developments led MGM to tap him as the studio planned *The Mysterious Island*. This time hurricanes plagued Williamson's Bahamas shooting, while in Hollywood the production was matched by a tornado of changing scripts, directors, and cast. MGM's producer, Irving Thalberg, lacked any comprehension of how to handle science fiction, suggesting fights with ray guns and failing to grasp the fundamental coherence and likelihood on which a Verne narrative depended.[3]

*The Mysterious Island* opens as oppression generates unrest in the eastern European kingdom of Hetvia, where Baron Hubert Falon is

One of Captain Nemo's divers emerging from the *Nautilus*, staged and photo-graphed on the sea floor of the Bahamas by the Williamson brothers for *Twenty Thousand Leagues under the Sea* (1916).

planning a coup. Offshore lies Mysterious Island, formed by the shell of a submerged volcano (à la *Facing the Flag,* another Verne submarine novel, published in 1896). The reclusive Count Dakkar (Lionel Barry-more) is the enlightened ruler of Mysterious Island, and his scientific workshops are a virtual utopia where all men are equal. The new spirit of science, represented by Dakkar in a plain smock, his hair rumpled, is contrasted with the old, aristocratic injustice meted out by the dapper Falon.

Dakkar naively fails to recognize his fellow nobleman's intentions and tells Falon of the upcoming launching of his submarine. Falon instantly recognizes its potential as a warship, a thought utterly for-eign to Dakkar. His ambition is to journey to the ocean depths, where he hopes to discover a race of antediluvian underwater men who have evolved in a parallel direction to mankind on the surface.

At the controls of the first submarine to be launched is Nikolai Roget (Lloyd Hughes), a skilled worker who is the fiancé of Dakkar's younger sister Sonia (Jane Daly). During the test launch, Mysterious Island is overrun by Hussars; in an extended, painful scene, the treacherous Falon tortures the count and Sonia in an unsuccessful attempt to gain their secrets. As in the 1916 version of *Twenty Thousand Leagues under the Sea,* divers come ashore from the submarine, remaining in full underwater gear, to attempt a rescue. Cannon fire damages the submarine as Dakkar is rescued by loyalists, but Falon takes over No. 2, an identical submarine.

As the pressure of the ocean bottom causes No. 1 to flood, its survivors are witness to the amazing sight of thousands of "ictholites," as advertisements dubbed these midget-size men of the sea. They welcome Dakkar when his torpedo kills a sea serpent. Meanwhile, Sonia has damaged the vertical controls on No. 2, and it too sinks to this secret domain. Nikolai and Sonia are reunited on the bottom, and Dakkar and his followers move to No. 2. By switching No. 1's air compressor to No. 2, they enable the second submarine to ascend to the surface. Dakkar kills Falon, and the scent of the dead man's warm blood drives the ictholites into a frenzy because they are accustomed only to the cold of the dark depths.

At first beguiling, these creatures turn menacing, and they release a giant squid that envelops No. 2. One of its tentacles enters the diving hatch, crushing Dakkar. Back ashore, his crew overthrow Falon's men. In a dignified, fitting close, the dying Dakkar orders his workshops abandoned and detonates them. Because he is the only man who can design another submarine, No. 2 becomes his tomb. In a comment prophetic of future cinematic Nemos, Dakkar's epitaph reads, "In the years to come, I do not wish to be remembered as one who brought into the world an instrument of death and destruction."

Like so many Verne films, *The Mysterious Island* ends with the postponement of the advancement of science as Dakkar and his submarine sink to a watery grave. Lionel Barrymore is unlikely but acceptable in the role, developing what became the standard portrayal. The two main characters embody different sides of humankind: Falon is destructive, whereas Dakkar is a man of peace, science, and exploration who is forced to abdicate his neutral stance and isolation.

The dying Dakkar (Lionel Barrymore) takes the submarine and his secrets to the bottom of the sea in *The Mysterious Island* (1929).

Lucien Hubbard received final credit for writing and direction, but even as *The Mysterious Island* was completed, *The Jazz Singer* (1927) heralded the arrival of sound. To compensate, extensive sound effects, a recorded score, and some dialogue scenes were added to *The Mysterious Island,* in particular the opening sequence. Dakkar promulgates some bizarre theories of evolution as bone fragments are washed up by currents from the bottom of the sea.

All this effort and color did not draw audience interest away from the all-talking black-and-white films when *The Mysterious Island* was released on October 5, 1929, and little of the enormous cost was recouped at the box office. *The Mysterious Island* had none of the resonance that *Twenty Thousand Leagues under the Sea* enjoyed amid wartime and fear of U-boat attacks. Grosset & Dunlap issued a lavishly illustrated photoplay edition of the novel, but the Verne name on a movie that mentioned neither Captain Nemo nor the *Nautilus* yet had submarines and

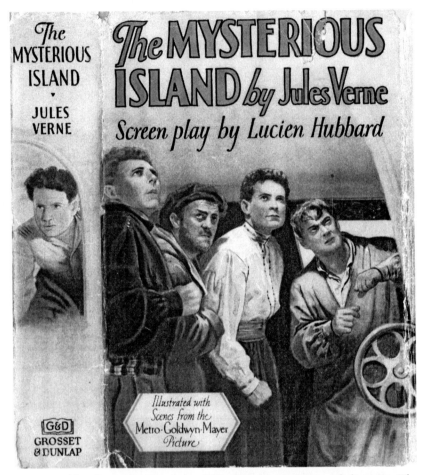

Lucien Hubbard's resolution of the difficulties in adapting and directing *The Mysterious Island* (1929) won him an equal credit with Verne on the dust jacket of the movie tie-in book, showing Dakkar *(right)* and some of his crew.

an inventor puzzled reviewers. Few if any realized that the film's Count André Dakkar was a facsimile of Captain Nemo, as revealed in the novel *The Mysterious Island*. As a result of this confusion and the unfortunate timing of its release, the 1929 version of *The Mysterious Island* did not begin to be recognized as a classic of early science fiction until the 1970s.[4]

Watched today, *The Mysterious Island* is one of the most imaginative movies of its genre and one of the few truly unpredictable American films of the era, with an ending and storyline that cannot be antici-pated as it unspools. The pace is gripping, suspenseful, and well con-structed, without a single dull sequence, although the plot is not for a moment credible. The strength of *The Mysterious Island* is its audacity; because of the numerous twists and turns, it leaves the viewer absorbed, not skeptical. The special effects are polished for their time, with some clever angles used in photographing the submarines, whose design fol-low Verne's vision more closely than in most films. Despite its tenuous relation to the novel, the movie is an enchanting delight, more entertain-ing than some more faithful versions.

The precedents in *The Mysterious Island* would reappear in the Ver-nian science fiction film cycle that began in the 1950s. Although the events in the film are certainly not those written by Verne, they have acquired a distinctly Vernian cinematic flavor that adds to the viewing. The melodramatic *Twenty Thousand Leagues under the Sea* of 1916 had already incorporated love subplots and torpedoes, and many more incidents from *The Mysterious Island* would reappear in later Verne movies. They include descents to the bottom of the ocean, repairs in the deep, underwater radio, volcanic island bases, sea monsters, the attack on a man of science by the outside world, the destruction of his base, the depiction of an Atlantis-type lost civilization, damaged and multiple submarines, and the injection of far more fantasy than Verne intended. For instance, the 1954 production *20,000 Leagues under the Sea* has a similar ending, with the dying Nemo destroying his laboratories and sinking with the submarine as he reflects on how the future will regard his invention. *Captain Nemo and the Underwater City* (1970) would use the idea of two submarines pursuing one another, one stolen and used against its inventor, along with the discovery of an inhabited city on the ocean floor.

The pattern of remaking silent successes continued to be followed, turning next to other stories presented already on both stage and screen: first *Michael Strogoff* and later *The Tribulations of a Chinese in China*. Despite the popularity of *Michael Strogoff* in the years prior to the Rus-sian Revolution, audiences in the United States had little interest in it after the revolution. In Europe, however, Verne's story of heroism on behalf of the czar had acquired distinct political implications, where it was brought to the screen by white Russian filmmakers living in exile. First was the 1926 spectacle *Michael Strogoff,* which was distributed domestically by Universal as a prestige item but was nonetheless cut from three to two hours in length, failing to achieve the anticipated popularity.[5]

A similar genesis a decade later led to a sound feature of *Michael Strogoff* titled *The Soldier and the Lady.* As with the 1926 film, in 1936 a white Russian, this time Joseph Ermolieff, produced French and German versions of the novel. Each film used much of the same action footage, with the Bulgarian army impersonating that of Russia. Ermolieff took his work to Hollywood and impressed RKO production chief Pandro Berman with the possibilities for a similar American production. The studio bought access to the French negative for $75,000; the preexisting long shots and battle scenes would then be intercut with new close shots of American actors playing the roles in English. Some 60 percent of the footage of *The Soldier and the Lady* were from the earlier version; the total budget of the RKO production was about $400,000 for eighty-five minutes, moderate for the time. (During World War II, Ermolieff went to Mexico and, using the same approach, in 1943 squeezed a fourth film from the original European footage.)

Failing to interest an American star in the lead of *The Soldier and the Lady,* RKO imported the Viennese actor Adolf Wohlbruck, who had played the role in Ermolieff's European versions. His name was anglicized to "Anton Walbrook" in the hope he would become, according to publicity, the screen's new dangerous lover. Others in the cast were moderately better known to American audiences: Elizabeth Allan as Nadia, Margot Grahame as Zangarra, Akim Tamiroff as Ogareff, and Eric Blore and Edward Brophy as the whimsical war correspondents. Mortimer Offner, Anthony Veiller, and Anne Morrison Chapin wrote the English version of the script, their plot following with few exceptions Verne's novel and Ermolieff's previous versions, only adding emphasis to some incidents. The principal change from the novel was having Zangarra save Strogoff from blinding through a bribe rather than revealing how his tears for his mother provide protection. Strogoff's mother dies when the blade passes before his forehead, her death serving as an effective focus for the camera as the apparent blinding takes place off-screen.

As a result of its patchwork construction of new and old footage, *The Soldier and the Lady* is never quite convincing; the blend prevents the picture from achieving either immediacy among the characters or the suspension of disbelief necessary for an historical adventure film. The seams are too apparent, and the epic aspirations are a distinct failure. Although the large-scale action footage is impressive, there is no sense of the enormous geographical distance. Only occasionally does *The Soldier and the Lady* capture the flavor of the historical Russian backgrounds, nor is Nathaniel Shilkret's musical score, sometimes drawing on classical passages, of much assistance.

*The Soldier and the Lady* is rather unevenly paced, at times almost too action filled, yet with the battles excessively brief—particularly at Pulev, where the reporters' antics mar the entire scene. The intended contrast between national types offered by Strogoff and the French and English war correspondents turns into rather tiresome humor, and such intrusions sometimes give the picture the feel of a "B" movie. The fight with the bear is similarly unconvincing, with Strogoff killing it in a series of bizarre cuts and angles that have a positively Eisensteinian construction, emphasizing blows instead of a struggle between the combatants.

George Nicholls Jr., a former editor, directed the new portions of *The Soldier and the Lady,* which fail to capture the dramatic highlights despite the abundant physical movement and some excellent photography by Joseph August. For instance, Strogoff's initial appearance is given no introduction whatsoever, unlike the fanfare surrounding the entrance of most such heroes in films of this era. Similarly, Strogoff lunges at Ogareff before the whip has even been raised to his mother, robbing the pivotal scene of its motivation—perhaps a constraint dictated by censorship. The courier's nobility does not become apparent until the film is well under way, when he aids Nadia and rescues Zangarra. Strogoff finally stands in sharp contrast to the cruelty and exotic dancers of the Tartar camp, well handled with abundant menacing shadows, atmosphere, and foreshadowing by close-ups on the character's eyes as he awaits being blinded. However, most of the film is over before this crucial scene, and Strogoff's journey is swiftly completed thereafter, allowing him to expose Ogareff to the grand duke and lead a charge that defeats the Tartars.

An advertisement for the British release of *The Soldier and the Lady* (1936), retaining the novel's title, *Michael Strogoff*.

*The Soldier and the Lady* acquires an almost European look because the new footage had to be compatible with the old. The discordant acting adds to this impression; both Fay Bainter as Strogoff's mother and especially Walbrook in the lead utilize a deliberately overdone, slow style. In contrast, the two correspondents—played by comedians—are irritatingly slapstick, and Tamiroff, Allan, and Graham perform in a standard Hollywood vein. In particular, Walbrook's bulging eyes and his reliance on two basic expressions, accentuated by his minimal dialogue, become a real detriment in the creation of a heroic character. This must have been a result of a lack of experience at the time or inadequate direction because Walbrook went on to a long career as a fine character and romantic actor, although primarily on the European continent.

*Michael Strogoff* was the film's original title—and was retained in Britain—but it attracted so little business that RKO gave it the new title *The Soldier and the Lady*. This change was odd because Strogoff is hardly a soldier, nor is Nadia, in terms of her social caste, a lady. The change in title did not boost the picture's popularity, and the production barely broke even at the box office. In 1946, Bell Distributing re-released *The Soldier and the Lady* as *The Bandit and the Lady,* with Bainter and Tamiroff now receiving top billing. In 1951 in England, Independent Distributing reissued the picture under the title *Michael Strogoff* but retained the original billing. For television, the movie's title was changed to *The Adventures of Michael Strogoff* but is now once more called *The Soldier and the Lady.*

Just as the silent, English-language release of the 1926 version of *Michael Strogoff* had spurred publisher interest, in 1937 Grosset & Dunlap and A. L. Burt issued separate editions of *Michael Strogoff* with dust jackets illustrating the new movie.[6] However, such highlights were becoming the exception. As Verne filmmaking waned, publishers were losing interest in the author. Forty-eight of his novels and a volume of novellas had been published in English during his lifetime, with the last new Verne translations appearing in 1923. Nearly all began to fall out of print by the 1930s, and outside of the musty shelves of second-hand shops few Verne stories were to be found beyond the evergreen classic titles.

Hence, it is no surprise that when the basic idea of *The Tribulations of a Chinese in China* was transformed into two unlikely if effec-

Henry Hull hires Donald Barry to arrange his death in *The West Side Kid* (1943), the first of two back-to-back productions of Verne's *The Tribulations of a Chinese in China.*

tive crime stories, neither credited the Verne name. First was Republic's unusual *The West Side Kid,* scripted by Albert Beich and Anthony Coldewey and produced and directed by George Sherman in ten days in April 1943 on a $50,000 budget. The title was explained by the advertising slogan, "A west-side gangster reforms an east-side family," although social lines are only a very subsidiary theme.

*The West Side Kid* opens as Sam Winston (Henry Hull) is berated by the board of directors of his newspaper and personally embarrassed by the fact that his frivolous, spoiled daughter, Gloria (Dale Evans, before winning fame as cowgirl Mrs. Roy Rogers), has backed out of her third wedding to pursue a newer, more exciting man. Sam's wife (Nana Bryant) is conducting an affair with his doctor, and she excludes her husband from a party in their house, while their idle son, Jerry, is in a perpetual alcoholic daze. Rather than financial disaster, as in the novel, it is disillusionment with work and family that drives Sam to contemplate suicide. Learning that one-time criminal Johnny April (Western star Donald Barry) has just been released, Sam, afraid to kill himself, proposes to arrange his own death for $25,000.

Johnny reluctantly follows Sam's routine for an evening, after which the doctor is found murdered. Johnny's attorney warns him that it will cost $25,000 to prepare a defense, giving the obviously reluctant Johnny a motive to carry out the job he has delayed completing. Johnny sends Sam a note saying it is time but actually only arranges for Sam's abduction; learning that his family does miss him, Sam asks to cancel their contract. There seems to be one addendum: Johnny and Gloria have fallen in love. However, Johnny realizes, from Sam's reaction, that she is not for him. He tells her he has to lie low, making her believe that life with him would compel her to join the criminal element but failing to tell her that he has been cleared of the murder. Observing Gloria's wedding to the man she had jilted at the opening of *The West Side Kid,* Johnny telephones his moll, Tootles, to tell her he is on the way.

Johnny has staged the outcome in a sagelike manner beyond that of the clichéd good-hearted underworld figure, combining the Wang part and several other characters in the novel to create the outlaw threat that brings Sam, in the part of Kin-Fo, to a realization of the value of his life. There is an uncertainty in the characterization of Johnny that, until the close, leaves the spectator wondering whether he is still a criminal and will yield to the temptation to take advantage of Sam's offer, a tension echoed in the book. Johnny's two incompetent associates provide amusement in the spirit of Craig and Fry in the novel, and Gloria's wedding provides a satisfactory romantic denouement. Unlike in Verne's novel, there is little action in *The West Side Kid;* rather, the story is completely one of character, demonstrating the possibility for an intriguing and unexpected narrative in a fifty-eight-minute movie intended for exhibition on a double bill.

A year later, another "B" with a running time of less than an hour again treated the same basic story. Rudolph C. Flothow produced a script by Eric Taylor, with the story credited to J. Donald Wilson. Although in many respects closer to Verne, this version was in a genre and series context that made the proximity all the less likely. *The Whistler* was the first in a series of mysteries from Columbia studios starring Richard Dix and

The second version of *The Tribulations of a Chinese in China* was the first episode in a famous mystery series, *The Whistler* (1944).

inspired by the popular radio show that related the surprising and ironic happenings seen by the narrator known as the Whistler, a shadowy man who walks by night, knows many strange things, and is identified by his signature whistle. The movie opens intriguingly as Dix meets criminal Lefty Vigran in a waterfront dive to ask him to arrange for the murder of industrialist Earl Conrad. Lefty passes along the arrangements through two intermediaries so that the crime will be impossible to trace, when he is suddenly killed by police. Only then is the viewer, seeing Dix return home, able to realize that *he* is Conrad and that the apparent murder is a form of suicide. Conrad dismisses his butler with a special retirement bonus and reveals to his secretary, Alice Walker (Gloria Stuart), that he cannot bear his wife's death.

A telegram informs Conrad that his wife is not dead, but a prisoner of the Japanese, and will be repatriated. Now he wants to live and tries to recall his order to Lefty, only to discover he is suspected of having betrayed Lefty. The killer follows Conrad, taunting him, believing he may simply frighten him to death. Conrad hides in a flophouse but is nearly killed in an attempt to rob him. Reported as an amnesia case by the newspapers, Conrad is recognized by a waterfront watchman, who calls the police. Meanwhile, Alice, who is in love with Conrad, learns that his wife died while incarcerated. The killer now realizes that his tactics have backfired and Conrad can identify him, so he desperately tries to finish his task, only to be shot by the police.

The waterfront pursuit takes the place of Kin-Fo's flight across China, and Conrad's reversal of his wish for suicide and unsuccessful search for Lefty parallel the comparable sections in *The Tribulations of a Chinese in China*. William Castle's direction maintains suspense despite the sometimes unlikely plot convolutions, following Conrad's steady descent from conscious determination to end his life to desperate, frenzied outpacing of the killer. In contrast to Dix's expressionless, square-jawed performance, J. Carroll Naish plays the unnamed psychotic assassin in chillingly cold-blooded fashion, determined to complete his assignment as a matter of professional pride, even after Lefty is dead. The seedy atmosphere provides a stronger sense of setting than the New York of *The West Side Kid* in offsetting the switch from the novel's China. Conrad's motivation in *The Whistler*, although different from Kin-Fo's—the loss of his wife rather than financial ruin—results in much the same outcome, especially with the murder assigned to another person who seems determined to carry it out no matter the change in circumstances.

Even as these years did not suggest that Verne was a box office draw, a series of developments were occurring that would set the stage for a Verne revival, beginning with the formation of the initial official groups of Verne enthusiasts. First among them was the Jules Verne Confederacy, which began in 1921 at Dartmouth Royal Naval College and published *Nautilus*, a literary magazine in tribute to Verne and his son, Michel. The teenage members saw in Verne an ideal favorite author and hero for British boys looking forward to a life at sea. Their most permanent legacy came with the publication in England of the Everyman's Library edition of *Five Weeks in a Balloon and Around the World in Eighty Days* in 1926. This volume was made possible because a former instructor of the "Julians" at Dartmouth had married and left teaching for a career in writing and publishing, and both books received new translations for this edition. The preface by two leaders of the Jules Verne Confederacy, K. B. Meiklem and A. Chancellor, was the best critical overview on Verne in English up to that time and contained a bibliography noting translators. Their work was updated in the 1940s and reprinted as late as 1966 by Dent-Dutton.

In France, the Société Jules Verne was formed in 1935 and began publishing a quarterly bulletin. Its efforts were interrupted by World War II, but the society almost immediately recommenced after the war. The American Jules Verne Society emerged when Willis E. Hurd penned the article "A Collector and His Jules Verne" for the August 1936 issue of *Hobbies,* recounting his discovery that most of Verne's novels available in English had received many different titles, had undergone various translations, and had often been drastically edited. As enthusiasts read Hurd's pioneering analysis of Verne, a small network formed. Another of the society's stalwarts, James Iraldi, assisted Stanford L. Luce in what became, in 1953, the very first doctoral dissertation on Verne in any language—by an American, not a European.[7]

Biographies about Verne also appeared in this period, replacing the often wildly inaccurate accounts given in newspapers and magazines during the author's lifetime. In 1940, Kenneth Allott's *Jules Verne* became the first volume on Verne in English, a scholarly treatise that sought to place Verne in the cultural and social context of such nineteenth-century literary movements as romanticism and positivism.[8] The first purely biographical book on Verne in English came three years later with *Jules Verne: The Biography of an Imagination* by George H. Waltz, an associate editor of *Popular Mechanics*. Both Allott and Waltz were indebted to Marguerite Allotte de la Fuÿe's 1928 biography, which was translated into English as *Jules Verne: Prophet of a New Age* in 1954. Allotte de la Fuÿe was a cousin of Verne (and no relation to Kenneth Allott), and although later research revealed her portrait to be largely apocryphal, the myths she promulgated still reverberate. Together, all of these sources provided the foundation for a new understanding of Verne necessary to his reemergence as an author relevant in the post–World War II era.

# 3

# Creating a Style, 1946–1955

Jules Verne's relation to science fiction was complex and about to become critical in Hollywood's undertakings of his work. Even if he was not the founder of science fiction (a position usually ascribed to Mary Shelley and *Frankenstein,* published in 1818) and did not create the tradition of fantastic literary travel, such as the trips to the moon by Baron Munchausen and Cyrano de Bergerac, Verne was certainly the first writer to popularize the genre for an ongoing series of novels. No less important is that Verne largely rejected fantasy to achieve a believability not previously attempted.

He believed that the literary qualities of the works by both Edgar Allan Poe and H. G. Wells would have gained by emphasizing facts.[1] Wells had taken science fiction into more imaginative realms, unbounded and untroubled by the limitations of possibility that so defined Verne's approach. Rather than Wellsian speculation, the Frenchman extrapolated from current technology, building on what was available in his time. Unlike Verne's intricately explained explosive launch and lunar orbit described in *From the Earth to the Moon* and *Around the Moon,* Wells's *The First Men in the Moon* (1901) offers a sphere coated with antigravitational paint and a fanciful visit to the verdant lunar fields and bizarre insect civilization. Verne explained the distinction to interviewers. "You will remember that [Wells] introduces an entirely new anti-gravitational substance, to whose mode of preparation or actual chemical composition we are not given the slightest clue, nor does a reference to our present scientific knowledge enable us for a moment to pre-

49

dict a method by which such a result might be achieved. I make use of physics. He invents. I go to the moon in a cannon-ball, discharged from a cannon. Here there is no invention."[2]

Through such means, Verne offered the first analysis, in fictional form, of the challenges of the scientific age, from space flight to urban planning, thus securing his reputation as "the prophet of the twentieth century." Nonetheless, because Verne's stories are set in his own time, limiting them primarily to issues, facts, and developments of the nineteenth and early twentieth centuries, his narratives seem fin de siècle, increasingly remote to readers accustomed to current science fiction writers and more up-to-the-minute predictions. Verne might appear an outdated historical curiosity; such creations as the *Nautilus,* the mobile Standard Island in *Propeller Island,* and the helicopter *Albatross* in *Robur the Conqueror* embody the nineteenth-century romance of technology, cloaked in Victorian luxury. Verne's science fiction has the unusual characteristic of prophecy set in the past, possibilities not then realized rather than the more typical forecast of imagined events in the years to come. This dichotomy and the problems it posed were about to underlie the distinct directions taken as the screen adapted Vernian science fiction.

By the late 1930s, when most American homes had a radio, adaptations of Verne novels had begun to be heard over the air. There were serials of such titles as *From the Earth to the Moon* and *Journey to the Center of the Earth,* each episode running a half-hour, over the airwaves in 1937. The following year Orson Welles adapted *Around the World in Eighty Days* in hour form for *Mercury Theater.* Welles and Cole Porter subsequently turned the novel into a stage musical, a condensation of which was heard on *Mercury Summer Theater of the Air* in 1946 and *The Railroad Hour/The Gordon Macrae Show* in 1950. Soon half-hour radio anthologies were regularly adapting Verne stories. First heard was *20,000 Leagues under the Sea* on *Favorite Story* in 1946, with the same series broadcasting *Around the World in 80 Days* in 1948; the story was also adapted for *From the Bookshelf of the World* in 1949 and *Hallmark Playhouse* in 1950. *20,000 Leagues under the Sea* appeared on *Family Theater* in 1950, *Hallmark Playhouse* in 1951, and *Family Theatre* in 1953. These renditions starred such major players as Ronald Colman,

Hans Conreid, Otto Kruger, William Conrad, Louis Jourdan, Raymond Burr, and Gene Lockhart.

Impelled by these broadcasts, the decline in Verne readership and publication reversed; the first book series published since the 1920s began in 1950, with Didier reprinting six Verne titles, some of which had been out of print for a decade or two. Verne was emerging once more as a classic, family author, regaining the status he had during his life and the immediate decade or two after his death. Together, radio programs and publications triggered the resurgence of filmmakers' interest in the author, with the first acknowledged screen adaptation to appear in fourteen years.

The initial manifestation of this attention was not a feature movie, but a serial, the first to present Verne since the 1922–1923 season and *Around the World in 18 Days*. The contrast presented by *Mysterious Island* (1951), a serial that multiplied the 1875 novel's science fiction elements under producer Sam Katzman for Columbia Pictures, could not have been greater. Richard Crane starred as Captain Harding (the standard W. H. G. Kingston translation of *The Mysterious Island* in 1875 having changed the name of Verne's hero from "Cyrus Smith" to "Cyrus Harding"), with Marshall Reed as Jack Pencroft, Ralph Hodges as Pencroft's adopted son Bert Brown, Hugh Prosser as Gideon Spilett, Bernard Hamilton as Neb, Terry Frost as Ayrton, and Leonard Penn as Captain Nemo. Even considering the low-quality performances expected of serial actors, Hamilton and especially Prosser are abysmal in their roles.

There were fifteen episodes to the serial, each lasting about twenty minutes: "Lost in Space," "Sinister Savages," "Savage Justice," "Wild Man at Large," "Trail of the Mystery Man," "The Pirates Attack," "Menace of the Mercurians," "Between Two Fires," "Shrine of the Silver Bird," "Fighting Fury," "Desperate Chances," "Mystery of the Mine," "Jungle Deadfall," "Men from Tomorrow," and "The Last of the Mysterious Island."[3] Curious additions were made, screenplay writers Lewis Clay, Royal K. Cole, and George H. Plympton deciding it was appropriate to add invaders from the planet Mercury who are searching for a rare radioactive metal to end all life on Earth in preparation for a Mercurian invasion, so that the film became the first of many to situate Verne as the prophet of the nuclear age. Yet as absurd as this interpolation is, it is

Advertisements for *Mysterious Island* (1951) stressed the interplanetary conflict.

not ruinous because the Mercurians are scarcely the only worry for the castaways. There are also pirates, the unpredictable wild man Ayrton, strange natives who worship the island's rumbling volcano, as well as the inexplicable presence eventually revealed as Captain Nemo.

The 1951 *Mysterious Island* begins in a straightforward manner, with five Union prisoners of war escaping via balloon from a Confederate prison—only to be blown far away by a tremendous storm that carries them to a remote Pacific island, where they witness the landing of a spaceship from Mercury. Harding, who jumped from the balloon to lighten it and save his friends, is carried from the sea by Nemo. However, Harding is found ashore and is about to be sacrificed by native volcano people when rescued by his fellow castaways. In succeeding installments, Bert is attacked by Ayrton, an earlier castaway stranded by pirates, but no sooner is Ayrton captured than he escapes again. In accord with standard serial practice, coherence and credibility are low priorities, and adversaries change sides on the least pretext; alliances between natives, castaways, the Mercurians, and the pirates are made and then reversed.

The details of the plot do not add up, and there are many apparent contradictions; some of the narrative is wholly inexplicable. In the first episode, although captives in Richmond, the Union prisoners wander the city at will. After the balloon crashes, the castaways discuss the urgent need to find Harding but do nothing to locate him. Nemo rescues Harding and questions him but walks away without giving him time to answer. Such faults become all the more evident under Spencer Gordon Bennet's lethargic directing.

Nemo finally explains himself to the castaways after appearing periodically as a near giant on mountaintops, wearing an enormous helmet resembling the one worn by Raymond Massey in the H. G. Wells film *Things to Come* (1936). Nemo's crew have perished, and the *Nautilus* has been destroyed; now he is on the verge of developing a machine to stop the Mercurians. Penn's mellifluous voice gives Nemo a certain classic note amid the bizarre plot, but there is no mention of his actual identity as Prince Dakkar.

A second spaceship from Mercury arrives as the radium unites with the molten volcano to create an eruption. Captain Nemo insists that he

Captain Harding (Richard Crane) and the castaways are shown the experiments by the white-haired Captain Nemo (Leonard Penn) to repel the invaders from Mercury in the *Mysterious Island* serial (1951).

will go down with his island, and as the island sinks into the sea, the castaways are rescued by a passing ship. Thinking no one will believe their amazing adventures, Spilett throws his reporter's notebook into the ocean.

The serial *Mysterious Island* is a peculiar combination of science fiction and adventure, neither fully one nor the other, lacking the sprightly, imaginative qualities found in many other serials that are more purely science fiction. No less preposterous was the first adaptation of Verne in the newest broadcast medium, television. On January 25 and February 1, 1952, "Twenty Thousand Leagues under the Sea" was shown in two half-hour episodes, "The Chase" and "The Escape," on the ABC live science fiction series *Tales of Tomorrow*. The George F. Foley Jr. production was directed by Don Medford, produced by Mort Abrahams, and adapted by Harry Ingram and Gail Ingram. Irascible Thomas Mitchell was miscast as Captain Nemo, and, instead of Professor Aronnax, his opponent is Leslie Nielsen as Commander Farragut of the *Abraham Lin-*

Captain Nemo (Thomas Mitchell) loses his daughter (Bethel Leslie) to Farragut (Leslie Nielsen) in *Twenty Thousand Leagues under the Sea* (1952).

*coln,* sent in search of the monster sinking ships at sea. After the *Abraham Lincoln* is struck by the *Nautilus,* Farragut is captured along with another officer, Peters (Brian Keith).

According to this adaptation, Nemo took to the sea because his wife left him for another man, not for political reasons. He has tried to create in the sea a free life for himself and his daughter but only does so through harming others, using the *Nautilus* to ram and sink ships, out of blind rage and without purpose, and forcing sailors who board the *Nautilus* to enter his service for the rest of their lives.[4]

In the most hackneyed of romances, Nemo's daughter, played by Bethel Leslie, predictably becomes her father's adversary when the right brawny man enters her cloistered existence. She becomes romantically involved with Farragut, in a situation that would become a cliché from

Nielsen's role in a later movie, *Forbidden Planet* (1956). The *New York Times* noted the lack of the novel's key episodes and the replacement with "a pretty girl," commenting, "Incredible as it may seem, the classic in prophecy was turned into a 'boy-meets-girl' story [that] resembled nothing so much as a soap opera staged in an aquarium."[5] Nemo's daughter finally convinces him to allow her to escape with Farragut and Peters and to cease sinking ships—for now any vessel may be carrying her, the one person Nemo loves.

The show suffers from all the hazards of a live production, with awkward camerawork, lighting, and a lack of any appropriate production design; the only sight from the *Nautilus* is a highly artificial model of the city of Atlantis, which Nemo claims sank after tyranny and misrule. Although Mitchell is the most obvious case, all the cast embody characterizations far afield from the natural logic and the proper spirit of Verne's narrative. Only in a few dialogue passages in which Nemo relates his love of the sea does the show resonate with the novel. Roger DeKoven supplies ponderous off-screen narration as Jules Verne in a thick French accent, all the more annoying because the story is so opposed to what he wrote.

The very same year as this inauspicious television beginning, the Canadian Broadcasting Corporation series *Tales of Adventure* retold the story. "20,000 Leagues under the Sea" appeared as a serial from September 13 to October 18, 1952, in six half-hour episodes adapted by Ray Darby and produced by Silvia Narizzano.[6] Radio and television brought not only adaptations but also stories of Verne's life. *The Hallmark Theater* offered an episode entitled "Out of Jules Verne," broadcast by NBC on March 21, 1954. Written by Elaine Ryan, it tells of Verne's most difficult years, when, after marrying a widow (Carole Mathews) with two children, he abandoned his hope of becoming a playwright in favor of business. However, Félix Nadar (Jack Kelly) encourages Verne to write once more, and his tale of a balloon's ascension appears simultaneously with Nadar's flight over Paris. Publisher Pierre-Jules Hetzel (Gene Roth) gives Verne a contract for many more fantastic novels, and prophecies flow from his pen, including the submarine. The next year, the radio version of the television show *Hallmark Hall of Fame* offered its own biographical half-hour episode on Verne.

Even as Verne was emerging on television, another new technology allowed a previously unimagined visual rendering of his stories: widescreen, with the new anamorphic process CinemaScope. Enhancing the potential for science fiction spectacle were ever more sophisticated special effects and Technicolor (the 1929 version of *The Mysterious Island* had been shot in two-strip Technicolor, which offered a far less lifelike palette, emphasizing green and orange hues). Fortunately, these technologies were combined in 1954 under the guidance of one of the twentieth century's imaginative geniuses. Walt Disney's cinematic transformation of *Twenty Thousand Leagues under the Seas* recognized how to bring it to a modern mass audience, utilizing motifs glimpsed in the 1929 and 1951 adaptations of *The Mysterious Island,* but without the serial's incompatible subplot (the Mercury invasion) or the distracting love interest used for *Tales of Tomorrow.*

Disney's rendering captures the mood and atmosphere of its source; whether in the *Nautilus* gliding gracefully beneath the waves or in the funeral on the ocean floor, the feeling of Verne's narrative is powerfully rendered intact into a new medium. The brooding shots of the submerged *Nautilus* and Nemo (James Mason) playing Bach at the submarine's organ are unforgettable, and Paul Smith's music expresses the various aspects of the story, enhancing the mood of the picture and foreshadowing the tragic outcome. The color becomes a prominent element of not only the decor but also the story itself, with interior photography by Franz Planer. The film's technical excellence was rewarded with two Academy Awards, for special effects and color art direction. Comparative viewing on the small and large screen reveals that the movie loses a major part of its strength and impact when reduced to television size.

Verne's vision of the assaulting *Nautilus* is perfectly realized from the opening shot, the submarine emerging out of the depths as a spectral phantom of destruction, portholes gleaming like eyes, engines screaming like an avenging angel as it bears down on a hapless warship. Although little of the *Nautilus* is futuristic by today's standards, the movie's submarine never becomes prosaic. Following the highly detailed design originated over a single weekend by Harper Goff (whose favorite movie was the silent version of the novel), many models of the *Nautilus* were built, and some earlier variations are visible in at least one of the opening shots

When Richard Fleischer directed *20,000 Leagues under the Sea* (1954), he used the same Bahamas undersea locations as the 1916 version and had the advice of J. E. Williamson, age seventy-three at the time and still active in production in the islands.

of the submarine attacking.[7] However, the life-size windows seem disproportionately large, making the *Nautilus* as a whole too small for its large crew to inhabit. The sets never attempted the enormous size Verne had given the rooms of the submarine because they would be unreal by today's standards, so the interiors are cramped, with noticeable ceilings in most shots. This is especially true in the salon with its pipe organ, not even close to as spacious as Verne designed it. Unfortunately, the result seems pitifully small for a combined library and museum. The art gallery's paintings, oddly enough, are primarily landscapes, a change from the portraits of revolutionary heroes mentioned in the book.

As with the 1916 version, *Twenty Thousand Leagues under the Sea*, the emphasis in the 1954 production is on the underwater photography, shot by Till Gabani, much of it taken off the Bahamas in Nassau and Jamaica's Montego Bay. More than twelve thousand working hours were spent in the deep. Indeed, J. E. Williamson, who directed the underwater portions of the silent film, was still working in the region and advised the crew as they encountered many of the same problems he had faced so many years earlier. However, such scenes as the crew harvesting underwater crops (influenced by Disney's series of short Technicolor "True-Life Adventure" films) now appear drawn out and extended to a later generation, lacking the freshness they had for earlier audiences unused to nature photography.[8]

The creativity with sets and miniatures is balanced by impassioned misanthropy as Captain Nemo proudly proclaims his estrangement from the civilized world. *20,000 Leagues under the Sea* combines nineteenth-century atmosphere and mood with twentieth-century technology, mingling the concerns of two centuries—oppression, totalitarianism, and science. Early on, Nemo speaks of having a mission with an end, which gives the tale a sense of destiny, an inevitable tragedy awaiting enactment. The film follows the initiative of the serial version of *Mysterious Island* to update Verne's predictions to include the atomic age: the submarine does not run on electricity, as in the novel, but on the secret source of the power of the universe, which Nemo has harnessed.

*20,000 Leagues under the Sea* divides into two halves, the first emphasizing psychology and mood through the landing at Rorapandi, a slave colony from which Nemo and his crew escaped. The second half keynotes action, from the *Nautilus*'s ramming of the warship that has left the island to the fight with the squid. Similarly, the film begins by following the outline of the book, but as incidents are added, it becomes increasingly remote from Verne.

Such deviations add up, especially in changing the characterizations and trying to end the plot on a note of closure—instead of with the uncertainty of the disappearance of the *Nautilus*, as in the novel. During the battle with the squid, Ned (Kirk Douglas) saves Nemo, restoring some of Nemo's reluctant faith in human instincts. He reveals a tentative plan to use Aronnax (Paul Lukas) as an emissary to offer the world the secret of atomic power on condition that nations disarm and end slavery. However, the *Nautilus* arrives at Nemo's base, Vulcania, to find the island surrounded by warships, which had been alerted by the notes in bottles Ned had thrown overboard. As Nemo sets a bomb, troops pour over the crest of the mountain, and one of the bullets hits Nemo. Returning to his cabin, Nemo announces, "I am dying, and the *Nautilus* is dying with me," signifying that he and the submarine with its source of power have failed to achieve the vision of a new world. Nemo and his crew wish to perish at the ocean bottom, but Ned, Conseil (Peter Lorre), and Aronnax escape in the dinghy as Vulcania explodes into a mushroom cloud and the *Nautilus* sinks. Unfortunately, the wrenching mood of the climax is hindered by the crew's apparently stoic, expressionless indifference and the interruption of Ned's slam-bang fight to escape. Aronnax suggests that Ned may have served humankind by delaying the secrets of nuclear power for a later, hopefully more peaceful generation. The end nonetheless comes as a surprise by taking the strongest possible conclusion, unlike most Disney denouements. Merchandise issued with the film indicates that a variety of different climaxes were considered, many of them having Nemo release the trio voluntarily.

For all its virtues, *20,000 Leagues under the Sea* is hardly a definitive adaptation of the novel. Although Nemo is treated with understanding, his actions are ultimately regarded as villainous, requiring his compensatory death to achieve the family entertainment Disney strived for. Ned becomes not only a contrast to Nemo but also the undoubted hero, with Nemo taking second place in the Douglas–Mason cast credits and in the narrative. The filmmakers felt the need to give variety and pace by balancing emotion with crude humor to appeal to youth rather than aiming purely at adults. The majestic, thorough telling of the story is contrasted with excessive comedy relief gauged at small children's limited ability to withstand the film's tension. The resulting oscillations, rather than blending together, diminish the totality.

The characterizations range from Nemo's genius on one pole to the educated Aronnax and Conseil and then to the physical Ned, Nemo's opposite. Paul Lukas is effective though a trifle leaden as the earnest, thoughtful Professor Pierre Aronnax. He is Nemo's intellectual equal, apparently the only other person on the ship so inclined, including the crew, and Nemo proudly shows him the wonders of the *Nautilus* and the ocean floor. Because both Aronnax and Nemo value science above life and look to the long-term goal of bettering humankind, a distant but respectful comradeship grows between them.

A French poster emphasizes the cast and battle with the giant squid in *20,000 Leagues under the Sea* (1954).

Ned, as portrayed by Kirk Douglas, is an instinctual, hard-drinking, outdoors person, introduced as he compares his girlfriends to fish in the song "A Whale of a Tale." He saves Aronnax and Conseil and even gets if not the girl (since there is none), then Nemo's pet seal, Esmeralda.[9] (Walt Disney added her to the crew, and she won a Patsy award as the year's best animal performer.) Ned also convinces Conseil to shift his loyalty to him, away from Aronnax. Conseil, passably played by Peter Lorre, is used mainly as a foil for Ned's humor, but the role began Lorre's shift from psychological menace to chubby comedian. Nemo and Aronnax's priorities, manners, and behavior contrast with those of Ned and Conseil, who form an emotional bond that esteems life above science, allowing small-minded individuality to triumph. They are able to extract a victory of sorts by simply surviving Nemo's aborted dream. This leads to a contradiction—Nemo is the visionary, yet Ned leads to a retrogression and triumph.

Ned's own surname, "Land," indicates his contrast with Nemo, the anonymous man of the sea; Ned stands for all those values of the surface world that Nemo fled. Ned is the primitive man, with unrefined, inextricably intertwined drives toward both good and evil. A strong dichotomy is drawn between this ordinary, unreflective man representing humanity at its unsophisticated best and worst and Nemo, a man of vast intellectual abilities but who is emotionally overwhelmed by the persecution he has endured. At the same time, Nemo is unable to save himself and his ship during the fight with the squid and must be rescued by Ned's brawn and vitality, sharpening the comparison between the two antithetical forces. Ironically, Nemo is saved from the squid by a gesture of the very type of unreasoning courage and humane selflessness that his own sophistication has left behind. The difference is reflected in their musical instruments, Nemo's pipe organ in the salon versus Ned's banjo in his cabin.

A fifth character, who did not appear in Verne's book, is Nemo's unnamed first mate, played by Robert J. Wilke, a supporting player in Westerns who was deplorably miscast. Literally everything Wilke touches goes awry. The remainder of the ship's crew are entirely undeveloped in their portrayals. Although they, like the captain, supposedly are survivors of similarly traumatic experiences, their impassivity and flat voices are at variance with Nemo's emotion, and no visible comradeship exists among them.

Although British sophistication is the precise ethnic opposite of what was needed for the role, James Mason provides a sterling performance as Captain Nemo. He drains his voice and manner of any relation to a particular nationality, and although the identity of that hated nation is never uttered, it is assuredly imperial England. Mason never read Verne's book and later remarked, "I was a bit reluctant to accept the part at first because Nemo is basically a serious, dramatic part in a film primarily aimed at children—and I wasn't sure I could find the right key."[10] Mason was correct to note that Verne's story would be toned down and Nemo's relative importance reduced, despite the slogan "the mightiest motion picture of them all." In fact, Mason has comparatively few lines and is almost a supporting character, with less time on screen than Douglas, Lukas, and Lorre, but he simultaneously carries the major acting burden. Despite the diminished role, Mason dominates and dignifies any scene in which he appears, even with sparse dialogue or a brief monologue. His performance gives the picture a pillar around which it coheres; it is hard to imagine the *20,000 Leagues under the Sea* of 1954 achieving even half its quality had Nemo been portrayed by any of the other actors who have played Captain Nemo over the years.

Although displacing Nemo from the central position, the script does not weaken the attitudes Verne gave him; only in providing an explanation for his past is Nemo's aura of mystery reduced. The details given are different from those in *The Mysterious Island,* but they are compatible. Nemo is frequently isolated from the others in shots and often shown alone in close-up. The extreme close shot of his eyes as he is about to ram the ship from Rorapandi was considered the largest close-up to that time because of its CinemaScope dimensions, and it provides a visual correlative for the submarine's apparent eyes when ships view it as an attacking monster. Nemo is a tragic figure—distant, apparently ruthless, outwardly defiant, yet intensely human. He worships the sea, finding its perfection a contrast with the injustice on the land. His is a soul in torment, painfully invoking the crimes committed against himself and his family to justify his agonized vengeance. Forced to believe that humankind is fundamentally evil, he has begun to question this assumption, the very rationale for his nomadic exile. His reprisals bring no satisfaction; the attacks he makes against warships and munitions transports are the result either of an unprovoked assault on his submarine, such as that of the pursuing *Abraham Lincoln,* or of sporadic and overwhelming rages against his adversaries. Following one of these paroxysms of destruction, Nemo undergoes an emotional catharsis, leaving him drained from the spent force of his hate. As he tells Aronnax after sinking the warship from Rorapandi,

> You call that murder? Well, I see murder, too, not written on those drowned faces out there, but on the faces of dead thousands! There are the assassins, the dealers in death—I am the avenger! Is murder a right reserved for that hated nation? They've taken everything else from me, everything but my secret, the secret of my submarine boat, and the energy that propels it. They tried, they cast me in a prison, and when they failed—when they failed, they tortured my wife and young son to death. Do you know the meaning of love, Professor? What you fail to understand is the power of hate. It can fill the heart as surely as love can.

Verne's militant avenger remains intact in the movie, but the man he imagined as an outlawed revolutionary is transformed into a man whose chief enemy is war. (Curiously, Verne's publisher had recommended using opposition to the slave trade as a justification for Nemo's attacks on ships, but Verne was adamant that Nemo be an exile from specific imperialist oppression; author and publisher ultimately compromised by leaving Nemo's background unknown, although he is clearly a victim of injustice.)

For the young director, Richard Fleischer, the son of a one-time Disney competitor, this was his first big picture, and his attitude toward the project was reflected in his later remark that the book was very difficult to translate to the screen because there wasn't really any story.[11] Equally important for the action was James Havens, an experienced hand at the marine elements in many Hollywood films, who directed the retake of the scenes with the squid, which cost an additional $200,000. The first version had placed the battle against the background of a sunset, which failed to conceal the manner in which the squid was manipulated with wires; the retake hid the wires by placing the scene in a violent storm, which serves as a parallel to the cauldron of Nemo's own emotions.

Both Fleischer and screenwriter Earl Felton had spent their previous careers doing low-budget Hollywood pictures. Felton effectively organized the novel's incidents into a screen treatment, one that is generally regarded as a faithful adaptation—to such a degree that in the public memory the movie has supplanted the novel.[12] The typical critical attitude and the fundamental flaws underlying it were expressed in the *Hollywood Reporter* review.

Felton's script and Disney's concept improve on Verne's original. The French author, who was touched by the philosophy that led to the Paris Commune of 1871, wrote on the presumption that anything was moral that tended to set up a revolutionary dictatorship of the world. His Captain Nemo was such a would-be dictator and Verne, in the original work, did not even take the trouble to disclose the nature of Nemo's grudge against society. And it paid slight attention to the morals of drowning hundreds of sailors because you are displeased with their masters.

In the Disney version, all this is changed. We are told that Nemo's wife and child were killed for political reasons and that he was condemned to slavery. Even so, despite his madness, he seeks world reformation rather than world revolution and is eager to give humanity the benefits of his knowledge.[13]

*20,000 Leagues under the Sea* was the fifth in a series of Disney live-action movies, many of them based on classic novels or historical characters, which Walt Disney began producing in 1950 and marked a shift from his emphasis on animation.[14] It was also his very first science fiction effort and the initial film produced and distributed under Disney's own corporate name, Buena Vista. Although *20,000 Leagues under the Sea* did top box office business, it ultimately brought more prestige than immediate actual profit because of the $5 million budget, high for the time. Most of the profit was derived from the re-releases in 1963 and 1971 as well as from the subsequent television broadcasts and video releases. The picture was backed with an enormous press campaign, including such promotions and collectibles as models, games, puzzles, toys, and costumes.[15] Disney also utilized storybook records

Robert Florey, who had first observed Verne filmmaking under Georges Méliès, about to direct a segment of "Operation Undersea" for the *Disneyland* series in 1954.

and publications—a coloring book, magazine, and books for youth from children to teenagers.[16] While no tie-in used the actual Verne text, artwork clearly inspired by the movie subsequently embellished the covers of many paperback editions, such as those published by Scholastic, Pyramid, and Bantam, demonstrating the cultural absorption of this visualization of the novel.

The new hour-long *Disneyland* television series, which had an estimated audience of thirty million weekly, served to promote the movie.

Preview clips, together with storyboards, diving gear, and the like, were shown on the very first show, "The Disneyland Story," broadcast October 27, 1954. The episode "Operation Undersea" documented the making of *20,000 Leagues under the Sea* and included clips from the movie and background footage on the production. The footage was effectively arranged to highlight both the film's special effects and the dramatic portrayal of Captain Nemo, and the episode won the Emmy award for best television documentary of the year. Narrated by Winston Hibler, "Operation Undersea" emphasized the undersea photography, commencing with a cartoon about man's attempts to plumb the deep before showing the difficult underwater shooting off Nassau, then the cannibal scenes shot at Long Bay, Jamaica. The diving suits were falsely described as built to Jules Verne's specifications, and one of the book's engravings was even doctored as apparent evidence. "Operation Undersea" concluded with a collage of scenes from the movie. The documentary is ultimately successful because it both reveals information about *20,000 Leagues under the Sea* and leaves much that is tantalizingly untold or only hinted at. The movie's narrative is held in abeyance, and the episode offers sufficient spectacle to entice newcomers to Verne (such as the squid fight) and hints at the movie's divergence from the original to intrigue those who knew the source (showing the dying Nemo).

"Operation Undersea" was first broadcast on December 8, 1954, to coincide with the movie's opening and was shown again in 1956 as well as for the picture's re-releases in 1963 and 1971. Yet another *Disneyland* episode, thirteenth in the series and broadcast January 19, 1955, was entitled "Monsters of the Deep." It featured Peter Lorre and told a story of the many creatures in the ocean as a lead-in to the battle with the squid and Kirk Douglas singing the song "A Whale of a Tale."

When Disneyland opened in California in 1955, there was empty space in the Tomorrowland section, and the Academy Award–winning sets from *20,000 Leagues under the Sea* were turned into an exhibit. In this way, Disney was responsible not only for producing the first Verne hit movie of the sound era but also for introducing Verne to the theme park, where the author had been presented only peripherally a half-century earlier though lunar "rides" in such venues as Coney Island. Although originally intended to last six months, the Disneyland exhibit

This board game of *20,000 Leagues under the Sea* (1954) was one of many tie-ins for the children's market.

became so popular that it remained in place until 1966. Visitors walked counterclockwise in a circular pattern from one room to another, with "A Whale of a Tale" played when they entered the exhibit. In the center of the circle was the final resting place of the *Nautilus*, its hull sunk deep into the sandy ocean floor, revealing only the deck.

Recorded narration by Thrul Ravenscroft greeted the visitors as if they were coming aboard the *Nautilus*, beginning with the wheel-house, crowded with steering controls. Next, visitors passed the chart room, the cabin from which the captain planned the *Nautilus*'s course. Adjoining Nemo's quarters was the cabin shared by Aronnax and Conseil. Pipes, steel, and rivets helped to link the once-separate set pieces together, and the central passageway through the submarine led into the salon, with its fountain and samples of marine life. The pipe organ played Bach's Toccata and Fugue in D Minor, recalling some of the film's most emotional moments. Seen through the porthole, the squid menacingly moved its seventy-foot tentacles. The pump room revealed the engines of the *Nautilus*, followed by the diving chamber, where the sea bubbled up through the hatch and underwater suits hung from the walls. Finally, banks of glowing lights indicated the power-supply room, the heart of the ship's atomic reactors. The sets eventually began to show their age, though, and could no longer compete for valuable space among newer attractions, and a story set a hundred years in the past seemed out of place in a Tomorrowland trying to envisage the twenty-first century.[17]

The spark that had been lit with radio and television productions of Verne might easily have died had not Disney focused on Verne for a movie spectacular, and Disney's entertainment talent fanned the flame into a bonfire. He proved how Verne could become a screen classic, one that has remained in the public consciousness to such a degree that even sixty years later the Disney interpretation overshadows other attempts to film the story. Moreover, Disney also situated the work to echo for residual benefit, exploited through books, records, associated television shows, and theme park attractions.

Walt Disney, with his wide-ranging entertainment background and future projects, was uniquely qualified to popularize Verne for new audiences and for both movie and television viewers. Just as Verne ushered in a new genre, science fiction, while relying on adventure, Disney refined and transformed first animation and then nature documentaries, live-action films, and theme parks. Like Verne himself, Disney had new ideas about how to create and refine storytelling ideas and techniques for a mass audience. Both men were fascinated by the challenges of presenting a glimpse of a future and its technology, of discerning how dreams might be realized. They knew that the core of their audience was youth, anchored by the family, and so addressed them with entertainment accompanied by a pedagogical element. For Verne, this element was geography and science, which Disney also used, along with (primarily American) history.

The television series, the Disneyland park, and the film opened simultaneously, and it was no coincidence: all had specific and broader relevance to the ongoing image Disney sought to create. The movie was not only situated as a key move forward in Disney's live-action filmmaking and as a logical advance from the True-Life Adventures but also fit within both his television and theme park plans. He sought to incorporate in his work a view of the past that was ultimately realistic if hero-centric; for instance, Davy Crockett meets a tragic end in the 1955 *Disneyland* television miniseries, no less dismaying to children than Nemo's climactic death. In *20,000 Leagues under the Sea*, Disney was able to continue burnishing his credentials in science, which would be presented in a serious, didactic manner in both his television series and Disneyland. The approach followed the Vernian pattern, offering glimpses of a near-term future of actual probability, not the speculation of H. G. Wells or the science fiction of space aliens found in the serial of *Mysterious Island.* Hence, Verne, *20,000 Leagues under the Sea,* and the sometimes paradoxical notion of science set in the past, with its limited forecast, fit in squarely with the Disney agenda in three separate media. Walt Disney certainly understood Verne, and had their lives overlapped, it is no exaggeration to say that Verne would have understood Disney because Verne did so much to adapt his own storytelling and theatrical productions to similar styles and audiences, expanding beyond the confines of his book publishers and happily allowing such talents as Jacques Offenbach to bring his lunar travel conception to the stage.

The 1954 version of *20,000 Leagues under the Sea* is undoubtedly the most influential Verne movie ever made, achieving a level of critical, commercial, and artistic success that launched a seventeen-year cycle of live-action adaptations of Verne's work. It is difficult to imagine the Verne cycle without Disney's trailblazing, but one more entertainer was necessary to prove that the success was not due just to the Disney name or to science fiction—Jules Verne was boffo box office.

**4**

# Establishing a Mythos as the Verne Cycle Begins, 1956–1959

Walt Disney demonstrated how color, widescreen, and special effects could serve to vitalize Verne for the screen and become crucial to the popularity of such a film, providing sights that audiences had never seen before, but he also proved that adaptations needed to retain the grounding in the author's nineteenth-century world. Even as Paramount, in adapting H. G. Wells's *The War of the Worlds* for the screen in 1953, had transplanted the time and place from turn-of-the-century England to modern-day California, such alterations did not influence Verne filmmaking. Disney's return to the author's own setting provided a crucial lead for subsequent Verne films, whose foothold remained appropriately in the nineteenth century.

This was most obviously true as *Around the World in Eighty Days* was brought to the screen in 1956 in a nearly definitive rendering of the novel, more faithful to its source than all but a few Verne movies. Silent versions, whether the one from Germany in 1914 or the American serial *Around the World in 18 Days,* had updated the story to contemporary times and were more pastiche than adaptation. Fortunately, in making the first large-scale screen rendition of the novel, producer Michael Todd consolidated and perpetuated Disney's precedents by returning to Verne's own time. Todd was a champion showman, who, like Disney, was able to ignite Verne's appeal to a mass audience, although in a contrasting genre, pure adventure, without science fiction. Critics and audiences joined in applause, and *Around the World in 80 Days* won five Academy Awards, including one for best picture, along with numerous other honors.[1]

Todd followed Disney's lead in creating his own exploitation and promotion.[2] Major tie-ins included two different-size seventy-two-page Random House hardbound color program books that sold widely beyond theaters and an illustrated Avon paperback of the novel, which was published again for the movie's 1968 re-release. Television promotions also served as an echo and supplement, no less than had been the case with *20,000 Leagues under the Sea.* The popularity that *Around the World in 80 Days* enjoyed was commemorated on the first anniversary of the movie's premier with a chaotic but highly rated all-star party in Madison Square Garden with eighteen thousand of Todd's "closest and most intimate friends," along with a thousand entertainers. On the scale of a political convention, CBS paid $175,000 for a live broadcast of this 1957 celebration, entitled *Around the World in 90 Minutes,* and as a result box office receipts increased.[3] The show also served to mark the transition of the release to a more traditional pattern. Whereas most movies had completed their theatrical showings by the time a year had passed, during the first year *Around the World in 80 Days* was exhibited only on a "road show" basis, opening in select cities with screenings twice daily. Tickets had to be purchased in advance—making them difficult to come by and rendering the movie an "event" more akin to a stage show than to a typical motion picture release.

The same year, on April 2, 1957, a special satire entitled "Bilko Goes around the World" appeared on *The Phil Silvers Show.* After the men of the army base go to *Around the World in 80 Days,* an attempt to get Sergeant Bilko a free flight to San Francisco leads to realizing he could fly military planes around the world in less than eighty hours. Bilko telephones Todd and interests him in promoting a contest to give $20,000 to the first person to make it around the world in that time. The producer appears as himself, holding his own with the professional comedians, effectively portraying just the type of promoter who would take credit for Bilko's idea.

*Around the World in 80 Days* was also the culmination of Todd's life and his brief filmmaking career; he died at age fifty in an airplane crash on March 22, 1958.[4] He had been interested in the novel since 1946, when he briefly sponsored Orson Welles's unsuccessful stage musical production of it, with music and lyrics by Cole Porter. Todd described the story as "a fairy tale for adults" but believed that a stage presentation must make the journey seem real, a goal whose cost would be prohibitive.[5] Ten years later, however, such a motion picture could be accomplished as a follow-up for Todd's involvement in the widescreen processes Cinerama and Todd-AO. Disney had shot 20,000 Leagues under the Sea in CinemaScope, using an anamorphic lens to squeeze a widescreen image onto standard 35 mm. stock. In making Around the World in 80 Days, Todd-AO sought to supplant CinemaScope by creating instead an image photographed and projected on a larger, wider film stock, 65 mm. However, this meant that two versions of Around the World in 80 Days would need to be shot because many theaters were able to show only 35 mm. film. Most scenes were photographed with the 35 mm. and 65 mm. cameras placed side by side, but sometimes portions had to be reshot for the benefit of one or the other camera; as a consequence, there are actually two different release versions of the movie.

The use of widescreen and a three-hour running time (including intermission) afforded the opportunity to show nearly all the principal incidents in Verne's story of global travel. Humorist S. J. Perelman wrote most of the script, although James Poe and John Farrow sued and won a share of credit for authoring the original draft, but many scenes were composed with minimal planning during the far-flung location shooting. Fearing budget overruns, Todd wanted to complete some of the most expensive sequences first to have promising footage to show possible investors.[6] His endeavor was a completely independent effort, and after the project had been shooting nine months and he was broke, he turned down offers to buy him out, relying on private funding until finally United Artists and Paramount Theaters came through with a releasing deal and the necessary cash to complete the work.

After a year of preparation, photography began in Toledo and Chincon, Spain, in March 1955, but veteran director John Farrow was relieved on the second day in favor of the much younger Michael Anderson. Talented designer William Cameron Menzies served as the associate producer. Kevin O'Donovan McClory directed scenes in Paris, the Middle East, Pakistan, Thailand, Hong Kong, and Japan before assisting in the editing of the 680,000 feet of film. The expected budget doubled to more than $6 million as filming took place in 112 locations in thirteen countries over 127 days. In the United States, the principal locations outside California were in Oklahoma and New Mexico, and five Hollywood studio lots were used, with most of the interiors shot at RKO.[7]

The result was what Todd called a show on film—a travelogue, a circus, a revue, a comedy, a mystery, a romance, a Wild West show, a bullfight all rolled into one. Numerous film clichés are employed, including a last-minute cavalry rescue, to create a triumph of farce.[8] Despite the awesome scale, the movie seldom dwarfs the story and characters, staying light and charming, and the amusing concluding credits animated by Saul Bass are a special treat.

In addition to scouting locations and directing some sequences, Todd fast-talked dozens of headliners into appropriate roles as cameo stars, agreeing to alphabetical credit, which placed Charles Boyer first on the list; others were impeccably cast in bit parts, such as Philip Ahn, although given only secondary billing. Some, such as Maurice Chevalier, demanded a high sum for a half-day's work, which Todd was willing to pay, but they also wanted special billing—so, for example, the role meant for Chevalier went to Fernandel instead.[9] All the cameo stars were chosen not for their prominence, but for the appropriate qualities they would bring to the role. For instance, when Gregory Peck proved unable to bring the proper tone of seriousness to the role of the cavalry colonel, location shooting paused until he could be replaced by one-time Western star Tim McCoy.[10] The importance of the cameos was to have been underlined by a modern prologue, with Phileas Fogg (David Niven) and Passepartout (Cantinflas) boarding an airliner. Charles Boyer arranges for their tickets, just as he suggests their balloon flight in the movie. Many of the other passengers on the plane are the "cameo" stars who later appear in the movie during Fogg's travels, and Fogg is reading a folio edition of Verne's novel. This framing device was shot but replaced with a nonfiction introduction featuring CBS newsman Edward R. Murrow discussing how the globe has seemed to "shrink" in modern times— while the screen itself literally grows (this introduction would be deleted in reissues, both with Murrow's death and when widescreen had become more commonplace).[11]

The assembled cast of cameo and lead players who appeared in the modern prologue shot for *Around the World in 80 Days* (1956).

Accompanied by Cantinflas, David Niven is reading *Around the World in
Eighty Days* in this frame in the original 65 mm. from the unused prologue for
the 1956 movie.

For once, a movie designed to feature a host of cameo stars and overseas locations had the ideal plot to integrate so many disparate elements.
*Around the World in 80 Days* centers around a journey begun for profit
and glory, depicting a race against time in an age of rapidly advancing

technology. National, ethnic, and occupational stereotypes are invoked and spoofed for a large share of humor. Yet this element is merely a leavening ingredient in the 1956 movie, unlike in some later, less successful imitations. Although amusing, the movie is neither smug nor burlesque, realizing that the story is ultimately a serious one, as shown in the transformation of Phileas Fogg. The integrity of the book is preserved by retaining Verne's satire of English manners and mores—on one level it is a travel adventure, but on another level it is also a satire, a rebuke to the insularity and imperialism of Great Britain, on whose global empire, in this story, the sun truly never sets.[12]

David Niven portrays Fogg as the man who has insulated himself from the outside world, governing his life by the clock. As in the book, his journey around the world, ostensibly initiated as a wager, is equally an unconscious flight from the minimal human contact he has at the whist table of the typically British Reform Club. He begins with contempt for everyone who is not English, from Americans to Asians, seeing them all as equally barbaric and foreign. His nemesis, Detective Fix, correctly diagnoses Fogg's method if not his motivation: Fogg is not a true traveler, but one oblivious to his surroundings, simply performing a mechanistic circumnavigation. The journey provides the opposite of his expectation: his anticipated, well-timed, and perfectly scheduled itinerary runs steadily more afoul of chance and circumstance, his mechanical plans breaking down completely. As Phileas Fogg encounters numerous foreign cultures, his unflappability is steadily shaken until his English reserve and imperturbability slowly succumb to the lure of adventure and romance.

Brought into the proximity of a wide variety of characters whose background is the opposite of his own, Fogg finds friendship with his faithful servant Passepartout (endearingly portrayed by the Mexican comedian Cantinflas) and love for the Indian princess Aouda (Shirley MacLaine), rescued from death by suttee. Cantinflas's differing nationality does not create a dissonance with Passepartout's character but complements it, and the casting of MacLaine is not incongruous because she was then new to the screen, although she never mastered an Eastern accent.[13] Aouda and Passepartout provide Fogg with an appreciation for human comradeship that he had never known before. By the end,

Fogg's win is predicated on his willingness to marry Aouda, despite such a wedding being highly unusual for the British aristocracy of the time.[14] The change in Fogg's character is complete as Passepartout and Aouda invade the sanctity of the Reform Club, signaling the end of the stuffy aristocratic English snobbery that Fogg formerly reflected. His counterpart is Detective Fix, delightfully played by Robert Newton, a character as fanatical as Fogg once was. Yet whereas the trip transforms Fogg and his adaptability to challenges earns him the mantle of heroism, Fix retains his obsession, leaving him a comical figure.

The sheer length of the film was the key stylistic difference from *20,000 Leagues under the Sea,* but Verne himself had realized that *Around the World in Eighty Days* was ideal for such epic treatment when he adapted his novel into a stage play even longer than the film. Only two sequences were added for the movie. One was a hiatus in Spain to allow Cantinflas a comedic episode as a bullfighter along with the appearance of several other Latin cameo stars; the casting of Cantinflas also guaranteed popularity in the Latin American market. Many Verne purists were dismayed by the inclusion of a balloon flight because no balloon is present in the novel, and it was of course the least practical form of transportation at the time, despite Verne's use of it in *Five Weeks in a Balloon* (1863). Although many viewers subsequently believed this balloon was a Vernian "prophecy" like the submarine, the balloon's actual, practical purpose in *Around the World in 80 Days* was to demonstrate the aerial potential of 65 mm., accompanied by Victor Young's soaring score (for which Todd had also bought the publishing rights, the album proving to be the first non–musical genre score to rack up vast sales).[15] Todd also intended the balloon to become the sequence most associated with the movie in public memory, and it became the logo in print advertising.[16]

*Around the World in 80 Days* confirmed Verne's position as a source of prestige movies that could do mammoth business and quite naturally led to more screen versions of his work. Hollywood's next two Verne adaptations return to the author's scientific stories, tackling distinct subjects with divergent challenges—and degrees of success.

As the possibility of space exploration began to fascinate much of the globe in the 1950s, increased attention would turn to Verne's outline for

The memorable on-screen balloon flight in *Around the World in 80 Days* (1956) and its prominence in advertising made the balloon an iconic image to evoke Verne henceforth.

a lunar journey composed a century earlier in the duo *From the Earth to the Moon* and *Around the Moon*. Popular fascination with these novels would reach its crescendo with their resemblance to the Apollo moon shots. Press coverage of Verne's sagas highlighted his meticulous research in the scientific journals of his day, and his thoughtful predictions, in contrast to H. G. Wells's reliance on imagination, won renewed respect.[17]

The novel *From the Earth to the Moon*, set at the end of the American Civil War, suggests that militarism might transition to space exploration, providing a new venue for the perfection of munitions. Verne imagined the Baltimore Gun Club, a group of eccentric Yankee artillerists, each lacking a hand, leg, arm, or nose, physically mutilated by their own explosive experiments. They decide to build a giant cannon to fire a projectile to the moon containing three fearless explorers. Although critics often dwelled on the validity of this premise to achieve a launch, the launch's larger purpose was to allow Verne's own ironic commentaries on nationalism, capitalism, and militarism.

With a spate of early 1950s films about fictional space journeys, Verne's novels were bound to emerge on the screen for the first time since the 1902 version by Georges Méliès, whose still widely seen adaptation had been excerpted in the prologue to Todd's *Around the World in 80 Days*. *From the Earth to the Moon* (1958) was one of RKO's last productions, released by Warner Bros. and produced by Benedict Bogeaus, which led one reviewer to impishly but accurately label the one-hundred-minute production "bogus Verne."[18] The role of Verne's Barbicane was originally conceived for the ailing Errol Flynn but went to Joseph Cotton instead, with George Sanders as his adversary Nicholl, here conceived as a religious zealot. Nicholl alternates between crazed villain and ambiguous hero, never achieving the consistency required to make such a characterization creditable. According to costar Debra Paget, playing Nicholl's daughter, Cotten and Sanders rewrote many of their lines on the set—diminishing the roles of their costars and favoring dialogue over action—although she believed they improved on the script by Robert Blees and James Leicester.[19]

*From the Earth to the Moon* is predicated on the same innovation that did so much to accelerate science fiction filmmaking, nuclear power. Already mentioned in the *Mysterious Island* serial, this innovation had been presented by Disney as Captain Nemo's discovery. *From the Earth to the Moon* portrays Barbicane as a contemplative arms inventor who has found the formula for an atomic explosive, described as "Power X." To test it, he raises millions of dollars to fire a shell and blow up the moon. However, when President Grant informs him that other countries regard this act as a dangerous Yankee provocation, Barbicane realizes he can use the armor plating developed by Nicholl as a coating for a manned projectile to travel to the moon and back to Earth.

Nicholl cooperates only to sabotage Barbicane's craft, but he is unaware that his own daughter has stowed away because she is in love with Barbicane's assistant. In a confusing finish, the craft breaks apart near the moon, leaving various compartments intact. One will take the lovers back to Earth, while another will land Barbicane and Nicholl on the supposedly habitable lunar surface, where they are now expected to live in harmony. This adaptation of *From the Earth to the Moon* made the same mistake as the *Mysterious Island* serial: it abandoned scientific plausibility.

*From the Earth to the Moon* compounded the overload of contradictory technical theory with cut-rate special effects, a rocket looking like a torch, and a comet resembling fireworks. The interior of the rocket is an unconvincing mix of nineteenth-century furnishing and vaguely futuristic contraptions—some of which prove demonstrably unnecessary, such as an elaborate spinning device supposedly required to allow the three men to survive blast-off, even though Nicholl's daughter stows away outside of it and remains unharmed. Director Byron Haskin admitted, "Up to the time that the damned missile was fired out of the cannon to go to the moon, it [the film] had a strange sort of nostalgic authenticity. I don't know what could have made it into a good film. It just lost all sense of credibility with this obviously phony looking projectile with big rooms in it and step ladders and that twirling sort of gyroscope contraption and so forth."[20] The movie was filmed in Mexico, so the Earth-bound portion of the sets and costumes have a distinctly inappropriate Western flavor. The musical score for the heavens was adapted from *Forbidden Planet*.

Humorless and pretentious, *From the Earth to the Moon* fails to discuss the very issues on which it attempts to pontificate. Such a result was not inevitable; the 1964 movie of the H. G. Wells novel *The First Men in the Moon* brought the Victorian qualities to the fore in a treatment that was charming, thrilling, and dynamic, overcoming the period setting by using a framing device, with a modern lunar landing discovering traces of the original journey. The most interesting touch of *From the Earth to the Moon* is the casting of Carl Esmond as "J. V.," a character revealed at the conclusion to be Jules Verne. Originally, he was to have found that the lovers had returned to Earth and to learn from them the outcome of the trip. Instead, this device was eliminated in favor of a closing epilogue wherein he lauds imagination.[21]

By 1958 and the release of *From the Earth to the Moon,* Verne films began to mention their famous predecessors to promote new adaptations.

Far from the "prophetic" works of science fiction such as the lunar novels and *Twenty Thousand Leagues under the Seas,* which rely on some type of advanced technology, was a novel outside the genre: *Journey to the Center of the Earth.* It is a fantasy set in a milieu where events trespass physical laws and the bounds of human possibility, an entirely different vein from stories relying on credible science.[22] *Journey to the Center of the Earth* nonetheless has appeared on the screen second only in frequency to the eighty-day races around the world of Phileas Fogg and his descendants and the undersea exploits of Captain Nemo, stories embodying Verne's other two primary genres, adventure and science fiction.[23]

With its publication in 1864, *Journey to the Center of the Earth* vivified geology, fictional scientific exploration, and prehistoric life in a manner that was new to literature.[24] Avoiding intrigue, villains, and satire, Verne provided a direct account of a contemporary descent following the route originally taken by Arne Saknussemm, an imaginary sixteenth-century alchemist. Saknussemm left behind instructions on how to locate the path in coded runic lettering on an old parchment, although the obvious question of just how he discovered the route is never broached. Saknussemm's relics—his initials carved in the rocks, a rusty knife—are found unpredictably on the new journey, serving as clues to the enigma of the earlier journey while confirming that those who follow are on the right path. (Scenes of the discovery of such relics have proven ideal for screen adaptations.)

The three travelers are a German professor, Otto Lidenbrock, his young nephew Axel, and Hans Bjelke, an Icelandic guide and hunter, each embodying contrasting and distinct types. Lidenbrock is the eccentric scientist who proceeds before realizing the consequences; he believes Saknussemm's expedition can be duplicated and is unconcerned with the obvious question of how it will end. Axel is the practical one, logically objecting to the entire idea of the journey, and the novel is told from his first-person perspective, even as Verne provides a corresponding, parallel psychological journey. Yet Axel solves mysteries that defy Lidenbrock's skill. The expedition becomes transformative as Axel frankly admits and then overcomes his own fears, striving to live up to the expectations of both his uncle and his sweetheart, Graüben, so as to become worthy to marry her upon his return. (The situation would be satirized in Edward Malone's quest to earn the right to marry Gladys Hungerford in *The Lost World,* Sir Arthur Conan Doyle's 1912 novel, which was in part inspired by *Journey to the Center of the Earth.*) The courageous Hans stoically facilitates Lidenbrock and Axel's journey without emotion or question, his thought glimpsed only externally in action. Together, the three men represent the science, spirit, and strength—head, heart, and hands; mind, soul, and body—that are necessary for such an endeavor.

As the world's largest volcanic island, Iceland was a logical place to begin the journey, and today its tourism industry touts the novel. The trip begins and ends on a perfect parallel: commencing with a peaceful descent into the extinct Icelandic volcano Snæfels and violently returning to the surface from the earth's interior in an eruption from a live volcano, Stromboli. The geographical expedition is varied by making it a trip back in biological and geological time—the deeper the explorers go, the farther they travel into the past. Lidenbrock, Axel, and Hans eventually encounter prehistoric animals and the primordial sea in which life began, and they finally sink into an abyss that transforms into a volcanic eruption, from which they are pushed vertically up to the surface—and back to the present—atop the molten material that was spewed over the surface of the earth in the planet's formation.

Hollywood writer-producer Charles Brackett, age sixty-six, was nearing the end of his career and had long cherished the dream of filming *Journey to the Center of the Earth*. He had been told that an expensive fantasy with a period setting could not be profitable until Disney's and Todd's Vernian successes proved the contrary.[25] Brackett's 1959 production for 20th Century-Fox wisely followed Disney and Todd's lead, emphasizing special effects, color, and widescreen. Brackett's screenplay was coauthored with Walter Reich, who had studied Verne with the intention of writing a biography but who had believed only the novel's premise was successful.[26] Even before the narrative begins, the title sequence perfectly captures in a visual metaphor the trip the characters and the audience are about to undertake. The camera moves steadily closer to an Earth revolving in space, until Earth comes so close that it fades to black, and finally out of the darkness emerge shots of spewing lava and a red volcano.

Verne's opening in Germany is switched to Edinburgh in 1880 to accommodate the stars and to eliminate the need for German heroes only fourteen years after the end of World War II. Otto Lidenbrock becomes Oliver Lindenbrook, played by James Mason, who was fifty at the time, the age Verne had given his hero. Although Mason had provided the authoritative movie portrayal of Captain Nemo in *20,000 Leagues under the Sea* five years earlier, his Lindenbrook is far less true to the source.[27] Instead of following Verne's characterization of an eccentric, the movie substitutes a note of temper, accenting misogyny, and Lindenbrook's elitist pretensions are mocked when he misinterprets the noise of a duck foraging for food as a code in a foreign language. Some of the changes derive from the fact that the part had been intended for Clifton Webb, who withdrew due to illness only weeks before shooting began and at age seventy was far too old for the role.

Lidenbrock's nephew Axel became favorite student Alec (Pat Boone), in love with the professor's niece Jenny (Diane Baker), equivalent to Graüben in the novel; Baker is included in the star billing despite a small role. Although cast to appeal to teen filmgoers, Boone perfectly incarnates Alec; Alec's passage from boyhood to manhood on the trip is evident in the film as for the first time he is required to demonstrate courage and heroism. Boone saw the science fiction assignment as a downturn in his career, and earnest persuasion and a percentage of the profits were necessary to convince him to take the role.[28] Although several songs were inserted for him, with music by James Van Heusen and lyrics by Sammy Cahn, they were minimized and concentrated early in the picture, preventing his musical persona from interfering with the narrative.

Brackett and Reich added human antagonists to Verne's inherent natural obstacles. Lindenbrook confides Saknussemm's note to a Swedish professor, Goetaborg, who then undertakes the trip himself. However, Goetaborg's sudden, mysterious death allows a variation on the romantic theme when his widow, Carla (Arlene Dahl), demands to join the Lindenbrook expedition, thus incorporating a more active, older heroine than Jenny would have been. Carla is also every bit as prickly and headstrong as Lindenbrook himself, and the trek becomes a humanizing experience for him as well. The eventual romance of a middle-aged couple stands in for the largely unseen one between the ingénues, Jenny appearing only briefly in lonely intervals, wondering what is happening to Alec and her uncle.

Carla also proves of practical use as the only one who shares a language in common with Hans. Actor Peter Ronson (née Rognvoldsson) was the decathlon champion of Iceland and the film's technical adviser, but he understood and spoke little English, just like the character he played. Hans was given stronger motives and turned into a source of mild amusement; perhaps best remembered by young viewers was his pet duck, Gertrude, who accompanies the expedition—even though Verne had described Hans as a duck hunter!

The only one-dimensional role was in the characterization given a modern descendant of Arne Saknussemm. A scientist in his own right, he poisoned Goetaborg when he learned of Lindenbrook's note. The second major casting switch took place after the first few days of shooting, with Thayer David replacing Alexander Scourby as the imperious count who believes the underworld is his by inheritance. (His motives actually approximate those of the menacing Silfax in Verne's other underground novel, *The Black Indies* [1877], who threatens to destroy a once-abandoned coal mine when his solitude is disturbed as the mine becomes active once more.) The count is the only one who will die on the trip, after making a meal of Gertrude.

By slowly easing the viewer into the complex plot with its myriad details (fifty minutes pass before the descent begins), the movie gives the journey an aura of possibility—following the pattern set in the novel, in which nearly half the book is consumed with deciphering the manuscript and the trek to Snæfels.[29] The use of actual caves provides an eerie sense of authenticity to the underground scenes, and filming took place in Carlsbad Caverns, New Mexico, descending to 1,100 feet, beyond the areas seen by tourists. The encounters with dinosaurs at sea are transferred to the beach, preceding the launch of the raft. The dinosaurs look (inevitably, perhaps) less than authentic: rows of sail-like spines were attached to the backs of two-foot Haitian iguanas prior to photography, and the iguanas were enlarged as necessary through double exposures and other effects, with their movements altered by increasing camera speed.[30]

The explorers stumble across the lost city of Atlantis, an incident that was borrowed from *Twenty Thousand Leagues under the Seas* but had not been used in the Disney movie.[31] Buried within the ruins is a giant reptile. Lindenbrook is seized by the live serpent's tongue but saved by Alec's quick intervention—echoing the scene five years earlier in which

Dinosaurs menace the travelers at the shore of the underground sea in *Journey to the Center of the Earth* (1959).

Nemo, played by the same actor, is seized by a tentacle of the giant squid in *20,000 Leagues under the Sea* and then rescued by Ned Land. Among the crumbled stones and pillars, Arne Saknussemm's skeleton points to a shaft. Gunpowder triggers an eruption, and Alec, Lindenbrook, Carla, and Hans take refuge in an ancient cup-shaped altar stone as they are carried to the surface in one of the most superbly visualized scenes. Shown schematically, they are pushed up through the chimney on top of rocks propelled by lava; the camera looks down directly at them as they are transfixed to the stone by the air pressure. They, in turn, watch the walls of the cavern race by and, looking up, see a gradually growing spot of light that represents the surface. Through these three key shots, the difficult concept of the return to the surface is ideally expressed in cinematic terms.

*Journey to the Center of the Earth* is visually a continuous feast for the senses and received Academy Award nominations for sound, art direction, set decorations, and special effects.[32] The story is ideal for widescreen treatment, and director Henry Levin imaginatively composed the staging and images to take advantage of the CinemaScope ratio of 2:35 to 1. Camera angles subtly reveal characters' position and nearby menaces, from Saknussemm to a monster's observant eye. CinemaScope, together with the long running time of 132 minutes and a $4.5 million budget, helps to capture a sense of the epic immensity of the heroes' journey (noted as 256 days prior to the discovery of the mushroom forest). Equally important are the sound effects and the score. Bernard Herrmann's music varies between the deepest sounds to loud, high-pitched music. He explained, "I decided to evoke the mood and feeling of inner Earth by using only instruments played in low registers. Eliminating all strings, I utilized an orchestra of woodwinds and brass, with a large percussion section and many harps. But the truly unique feature of this score is the inclusion of five organs, one large Cathedral and four electronic. These organs were used in many adroit ways to suggest ascent and descent, as well as the mystery of Atlantis."[33]

Although *Journey to the Center of the Earth* is not an overpowering film in the manner of Disney's *20,000 Leagues under the Sea,* it also does not show its age. Though leavened with humor, the amusing ingredients are incidental to the plot and situations, becoming an integral element of the long trek. It stands up well to repeated viewing and different generations of viewers. On American television, it became popular in the late 1960s and was simultaneously re-released overseas well into the 1970s before becoming a staple video release.

To promote the film, a series of book tie-ins were issued in hardback and paperback in the United States and England, showing scenes from the movie on the cover, but unlike the publications issued for *20,000 Leagues under the Sea,* they were directed largely at adult readers and used translations of the Verne text. Although *Journey to the Center of the Earth* was republished in England and the United States on some fifteen occasions in the fifty years between the first film of the novel, Segundo de Chomon's 1909 *Voyage au centre de la terre,* and Brackett's version, it has been republished more than fifty times in the years since the 1959 movie.[34] The steadily growing popularity of *Journey to the Center of the Earth* on the screen has made it the third most widely read Verne novel after *Around the World in Eighty Days* and *Twenty Thousand Leagues under the Seas.* This suggests that accelerating interest in the novel, continuing enjoyment of the 1959 movie, and the frequency of other subsequent film, television, radio, and stage adaptations have become mutually reinforcing, each fueling the demand for the others.

Coming on the heels of the enormous box office success of *20,000 Leagues under the Sea* and *Around the World in 80 Days, Journey to the Center of the Earth* proved a wise investment, becoming the third top-grossing Verne picture in a mere five years in the global marketplace. Despite the stumble of *From the Earth to the Moon, Journey to the Center of the Earth* confirmed a cinematic cycle, and within a short time four new Verne movies were showing or in production. On September 28, 1960, *Variety* headlined, "Jules Verne as His Own Hero: Rivals Bible as Film Source." Together, Disney, Todd, and Brackett had proven how Verne could be a source of popular entertainment for a mass audience around the world.

Interest in Verne himself was also on the rise. Issued in the wake of Disney's *20,000 Leagues under the Sea* was *Jules Verne: His Life* (1956) by Catherine O. Peare, the first Verne biography in English aimed at children. It was heavily fictionalized and indebted to the earlier books by George Waltz and Kenneth Allott, but most especially again to the biography by Marguerite Allotte de la Fuÿe. Peare's volume was reprinted five times in the next ten years, and its success would lead to two new biographies of Verne for youth, Russell Freedman's *Jules Verne: Portrait of a Prophet* (1965), the most mature such effort, and Beril Becker's *Jules Verne* (1966). The nadir was reached with Franz Born's *Jules Verne: The Man Who Invented the Future* (1964), a book whose many errors were compounded by a wretched translation, yet this volume was directly marketed to schoolchildren in the classrooms of America by Scholastic Book Services well into the 1970s.

Nonetheless, Verne became fashionable once more for literary-minded adults as the faulty nineteenth-century renditions were replaced with improved translations, a movement quietly encouraged by the interest of legitimate publishing houses (rather than pirates) when European copyright protection expired fifty years after Verne's 1905 death. One of the first to take up the pen was Willis T. Bradley, a Massachusetts academic who sought to provide a more faithful version than "the free and silly adaptation made for British schoolboys nearly a hundred years ago," as noted on the dust jacket of the hardcover edition of his translation of *Journey to the Center of the Earth,* published in 1956. Bradley continued with Verne's horror story "Frritt-Flacc" (1884), and the first translation of *The Eternal Adam* (1910) appeared in the March 1957 inaugural issue of the science fiction magazine *Saturn.*

Beyond Bradley's efforts, between the late 1950s and 1970s fifteen Verne novels reappeared from various publishers.[35] Most important would be the Fitzroy Edition of Jules Verne, edited by Idrisyn Oliver Evans. In 1956, Evans compiled *Jules Verne, Master of Science Fiction,* published in London and including excerpts from fourteen of the author's novels, accompanied by a critical introduction. Two years later Evans began editing the Fitzroy series, which ran through 1968 and issued forty-eight separate stories in sixty-three volumes, eventually including many of Verne's later works that had never before appeared in English.[36] Evans's efforts made the vast majority of Verne's works again available, and paperback versions of some titles in both the United States and England made the series even more widely read. In 1966, Evans offered *Jules Verne and His Work,* combining biographical and critical approaches to demonstrate the depth of Verne's cultural impact and becoming the first in that era to perceive that resurgence of interest in the author and the reading of his stories were intertwined with the appearances of his work on screen. Verne had become more than the "prophet" of the technological age; he was now also a vital source of modern entertainment on the screen and printed page, as much in vogue as when his books were best sellers during his lifetime.[37]

# 5

# The Height of the Verne Cycle, 1960–1962

Verne filmmaking was about to move beyond spectacle and entertainment for the whole family. Average filmgoers were younger, and science fiction had emerged as a successful draw that could make lower-budget filmmaking just as profitable as its more expensive counterpart. Verne became one of the names to lure this new audience, who had often learned of him through the revival in Verne publishing. The peak year was 1961, when four Hollywood Verne movies were released, as well as several imports along with television broadcasts. The apex was reached when *Daily Variety* and *Hollywood Reporter* ran separate reviews of two Verne movies—*Master of the World* and *The Fabulous World of Jules Verne*—on a single page in their April 26, 1961, issues.

Only one overseas Verne adaptation had appeared on the American screen in the years since the silent era, *Captain Grant's Children*, which arrived from the Soviet Union in 1939. Now, Hollywood sought to cash in on foreign-made Verne films, dubbing them into English. From Czechoslovakia came a 1956 adaptation of *Facing the Flag*, released theatrically in the United States in 1961 under the title *The Fabulous World of Jules Verne*. The previous year, *Michael Strogoff*, a 1956 European coproduction with Curt Jurgens in the lead, was shown to American cinemagoers; it was later retitled both *Revolt of the Tartars* and *Secret Mission to Siberia* for television. Although both *The Fabulous World of Jules Verne* and *Michael Strogoff* flopped theatrically in the United

States, the latter had been a major hit in Europe and had inspired an original, Franco-Italian cinema sequel, again starring Jurgens, entitled *The Triumph of Michael Strogoff* (1962).[1] It was shown on American television, as was an unacknowledged 1960 Japanese version of Verne's novel, *King of the Mongols* (also titled *Genghis Khan and His Mongols*). *La Jangada,* produced in Mexico in 1959, was based on Verne's 1881 novel of the same title and retitled *800 Leagues over the Amazon* for television in the United States, while *Shipwreck Island* (1961) was a Spanish version of *Two Year Holiday* (1888). Although both of these Spanish-language films were sparsely broadcast, they would far outclass subsequent Hollywood versions of these same novels.

Hollywood had already resumed filming the author directly for the small screen, and the influence there would continue to grow. The October 19, 1959, episode of the film noir series *Peter Gunn,* starring Craig Stevens, returned to the concept at the center of *The Tribulations of a Chinese in China.* In the *Peter Gunn* episode entitled "Death Is a Red Rose," a man arranges for his death so his family can inherit his life insurance, but then he regrets the decision and asks for detective Gunn's assistance.[2] Boris Sagal directed a script by Lewis Reed and Tony Barrett, with story credit given to Blake Edwards, the series creator. In fact, the television script was a remake of a 1951 radio segment of another Edwards series, *Richard Diamond—Private Detective;* neither attributed Verne.[3]

A Verne story was explicitly folded into the December 3, 1960, episode "Foggbound" of the CBS Western series *Have Gun—Will Travel.* In San Francisco, Passepartout (Jon Silo) requests the assistance of series lead Paladin (Richard Boone) on behalf of his master, Phileas Fogg (Patric Knowles), whom he bluntly describes as mad. Because of his refusal to duel with Colonel Proctor (Peter Whitney), who is stalking him, Fogg has missed his train and must catch it at its next stop in Reno.

On the way, Fogg encounters Proctor and gamely defends himself. When Paladin suggests taking an evasive route, Fogg lectures him on British behavior, only to be told that the world cannot always be approached according to the standards of a game of cricket. As Passepartout seeks a boat along the Truckee River, there is the hint of a romantic possibility between Aouda (Arlene MacQuade) and Paladin (a convention for most of the heroines appearing in the series), especially given Fogg's indifference to her.

Proctor shoots and wounds Fogg without warning, but Paladin fires in return, Proctor's body disappearing down the river. Fogg speaks of leaving Aouda behind because as an expert Punjab horsewoman she seems to prefer the West to England. At that moment, she asks Paladin to ask Fogg if he will marry her. Replying in the same manner, using the silent Paladin as intermediary, Fogg accepts, and the party then proceeds on their journey. Only in this change in the resolution of the romance between Fogg and Aouda does episode writer Shimon Wincelberg take any notable liberties with Verne's concept. The only missing element is Fix, but a second antagonist would have been unwieldy in a single half-hour episode. "Foggbound" is a credited adaptation of a portion of *Around the World in Eighty Days* within the larger context of the typical conventions of a *Have Gun—Will Travel* segment. The recent success of the Michael Todd spectacular in theaters made the idea seem promising for *Have Gun—Will Travel* because Paladin often encountered actual or literary characters in a credible manner in various episodes. Andrew V. McLaglen's direction includes some attractive exteriors on the Paramount Ranch but conveys little of the humor of the Verne source. Knowles is appropriately cold, aloof, selfish, overbearing, and single-minded as Fogg, and Silo is an effective Passepartout. However, both MacQuade and Whitney fail to embody Verne's concept of their respective roles. The incidents in this episode, as ingenious as they are, do not quite live up to the premise, and "Foggbound" suffers from much of episodic television's general tendency to adjust every original idea to each particular series' normative standards.

Two other Verne adaptations for television were on anthology shows, and although still requiring adjustment to the constraints of running time and genre, they did not need to accommodate reappearing characters and settings. Ironically, both were versions of the same story, *Master Zacharius* (1854), although, like "Foggbound" and "Death Is a Red Rose," one was acknowledged as such, whereas the other was not. Considerable liberties were taken with *Master Zacharius,* carrying Verne's idea one logical step further to embellish the science fiction element by portraying the outcome of the clockmaker's experiments as the creation of human automatons operating on a clocklike mechanism.[4]

The first broadcast of an adaptation of *Master Zacharius* occurred on January 3, 1961, with "The Changing Heart" episode of *Alfred Hitchcock Presents*. It was scripted by Robert Bloch and directed by Verne enthusiast Robert Florey. This version was uncredited, necessarily condensing the story's themes to fit a thirty-minute show. Nonetheless, of the two versions, this one actually retains greater fidelity to the duality and menace of Verne's clockmaker (memorably played by Abraham Sofaer), who believes he has conquered time. Despite the American setting, there is a European flavor as the clockmaker possessively retains a hypnotic control over his granddaughter, Lisa (Anne Helm), that gradually gives evidence of his increasing madness. She becomes broken-hearted and ill as she is kept inviolate from the outside world and Dane, the man she loves (Nicholas Pryor). Weeks later, when Dane is able to return to the clockmaker's shop, it is now suddenly quiet, with all the hitherto noisy clocks having stopped at the same time. The clockmaker is dead and surrounded by broken springs, mechanisms, and dismantled watches, but he has left a scrawled note claiming that his experiment has succeeded. And in the next room is the granddaughter, apparently recovered. However, Lisa appears strangely doll-like, and a loud ticking breaks the silence, emanating from within her. The clockmaker had used his knowledge of miniature automatons and wind-up figures to turn her into one, giving her a new but inhuman kind of life.

A few weeks later, on January 29, NBC broadcast the official adaptation of *Master Zacharius,* a one-hour show entitled "The Terrible Clockman" for the series *The Shirley Temple Theater.* The clockman in this version is not Zacharius himself, but his latest triumph to calculate time, a giant human-shaped statue with a clocklike face and arms for the hands of the clock—all intended as a gift for the king of Bavaria during his forthcoming visit to the village. However, Zacharius's daughter, Gerande (a blond, thirty-three-year-old Shirley Temple), has been followed by Ignacious Van Der Graf, a stranger who brings darkness and storms wherever he goes and is able to appear and vanish at will. Van Der Graf, a demonic alchemist, demands that Zacharius allow him to marry Gerande regardless of her love for Aubert, her fiancé and her father's assistant. When Zacharius refuses, more than just his clocks stop; the ticking mechanism in the clockman turns into an audible beating heart as it comes to life as a walking robot and escapes. The clockman thus becomes the scientific prediction audiences expect from Verne, despite the original story having been a pure fantasy.

Not only does Van Der Graf cause the townsfolk to lose all track of time, but he also changes day into night and causes snow during the summer. The clockman stalks the streets, murdering a young couple and terrorizing the people, who blame Zacharius. The clockman also abducts Gerande and takes her to Van Der Graf's lair in the Black Castle, but when she spurns Van Der Graf's marriage proposal, he transforms her into an old woman. Aubert arrives to save her, disconnecting the clockman's mechanism, and the dying robot turns on Van Der Graf and kills him before falling to pieces. Villainy has turned destructively back on itself, and with the magician's death Gerande regains her youth as time returns to normal.

Temple's out-of-costume introduction casts the Verne story as a science fiction fairytale, a look enhanced by the fact that the William Asher production was shot live. The mood is furthered by the show's clear stage limitations, its artificial decor and medieval setting, and the extraordinarily bright and colorful hues. Allen Reisner's direction facilitates fast camera movements, and the sense of evil is furthered by the dramatic lighting and shading (such as the lightning that whitens Van Der Graf's face), sound effects, and musical score. Eric Portman and Sam Jaffe vividly etch Van Der Graf and Zacharius, respectively, but some mediocre acting by the supporting players causes the story to drag when they alone occupy the screen.

Although one of the best-made Verne television shows, "The Terrible Clockman" has little fidelity to Verne's conception. Unlike Bloch, writer Bernard Schoenfeld eliminated the tragic, Faustian duality in *Master Zacharius,* instead splitting the original characterization by adding Van Der Graf. Rather than Verne's tale of a man tempted by the devil, "The Terrible Clockman" elides Verne's specific religious connotations and shifts to emphasize a Frankenstein-style conflict and a time-warp theme. Zacharius must still choose between having all his clocks stop or marrying Gerande to the sorcerer, but he never considers accepting, and his complicity instead comes through his having built what becomes the terrible clockman. Nonetheless, the show is gripping, and the new themes provide an arresting manner of presenting Verne.

Like these two television productions of *Master Zacharius,* other Verne movies at this point also enhanced the science fiction aspects of their source. Two were influenced by the success of Disney's *20,000 Leagues under the Sea,* whether its narrative pattern or the persona of Captain Nemo and the goals established for him. None of the new films had the budgets of those that came before, but some were no less inventive.

A decade after the serial of *The Mysterious Island,* Columbia Pictures again presented the story, this time in the form of a 101-minute feature. Disney's *20,000 Leagues under the Sea* was not only an impetus but also a shadow hanging over a potential sequel because Nemo had been killed off in the earlier film, and viewers who assumed it was a faithful rendering would be surprised at his reappearance. The script developed by Crane Wilbur years earlier was sold to Charles Schneer, who regularly produced vehicles for Ray Harryhausen's stop-motion special-effects wizardry.

Just as filmmakers in 1929 believed the way to enliven the novel was by adding a race of underwater men, and the creators of the 1951 serial felt compelled to enrich the tale with invaders from outer space, the 1961 version of *Mysterious Island* augmented an otherwise faithful retelling of Verne's story with giant creatures. The animals' creator, Harryhausen, noted, "The story was changed to embrace the entertaining visuals which can be produced by special effects and animation. . . . We felt it important for audience acceptance to inject other elements to keep the film more unusual and interesting pictorially."[5]

Michael Craig starred as Captain Cyrus Harding, Michael Callan as Herbert Brown, Gary Merrill as Gideon Spilett, Dan Jackson as Neb, and Percy Herbert as Pencroft, here a Confederate soldier.[6] Bernard Herrmann, who had scored *Journey to the Center of the Earth* two years earlier, again provided a virtuoso Vernian musical background. The escape from Richmond and the journey to the island via balloon in a storm are vividly portrayed in a colorful, dramatic sequence. Cy Endfield's direction of the escape and of life on the island accentuates fast

The death of Captain Nemo (Herbert Lom) in *Mysterious Island* (1961).

pacing through frequent changes of camera position as well as action in the frame, a style that also combines ideally with Harryhausen's effects. These portions and the first half of the picture closely follow the novel, with the exploration of the island, settlement, and discovery of Granite House. Two women, played by Joan Greenwood and Beth Rogan, also shipwrecked, are the major addition. The monsters begin as a subsidiary plot device but become more important as the second half diverges sharply from the novel.

A sea chest washes ashore, and the castaways, having read *Twenty Thousand Leagues under the Seas*, realize it is from the *Nautilus*. Hence, they are ready for Captain Nemo's appearance after he explodes a pirate ship. He emerges dramatically from the deep in a sea-shell-style diving suit, warning the castaways that "contact with my own species has always disappointed me." Spilett, the cynical war correspondent, is eager for a scoop with Nemo's story, whereas Harding, a military man, considers him a butcher. For his part, Nemo regards both men as instruments of war and deals with them warily, minimizing natural antagonism because of their mutual need.

Mason could not be obtained to extend his previous portrayal of Captain Nemo, and the part was placed in the hands of Herbert Lom.

He portrays Nemo in an extremely limited range, using a single dour note of fatalism and an unemotional monotone. There is none of the tortured emotion and brooding charisma achieved by Mason or Lionel Barrymore in *The Mysterious Island* (1929) and Robert Ryan in *Captain Nemo and the Underwater City* (1970). These faults are all the more glaring because Nemo is made such a key character. Lom's Nemo is a man who sometimes fails to notice the obvious, becoming overshadowed by Harding's science even aboard the *Nautilus:* when volcanic eruptions preclude completing the castaways' boat, Harding, not Nemo, realizes the submarine's pumps can be used to float the pirate ship.

For this 1961 film, Nemo's submarine had to be more modest in its interior decors, but the exterior offers a fresh conception. However, Nemo is trapped aboard when the grotto caves in, so his secrets are lost to science. As Nemo dies, Lom provides nothing more than a glassy look of emptiness on his face. His performance is the only failure in a lively and colorful film exemplary in most other respects. Once again, the script transforms Nemo into a frustrated beneficiary of humankind, and the giant animals are an attempt to end war by literally increasing the food supply; surely a more accurate reflection of the concerns Verne gave Nemo would have demanded mentioning nationalism, imperialism, and totalitarianism as causes of war. The picture opened in December 1961, and the reaction at the box office was lukewarm; audiences seemed to prefer Harryhausen's work in mythological fantasies rather than in pure science fiction. Over the years, however, this version of *Mysterious Island* has steadily gained popularity and has become a staple of the small screen; it was even theatrically reissued in 1978, after having already spent a decade on television.

The challenge that the filmmakers of *Mysterious Island* had overcome would be faced again when making a screen version of *Hector Servadac* and would be resolved in a similar manner. This novel, named for its principal character, is Verne's second excursion into "outer space" after *From the Earth to the Moon* and *Around the Moon*. Although abandoning the technical exactitude of the lunar journey, *Hector Servadac* is perhaps Verne's most astounding novel, ingenious and surprising: when a comet, Gallia, grazes Earth, it sweeps up a small portion of the Mediterranean, taking a group of travelers on a two-year round trip through the solar system.

The *Nautilus* trapped in a grotto in *Mysterious Island* (1961).

The interior of the *Nautilus* in *Mysterious Island* (1961).

In a series of incidents, the cosmic castaways come to understand the celestial cataclysm and learn to survive on the comet's natural resources. Whether they are enduring the heat of approaching Venus or the cold of nearby Saturn, some human behavior remains immutable, despite the palpable emergency that draws together most of the travelers on Gallia. A few obstinately stand apart, including an eccentric and selfish French scientist, a greedy moneylender, and the British garrison at Gibraltar.[7] *Hector Servadac* is, along with *Journey to the Center of the Earth* and *The Secret of Wilhelm Storitz* (1910), one of the few books in which Verne's imagination is wholly unfettered by probability. For instance, he adopts an idea he had once criticized in Edgar Allan Poe's "The Unparalleled Adventures of One Hans Pfaall": a balloon ascending beyond Earth's atmosphere; now Verne uses a balloon as a vehicle for the castaways to avoid the impact as the returning meteor strikes Earth.[8]

*Hector Servadac* was first filmed as *Valley of the Dragons* (1961), retitled *Prehistoric Valley* in England, and advertised as based on a novel by Verne entitled *Career of a Comet*—one of the English-language title variants of *Hector Servadac*. Donald Zimbalist, son of executive producer Alfred Zimbalist, had stumbled across the volume in a British used-book store, which earned him story credit. Just as *Mysterious Island* required the addition of monstrous creatures to enliven its narrative on a limited budget, the elder Zimbalist's keen eye for exploitation conceived merging *Hector Servadac* with recycled footage from the 1940 Hal Roach production *One Million B.C.* Advertising the process as "Monstascope," the filmmakers shot the eighty-minute black-and-white picture at the Hollywood studios of Columbia Pictures for a mere $135,000.[9] Considering the recent success of *Journey to the Center of the Earth* only two years earlier, a movie that associated Verne with dinosaurs in the public's mind, Zimbalist's notion situated *Valley of the Dragons* as a follow-up.

With Byron Roberts producing, Zimbalist asked writer-director Edward Bernds to devise a screenplay he would also direct. Unfortunately, the producers never realized that the copy they had of *Career of a Comet* was in fact only the first volume of *Hector Servadac*. As a consequence, the movie does not include any of the events from the novel's second half, and Bernds later wished he had known about the second volume because he thought the return of the comet to Earth "would have made a most interesting film."[10]

Valley of the Dragons has been undervalued because of the inherent absurdities of its particular branch of science fiction: the representation of prehistoric life. In fact, however, much of Valley of the Dragons stands on a par with a more artistic adaptation, Karel Zeman's On the Comet (1970), which saw even more limited theatrical release in the United States than Zeman's The Fabulous World of Jules Verne. Zeman, filming in Czechoslovakia, was known as the true heir to Georges Méliès for his combination of animation, puppets, models, and live action in a manner evocative of the engravings in the first French editions of Verne's works. On the Comet almost entirely jettisoned the plot of Hector Servadac in favor of a reinterpretation that emphasized its whimsy and without explanation recapitulated dinosaurs from an earlier Zeman movie.[11] Both Zeman and Bernds faced the same problem—visualizing Verne's lively events would have required a budget they lacked—but Bernds's script offered a more convincing rationale for the dinosaurs' presence. The first third of Valley of the Dragons, which resembles the novel, is exciting in a simple way, especially for young audiences. For good or bad, Valley of the Dragons remains down-to-earth in its presentation and emotion, avoiding the risky and ultimately disappointing flights of high fancy attempted in On the Comet.

The opening credits of Valley of the Dragons unroll effectively over an approaching, spinning globe, and the Verne source is twice cited as Career of a Comet. An unusual introduction follows, more strongly acknowledging the debt than other American adaptations of this time did:

Jules Verne was an imaginative genius a hundred years ahead of his time. He wrote of a marvelous submarine, a record-breaking trip around the world, a journey to the center of the Earth, a flight to the moon. Many of his imaginings have come true. Who is to say that all of them will not. In his great book, Career of a Comet, Jules Verne tells of a mysterious adventure in time and space, and the story begins in North Africa, in Algeria,

May 16, 1881, in the crowded streets, the bazaars, swarms [*sic*]
of humanity. Outside the city, a silent group of men—Michael
Denning, soldier of fortune from County Claire, Ireland; Captain Hector Servadac, of the French Army.

Subsequent dialogue indicates the two men have quarreled over a woman
and are about to fight a duel. Opening on an obviously painted Arabian
backdrop does not hurt *Valley of the Dragons* as presented in this fantastic context, and the surprising attention to period and manners helps
to make the fantasy more credible. Cesare Danova plays Servadac in a
dignified, military fashion, and Sean McClory is the more emotive Irish-
man Michael Denning, who replaces Verne's Count Wassili Timascheff.

The scene that ensues demonstrates how special effects can be handled impressively even in black and white on a low budget; for instance,
they are far superior to the color results in the 1958 version of *From
the Earth to the Moon.* A violent windstorm interrupts the counting of
steps; the duelists are knocked over, and the comet appears, shedding a
stream of sparks as it approaches Earth's atmosphere. The men claw at
the ground in an attempt to hold their place against the wind, and those
acting as seconds are pulled through the air by gravity back to Earth.
An onrush of water covers the camera, and as the comet hits, it seems
to explode, with two pieces of land torn apart as if in an earthquake,
trees aflame and lightning striking. Earth's horizon spins off into space,
and as the storm dies down, the comet apparently recedes. The duelists
get up, noticing that the nearby city has disappeared in this calamity of
nature.

Postponing their duel and heading to where the city used to be,
they instead find themselves in a tropical forest. At night, Servadac, the
astronomer and scientist of the duo, surmises from the stars that Earth's
orbit has changed. Building a fire attracts growling, humanlike creatures, apparently Neanderthals. Having emptied their pistols at them,
Servadac and Denning take up the spear and hatchet dropped by the
Neanderthals, an action that, together with the two men's tattered
clothes, suggests their increasing distance from civilization literally and
metaphorically. As the two observe a giant sloth eat a serpent and a
battle between dinosaurs, the use of long stretches of footage from *One*

Servadac and Denning look back at Earth from the comet in *Valley of the Dragons* (1961).

*Million B.C.* becomes surprisingly effective, fitting into the story and avoiding any patchwork quality. Saving each other's life confirms the friendship between Denning and Servadac as they laugh together about the lady who had urged them to duel.

That night, the moon seems enormous until they recognize that what they are looking at is actually Earth. Servadac realizes there must have been a collision with a comet, carrying away an envelope of the earth's atmosphere. He explains that the combined movement of the comet with Earth's rotation prevented a direct collision, and the variety of life around them provides apparent evidence that their celestial body may be striking Earth every one hundred thousand years. After observing a herd of Ice Age animals, Denning and Servadac sight a group of cave people and adopt some of their furs and leather for new clothing. Chased by a mastodon, Servadac falls over a cliff; he survives, but both he and Denning assume the other is dead. From this point, Verne is left behind, and the plot of *One Million B.C.* comes to determine the incidents in *Valley of the Dragons*, which accordingly suffers from the earlier film's caveman hokeyness.

Servadac floats downstream until rescued by a blond cave girl, Deena, amazed at his clean-shaven face in contrast with the unkempt beards on the men of her tribe. As she nurses his broken leg, they begin to learn each other's language, and Servadac dubs her "chérie" as they kiss. Denning saves an old man from a rival tribe and is given food by his daughter, Nateeta (Danielle de Metz). Meanwhile, after a romantic interlude with Deena, Servadac discovers sulfur and realizes he can make explosives; as *Variety* humorously noted, Servadac and Denning's sole contributions to Neolithic culture are gunpowder and the smooch.[12] The minerals are in a cave where Deena and Servadac are attacked by Morlocks from the previous year's filming of H. G. Wells's *The Time Machine* at MGM.[13]

When Deena is seized by men from Nateeta's rival tribe, her fragmented modern speech catches Denning's attention, but a volcanic eruption traps some of her people in a cave. Servadac's gunpowder, which might otherwise have seemed too lamentable an extension of his military background, creates a rockslide to crush the dinosaurs menacing them. Only in this sequence does the mix of old and new footage become jarring; some of the shots of reptiles are clear mismatches, projected through an anamorphic widescreen lens.

The tribes are ready to resume their old antagonism until Servadac and Denning remember that they, too, met to duel, and so they set an example by laying down their weapons. The strand of social comment that began with Servadac's thoughts of gunpowder by the river finally end as cooperation emerges triumphant over warlike inclinations. Servadac reveals that in his study of the heavens he has learned they are in a new orbit that should take them back to Earth in seven years, giving them plenty of time to prepare; with Deena and Nateeta's companionship, he and Denning realize that the time waiting will not seem so long.

Just as Verne gave the conquest of the seas to the rebellious outcast Captain Nemo, he created a more enigmatic inventor to rule the skies: Robur, in an aerial machine even more visionary than the *Nautilus*. In the first of his two novels dealing with this character, *Robur the Conqueror,* published in 1886, Verne created the magnificent *Albatross*. One hundred feet long by twelve wide, the airship has a hull shaped like an ocean-going vessel, a deck and cabins, and propellers at the bow and stern, and it is powered by electricity drawn from the skies. Vertical maneuvering is provided not by wings, but by two contra-rotating screws apiece atop thirty-seven separate masts along both sides and the middle of the deck. This forest caused English translators to dub the *Albatross* "the clipper of the clouds." Instead of an airplane, the *Albatross* is an enormous helicopter, a technology that was in its relative infancy during Verne's day, making his recognition of its potential all the more notable.

The members of a club for balloonists scoff at Robur's theories on flight, so he abducts their two leaders, Prudent and Evans, and flies these stubborn men around the world to convince them that his own heavier-than-air invention is superior to lighter-than-air balloons. Returning the men, Robur proclaims:

> My experiment is finished; but my advice from now on is to be premature in nothing, not even in progress. Science should not precede the mental capacity of the times. It is evolution and not revolution that we should seek. In a word, we must not be before our time. Today would be too soon for me to claim to overcome such conflicting and divisive interests. Nations are not yet fit for union.
>
> I go, then; and I take my secret with me. But it will not be lost to humanity. It will belong to you the day you are educated enough to profit by it and wise enough not to abuse it.[14]

The *Albatross* ascends into the air, carrying away Robur and the science of the future.

Eighteen years later Robur returned in *The Master of the World* (1904) as the culmination of several apocalyptic late novels that reflect Verne's disillusionment with the potential of science to better humankind. Not satisfied with having conquered the air, Robur has designed a new machine: the *Terror* is an automobile, ship, submarine, and airplane all in one, shaped like a spindle and using wheels, propellers, and retractable wings. With it, Robur launches a campaign of fear, his machine appearing on the roads, on the seas, and in the skies of America. When the nations of the world offer $20 million for the *Terror,* Robur responds with a written refusal.

> This invention shall be neither French, nor German, nor Austrian, nor Russian, nor English, nor American.
> The machine will remain my property, and I shall make use of it in the way I think fit.
> With it, I have complete power over the whole world, and there is no human power capable of withstanding it in any circumstances whatsoever. . . .
> Let the Old World and the New World know they are powerless against me, and I am all-powerful against them.
> And this letter I sign: Master of the World.[15]

Robur and the *Terror* rule the earth, air, and water but are destroyed by the fourth element, fire. Believing he is a god who has conquered all, Robur flies the *Terror* directly into a storm, daring the greatest violence of the elements. The *Terror* is struck by lightning and falls into the sea, killing Robur and his crew.

Outlawed and feared, in what sense does he seek to be "master"? Verne may mean that Robur is not a political dictator but a master engineer. *Master of the World* does not answer the questions raised by *Robur the Conqueror;* instead, it multiplies them, and when it ends Robur's life, it leaves his true motivations and background never to be known.

*Robur the Conqueror* and *Master of the World* have often been compared with *Twenty Thousand Leagues under the Seas,* but beyond structural similarities they are entirely different. Although far less is told about Robur than about Nemo, the twelve men navigating the *Albatross* are endowed with personalities, unlike the nearly anonymous crew of the *Nautilus.* Robur is a far more terrifying creation than Nemo, whose torment is palpable; Robur is the warning of the more modern danger of a cold inhumanity unaffected by social dreams—an enigma that cannot be resolved by any Dakkar-style explanation.

American-International Pictures (AIP) was a company launched in the 1950s to attract the young audience, largely through horror and science fiction. In 1960, the company turned to the classics with a version of Edgar Allan Poe's *House of Usher,* starring Vincent Price, produced by James H. Nicholson, scripted by Richard Matheson, and including a score by Les Baxter and production design by Daniel Haller. The same team turned to Verne as a promising follow-up, and after contemplating several possibilities, including *Off on a Comet* and *In the Year 2889,* decided on a combination of *Robur the Conqueror* and *Master of the World.*[16] With Matheson, for the first and only time a renowned science fiction writer scripted Verne. Having already adapted two other Verne stories for television films that remained unproduced (one of which was *Facing the Flag*), including the pilot for a small-screen series of Verne tales, Matheson was so immersed in the Vernian universe that he was able to brilliantly combine episodes and characters from both *Robur the Conqueror* and *Master of the World* into a single script, celebrated with a special Ace paperback containing both novels and issued to coincide with the movie's release.[17]

*Master of the World* begins as John Strock, representing the U.S. government, wants to use a balloon to fly over the unclimbable Great Eyrie and investigate the disturbances at the mountain. However, no sooner do Strock and his fellow balloonists, Prudent and Evans, along with Prudent's daughter, observe that the Great Eyrie is in fact a crater than a missile is fired at and strikes the balloon in such a way that the balloon crashes inside the crater. They are taken aboard the *Albatross,* and Robur soon declares his mission to be world peace, demanding disarmament and bombing the military of any nation that refuses, from an American warship and the British fleet to the combatants in a North African war, an echo of the attack on slavers in Dahomey in *Robur the Conqueror.* Prudent's servant in that novel is replaced on screen with his daughter, Dorothy (Mary Webster). The servant's dunking at the end of a rope in *Robur the Conqueror* becomes Robur's punishment of Evans for his plot to escape in the movie.

The movie concludes with the aerial pause over an island for repairs, which facilitates the demise of the *Albatross* when she is blown up by Robur's prisoners. Only they survive; despite Robur's order to abandon ship, his crew chooses to remain with him and go down with the *Albatross* and their dream for world peace.

William Witney directed, and Price starred as Robur, with Charles

# ROBUR
## DER HERR
## DER 7 KONTINENTE
### (MASTER OF THE WORLD)

EIN FARBFILM

A German program for *Master of the World* (1961) pictures the *Albatross* over London, with Vincent Price as Robur the Conqueror.

Bronson as Strock, Henry Hull (who had already starred in *The West Side Kid*) as Prudent, and, cast ideally at the last minute in the thankless role of Evans, David Frankham (who months earlier had appeared as Aubert in "The Terrible Clockman").[18] Supporting players were chosen from among AIP regulars as well as television performers Witney knew.[19] Witney remarked,

> I picked all the crew; we had interviews, they showed up, and I picked 'em. I think Nicholson wanted to use Wally Campo as Turner and Richard Harrison. I've worked with most of the people before, the other members of the cast; we just had an interview, and I'd say, "This guy looks like it," and "That guy looks like it"—you know, that's usually the way you did it. Vito Scotti had worked for me in the *Mike Hammer* (1956–1959) television series. I made a lot of those, and I liked Vito. The first time I used him, he needed a job, and I got him working, and he worked like hell. He was a cute little guy, and he had so much talent, and that's how he came in; we didn't have anybody else that even looked good for his part of the chef of the *Albatross,* a good little cameo part.[20]

The film *Master of the World* eliminates the urge for exploration that Verne's Robur shares with Nemo, but although taking liberties with the sources it still taps into the prevalent themes of the Verne canon, adopting the tone of such works as *The 500 Millions of the Begum* (1879), *Propeller Island,* and *Facing the Flag.* In this way, *Master of the World* expands on the framework of the novels *Robur the Conqueror* and *Master of the World,* adding significantly to the vague threat that Verne had Robur portend. The title is literally fulfilled as the inventor is given weaponry to achieve the recognition, acceptance, and fear that Verne's Robur embodies.

The movie shifts the story from the years of the novels to 1868, the same time as *20,000 Leagues under the Sea,* enhancing the similarity. The dialogue, however, is more redolent of 1961 than of more than a century earlier. Dorothy becomes the center of a stale romantic triangle made up of her, the jealous Evans (her fiancé), and Strock. This triangle complicates her suitors' motivations and amplifies the heroic posture of Strock, whose persona is simultaneously undercut by the modern ambience of Charles Bronson's performance, which grates against the period atmosphere. According to Matheson, Bronson was miscast and "knew it too and was rather surly about the whole thing. I think he felt badly because he knew it was not his kind of role."[21]

Producer Nicholson was personally and enthusiastically committed to the project, having been involved with every stage of its development, and he frequently visited the set, although never interfering with the shooting. Nicholson chose Witney because he owed AIP a picture and had extensive experience in process, backgrounds, and aerial footage, including helicopter shots in the High Sierras. One of Witney's serials, *The Fighting Devil Dogs* (1938), had involved an inventor challenging the world from an airship, and even Witney's family fare (such as his Roy Rogers Westerns) was noted for its undercurrents of violence. Given the limited schedule, budget, and subject matter, Witney was the perfect director; he also modified the script to heighten Robur's hubris.

Unfortunately, *Master of the World* was never clear in either treatment or publicity as to whether it was aimed primarily at a youth or adult market.[22] Perhaps as a result, the movie won neither audience, and *House of Usher* proved so much more popular that henceforth AIP decided that its Vincent Price series would be grounded in both Poe and the horror genre, not in Verne. However, when *Master of the World* premiered on television during the height of the anti–Vietnam War movement, viewers found it unexpectedly relevant. Through television broadcasts and video releases, including a restoration that recaptured the highly saturated color schemes that Witney sought, *Master of the World* won a wide following. The small screen's foregrounding of the movie's disquisition on pacifism makes some cheap effects less noticeable, including inappropriate battle footage (some of it tinted black and white) taken from several Alexander Korda movies.

Despite such shortcuts, *Master of the World* was AIP's most ambitious production up to that time, and no expense was spared in depicting its centerpiece, the delightful *Albatross*. Supposedly made of an especially strengthened but nonetheless lightweight paper, the *Albatross* is a giant, dirigible-shaped helicopter resembling an ocean liner with several decks and balconies. This eccentric, complicated, and truly Vernian airship is an intricate combination of the old and the new, a futuristic craft constructed from an archaic point of view.[23] The *Hollywood Reporter* described the *Albatross*, with all of its complicated mechanisms fully operational, including the thirty-nine propellers emerging from the deck, their elaborate connecting rods resembling the pipes of a refinery, as a "spectacularly beautiful" miniature creation: "The success of this aspect alone gives a lift to the entire production."[24]

Those responsible for the model *Albatross* were Tim Baar, Wah Chang, and Gene Warren of Project Unlimited. Recalled Witney, "All the sets were built by a fellow that was the art director on this picture, Daniel Haller, and he became a damned good director later on, and he was a genius. The guy's sets were beautiful; the only problem was that I didn't really have time to move his sets around enough to show how beautiful they were."[25] Another disadvantage was the cinematographer, as Witney noted; by the time the problem was recognized, shooting had already progressed too far to replace him.

> For the shooting, they gave me a cameraman, Gil Warrenton, who was quite old and was very slow. I never worked with him before, and I never worked with him since. The first morning we were shooting in the hallway set, I looked at his lighting. I said, "You don't seem to understand; we are in color." I wanted some weird lights streaming down; I wanted green, purple, some flashing ones. "I want some action with your lighting throughout the picture." He said, "Gee, I don't know if I can do it, get another cameraman," so I told Nicholson. But anyway, Warrenton caught on in the second half of the picture, but if he would have had a little understanding, it would have improved the picture a heck of a lot.[26]

Having to shoot in a mere fifteen days, including shifting to a variety of sets, presented a more strenuous schedule for *Master of the World* than many "B" pictures of the studio era.

The potential disadvantages of a picture relying so heavily on process shots to convey its aerial setting were turned to advantage. Witney

Advertisements for *Master of the World* (1961) highlighted the *Albatross* and often situated the film in the tradition of its famous Verne film predecessors.

noted, "As far as the camera movement goes, on process you can only move in and out, you can go across the screen, dead center across it, but you can't do too many things because the light has to stay off the screen. But usually with most of your process, you're either going to stay parallel to the screen and your movement, or you've got to go straight in and out because the screen is flat. You can't put it at an angle because it distorts in the background."[27] The feeling of flight is superbly captured with frequent exterior views, re-created gracefully, majestically, and leisurely as experienced by the story's characters, without trying to conceal the monotony imparted by the steady hum of the suspensory blades. The movements of the *Albatross* and the sensation of soaring are perfectly amplified in Les Baxter's symphonic score (issued on a separate soundtrack record), which the *Hollywood Reporter* labeled the loveliest of its sort since Victor Young's for *Around the World in 80 Days*.[28]

Thematic similarities between *Master of the World* and *20,000 Leagues under the Sea,* a film that much impressed screenwriter Matheson, have sometimes caused the two pictures to be compared. Although *Master of the World* did not benefit from the epic treatment, large budget, and spectacular visual production of *20,000 Leagues under the Sea,* it has compensating strengths. Perhaps better than any other Verne picture made in America, *Master of the World* captures the essential spirit and totality of the visionaries of the Nemo–Robur school, including the tragic flaws of excessive ambition and overconfidence in their power. Whereas *20,000 Leagues under the Sea* situates Ned, not Nemo, at the center, in *Master of the World* Robur dominates, and characterization, performance, and humor combine no less effectively to convey the message.

Although sharing with *20,000 Leagues under the Sea* such concerns as the alienated scientist with a loyal crew who use their technology to isolate themselves and combat war, *Master of the World* is a far harsher, more politicized film. Disney's Nemo lives apart from his fellow beings, but Robur, a man of moral absolutes, is at war with humankind. Nemo's purposes are spurred by a personal desire for revenge, whereas Robur's motivations are left abstract, without any attempt at psychological rationalization—disproving the earlier film's assumption that such an explanation is necessary. Robur is thus given a misanthropic strength lacking

Directing *Master of the World* (1961), William Witney demonstrates a scene, seizing Henry Hull as Prudent, with Vincent Price as Robur *(in white coat at left)*.

in Nemo's vacillation and occasional glimpses of compassion, traits to which Robur never surrenders.

In one of his best and most restrained performances, Vincent Price plays Robur as a character simultaneously loftier and more congenial than Nemo.[29] Witney saw the role as outside of Price's recent horror persona.

> When I first met him, I had never met him before. He was just a delight to work with; he was enthusiastic, knew his lines, and the cast all looked up to him. He gave everybody an even break, and he was just one of the nicest people I've worked with for a long, long time. As far as considering him from the horror pictures, that never even crossed my mind. An actor is an actor; he can play a dirty rotten SOB in one role and a romantic lead in the other, and it's the part he's playing.[30]

Price remarked of *Master of the World*, "I thought it had a marvelous moralizing philosophy. I adored it. A man who sees evil and says 'Destroy it'—and if it's the whole world, then it's got to go!"[31] Describing himself as a citizen of the world to his prisoners' nationalistic dismay, Robur leads a multiethnic crew exuding a personality, fellowship, and competence that is wholly lacking in the crew of *20,000 Leagues under the Sea*. He grasps a Bible and quotes from scripture at both the beginning and the end.

Even more arresting is the sharp delineation of the individual characters into polemical representatives of inherently opposite ideologies, ideally portrayed by Price and Hull. Robur the aggressive pacifist is sharply contrasted with Prudent the wealthy military industrialist, Strock the pragmatic, unenlightened government agent, and Evans the conservative Victorian. They engage in a lively and rhetorical debate over the merits of Robur's goal and methods—an irresolvable argument because each of the men commences from a different base of values. The righteousness of Robur's cause as well as the ruthlessness of his methods and the hypocrisy of his adversaries are given a full hearing. Determined to impose peace on the world even at the price of war, Robur finds his prisoners to be adversaries who cannot be converted to his beliefs and who will ultimately destroy him.

*Master of the World* maintains a troubled admiration for Robur, a product of the scientific age with enormous potential for good but also a disregard for the humanism Verne valued. Matheson capitalized on the typical dilemma of Verne films, the portrayal of a once possible future set in the past, to turn the audience's sympathy away from Robur's prisoners toward the inventor. Robur's passion for peace is far from fanatical, and from the perspective of the twentieth century's experience of two world wars and a cold war, his methods seem less problematic in that he represents the unrealized goal of an impartial world policeman, for whom there is no "just war." Ultimately, there is compassion for Robur and his fate rather than for his enemies, who are not only equally ruthless but also selfish and parochial.

Although Verne always believed that the true conquest of the air lay with heavier-than-air machines, his very first hit novel, *Five Weeks in a Balloon*, forever linked his name with lighter-than-air travel. Even as one aerial novel was brought to the screen, so was this novel of exploration across Africa, establishing the pattern that would become typical of his "Extraordinary Journeys": science combined with geography. Many other authors would have ignored the technical problem of steering a balloon, but Verne proposed a device to heat and cool the hydrogen, allowing the balloon to rise and fall to find a favorable air current. Regardless of the technical feasibility of this device, this attention to the matter reassured the reader in a manner that was new to such fiction in 1863.[32] As the centenary of the book approached, an attempt was made to duplicate the book's flight, but the balloon was forced down four hundred miles inland from Zanzibar, and neither of the two movie versions fared much better.

The first film, released in 1961, was *Flight of the Lost Balloon*, a ninety-one-minute venture by the Woolner Bros. Set in 1878, the plot depicts how Dr. Joseph Faraday (weakly portrayed by Marshall Thompson), taking the place of Verne's Dr. Samuel Ferguson and the servant Joe, has developed a balloon with two gas bags, one inside the other, so that it can be made to rise or fall by heating the buoyant elements (per Verne's idea). In the debate at the London Geographical Society over how to find the missing Sir Hubert, Faraday suggests that rather than launching a five-month safari, they use his balloon *Victoria* to carry three men on a five-day aerial trip to Lake Victoria, where Sir Hubert was last heard from. Sir Hubert's fiancée Ellen (Mala Powers) volunteers for the aerial journey.

Despite the film's title, the balloon never becomes lost, but, reversing Verne's direction, the balloonists pilot the *Victoria* eastward across Africa after a villainous Hindu, the only man to know the explorer's whereabouts, also joins the trip. The Hindu hopes to use Ellen to force Hubert to tell the whereabouts of Cleopatra's treasure—the original title of *Flight of the Lost Balloon* having been *Cleopatra and the Cyclops*. But Hubert himself turns out to be a greedy fraud, willing to allow Ellen to be tortured rather than reveal his secret. When Faraday helps Ellen and Hubert to get away from the Hindu, Hubert tries to load the balloon with valuables but is crushed by the treasure chests in Cleopatra's tomb. Ellen departs with Faraday, and to escape they empty the balloon of all the valuables except one magnificent diamond, perfect for a wedding ring.

Advertising art for *Flight of the Lost Balloon* (1961) pictured the attacking birds from the novel *Five Weeks in a Balloon*.

Into this framework are woven a number of incidents from the novel, such as the attack of birds on the balloon (the central scene depicted in advertising art for *Flight of the Lost Balloon*), an encounter with cannibals, and the sacrificial leap of one of the passengers to keep the balloon aloft. Some of the aerial scenes are bolstered by Hal Borne's pleasant musical themes as well as attractive color and costumes. Puerto Rican locations substitute well for the African setting until the castle is reached, supposedly on an island in the midst of Lake Victoria, but clearly more redolent of Spanish ruins.

*Flight of the Lost Balloon* was made on a low budget with thoroughly unconvincing special effects, although the use of the anamorphic widescreen Spectrascope demonstrated the filmmakers' ambition. *Flight of the Lost Balloon* could not compete with more prestigious releases, and after its shooting was completed, a powerful rival emerged. Irwin Allen desired to be first with a film of *Five Weeks in a Balloon,* released through 20th Century-Fox. Admitting that the novel was in the public domain in the United States, Allen insisted there might be complications on the overseas copyright.[33] Hence, the makers of *Flight of the Lost Balloon* agreed to drop all references to Verne. Associate producer and director Nathan Juran took credit for story as well as screenplay, and cinematographer Jacques Marquette doubled as executive producer. *Flight of the Lost Balloon* was a credible effort for its investment, with Juran's adept direction overcoming many of the acting, budget, and script shortfalls; he had helmed several of Ray Harryhausen's films, including the superlative version of H. G. Wells's novel *The First Men in the Moon.*

Actually, *Flight of the Lost Balloon* is no less true to its source than the film Irwin Allen made the next year, capitalizing on the Verne name and title, *Five Weeks in a Balloon.* Indeed, there are some surprising similarities between the two, a result of both the formulaic conventions for African pictures of the period and perhaps something more, as the pictures' chronology might suggest. Both *Flight of the Lost Balloon* and *Five Weeks in a Balloon* preserve Verne's episode in which the aeronauts are accepted by the natives as moon gods because of the shape of their vehicle, revive an inebriated local monarch, but are exposed when the real moon comes into view. The filmmakers' of both film versions, however, believed it necessary to substitute other themes in place of Verne's simple concern with exploration. In *Five Weeks in a Balloon,* the motivation is opposition to slavery and a race to plant the British flag in unexplored territory, the latter a concept apparently so obscure and irrelevant to today's audiences that it had to be treated in a comedic vein. Recognizing that an entirely new story was given to the film, Pyramid's movie paperback tie-in was not even an edited or children's version of the Verne novel, but an original with the same title by Gardner Fox.

There are a few genuinely exciting scenes in *Five Weeks in a Balloon,* indicating what it could have achieved if not drenched in silliness. The opening and concluding sequences are interesting, from the outset to the arrival in Zanzibar and from the landing in the desert to the final crash, showing that *Five Weeks in a Balloon* could have been an effective light adventure comedy if handled more deftly. However, Allen as producer, director, and coauthor of the script brought to the 101-minute *Five Weeks in a Balloon* his typical lack of story sense and tendency to overload productions. Too many comedians and lightweight performers are given roles, with the result that all the dramatic needs are placed on Sir Cedric Hardwicke as Dr. Samuel Ferguson, who was overwhelmed and far too old for the role. Fabian is inoffensive as Jacques Verlaine, who replaces Verne's Joe, and merely smiles and toots the balloon's whistle. The crew of the balloon acquires a chimp and no less than five superfluous stars as additional passengers: Richard Haydn as an idiotic general, Red Buttons as a bumbling reporter, Barbara Luna as a stowaway slave, Barbara Eden as a spunky missionary, and Peter Lorre as the dealer who wants to enslave her.

Although the problem of weight is established early in the picture, the balloon apparently has no problem carrying all the added passengers, from an intended two passengers to ultimately seven. This creates an inherent travesty of the basic idea; in *Flight of the Lost Balloon,* there at least was constant, accurate attention to the problem of how many pounds the *Victoria* could lift and carry. Not one of the five added passengers plays a character in the Verne novel, and the need for each is ambiguous; together, they form an unwieldy group, providing mere decoration in the hope that some laughs might occur. They also make possible not one but two romantic subplots. There are stops in several artificial and drab Arab cities, where hilarity is meant to be derived from

Verne films of the 1950s and 1960s often had sheet music tie-ins, as in this example from *Five Weeks in a Balloon* (1962).

the caricatured vulgar natives snorting noisily (such as a drunken Billy Gilbert)—an example of the level of authenticity that exists throughout. Sharing the writing blame with Irwin Allen are Charles Bennett and Albert Gail.

Metaphorically, *Five Weeks in a Balloon* never gets off the ground. Only an aging Peter Lorre, at his pop-eyed chubbiest, provides some genuine chuckles with his dry wit. He regards himself as an honest slave trader, and when, despite his lazy nature, he is pressed to work, he replies, "I'm not a slave; I sell them." However, even Lorre looks ill most of the time, and he can hardly be blamed. Filmed two years before his death, *Five Weeks in a Balloon* was his third and final role in a Verne movie after playing Conseil in *20,000 Leagues under the Sea* (1954) and a ship's steward in *Around the World in 80 Days* (1956).

Indeed, *Five Weeks in a Balloon* attempted to be a small-scale version of *Around the World in 80 Days,* with travel, a balloon, evocative credit animation, and cameo stars: Billy Gilbert, Herbert Marshall, Reginald Owen, Henry Daniell, and Mike Mazurki. The music by Paul Sawtell is pleasant and appropriate, featured as background throughout and enhancing the mood of many special-effects shots. In the words of the title song by Jodi Desmond, sung by the Brothers Four, "Here I am up high in the sky, and as happy as can be, and you'll be too when you've been through *Five Weeks in a Balloon,*" and its recording provided a commercial tie-in with the youth market.

*Five Weeks in a Balloon* has CinemaScope and a range of Deluxe color that indicate its budgetary advantages over *Flight of the Lost Balloon.* So, too, the vehicle in *Five Weeks in a Balloon* is seen to advantage by comparison with the vehicle in *Flight of the Lost Balloon;* there are a number of effective montages as the balloon is superimposed over maps and other backgrounds to indicate its progress. Presumably because *Flight of the Lost Balloon* had already used the name *Victoria* for its craft, *Five Weeks in a Balloon* felt obliged to invent a new one, *Jupiter.*[34] The movie simplifies Verne's method of controlling and maneuvering the balloon through rising or falling but remains true to the basic concept. The aerial exteriors of the *Jupiter* are majestic and certainly convincing, but the artificial ribbons and unicorn design festooning the enormous gondola are excessively elaborate and impractical. Interior views of an oversize cabin reveal the same inattention to probability as the overloading of the passengers.

The cycle of cinematic adaptations that had begun with Walt Disney's *20,000 Leagues under the Sea* was about to shift after one more contribution by this producer. Even before he began that production, he had been thinking about filming Verne stories. While Disney prepared his second television special for a Christmas 1951 broadcast, he discussed various Verne books with the show's director, Robert Florey. Florey presented Disney with several Verne mementoes and early French editions that fomented Disney's further interest in filming the author's stories, and their talks resumed when Florey returned to the studio as the *Disneyland* television series began, including the episodes on the making of *20,000 Leagues under the Sea.*

The commercial success of *20,000 Leagues under the Sea* further suggested a Verne follow-up, and Disney decided to utilize *The Children of Captain Grant,* a novel that had a premise ideal for Disney treatment in several respects, particularly its youthful leads. Mary Grant, sixteen years old, and her brother, Robert, twelve, initiate a search for their mariner father, lost at sea. Professor Paganel, an absent-minded savant, joins them, providing amusement and serving as a fount of knowledge during an uncertain journey spurred by a damaged note from Grant found in a bottle in the ocean, with only a latitude number and the word *Indian* still clearly decipherable. The same elements that attracted Disney were what had made the novel one of Verne's most successful: deciphering the note facilitates the portrayal of several remote, exotic lands on the nineteenth-century frontiers in South America, Australia, and New Zealand, all with youthful heroes.

Disney bought cinematic rights to *The Children of Captain Grant* from the Verne estate in 1958, but an adaptation posed several difficulties.[35] One of the titles given by translators, *In Search of the Castaways,* was selected for the planned movie, but in 1960 Disney decided to film the better-known Johann Wyss novel *Swiss Family Robinson* first. Its success demonstrated the box office viability of a shipwreck tale, and the *Swiss Family Robinson* scriptwriter, Lowell Hawley, was assigned to the Verne novel. Whereas Verne had concentrated on Grant's son, Robert, the gender priority would be reversed for the movie because teenage actress Hayley Mills had begun a meteoric rise to stardom under Disney's guidance. This turned *In Search of the Castaways* (1962) into a vehicle for the new star as Mary Grant, with the slogan "A Thousand Thrills and Hayley Mills"; Keith Hamshere assumed the now secondary role of her brother, Robert.

Although Mills would bring younger filmgoers, attracting their parents and providing further box office insurance was the casting of Maurice Chevalier as Paganel. Chevalier provides a mild version of his typical Gallic persona in a manner that does little to distort Verne's character and serves to balance Mills's primacy. Moreover, because Mills had sung during her film for Disney the previous year, *The Parent Trap,* the casting of Chevalier also allowed the augmentation of the musical element, with four tunes by Richard M. Sherman and Robert B. Sherman added at pivotal portions of the narrative.

By the end of the journey, Verne had Mary wed a ship's captain, a romance only glimpsed on the written page. This subplot, naturally, had to be on-screen for *In Search of the Castaways,* so the beginning of the novel is slightly altered. Paganel, rather than accidentally joining the search for Grant, in the film accompanies the children aboard a yacht owned by Lord Glenarvan (Wilfrid Hyde-White) to deliver to Glenarvan the note found in a bottle. Here Glenarvan is situated as Grant's former employer and is ultimately convinced by his own teenage son, John (Michael Anderson Jr., whose father directed *Around the World in 80 Days*), to make the search.

From the outset, *In Search of the Castaways* has clear strengths and weaknesses, and some unfortunate Disney conventions are quickly apparent. There is the usual fragmented family structure emphasizing patriarchy, with the maternal figure of both the Grant and the Glenarvan families conveniently dead, thus eliminating Lady Helena Glenarvan's function in the novel as a model for Mary. Puppy love abounds in the scenes between Mary and John, although the performers were closer in age and more suitable for a 1962 audience than those established in the novel. During the journey, Mary becomes increasingly feminine and less practical, the opposite of what such an odyssey should induce, changing from pants in South America to a Victorian dress in Australia.

After not quite an hour of the film and after experiencing both an earthquake and a flood in South America, Paganel realizes that Grant's message must instead indicate Australia, where smuggler Frederick Ayrton (George Sanders) and his ruffians take over the yacht. Mary, Robert, Paganel, and the Glenarvans are captured by Maoris and placed in a precarious, high-perched prison where they encounter Grant's half-mad mate, Bill Gay (Wilfred Brambell). Laughing hysterically and repeating, "I be smart!" Gay is patterned after the eccentric Ben Gunn of Robert Louis Stevenson's *Treasure Island* (1883), filmed by Disney in 1950, and his character is the primary divergence from Verne's novel offered by *In Search of the Castaways*. With Gay's help, they escape and find Grant (Jack Gwillim), whom the Maoris have held captive to bargain for guns against Ayrton, and the heroes retake Glenarvan's yacht. After a reunion of Grant and his children, Grant, Paganel, and Glenarvan realize that John and Mary are in love.

A sharp contrast exists between the two native types portrayed— on the one hand, the English-speaking, noble Indian Thalcave (Antonio Cifariello), whose perfect rifle shot saves Robert from the talons of a giant condor and who rescues them in the pampas, and, on the other, the grimacing, primitive Maoris. The Maoris' behavior is clearly meant to amuse younger audiences, one of the abundant silly touches that mark *In Search of the Castaways* as aimed at the preteen audience, with little appeal for older viewers, so unlike Disney's earlier *20,000 Leagues under the Sea*.

Indeed, *In Search of the Castaways* is also far more light-hearted than *Swiss Family Robinson* and consequently less memorable. Lacking the quality acting and epic scope of either *20,000 Leagues under the Sea* or *Swiss Family Robinson*, *In Search of the Castaways* clocked in at ninety-eight minutes and is among the more faithful if compressed Verne adaptations. Ironically, reviewers criticized the movie for retaining some of Verne's more implausible incidents, believing they had been added by Disney and thus classifying the film as juvenile. Although the pace is fast and there are some harrowing incidents, the episodic construction may have been unavoidable considering the novel's sprawling narrative, and Verne's own play version had not met with the same phenomenal success as his staging of the novels *Around the World in Eighty Days* and *Michael Strogoff*. The best aspects of *In Search of the Castaways* are the color, photography, and special effects; Disney house director Robert Stevenson filmed at England's Pinewood Studios.

The Verne authorial signature remained central, with "Jules Verne's Fantasy-Adventure" announced above the title, the credits superimposed over a shot of a bottle thrown into the sea and floating away, suggesting

Many of the advertisements for *In Search of the Castaways* (1962) linked the appeal of both Disney and Verne together.

the genre. Graphic advertising was even more pronounced, proclaiming, "Only Walt Disney could tell this incredible Jules Verne adventure!" However, *In Search of the Castaways* lacked the television promotions that had been produced for *20,000 Leagues under the Sea,* even though those programs would be rebroadcast a year later during the first major theatrical re-release of Disney's first Verne production. That event would also be marked with the republication of some of the many book tie-ins from the 1954 advent of *20,000 Leagues under the Sea,* but the situation was different for *In Search of the Castaways.* Other tie-ins for Verne books filmed at the same time had by that time crowded American bookstore shelves, whether the Ace paperback of *Master of the World,* the Permabook paperback of *Mysterious Island,* or the editions of *Journey to the Center of the Earth.*[36] However, *The Children of Captain Grant* had not been published in English for two decades, and perhaps as a result for *In Search of the Castaways* there was only a small paper-back printing in England from Icon in a shortened version edited by Robert Hamer. With the movie's final theatrical reissue in 1978 as the second feature on a double bill, a novelization by Hettie Jones was published by Pocket Books.

Alfred Zimbalist, producer of *Valley of the Dragons,* explained the conceptions behind Verne productions. He called Verne a name that has never had a flop, in which the players were of secondary importance—Verne himself was the star. "Jules Verne," said Mr. Zimbalist, "is as big a name as Marlon Brando. Verne is for any size budget. Verne is the purest kind of escapist, and at the same time he is timely. His books have imagination, adventure, danger, even terrible beasts. You don't have to go in for violence with Verne. You can even try a little comedy here and there."[37] The three years from 1960 to 1962 marked a golden age in Verne filmmaking. Even if the quality was increasingly variable, never again would so many adaptations be produced in such rapid order. However, the trend toward fealty in Verne films, having thoroughly mined one vein over a decade, was about to shift toward new content, style, and target audiences.

# 6

# The Cycle Changes, 1963–1971

The shift in tone of the next few years was crystallized in a note above a title. *The Three Stooges Go around the World in a Daze* began, "Acknowledgment is hereby made to Jules Verne, on whose classic, *Around the World in Eighty Days,* this film is based—Sincere apologies, The Producers." Rather than aiming at family filmgoers generally, Hollywood Verne adaptations began to polarize around either adults or preteens. The first Verne television series would also demonstrate animation as a viable style for bringing Verne to the screen.

Most importantly, a certain exhaustion of the existing trend became evident as filmmakers, in the search for fresh perspectives, turned away from adaptations toward pastiche and satire of the author's stories. This trend continues to this day in both Hollywood and foreign films, an evolution from literal adaptations to the creation of films inspired by Verne stories and thus freed from their precise confines or dated aspects. Filmmakers used Vernian characters, icons, and vehicles in narratives and contexts outside of those the author created. New variations on his ideas or futuristic elements beyond Verne's vision or intent developed, while still retaining the canonical elements, plot structures, and thematic motifs. Although this trend had begun in the early silent era with *Around the World in 18 Days* and reappeared in the "Foggbound" episode of *Have Gun—Will Travel,* in 1963 it would reemerge with *The Three Stooges Go around the World in a Daze,* to be followed by *Those Fantastic Flying Fools* and *Captain Nemo and the Underwater City.*

Despite star billing for the Stooges, Phileas Fogg and Verne received full notice in advertising for *The Three Stooges Go around the World in a Daze* (1963).

This was also the rationale allowing for a series format in several Vernian animated television presentations.

The new pattern was nowhere more apparent than in the initial offering. As the title *The Three Stooges Go around the World in a Daze* suggests, Larry, Curly, and Moe did bring their zaniness to a 1963 parody of the novel. As in the serial *Around the World in 18 Days,* the novel was updated to center around a descendant, the great-grandson of the hero whose adventures Verne chronicled. Phileas Fogg III is played by Jay Sheffield, with the Stooges as his servants, a sort of tripartite Passepartout who accompany him on the global trek, joined by a damsel rescued from distress (Joan Freeman). Moe's son-in-law, Norman Maurer, wrote the screen story as well as produced and directed this ninety-four-minute Columbia Pictures film from a screenplay by Elwood Ullman.

The story opens with a criminal reading Verne's novel and deciding that the bank robbery of which Fix suspected Fogg might never have been traced to the real culprit had Fogg conveniently disappeared during his travels. The criminal dares Fogg's descendant to repeat his ancestor's journey without spending any money and simultaneously implicates him in a bank theft. However, Fogg and his friends continually manage to escape both danger and a Scotland Yard detective, arriving back in England apparently a day late but of course having made the same original date error. The picture is far more of a Three Stooges vehicle in all its other details, and subsequent pastiches would be more canonical.

*From the Earth to the Moon* (1958) was not distributed in England until the early 1960s, and this labored effort may have prompted producer Harry Alan Towers to return to the spirit of Georges Méliès, whose *A Trip to the Moon* had actually been as faithful as the recent movie. Towers had a childhood background in the classics, recognizing their evergreen quality as a basis for filmmaking and possessing a skill at exploiting them through modern and budget-minded showmanship. He wisely decided on a jaunty, tongue-in-cheek romp, writing an original screen story (under his pseudonym "Peter Welbeck") inspired by Verne's writings, principally the first part of his lunar saga. Towers's decision not to encompass the novel *Around the Moon* is not so surprising considering that the two books have been as often reprinted separately as together. Moreover, the sequel shifts toward materialistic science fiction, away from the satire of American culture in *From the Earth to the Moon,* which was Towers's focus.[1]

His production was shot in Ireland under the capable direction of Don Sharpe, and the British release title was the perfectly appropriate *Jules Verne's Rocket to the Moon.* In the United States, the distributor, AIP, tried to cash in on the current popular success of the epic avia-tion comedy *Those Magnificent Men in Their Flying Machines* (1965, on which Sharpe was a second unit director) by retitling the Verne film *Those Fantastic Flying Fools.* Apparently this title variation, one of sev-eral imitations of *Those Magnificent Men in Their Flying Machines* in circulation that year, 1967, was not successful. The ninety-five-minute Towers picture was later given some showings as *Blast-Off!* and televi-sion opted to revert to the title *Those Fantastic Flying Fools.*

Unlike the all-American lunar journey in *From the Earth to the Moon,* Towers chose to follow an idea more akin to what Verne imag-ined, a launch involving participants from several nations, an idea that seemed just as much "science fiction" in the Cold War era as the rocket itself. Director Sharp recalled the production:

> Dave Freeman, who wrote a lot of the Benny Hill shows, wrote a lovely, tight script. . . . We had a marvelous cast. Harry had done a preliminary budget . . . visited all the locations, and then Harry did a realistic budget. He found that the actual amount it was going to cost [reportedly $3 million] was way in excess of what he'd budgeted, so he had to get more money. He first went to [Constantin Films in] Germany and they approved of the screenplay and cast, but they thought if they were putting in more money, Gert Frobe should have more screen time, to which Harry agreed. He then went to Nat Cohen [at England's Anglo-Amalgamated], who wanted more with Terry-Thomas and Lio-nel Jeffries. Then he went to America and [AIP's] Sam Arkoff wanted more with Troy Donahue. So, because of all these man-dates, we had to expand the bloody script, and what had been a tight, fascinating comedy became overblown. If Dave and I had been as cynical . . . we'd have written it in such a way that you could cut things out. Instead, we worked our socks off to inte-

An advertisement for an early 1970s television broadcast of *Those Fantastic Flying Fools* (1967).

grate all the new scenes and, eventually, you couldn't take anything out because it was all part of the fabric.[2]

*Those Fantastic Flying Fools,* superior to *From the Earth to the
Moon,* is an enjoyable pastiche in the style of the post–World War II
British satirical comedies typified by Ealing Studios. In fact, the Towers
version is the more believable film simply because it does not strain to
make its mechanisms seem credible by today's standards. Towers lampoons the whole notion of Victorian scientific progress, the humor deriv-
ing from the misfires and disasters to which scientific experimentation is
prone. The pace is sprightly, and Patrick John Scott provides an appropriate musical score. *Those Fantastic Flying Fools* unfolds in a series of
set pieces, varying in amusement, with each character introduced in a
vignette. Most of the scenes manage a Vernian air, especially the concluding sequences of the rocket's transport and launch.

In place of the Baltimore Gun Club, Professor Siegfried von Bulow
lectures to London's ineffectual Royal Society for the Advancement of
Science. Von Bulow, played by Gert Frobe as an excitable German eccentric, most of whose inventions fail, takes the place of Verne's Barbicane,
a man only a bit less fanatical. Von Bulow suggests firing a projectile
to the moon from a 310-foot cannon drilled directly underground into
a mountainside, and he has developed Bulovite, a superexplosive, to
launch the moon ship. The filmmakers wisely realized it is unnecessary
to hint at nuclear power; Bulovite, like Verne's gun-cotton, is sufficiently
threatening in the hands of its careless, accident-prone inventor.

Phineas T. Barnum (Burl Ives), whose first name is so often confused with Verne's "Phileas Fogg," supports von Bulow's plan in hopes
of recouping the lost Barnum fortune.[3] Barnum also suggests his midget
star, General Tom Thumb, as a passenger conveniently sized for the
moonship. In *Those Fantastic Flying Fools,* millions of dollars are raised
for Barnum's moon shot amid growing entanglements with scientific,
romantic, nationalistic, and business threats to the endeavor. The last
of the needed funds are provided by a French banker, who requests only
that his rival for a beautiful girl be the one sent to the moon. The rival is
the rocket's designer, Gaylord Sullivan (Troy Donahue), a fearless Yankee
balloonist who takes the place of Verne's French astronaut Michel Ardan.

However, the moonship is sabotaged by a crackpot scientist (Terry-Thomas) and a gambler who have wagered against the flight's success. At the last moment, the launch is aborted, Sullivan removed back to land, but a Russian spy has entered the rocket unseen. The only character who is crazier than von Bulow, he triggers the mechanism from inside. Barnum and his friends believe the projectile was launched empty, but in the final scene Russians haul the crashed capsule across a bleak landscape, either Siberia or the moon. This anticlimactic, Russo-dominated ending may have hindered the potential popularity of *Those Fantastic Flying Fools* at a time when the space race between Americans and Soviets seemed a vital issue, hardly appropriate for humor.

As filmmakers began to transform the author's work to animation, they started with some of his best-known stories already filmed in live action. *Journey to the Center of the Earth* not only found a home on the large screen but also was adapted for television. It was a Saturday morning television cartoon during the 1967–1969 seasons, when ABC aired a sequence of seventeen animated films under the series title *Journey to the Center of the Earth.*[4] They were directed by Hal Sutherland, with Louis Scheimer and Norman Prescott producing for Filmation (helping to launch the studio) in association with 20th Century-Fox Television, using the plot based on the studio's 1959 movie. The narration of the prefatory sequence sets the premise and mood:

> Long ago, a lone explorer named Arne Saknussemm made a fantastic descent to the fabled lost kingdom of Atlantis at the earth's core. After many centuries, his trail was discovered, first by me, Professor Oliver Lindenbrook, my niece Cindy, student Alec McKuen, our guide Lars, and his duck Gertrude. But we were not alone. The evil Count Saknussemm, last descendant of the once noble Saknussemm family, had followed us, to claim the center of the earth for his power-mad schemes. He ordered his brute-like servant Torg to destroy our party. But the plan backfired, sealing the entrance forever. And so for us began a desperate race to the earth's core, to learn the secret of the way back. This is the story of our new journey to the center of the earth.

This preface, with many of its visuals repeated over the closing credits, situates the series as simultaneously an alternate version of the 1959 movie and a possible sequel, and it is open to either interpretation. There are clear similarities and differences; this time the Lindenbrook expedition includes the professor and Alec, but Hans becomes Lars (given a humorous Swedish accent), and Cindy takes the place of both Jenny and Carla but is no one's love interest. Gertrude, well remembered by young viewers of the movie, had to be revived from her ignominious end as Count Saknussemm's last meal.

Voices were provided by Ted Knight as Lindenbrook and Saknussemm, Jane Webb as Cindy, and Pat Harrington Jr. as Alec, Lars, and Torg. Lindenbrook took over the duties of first-person narration from Alec. The sequential episode titles included "Land of the Dead," "Living City," "Creature World," "Ocean of Destruction," "Perils of Volcano Island," "Frozen Furies," "Caveman Captives," "Arena of Fear," "Sleeping Slaves of Zeerah," "Return of Gulliver," "Labyrinth Builders," "Moths of Doom," "Trail of Gold," "Revenge of the Fossils," "Creatures of the Swamp," "The Living Totems," and "Doomed Island." Unlike the careful plotting of the movie, the series is geared strictly toward children, with cheap animation. The characters' catch phrase, "No stopping—we've got to keep moving," could have been the motto of the series itself, and its logo was a silhouette of the four main characters running, with Gertrude flying just ahead. They search for Atlantis as the spot that will show them how to get back to the surface. Each episode consists of a repetitive sequence of incidents relating a peril, such as a man-headed spider, and an improbable escape, such as fleeing a volcanic eruption by riding a wave of lava surfboard style. With these incidents placed back to back without pause, there is no attempt at logic or development; endemic of this approach is the lack of any opening or ending episodes to the series. However, more has been derived from the novel than might be expected; in the episode "Revenge of the Fossils," Lindenbrook discovers and accidentally revives a race of prehistoric men, who become menacing, and in "Creatures of the Swamp" the adventurers journey via raft. In conjunction, Whitman issued a jigsaw puzzle, a coloring book, and a Big Little Book volume.[5] The series, with its storyline dominated by children, seems to have made a deep impression on those

Among the promotions for the animated series *Journey to the Center of the Earth* (1967–1969) was a puzzle.

who saw it and served as the true source of inspiration for many film-makers who would film the novel in the 1980s and beyond.

Other television series would offer Phileas Fogg in animated adventures. *Cattanooga Cats,* a 1969–1971 ABC series, was a weekend children's cartoon show with singing feline hosts and episodes that included segments of different cartoons of varying length. Installments of *Around the World in 79 Days,* a sequel to the Verne novel, were irregularly offered. Opening in a manner similar to *The Three Stooges Go around the World in a Daze,* in present-day London, Finny Fogg, great-great-grandson of the legendary Phileas Fogg, learns of his recently deceased relative's strange will. Finny, penniless himself, may inherit the Fogg fortune on condition that he go around the world without using modern transportation and break the previous Fogg's record. Otherwise, the fortune goes to Phileas Fogg's loyal retainer, Crumden, and his pet monkey, Smirky.

Jenny Trent, a reporter for the *World News,* and her assistant, Happy, a photographer, overhear this news. Finny, without money to finance his trip, is given his great-great-grandfather's balloon, and while photographing the launch, Jenny and Happy are carried away with Finny, which forces them to make the trip as well. Unknown to them, Crumden, Smirky, and Crumden's appropriately named lackey, Bumbler, pursue Finny, determined to prevent him from winning his race against time. Crumden has built a supercar, the *Fierce Arrow,* which can transform in more ways than the *Terror* from Verne's *Master of the World.* The *Fierce Arrow* is alternately able to be driven on roads, to fly in the sky as a dirigible, to burrow underground, and to deploy a large armament—all in the first episode of *Around the World in 79 Days* entitled "The Race Is On."

Fogg's schedule is constantly delayed by his enemy; for instance, when the balloon lands in Paris, Crumden steals the *Mona Lisa* and tries to make the local police blame Finny. The format allowed the show's characters to travel to many corners of the globe, from Switzerland to Arabia, India, Australia, Hawaii, Argentina, and even the South Pole. Voices were supplied by Bruce Watson as Fogg, Janet Waldo as Jenny Trent, Don Messick as Happy and Smirky, Daws Butler as Crumden, and Allan Melvin as Bumbler; the show's producers-directors were William Hanna and Joseph Barbera.

In the wake of the beginning of Verne adaptations as children's cartoons, he was adapted for a similar age group in live action. *Strange Holiday* (1969, retitled *Boys of Lost Island* for video release in 1992) is actually one of the most faithful of Verne films, but that is primarily a result of the picture's modest scope. It was based on the 1888 Verne novel *Two Year Holiday,* which after many years of languishing in obscurity had been reprinted twice in the 1960s, including a juvenile condensation in 1967.

*Two Year Holiday* is Verne's only narrative written expressly for young people, relating how fifteen boys who had been attending school in New Zealand are shipwrecked while on a vacation cruise. Like the prototypical Robinsons before them, the marooned boys attempt to convert wildlife into pets (with a notable lack of success), find a fellow castaway on a Friday (in this case a woman), and must overcome an onslaught of pirates. However, no longer is the emphasis on survival, but instead on the process of setting up a social system, examining the boys' interrelationships and their politicization.

The boys gradually change from castaways to colonists of their desert island, reproducing their known society and a school of their own rather than reverting to primitive instincts. Rivalry inevitably arises between the oldest boys, aggravated by their divergent citizenships: two are French brothers and one an American among a largely English group, and *Two Year Holiday* reflected Verne's sentiments toward the dominant nations of his day. Although the eldest of the French lads proves the most capable and caring, the need for leadership arouses the British boys' chauvinistic instincts, and the intercession of a more mature American is needed to unify them all. Today, *Two Year Holiday* is read in a different context because of its antithesis, William Golding's *Lord of the Flies* (1964); Verne believed that, for better and worse, a group of boys would emulate European society, with its strengths and weakness, not revert to savagery, as in Golding's novel.

*Strange Holiday* compresses *Two Year Holiday* into seventy-five minutes, following the outline of the book and adding little that is new. The boys prudently go about surviving the shipwreck, finding the cave of a dead Frenchman who had been shipwrecked long before, and making it habitable. The sensible Gordon (Van Alexander) is elected as their leader, and Doniphan's (Mark Healey) attempt to establish separate quarters is dropped. They happily agree not to punish the younger Briant (Jaeme Hamilton) when he confesses that he foolishly loosed the

An advertisement for *Strange Holiday* (1969) emphasized the juvenile and family appeal.

ropes that had moored their boat, causing their situation. Further exploration by Doniphan after another storm reveals a second shipwreck and three ruffians.

Little time is allowed for characterization or more than the sketchiest notice of the conflicts between the children. However, in the film, Moco (Jaime Messang), portrayed as a native who is wiser than his white comrades in the means of survival, receives more attention than he does in the novel. He devises a scheme to impersonate demons that convinces the pirates that the island is haunted, with the result that two of them kill one another and the third is captured. To heighten the contrast with the boys, the shipwrecked young lady (Carmen Duncan, the best performer in an amateurish group) spends her first minutes after regaining consciousness fixing her hair, while the lads watch her, bored. They discover that the ship's carpenter has also survived, and with his help the boys figure out that they are on an archipelago and repair the ship, finally sailing to safety.

The script is obscured by the dreadful elocution of the child actors, all of whom appear to be the appropriate ages, between eight and fourteen. However, much of the novel's charm is eliminated by altering the setting from Verne's time to the present. Although this decision was doubtless made in part due to budgetary constraints, the change was probably also deemed the best way to intrigue the audience of children the picture was addressing.

The movie had minimal release and television showing, reflecting the form's typical low cost, inept acting, and mediocre direction. Produced, written, and directed by Mende Brown, the picture was filmed by Mass-Brown Pictures in Australia and shot in color and widescreen in studios in Sydney and around the nearby coastline. Much of the location photography and general art direction is quite pleasing and the best part of the picture. However, the score by Tommy Tycho is loud, intrusive, and pointless, and the opening and closing credits are ruined by ludicrous voice-overs of a boys' choir singing "Row, row, row your boat." *Strange Holiday* is a minor Verne film in a lesser vein, attempting and accomplishing little.

Although also aimed predominantly at youth, a pastiche released at the beginning of 1970 was far more ambitious, MGM's $1.5 million original sequel to Verne's Nemo novels, *Captain Nemo and the Under-water City*. In the manner of *The Mysterious Island*, this sequel opens at the time of the American Civil War, except that this time drowning passengers from a shipwreck are rescued by the *Nautilus* and its crew. They include a widow, her young son, the engineer Lomax, two petty criminals, and Senator Robert Fraser (Chuck Connors), who is on a vital diplomatic mission for President Lincoln. Captain Nemo (Robert Ryan) takes them to his home, Templemer (pronounced "Templemeer"), a huge glass-domed metropolis on the ocean bottom and inhabited by the families of his crew, which the newcomers may roam but never leave lest the world bring warfare to this secure domain. Exploring the city's adjoining farms, they see the new domes under construction to house the thriving population.

As in other underwater Verne films, the diving scenes and Nemo's ocean husbandry are important elements, filmed in the Mediterranean off of Malta. They were likely the motivation for the selection of James Hill as director; his helming of the box office hit *Born Free* (1966) associated him henceforth with wildlife stories. However, in this case his approach to Verne was more evocative of his atmospheric, well-paced direction of one of the era's best Sherlock Holmes films, *A Study in Terror* (1965), another pastiche that carried forward the patterns of the original canon.

Despite the utopian setting, only the widow (Nanette Newman) and her son are happy to remain in Templemer, and she and Nemo fall in love. Other characters remain unchanged. Lomax dies when his claustrophobia leads him to destroy one of the three oxygen machines that allow the inhabitants to breathe; these devices make gold as a by-product (rendering it worthless except as a raw material in Templemer), intriguing the criminals. Fraser begins a romance with Mala (Luciana Paluzzi), fiancée of Nemo's mate Joab (John Turner), and Nemo simultaneously begins to groom Fraser as his successor, giving him credit for a successful attack on an enormous sea monster, Mobula. This approval prompts Joab to become jealous both personally and politically, and he conspires with the criminals to allow them, along with Fraser, to depart in the new, enlarged submarine, *Nautilus II*. Nemo engages in a pursuit in the first *Nautilus*, initiating a battle during which the second submarine is

The *Nautilus* leaves through the gate of Templemer in *Captain Nemo and the Underwater City* (1970).

destroyed, Joab killed, and only Fraser and one of the criminals succeed in swimming to the surface. They decide to keep silent about their experiences, knowing they would not be believed.

*Captain Nemo and the Underwater City* successfully carries Verne's ideas a logical step further with an urban concept redolent of Verne's *The 500 Millions of the Begum* and *Propeller Island*. So, too, the indictment of gold fever is a familiar theme in the author's novels, and in *Twenty Thousand Leagues under the Seas* Nemo had used gold salvaged from sunken shipwrecks to finance revolutions. The handicap of Verne's dated predictions in *Twenty Thousand Leagues under the Seas* is overcome by focusing not on the submarine, but on the city, taking the film into a domain that is still science fiction yet with a notion that has become credible by the 1960s. For all the resulting originality, *Captain Nemo and the Underwater City* follows the character types and archetypal situations found in Hollywood adaptations of Verne works in the preceding dozen years: the captain takes prisoner a group embodying a variety of different tendencies, emotions, and types from the earthly world. Like John Strock in *Master of the World*, Fraser believes he must continue his mission despite its unforeseen interruption, and the invocation of Lincoln in effect sanctifies the subterfuges Fraser engages in to return to the surface.

As a result, *Captain Nemo and the Underwater City* is compatible with Verne narratives and concerns. Nemo and his dreams live on, if in a more familial way than Verne ever imagined; while helping the citizens of Templemer, Nemo is still driven by disgust for the world of the surface. The undersea realm is simply an enlarged version of the submarine, and Nemo's own romance with the widow in no way affects the seriousness of his character. Although sympathetic, he remains credible and zealous in the mold of his best previous incarnations, still a man with strong beliefs about war. The Nemo portrayed by Robert Ryan is a craggy figure, lacking James Mason's tragic depth but also far more appropriate than either Leonard Penn or Herbert Lom in the 1951 and 1961 versions of *The Mysterious Island*.[6]

*Captain Nemo and the Underwater City* is also very much a film of the 1960s. The Nemo it offers is bent on creating a Great Society under the seas. The parallel and resemblance to Lyndon Johnson is more than coincidental, especially in Ryan's casting, his craggy face recalling the president. An LBJ crossed with undersea explorer Jacques Cousteau, this Nemo is distant and difficult to know but fundamentally benevolent, a visionary social experimenter enjoying his role of metropolitan mayor. Just as the Nemo of *20,000 Leagues under the Sea* (1954) was concerned with nuclear war and the Nemo of *Mysterious Island* (1961) with world hunger, the Nemo of *Captain Nemo and the Underwater City* attempts to create a perfect community. In Templemer, there is freedom without urban blight, growth with peace, and equality without social unrest. The only threats are external: Mobula and the newcomers Nemo brings to the city.

The utopia of Templemer, visualized as a live-in, perpetual Disneyland, represents an attempt to forge a union of Jules Verne with the popular mythology that had grown around James Hilton's novel *Lost Horizon* (1933). Templemer is a secular, underwater Shangri-La, an eternal dream world for humankind, a refuge safe from the ravages of war and the threat of an apocalypse on the surface of the world. The Nemo of *Captain Nemo and the Underwater City* is a high lama of peace, a

In *Captain Nemo and the Underwater City* (1970), Captain Nemo (Robert Ryan) reveals to one of the shipwreck victims, played by Nanette Newman, his plans for an even larger undersea metropolis.

leader whose followers are in a promised sanctuary. The only loss is the liberty to have contact with the brutalities of the outside world, a loss the residents do not miss. The arrival of the strangers in Templemer proves, however, as it does in Shangri-La, that for some even paradise is flawed. Similarly, love almost tempts away some of the inhabitants of Templemer, when Mala nearly agrees to follow Fraser to his world. However, among Templemer's natives, only Joab is truly corrupted by the outsiders' presence.

Verne, of course, had the *Nautilus* manned by a crew whose families had been lost in the Sepoy Revolt of 1857. However, if one accepts the film's premise that Nemo's crew had relatives to retrieve after building the *Nautilus, Captain Nemo and the Underwater City* becomes an enjoyable film. The script is by Pip Baker, Jane Baker, and R. Wright Campbell; Bertram Ostrer produced, and Steven Pallos was executive producer, having dreamed of bringing Verne to the screen since serving as Alexander Korda's associate more than thirty years earlier. The decor, photography, and effects are top-notch, with a beautiful, almost watery score by Angela Morley.

After Verne adaptations had broadened to regularly encompass pastiche and animation, by the end of the 1960s they shifted further to appeal to a new audience, adults, beyond the previous focus on youth and the family. This was a result of publications that altered Verne's reputation. As I. O. Evans's Fitzroy series of Jules Verne's works reached its height in the 1960s, the 1965 translator's preface by Walter James Miller for his new edition of *Twenty Thousand Leagues under the Seas* published by Washington Square Press, revealed the extent of the damage done by earlier translators. Miller, a New York University professor with a background in both engineering and literature, was uniquely qualified to challenge the decades of misreadings of Verne. He delineated in a clear, unmistakable manner the typical textual problems that had plagued translations of this and other Verne novels. Miller was not the first new translator of *Twenty Thousand Leagues under the Seas,* but previous revisions did not indicate the problems with the 1873 Mercier version. Others followed Miller's effort, and by the end of the 1960s new translations of *Journey to the Center of the Earth, Around the World in Eighty Days, From the Earth to the Moon,* and *Around the Moon* were also available. A new Verne organization emerged in the United States, the Dakkar Grotto, formed by Ron Miller and Laurence Knight, which resulted in two issues of a journal titled *Dakkar* after Captain Nemo's original Indian name.

Verne's 1884 novel *The Star of the South* was reprinted for the first time in decades in 1966 in the Fitzroy series as *The Southern Star Mystery.* Editor I. O. Evans opined in the introduction that the book "would indeed lend itself to adaptation for the cinema, if the director could, somewhat improbably, be persuaded to refrain from his natural urge to make the heroine join in the wild rush across the veldt, having to be rescued from fantastic perils, holding up the expedition, and generally making herself a nuisance at every turn."[7] Perhaps his idea was read, for what he cautions against is precisely what was done—save for having an active rather than passive heroine in Columbia Pictures' fifth Verne film, *The Southern Star* (1969), produced by Roger Duchet, a Franco-British Nat Wachsberger coproduction.

The book itself had been the result of a "collaboration" between Verne and Paschal Grousset (1844–1909), who wrote the first drafts of both *The 500 Millions of the Begum* and *The Star of the South* but received no public recognition for his contribution. Publisher Pierre-Jules Hetzel had sent Grousset's manuscripts to Verne beginning in 1877, when Grousset was a young and untried author with many literary notions similar to Verne's.[8] Although the arrangement might seem unfair, in fact it was necessary because Grousset, in exile for having been a leader of the Paris Commune, had escaped New Caledonia and become established as an author in England. He was able to return to France after the amnesty of 1880, but not until *The Wreck of the Cynthia* in 1885 was proper credit given to both Verne and Grousset as coauthors—even though that book was almost entirely Grousset's effort.

*The Star of the South* relates the discovery and theft of an enormous diamond (the "star") in South Africa, a country that was a frequent setting for Verne novels. The narrative mocks Verne's readers' expectations of science fiction by pivoting on a young inventor's belief that the Southern Star has been successfully manufactured by artificial means. Instead, the diamond turns out to be the product of ordinary mining. The book is simultaneously a love story, a simple adventure, a comedy, a parable of greed, an exposé of imperialism in South Africa, and a denunciation of racism of all types.

The movie eliminates the facade of science fiction to concentrate appropriately on the adventurous chase across the wilds of Africa.[9] To satisfy the need for an American star, the novel's engineer lead was modified for the antiheroic persona of George Segal as a pseudo-geologist with the excessively coincidental name "Dan Rockland." Similarly, the book's intellectual heroine becomes a mature tomboy who knows the region and languages, sharpshooter Erika Kramer. She is played by Ursula Andress, who had costarred with Jean-Paul Belmondo in a hilarious 1965 French version of Verne's *The Tribulations of a Chinese in China*, released theatrically in the United States to critical acclaim in 1966 as *Up to His Ears*.

However, Erika's loud, vulgar, and imperious father, a stereotype of the wealthy, uncultured European imperialist, remains just as he was in the novel and is ideally played by Harry Andrews. His characterization is enhanced by the film's transferring of the affection for the pet ostrich from the daughter to her father. As Erika admits, there are only three things in her father's life: diamonds, his pet ostrich, and herself, in that order.

The novel's assorted villains of the diamond fields, the hero's rivals, are for the movie transformed into the head of Kramer's security force, Karl (Ian Hendry), as well as the predecessor he betrayed, the hard-drinking, vengeful Plankett, played by Orson Welles. Dan is also a contrast to Karl; although both men are fortune hunters, Dan merely takes advantage of circumstance, unlike the murderous Karl and the more off-handedly cruel Plankett. The search for the diamond becomes secondary to the personal conflicts of revenge, rivalry, and betrayal.

The crucial role of the principal African, Matakit, is written in a manner completely faithful to the novel and expertly portrayed by Johnny Sekka. Dan's friendship with Matakit, who is a skilled thief, is an interracial, equal partnership, with the mutual respect of one con artist for another, whereas in the novel their friendship is based on belief in the other's honesty. *The Southern Star* effectively depicts the currents of racism and exploitation in Africa, and the attitude toward natives distinguishes the villains, especially well captured by Welles's offbeat, effeminate mannerisms as Plankett. When Matakit is accused of having stolen the Southern Star, he is pursued by Karl, who wants the diamond, but also by Dan, whose motive is different—to prove Matakit's innocence. Erika joins Dan when he, too, is falsely implicated, and she is fully his equal in the wilds as they learn to depend on each other. Karl conspires to have Dan killed but is finally shot by Plankett himself, who returns to the wreckage of his jungle outpost.

The location of *The Southern Star,* despite the title, is transferred from the South Africa of the novel to French West Africa and moved forward to 1912 to allow for the introduction of some amusing early automobiles. However, the crucial ambience is maintained, especially in Raoul Coutard's photography of Senegal, with the entire cast on location shooting in 140-degree temperatures.[10] Director Sidney Hayers shows the hero and heroine as compatible with their frontier environment, a crucial element from the novel, whereas the others see the jungle terrain only as an adversary. Underlining the vistas and the trek is a marvelous score by George Garvarentz. The title song, synchronized with the per-

An advertisement for *The Southern Star* (1969) reveals the range of appeals offered to moviegoers.

fectly matched visuals of the opening credits, was sung by Matt Monro, who shortly before had helped establish the African setting of *Born Free* with its theme song, one of the signature melodies of the decade.[11]

Kramer is crushed by the loss of the Southern Star until Dan explains that it may never have been stolen, merely eaten by his pet ostrich, which then promptly loses itself amid a herd of ostriches. However, Matakit finally reveals to Dan that he did indeed take the diamond and still has it. Unlike Kramer, Dan, Matakit, and Erika are only amused by wealth, which for them is transitory and never the ultimate goal. The ending is also in the same spirit as the book's conclusion, in which the diamond explodes naturally from the local heat as soon as it is recovered. Screenwriters David Pursall and Jack Seddon (working from a scenario by Jean Giono, acknowledged only in the European credits) tell the story in a deliberately tongue-in-cheek, whimsical manner, although the lightheartedness fades by the end of the journey. Unfortunately, this 104-minute attempt to exploit the clichés of African adventures and treasure hunts never acquires the necessary originality, but it remains an exciting tale with a surprise ending. Adding to the lack of old-fashioned heroism is the emphasis on Erika's sexuality and Plankett's homosexuality, all combining to give *The Southern Star* the feel of an African adventure very much of 1969, unlike movies from previous decades.

With a similar adult tone, *The Light at the Edge of the World* was released in 1971. Although advertised as a successor to Jules Verne's science fiction, it is instead strictly a story of adventure, pirates, and survival in a vein far different from the Hollywood buccaneer formula that reigned from the 1930s to the 1950s. The novel on which it was based, *The Lighthouse at the End of the World,* was Verne's first posthumous novel, published within months of his death in 1905. The book focuses on the tradition of the "wreckers," land-bound pirates who are even more vicious than their brethren of the sea: they use shore lights to lure ships onto coasts at night and run them aground, then kill any passengers and crew who might survive and ransack the wreckage for profit. The height of such activity was from the seventeenth to the early nineteenth centuries, and the best-remembered adventures of such villains are two books with enduring popularity in various media, Daphne du Maurier's *Jamaica Inn* (1936) and Russell Thorndyke's series on Dr. Syn of the Romney Marsh that began in 1915.

*The Light at the Edge of the World* was a National General Pictures release, produced by Kirk Douglas in a European association with Alexandre Salkind and Ilya Salkind. Perhaps recognizing the excessive humor he had injected into *20,000 Leagues under the Sea,* Douglas had considered filming a grimmer Verne story, *Michael Strogoff,* in the early

Advertisements for *The Light at the Edge of the World* (1971) promised familiar Verne motifs but delivered an entirely different genre.

1960s, to be shot in Russia, and *The Light at the Edge of the World* had been discussed for a decade among various producers before Douglas was approached for the project.[12]

The new film marked the emerging sharp delineation among Verne screen interpretations. The pastiches had continued the family focus, and there was also an increasing turn toward the juvenile, represented by the animated series and *Strange Holiday.* By contrast, *The Southern Star* tried to appeal to a more adult audience, and *The Light at the Edge of the World* followed in its footsteps to move the author even farther in this direction. This was evident in the "mature" rating assigned to both *The Southern Star* and *The Light at the Edge of the World* as the motion picture rating system emerged; print advertising for *The Southern Star* blatantly accentuated Ursula Andress's sex appeal.

The general outline and principal characters of Verne's novel are followed in *The Light at the Edge of the World,* but the novel is spare, and some complications inevitably had to be added for the screen. Doing so involved three writers: Tom Rowe for the screenplay, Rachel Billington (novelist and the director's wife) for additional dialogue (what little there is), and Bertha Dominguez for additional ideas. Douglas plays William Denton, equivalent to Verne's Vasquez, one of three keepers at a lonely Cape Horn lighthouse, trying to lose himself and his memories of disillusionment in the California gold fields. Denton mocks his associates for their devotion to the job until they are killed by Captain Jonathan Kongre's (Yul Brynner) cruel crew. Denton flees, simultaneously trying to stay alive on the barren island, avenge his comrades, and foil Kongre's plans to loot ships rounding the cape.

The opening has a certain rustic beauty and mood of melancholy, expressing the lighthouse keepers' monotonous existence and isolation, and Denton's loneliness recurs throughout the story. Douglas plays the central character as an unattractive antihero, never concealing his fifty-five years and wearing the same grimy clothes throughout. Although capturing some of the lighthouse's mystique, the atmosphere of the locale, shot on Spanish locations with a largely foreign crew, receives little development, with only a fragment of coastline used. The Cape Horn setting is never made explicit but must be inferred, and only at the end is the precise year finally given as 1865.

Within this context, a brutal story unfolds. As in the novel, Kongre and his men are not the romantic buccaneers usually portrayed in movies. When their ship comes into view, Denton sees an array of half-clothed men of many races; although Kongre is better dressed, he is no less vicious. After hiding in a cave, Denton is tricked into returning to the lighthouse, and a pet monkey whom Denton cared for even while starving is disembowled. Denton dives over a cliff into the sea, momentarily convincing the pirates that he is dead.

Denton does manage to save one wrecked ship's engineer, Giuseppe de Montefiore (Renato Salvatori), John Davis in Verne's tale. The movie adds a second survivor, a beautiful maid (Samantha Eggar) who assumes the identity of the lady she served, a member of the English nobility. Kongre notes her resemblance to a photo in the lighthouse of Denton's former sweetheart and uses the similarity to taunt him. Even after Denton learns the truth, he cannot comprehend her preference for serving as Kongre's mistress rather than escaping to fight. At the end, her pragmatism only results in her death at the hands of Kongre's men when he tires of her.

The latter part of *The Light at the Edge of the World* becomes steadily more disjointed and confused, incidents following one another with little coherence. At nearly every turn, Kongre finds himself defeated by the indefatigable and usually unarmed Denton, the rivalry becoming ever more personal and primitive. Denton must shoot his captured friend Montefiore rather than see him tortured on board the ship but then turns the pirates' own battery of cannons on the vessel, killing nearly all aboard. Although Denton must become a killer to survive, he does not revel in destruction, as do his enemies, and all his actions are guided by the desire to restore the lighthouse as a beacon of safety. Kongre and Denton engage in a personal battle to the death atop the lighthouse as it catches fire, with Denton the last survivor as the lighthouse keeper's relief ship comes into view to witness the end of the destruction.

*The Light at the Edge of the World* was released in the summer of 1971, initially in a 120-minute form and later in one cut to 101 minutes. The longer version has been shown on cable television, and a still further shortened cut finally appeared on commercial television for the first time in 1988. Whichever cut is examined, one notices lapses in story and motivation; the extended version does contain a longer romantic sequence later recapitulated in dialogue. Nonetheless, even the 101-minute version is filled with irrelevant scenes that add little to the narrative except violence and vulgarity.

Throughout the film, a tone of violence is maintained, accenting sadism, barbarism, and cruelty, although no more so than some of Verne's own shipwreck novels, such as *The Chancellor* (1875) and *A Fifteen Year Old Captain* (1878). Nonetheless, the distasteful incidents in *The Light at the Edge of the World* do serve a purpose, although the justification for many of them specifically is debatable. Like other genre films of its era, *The Light at the Edge of the World* sought to deconstruct the myths underlying its particular type, in this case the pirate adventure, taking its cue from the "spaghetti" Westerns of the 1960s. Choosing a Jules Verne story, with the connotations of a safe author for young people, was a striking way to deromanticize pirates, depicting them as they truly were—misfits and social outcasts, menaces to society, the opposite of the usual cinematic portrayal of swashbuckling beneath the skull and crossbones. *The Southern Star* also had a revisionist aim, but a milder, more humorous and truly adventurous approach.

Theatergoers would be reminded of the ongoing Disney–Verne relation with the 1970 re-release of *In Search of the Castaways,* followed a year later by the third theatrical re-release of *20,000 Leagues under the Sea.* Simultaneously, Walt Disney World opened in Florida and included a ride explicitly based on *20,000 Leagues under the Sea.* The personnel were dressed in the crew's uniforms, and the tedium of waiting in line was relieved by a diagram of the *Nautilus* in profile and a facsimile of the map to Nemo's Pacific base, Vulcania. The surface and interior of the twelve submarines were modeled on those of the movie, and each carried thirty-eight passengers, traveling through an 11.5-million-gallon tank. The ride itself observed certain modern expectations of what such a trip would require, especially in the sound effects. The voice-over narrator introduced himself as Captain Nemo, inviting passengers on a voyage twenty thousand leagues under the sea. As pipe-organ music played softly in the background, Nemo described the underwater fauna, including a giant clam. Divers harvested food from the deep as the *Nautilus* descended beneath a storm, passing an old sunken shipwreck.

As the *Nautilus* submerged beneath the polar ice caps, strange fish that created their own light could be seen. The ship could not go deeper because of limits beyond which man and his tiny efforts cannot survive, a line taken almost verbatim from the movie. Just as the *Nautilus* passed the remains of what appeared to be Atlantis, an undersea volcano caused the tottering ruins nearly to fall on the submarine. When the crew reported a sea serpent ahead, Nemo told them it was a myth like that of the mermaid, but moments later she too appeared. (The monster had a silly face, in an incident duplicated from the older Disneyland submarine ride with its modern-day setting.) A vessel identical to Nemo's appeared in the distance in the grip of an enormous squid fully the size of the *Nautilus*. However, electrical sparks flashing inside and outside the ship allowed the visitor's vessel to escape and tranquilly surface back where the ride began, at Vulcania.

Although consciously consecrated more to the Disney adaptation than to the Jules Verne novel, the ride included episodes from the book that the movie overlooked, especially the visit to Atlantis, an undersea volcano, and the trip beneath the pole. Outside of the Magic Kingdom, at Disney World's nearby Epcot, there have been a variety of homages to Verne and exhibits of *Nautilus* models and diving suits used during the movie's production. The mythic Verne was unforgettably promulgated in this context, even as beyond Disney World and Epcot, both in studies and films, a steadily wider understanding of the author became evident.

Amid this wide swath of popular culture, a bifurcation developed when Verne became a name attracting not only children but also mature filmgoers as he emerged as an author for adult consideration. The Verne cycle had evolved in approach and function, embracing the ethos of an age of social and generational transformation. This evolution ranged from the violated utopia of *Captain Nemo and the Underwater City* to a more realistic approach in treatments of feminism, race, and colonialism in *The Southern Star* and the acceptance of violence in *The Light at the Edge of the World*. By 1971, Verne was a name for the modern world, yet that trend was about to change completely.

# 7

# Toward a New Aesthetic, 1972–1979

Verne's ongoing renown was highlighted by two contrasting events in 1972. He received a Mardi Gras tribute, with coins and a Fat Tuesday parade composed entirely of floats suggested by various novels. The first network biographical show appeared in nearly twenty years, the "Jules Verne" episode of the series *Nothing but Biography* on NBC. Roland Winters was ideally cast in the title role, and producer Frank Michelli utilized the knowledge of noted Verne translator Walter James Miller. However, this show, along with the shift in audience suggested by *The Southern Star* and *The Light at the Edge of the World*, was followed by a reverse, as Verne henceforth appeared only irregularly on the big screen. Instead, the author shifted to the home and family audience on television largely in the form of animated versions, through which children gained their own entree to the author.

Just as Victorian-era schoolchildren were initially presented with Verne though story magazines, after World War II Baby Boomers and their offspring received an introduction through special editions for the younger audience. These publications ranged from abbreviated editions of perhaps a hundred pages to thin books that emphasized illustrations. Going beyond the weakest of such translations, these texts were purged of subtleties and subplots. Drastically rewritten in a more modern and inherently less literary language, these versions themselves would be edited and rewritten many times over in ever more diminished form as the years went by. Although satisfying a lucrative market, they fostered the impression of a writer more important for his general ideas than for his style and content, and their ability to serve as a transition and lure to reading the original works became ever more doubtful.

One unique form of such literature that emerged in 1947 was the comic book. That year saw the first Sunday serialization of *Twenty Thousand Leagues under the Sea,* later published in shorter form as part of a series, Classic Comics, that evolved into the beloved Classics Illustrated. The Gilberton Company issued all of the most famous and many of the less-known Verne titles in the series, selling them in the millions to American youth through 1970. Filled with bright, vivid color art and energetic and faithful adaptations, these comic books successfully guided many incipient readers to bookstores and libraries. Gilberton's founder, Al Kantor, was a white Russian immigrant whose favorite story was, appropriately enough, *Michael Strogoff,* and it was consequently the first of the ten Verne novels published in the series.

Most of the stories that Hollywood would adapt had already appeared in Classics Illustrated form—*20,000 Leagues under the Sea, The Mysterious Island, Around the World in 80 Days, From the Earth to the Moon, Journey to the Center of the Earth,* and *Off on a Comet*—except for *Robur the Conqueror* and *Master of the World,* whose comic book versions appeared simultaneously with the release of their movie version, *Master of the World,* in 1961. Classics Illustrated ended domestically in 1962, the final ten titles including no less than three Verne adaptations; the last was *Tigers and Traitors* (utilizing all of Verne's *The Steam House*). New titles, including some by Verne, appeared in the Classics Illustrated overseas editions. From the mid-1970s to the present, many other comic book publishers in America issued the best-known Verne titles (but seldom the more obscure ones), including Marvel, King Classics (translated from a Spanish series), and Four-color and Dell with a number of comic book film tie-ins (not only for the Disney films *20,000 Leagues under the Sea* and *In Search of the Castaways* as well as for the big-budget films *Around the World in 80 Days* and *Journey to the Center of the Earth,* but also for *Master of the World* and *Mysterious Island*). One of these comic book series, from Pendulum, was reissued with audio and visual tapes, and in this way the ultimate confluence of the comic book as a lead-in to animation was created. Already during the late 1960s and early 1970s, juvenile audio adaptations were for sale on the medium of vinyl records.

These tendencies toward Verne children's editions, in particular comic books, although largely beginning in the United States, spread globally. The saturation of the international market with these forms as well as the visual style absorbed by two decades of youth suggested to filmmakers that they transform Verne from a property presented in live-action, theatrical features to a presence largely in television animation. These animated series included not only *Journey to the Center of the Earth* (1967–1969) and various versions of *Around the World in Eighty Days* but also a number of half-hour or longer specials for various anthologies of children's classics. In this form, many of the best-known novels have been adapted, often on multiple occasions, including *Five Weeks in a Balloon, Journey to the Center of the Earth, From the Earth to the Moon* and *Around the Moon, Twenty Thousand Leagues under the Seas, Around the World in Eighty Days, The Mysterious Island, Hector Servadac,* and *Master of the World.* Not all are juvenile; by concentrating on a specific aspect of the story, such films have sometimes equaled and perhaps exceeded the achievements of their live-action counterparts.

The cycle began in 1972 with the *Festival of Family Classics* series, when producer-directors Arthur Rankin Jr. and Jules Bass offered a lively, entertaining version of "Around the World in 80 Days" for very young viewers that effectively dramatized the story in an easily comprehensible fashion. This animated rendition begins at the club with a discussion of the bank robbery, which effectively transitions to a discussion of global travel and Fogg's precise outline of a journey around the world, the number of days and planned stops demonstrating how such a journey could be accomplished. This outline is amplified throughout by the periodic display of a gauge showing days elapsed and days to go.

Narrative inflections are made to suit the intended audience, particularly with additional humor. No sooner has Fogg left the train station than Detective Fix impresses the clubmen with his ratiocinative skills, persuading them to offer one thousand pounds for the bank robber's capture. At a Suez fruit stand, Passepartout encounters Fix for the first time and gains a monkey companion, Abdul. In India, with the railroad incomplete, Passepartout locates an elephant, Bon Bon, not realizing that the mahout is Fix disguised. Fix abandons Fogg and Passepartout when they interrupt the marriage of the lovely young Aouda to an aged rajah—eliminating the explanation of suttee to children. Fortunately, Bon Bon has a mind of his own and provides a rescue. Upon arrival in Calcutta, Fogg sets the elephant free to return to the wild (another shift endemic to young viewers).

Fix inadvertently places Passepartout on the same vessel that Fogg has secured in Hong Kong, and when Fix sabotages the sails, Fogg uses the anchor to have a whale tow the vessel to Yokohama. An ellipsis occurs from the departure across the Pacific to the transcontinental rail journey from San Francisco to New York, and there is a quiet interlude as Aouda waxes poetic over her first view of falling snow. Passepartout suspects the Atlantic sea captain, who is Fix with one more plot wherein only enough coal to navigate halfway to England is loaded onto the ship. However, Fogg orders the burning of parts of the ship as fuel, with Passepartout and Aouda as his crew, one of the few screen incarnations in which she takes such direct action. They arrive in England minutes late for their train connection, but Fogg rigs a carriage powered by rockets that flies them to London. Missing the deadline by only minutes, Aouda and Fogg decide to marry, and Fix apologizes, having learned that the robber has already been caught. Fogg, suddenly remembering, is next shown entering the club as he explains the gain of a day by traveling eastward.

The accents are wild variations on expectations, and the character designs by Paul Coker Jr. etch a handsome Fogg, beautiful Aouda, and pleasant servant Passepartout; a choleric Fix and others are marked by enormous warts on their noses or chins.[1] The animation style itself, by Mushi Studios, is adequate considering youthful viewers and not as minimal as some later renditions. Leonard Starr's adaptation credibly spans the changes necessary along with the condensation, creating imaginative additions that are unique to this version. For once, too, there is no balloon journey, although such inventions as the rocket flight are more egregious. Perhaps the comparative fidelity may be explained by the program's production as part of a series of animated versions of classic stories; this program originally appeared in two half-hour parts on November 12 and 19, 1972.

Fix, Fogg, and Aouda in the animated "Around the World in 80 Days" (1972) on *Festival of Family Classics*.

Several weeks earlier, also premiering in two parts on *Festival of Family Classics*, on the October 1 and 8, 1972, broadcasts, Rankin and Bass had offered "20,000 Leagues under the Sea." Far more than "Around the World in 80 Days," "20,000 Leagues under the Sea" stands out as a serious, generally laudable adaptation, one that might be surprising considering the intended audience. The characters remain as

Verne created, with only Conseil becoming younger and renamed Conrad, although his function is identical.

What sets the Rankin and Bass version apart from other children's animated tellings is the stark portrayal of Captain Nemo. He constantly challenges Aronnax, Conrad, and Ned—and by extension the audience—from the moment he tells them they are prisoners of war. "I have renounced the life of so-called civilized men on Earth, a life you mistake for liberty," he tells them. Although never losing a certain unusual heroism, he also clearly suffers from bitterness and hubris—for instance, regarding the entire undersea world as his personal domain. The journey to the South Pole and the claiming of it in his name also become an extension of the reckless desire to prove his own mastery over the natural world, and the near-fatal entrapment under the ice is vividly portrayed. At the same time, he lives compatibly within his surroundings, resisting Ned's desire to go hunting when a pack of whales playfully but dangerously surrounds the *Nautilus.* This incident further serves to underline the distinction between these two men, the conservationist Nemo and the hunter-harpooner.

Ned recites the perils of life aboard the *Nautilus,* which keeps him from becoming the brawny icon personified by Kirk Douglas in the Disney version. Aronnax's curiosity about the sea and his appreciation for the experience Nemo is offering serve as an effective counterpoint for Ned's simpler wish to escape and allow Nemo to be understood in a more sympathetic light.

Another strength of Richard Neubert's adaptation is that he began the process by focusing on episodes of the novel that had been elided by Disney. Thus, in this animated version, the Arabian tunnel is traversed, Nemo showing Aronnax the harvest of treasure from Vigo Bay, and in the pearl fisheries off Ceylon Ned's harpoon saves Nemo from a vicious Hammerhead shark. Nemo takes Aronnax to Atlantis, telling him of the catastrophe that sunk it but finding a lesson in it: "The world needs new men, not continents."

An animal companion is added, just as the Rankin and Bass "Around the World in 80 Days" offered the monkey Abdul. Relieving the tension throughout "20,000 Leagues under the Sea" is a playful dolphin, Fifi, who rescues Aronnax and Conrad when they fall overboard and follows

Conrad, Nemo, Aronnax, and the *Nautilus* accompanied by Fifi in the animated "20,000 Leagues under the Sea" (1972) on *Festival of Family Classics*.

them throughout the *Nautilus*'s journey. The dolphin provides a deus ex machina when needed—for instance, rescuing young Conrad from a menacing giant spider on the underwater expedition to Crespo.

From the depth of the Sargasso Sea, after Nemo uses the *Nautilus* to save Fifi from a giant electric eel, an equally enormous octopus must be fought on the surface, with Nemo saving Ned and Fifi rescuing Conrad. Nemo excuses Ned from having to offer thanks, saying, "We fought together to save our ship and all our lives, no more, no less." Along with the emphasis on character, dates are provided that help to better understand the ten-month, twenty-thousand-league journey; for instance, Nemo sets foot on the pole March 23, 1868.

Ned signals to a nearby warship that flies no flag, only to have his life endangered by its cannon fire. Another shell kills one of the crew, causing the captain to turn the *Nautilus* on the attacker. The calm of the underwater burial follows the battle. By combining the ramming of the warship and the underwater burial, Nemo's actions are revealed in a comprehensible, not censorious, manner; no other version has so succinctly combined all these motifs so central to understanding his characterization.

Only by ultimately trying to explain the source of Nemo's anguish does the Rankin and Bass version come up short. Nemo tells Aronnax that he has lost everything he loved and cherished through war, and later, while playing the pipe organ, he reveals a picture of his late wife and children. They had been killed while crossing the Atlantic on an unarmed ship that he commanded, which was sunk by a warship, leaving him the only survivor. He cannot escape the sense of unreasoning loss. This explanation fails to clarify either the presence of Nemo's crew or the creation of the submarine. After Aronnax, Conrad, and Ned flee in the dinghy during the *Nautilus*'s encounter with the maelstrom, evading its depths with Fifi's help, Aronnax speculates about Nemo that "only death could have released him from the sorrow he carried in life." The survivors feel more than simply exultation in their freedom on returning to dry land, Aronnax noting at the conclusion that "I know the rest of our lives will be haunted by dreams of our voyage."

There are some striking images, such as Ned first seen, after the ramming of the *Abraham Lincoln,* seemingly walking on water but in fact standing on the *Nautilus* only inches below the surface. The design of the *Nautilus,* inside and out, is original and arresting. Nemo claims it runs on electrothermal conversion of salt water to energy; there is, thankfully, no intrusive allusion to nuclear power. The divers both swim and walk on the bottom of the sea, allowing a variety of movement.

From a stylistic standpoint, although the animation is still sometimes disappointing, it is an improvement over the animation of "Around the World in 80 Days." The character designs by Paul Coker Jr. effectively capture Nemo, Ned, Aronax, and Conrad as individuals, but there is rarely sufficient detail for facial expression. In contrast, the scenes of action contain a surprising element of detail, skill, and originality. For instance, at the beginning, what is believed to be a floating reef causing collisions at sea is shown through a series of still drawings that evoke the era. The sound design is far more sophisticated and helps to evoke the voyage. This Rankin and Bass version proves that it is possible to tell Verne's novel with a degree of fidelity for younger viewers; it need not be "dumbed down," nor is the forty-four-minute running time a disadvantage. The animation provides a liberating, fast-paced way to tell the story that is freed from the necessary correspondence of realism entailed by the more mimetic live-action approach.

The following year, 1973, an entirely different tack was taken in the William Hanna and Joseph Barbera version of *Twenty Thousand Leagues under the Sea*, one of the masterpieces of Verne animated filmmaking. In a manner typical of Hanna-Barbera Productions, corners are visibly cut in the visuals, but Draper Lewis offers a deeply introspective, entirely original dramatization. Rather than action, Lewis chose to concentrate on one aspect of the novel, providing a vibrant reinterpretation of Captain Nemo beyond the nuclear age, this time as a nineteenth-century ecologist.

A disarming opening dialogue between two crew members aboard the *Anna Marie* is interrupted by the sinking of their vessel. A government official hears an earful from panicked sailors, describing the global situation as shipping draws to a standstill. Professor Aronnax is consulted; suggesting a giant narwhal as the cause, he joins the search by the *Abraham Lincoln*. Also aboard is powerful harpooner Ned Land, whose brother was drowned aboard the *Anna Marie*, giving him a stronger motive. After a year searching the seas, they finally find their quarry. Ned's harpoon bounces when he hurls it at what they think to be the narwhal, and so he suspects the truth. When the *Abraham Lincoln* is struck, Ned and Aronnax fall into the ocean but are quickly rescued—not by a surface submarine, but by divers.

Maintaining the sense of mystery, the first glimpse of the *Nautilus* is hardly forbidding, but caring—two apparent doctors are reviving Aronnax and Ned. Only later are they summoned to dinner with Nemo as he plays classical organ music. Crew members armed with ray guns discourage Ned's initial threats. This is the last such confrontation, despite the ongoing tension resulting from Ned's determination to be free. Nemo explains that he is not a man of violence but sinks only those who slaughter and pollute the deep. This is the reason for his existence and the purpose of the *Nautilus*. He invites Ned and Aronnax to a walk on the ocean floor, easing the captives farther into the beauty of his world. The dangers are real; Ned's harpoon saves Nemo from a marauding shark. Despite his gratitude, Nemo cannot grant the only real gift Ned wishes lest he and Aronnax reveal Nemo's secret to the outside world.

Although inexpensively assembled, Andrea Bresciani's production design with its bright palette distracts from the repetition of shots and lack of actual movement. The orange of Nemo's red hair matches the color of the diver's helmets, which contrast with the greens and blues of the sea around them. However, unlike in many other animated versions, the visual characterization is in a realistic, not exaggerated, vein; there is no muscle-bulging Ned or uniformed Nemo.

Aronnax asks Ned to delay any attempt at escape; the scientist is delighted with the opportunity to catalog the creatures of the deep, and they see the underwater ruins of Atlantis and traverse the polar seas. Overhearing Ned planning an escape, Nemo allows them ashore, knowing they will be pursued by ferocious natives, but then he surfaces in time to rescue them and turn his electric current on their pursuers. Nemo has shown his own captives that their safety depends on him.

Passing through the Arabian tunnel reveals underwater life that produces luminescence. However, an earthquake traps the *Nautilus* in the tunnel; only through Aronnax's suggestion do they break through the fallen rocks. During this crisis, Nemo is shown giving hope to a frightened crewman, and this is perhaps the warmest, most humanitarian screen incarnation of the captain.

Waking to silence aboard, the captives are shown the Sargasso Sea, filled with hulks of derelicts; Nemo wants to reveal what might happen to the oceans. Adding to the tension is the glimpse of a giant octopus slithering from the depths; only such a strange beast exists in this region so devoid of life. A tentacle grabs Ned, and this time it is Nemo who saves his life; the two men are at last reconciled, despite Ned's ongoing plan to escape.

As Nemo turns his attention to a nearby whaler, it is revealed as a gunboat in disguise, neatly conflating the dual menace to both peace and the environment. Nemo is wounded, and Ned leads Aronnax in taking advantage of the opportunity to escape, but the maneuver only leads all three into the whirlpool. Nemo's last action is to warn them of the peril, and the *Nautilus*, damaged by the cannon fire, goes down.

Ned and Aronnax are thrown free but realize no one will believe their tale because they have lost the scientific evidence contained in their journal. As in the Disney live-action version, they are haunted by Nemo's words. However, at the Sargasso Sea he had warned not of atomic power, but of a no less insidious catastrophe. "It will not happen in your day or in mine, but the day will come when all the oceans of the world will be like this unless we stop all those who knowingly seek to obliterate all that is beauty, all that is purity, all that is wild." Aronnax adds, in tribute, "Yes, Captain Nemo, all that is life."

Suspense steadily builds as the story is retold in a manner compelling for both youth and adults. The elimination of Conseil is indicative of the decision to lay aside all humor for an entirely serious depiction of the voyage, paring it down to a compelling single message in a slim forty-six minutes. Tim Eliott, Ron Haddrick, and Don Pascoe effectively voice the roles, and the score is entirely appropriate; only in the design of the *Nautilus* is there a disappointment. Hanna-Barbera proved that an animated version could be as full of nuance and subtlety as any live-action version.

By contrast, when animation was used for a Verne television series, the results had little resemblance to the novels. *Around the World in 80 Days*, on NBC from 1972 to 1973, had a plot instantly conveyed in its theme song: "Around the world in eighty days, so Fogg may marry Belinda Maze—around the world, with Passepartout!" Produced by Walter J. Hucker and Air Programs International of Australia, voices were supplied by Alistair Duncan as Phileas Fogg, Ross Higgins as Jean Passepartout, and Max Obistein as Mr. Fix. It was broadcast in sixteen

Art for the comical animated television series *Around the World in 80 Days* (1972–1973).

half-hour episodes, and three of the episodes were also grouped together and released as a single feature-length cartoon.

The incidents are almost entirely new, using only the basic idea and the character outlines of the main trio in the novel, with their traits slightly modified for the target children's entertainment. To prove himself worthy of marrying Belinda, Fogg accepts a bet with her father, Lord Maze, hinging on whether he can circle the globe in a certain amount of time, unaware that Maze has hired the detective Fix to foil him. Fix continually appears in disguise, trying to prevent Fogg from reaching his destinations on time. Only after Fix's skullduggery is revealed does Passepartout realize what has happened, crying, "Fix tricks! Fix tricks!"

Fogg remains unflappable, uttering aphorisms as he predictably devises schemes to outwit his foes. His vocal intonations imitate Ronald Colman, and he is sometimes assisted by his occasional companion, the intrepid Belinda. In this incarnation, Passepartout is more of a friend and sidekick than a servant, and the pair are accompanied by a pet monkey, Toto. Despite the obvious juvenile shortcomings, the series is intelligently crafted and was the first Australian-produced cartoon series to be seen on American network television.[2]

The same Australian company and producer began a series of animated television specials based on various Verne novels. The Air Programs International animated version of *The Mysterious Island* in 1975 successfully rearranged key highlights of the plot, changing the relation of events to one another, while still retaining the spirit of the novel. Not only is there Ayrton, the pirates and the *Duncan,* and the miraculous intervention by Captain Nemo, but there is also the novel's reliance on geology and the climax with the volcano. In this way, John Palmer's script effectively condenses the story to forty-eight minutes, and although suggesting new causality on some specifics, there is no substantive alteration in the overall basic themes. The same is true of the characterizations; only Gideon is turned into a long-winded writer who keeps their daily diary, recapitulating events and constantly wondering if anyone will believe their account. As usual, Nemo is more central on screen than in the novel. The animation directed by Leif Gram is effective and moderately imaginative, as in the depiction of the *Nautilus* and of the rocky grottos and jungles of the island.

Harding falls from the sinking balloon in the animated *Mysterious Island* (1975).

The story is told in flashback from an indeterminate point on the island through the words of Neb, Herbert, and Gideon. Union shelling had blasted a hole in their Confederate prison in Richmond, and Neb, Herbert, Gideon, sailor Jack, Captain Harding, and Top the dog escape via balloon. They christen the refuge to which the balloon takes them "Mysterious Island" when they find Harding safe since he fell from the balloon while still over the sea. A cliff house cave seems to have been made by the hand of man somehow melting the rock (as it turns out, Captain Nemo created this space for them). Through a well in the back, strange noises and lights are observed, adding an extra dimension of science fiction to the mysteries around them.

Exploring the island, Herbert becomes separated, lost, and frightened, like Axel in the novel *Journey to the Center of the Earth,* but with a different outcome; he is attacked by Tom Ayrton. After being subdued by the castaways, Ayrton finally reveals the story of his betrayal of Captain Grant and the *Duncan* that caused him to be marooned for eleven years. Herbert becomes ill, which fills Ayrton with remorse, until, unable to believe his eyes, he sees a figure in the night who exudes a bright beam of light and leaves a medicine chest.

Herbert recovers, but when they again hear rumblings from underground and perceive strange lights, Harding resolves to explore the seemingly dormant volcano. From the peaceful summit, he spies a ship on the horizon; it is the pirate vessel on which Ayrton had once served. That night, Herbert, the best swimmer, tries to loosen its anchor but is interrupted by the pirates, who proceed to shell the island. The castaways under bombardment are trapped in the cliff house cave, as they were in Richmond, but then the pirate ship suddenly explodes.

As Jack plans to build a boat, Top spots a chest floating nearby that contains the tools they need as well as a wireless receiver that emits a message to follow a wire down the well. There, deep under the island, they notice the boiling rocks and water as an automated boat takes Herbert, Neb, and Harding to a submarine. Captain Nemo explains that he is dying and can no longer protect them; his tomb will be the *Nautilus,* trapped in the grotto. The castaways return to the cliff house and find the volcano active again, as Nemo warned. The eruption destroys their vessel just before launch, and only the timely arrival of the *Duncan* for Tom saves the group.

The 1976 animated version of *Master of the World,* again produced by Hucker for Air Programs International, hewed closer to the title novel but was still inflected by *Robur the Conqueror* and adopted some of the elements of the 1961 movie adaptation of both novels. The new version also changed its setting to 1910, allowing the surrounding technology to become more of a possible rival to Robur than was possible in the year in which the movie was placed, 1868.

The emphasis in the animated film is initially on speed, appropriate to the novel, with the pretitle sequence revealing Robur's air-land-sea machine's interruption of a road race as it passes ahead of the other vehicles. (The *Terror* is actually never mentioned by name, although its name can be glimpsed on the craft in one shot.) The next scene is a contrast. In Morganton, North Carolina, the inhabitants huddle in the church, fearful of the next, unpredictable disturbance of the mountain, the Eagle's Nest (instead of the Great Eyrie). Buzzards fill the air, foreshadowing not only the importance that flight will have in the narrative but also aerial depredations.

John Strock of the federal police is a square-jawed, wily hero chosen by the inspector's daughter Amelia as her consort. Hoping to participate in the auto race, Strock is established as a competitor to Robur beyond simply his status as representative of the government. Strock will also prove to have the proverbial nine lives, emerging unscathed from numerous brushes with death and coming to represent the world itself, which will somehow survive the threat Robur poses.

The two police who appear with Strock periodically provide a contrast. The Caucasian, Walker, is the comic, gullible figure, and correcting him is another officer, Hart, an African American. The latter's character deliberately reverses the stereotype of the servant Frycollin in *Robur the Conqueror,* also removed from the plot of the 1961 movie.

The source of the Eagle's Nest mystery remains uncertain when Strock is assigned to a new case. A radio broadcast from a "Master of the World" refers to an attack on Washington, D.C., and the master's ability to control science. (It is in this way, rather than with the 1961 movie's "voice magnifier," that Robur communicates his threats to those around him; radio transmission is a more dramatic way of conveying messages than the book's written letters.) Strock realizes the threat is in fact aimed at the Weldon Institute of Science, which Professor Robur had left three years earlier after a dispute over whether the future belonged to balloons or, as Robur asserted, to heavier-than-air craft. Strock saves Weldon just in time as the institute is destroyed.

The high-pitched whir of Robur's craft eventually becomes an effective device for signaling its presence, whether on-screen or off. Robur is here depicted as a bald, eyebrowless, goateed megalomaniac without redeeming qualities. The lack of humanity that he and his crew embody is amplified by their being shown in suits that resemble something worn by an extraterrestrial or alien and headpieces emphasizing goggles and gas masks.

French advertising art for the 1976 animated *Master of the World,* showing the masked Robur, his vehicle the *Terror*, and Strock in pursuit at the wheel of his automobile.

A series of attacks on bridges, trains, and factories are shown in black and white to evoke newsreels. Strock realizes that all the attacks occur in a circle around the Eagle's Nest, so it must be Robur's base, where he returns for fuel. Strock suggests that to attract Robur they should announce the maneuvers of two new high-speed destroyers. Robur's machine, like Captain Nemo's *Nautilus,* evades the naval shells and torpedoes and rams one of the ships. That night, Strock, Hart, and Walker spot signal lights from the machine to a truck bringing fuel. Strock clings to the machine's anchor rope and is dragged unconscious on board. When he awakes, he sees his plan foiled when the other destroyer traps the machine at the edge of Niagara Falls but must beach itself to prevent going over, while Robur's machine ascends into the air.

His machine proves to be a vertical-take-off-and-landing craft that can descend into the Eagle's Nest, an elaborate scientific base reminiscent of Vulcania in the 1954 movie *20,000 Leagues under the Sea.* Robur brings a special bomb aboard, which he uses to destroy the Eagle's Nest upon leaving it, planning to build his new headquarters in the ashes of Washington, D.C. However, an electric storm interferes with the radio broadcast of his new threat, and Robur defies the elements even when his crew warn him of the danger; his machine is struck by lightning and crashes into the Potomac.

Robur and the machine are lost, but once again Strock, representing humanity, survives. At the end, he muses prophetically, like Disney's Nemo, "Today, when I think back, I wonder whether we can ever use science purely for the good of mankind or whether someday, flying out of peaceful skies on wings of steel, will come a new and even more terrible master of the world." Unfortunately, in this climax, the novel's sense of Robur's mastery is diminished into that of a routine conqueror with geopolitical goals, and the elements seemingly protect the seat of the American government, giving this *Master of the World* more of the feel of a 1950s monster film.

A surprising amount of incident is included under Leif Gram's direction in this fifty-minute adaptation by John Palmer of Verne's equally compact novel. However, the ideas are not as effectively combined, as was the case with the 1961 movie, and most of the nuances are lost in a rather one-dimensional telling, amplified by the typecast voicing of

John Ewart, Tim Eliott, Matthew O'Sullivan, Ron Haddrick, and Judy Morris. However, *Master of the World* is also rather more basic in its story than *Robur the Conqueror,* and Robur in *Master of the World* has become a character of pure malevolence. The animation itself is colorful and atmospheric, and, although clearly aimed at younger viewers, the style also effectively enhances the story's tone and characters.

In the same year that they offered *Master of the World,* 1976, Hucker and Air Programs International tackled an oft-filmed novel and proved the full potential of a single forty-eight-minute animated television version. *A Journey to the Center of the Earth* (distinguishable from other versions as the only one to retain the article *A* from the initial errant English-language translation in 1871) was directed by Richard Slapczynski and scripted by Leonard Lee and was the best of the company's Verne adaptations.

Although diverging considerably from the book in numerous details, *A Journey to the Center of the Earth* treats the story and characters with commendable respect and verve. The likelihood of the story is enhanced by a huge spherical miniature model of the earth; with it, Professor Lidenbrock apparently proves that if the interior were as hot as supposed, the whole planet would explode—just as his model had done. The Hamburg Scientific Society ridicules his conclusion that the interior of the earth must be much cooler than generally thought and may even contain life.

Lidenbrock is the town's accepted eccentric, and this trait combines with his genius to form a three-dimensional character. His housekeeper's and neighbors' bemused, accepting reactions to his experiments add a humorous sidelight as in the novel. With this careful establishment of the personalities and treatise (as in the 1959 movie), the program is slow to start, using half its running time before the descent gets under way.

Lidenbrock is inspired by an old runic book by Arne Saknussemm, in which invisible writing is brought out by heat, but the heat also burns up the clue before it has been fully read. Arriving in Iceland, Lidenbrock and Axel discover the locals fear the slumbering volcano Scartaris, for legend has it that centuries ago an expedition of fifty men went down it, and only one returned more than a year later, refusing to tell what happened (all shown impressionistically). Only one local resident, Hans, volunteers to go with Lidenbrock and Axel; for once, he is a believable and courageous character and not a source of humor. Following the news of the trio are two disbelieving scientists from Hamburg, Kippner and Benz. They are jealous of the fame Lidenbrock's exploits might garner, and the scenes with Kippner and Benz, although a rather hackneyed plot device, provide a more likely interjection of an antagonist than the 1959 movie's introduction of rival expeditions.

The expedition soon runs out of water, and Axel faints and becomes lost. Here and at several other points in the story, the visuals adopt Axel's subjective point of view, approximating the novel's first-person narration. The novel's separate episodes of Axel's rescue and the finding of water are effectively conflated, and the three explorers also find the skeletons of the many other men who had traveled with Saknussemm—an eerie sequence that provides one of the few screen attempts to seriously suggest the outcome of the first expedition to the center of the earth.

Arriving at the underground sea, they find Saknussemm's raft, perfectly preserved after two hundred years. Their compass useless, they sail aimlessly and go even farther than Saknussemm, entering into a swamp, where their raft is wrecked. They walk through a giant mushroom forest, pass a saber-toothed tiger, and enter a cave. Better than any other version, the animated *A Journey to the Center of the Earth* thoroughly mixes different types of prehistoric life in the way Verne intended.

The travelers are menaced by giant insects with luminous eyes (who had earlier appeared in a hallucination to the thirsty Axel), and Lidenbrock fights back with dynamite. The explosions in turn cause a flood of high-pressure boiling water that returns them to the surface of the earth out of the volcano Stromboli. Back in Hamburg, Lidenbrock and Axel find Kippner and Benz placing a memorial plaque to the presumably deceased explorers. Doubts regarding the details of their story are met with proof as Axel pulls a huge egg from his knapsack, which promptly hatches a baby pterodactyl. This unacknowledged borrowing from Sir Arthur Conan Doyle's *The Lost World* is an appropriate homage considering the latter's inspiration from Verne.[3]

The visual treatment is both lively and realistic, with considerable pictorial detail and imaginative and effective color schemes foreshadowed by the same company's animated adaptation of *The Mysterious*

A dinosaur startles the explorers in the 1976 animated *A Journey to the Center of the Earth*.

*Island* a year earlier. For instance, kaleidoscopic light effects introduce the underground sea, and the caverns are initially patterned in shades of red, but blues are added as they reach the antediluvian world. Despite the ostensible limitations of its medium as an animated television program, *A Journey to the Center of the Earth* retains more of the original novel and adds fewer melodramatic elements than any of the live-action feature versions. Changes (such as switching from lava to boiling water as the device that carries them to the surface) or additions (as in the giant Earth model) are compatible with Verne. Many of the episodes are handled far more effectively than in the live-action version (such as its sequence of Axel lost and alone in comparison with the 1959 movie), making the 1976 rendition a competitor for the best adaptation in any form.

This animated telling would demonstrate in particular the advantages in creating a surreal underground world when only a year later the novel was remade as a Spanish coproduction, the first Verne live-action movie in six years. Although shown elsewhere a year earlier, it received distribution in 1978 in the United States by International Picture Show under the title *Where Time Began*, although initially titled *Jules Verne's Fabulous Journey to the Center of the Earth*. Made for $2 million (less than half the budget of the 1959 film, without considering inflation), *Where Time Began* was shot over a period of five months. With a running time of only ninety minutes, it was scripted by John Melson, Carlos Puerto, and Juan Piquer Simón and uses most of Verne's original major incidents. Producer-director Juan Piquer Simón had read all of Verne's novels as a boy and eagerly turned to the author for inspiration as he helmed his first film. He subsequently wrote, produced, and directed two other Spanish adaptations of Verne, turning *The School for Robinsons* into the disappointing Hollywood-financed *Monster Island/Mystery of Monster Island* (1981) and then *A Fifteen Year Old Captain*, along with elements of *Travel Scholarships* (1903), into the satisfactory African adventure *Los Diablos del Mar* (Sea Devils, 1982).

*Where Time Began* opens with a precredit discussion of the interior of the earth by a group of geologists, with Professor Otto Lidenbrock (Kenneth More) commenting that the only way to prove any of the theories is through an actual descent. The credits follow, superimposed over a pleasant salute to the Vernian visual style of Georges Méliès, using excerpts from *An Impossible Journey* (1904) and the seldom seen *Two Hundred Thousand Leagues under the Sea or a Fisherman's Nightmare/Under the Sea* (1907), but marred by an inane song on the soundtrack. Piquer Simón intended a tribute to his fellow countryman, Segundo de Chomon, who had first filmed *Journey to the Center of the Earth* almost seventy years earlier.

Piquer Simón moves up the date of the story to 1898 to make it more contemporary for the audience in both technology and social mores (such as the status of women). In Hamburg, an aged man tries to sell several old volumes to a bookstore; Lidenbrock ends up buying them. Arriving home, Lidenbrock finds the soldier Axel (Pep Munne) accidentally kneeling before his niece Glauben (instead of the novel's Graüben, played by Yvonne Sentis), and assuming there has been a marriage proposal, he gladly but offhandedly offers his consent. Glauben notices the small note that falls from one of the books, and together Lidenbrock, Axel, and Glauben, with the help of the cinematically referential device of a magic lantern, discover the key to Saknussemm's code.

Under the same necessity to add a feminine lead as other versions, *Where Time Began* follows a vastly simpler method. Glauben wants to go on the trip, and her practicality proves a valuable assistance to the absent-minded Lidenbrock and equally ill-prepared Axel. By contrast, it is Axel who is uncertain, hesitant, and reluctant; the juxtaposition of his equivocation with Lidenbrock's certainty and Glauben's eagerness provides humor absent from the novel. Axel is still the narrator of the journey, his exposition helping to expedite the plot, even as his failure to recognize his own frailties is amusing. By contrast, Hans (Frank Brana) is closer to the man of brawn Verne described; the only concession to humor is in showing how he imagines the pay for his efforts—sheep for his flock.

The exteriors of the entrance and exit through craters, taken at the Lanzarote volcano in the Canary Islands, provide a barren, otherworldly appearance that almost resembles a moonscape. Although the reddish plains scarcely resemble Iceland, a series of extreme dramatic zooms impressively isolates the cast amid the desolate location, providing a more dynamic lead-up to the descent than in the 1959 movie. The plunge into the earth was shot a half-mile inside caves near Madrid, with the lighting effectively dark and claustrophobic. The humidity was 99 percent, and the cast and crew remained for ten days in this environment, working more than nine hours each day.[4] The caverns are convincingly varied and realistic, without the interspersing of obvious and jarring studio sets that were a distraction in the 1959 version.

In a cave of winds, Lidenbrock loses Saknussemm's book that helped guide them through the first forks in their path. When Hans's pickaxe thrust releases boiling water, it burns the hand of a man Glauben had glimpsed in the darkness—who finally introduces himself as Olsen (Jack Taylor). Olsen says he entered (and will leave) the interior of the earth through another opening and has been traveling alone for two months. As in the 1959 version and its imitators, the filmmakers of *Where Time Began* believed that it was necessary to add a second expedition that meets up with the Lidenbrock group. Although Olsen is even less related to the novel, his actions are not as disruptive as those of the modern, villainous Count Saknussemm in the 1959 film.

The underground sea seems to exert a healing physical power over the members of the expedition. As Hans builds the raft, Lidenbrock, Axel, and Glauben explore the shoreline, including the forest of giant mushrooms. Claiming he has scientific experiments of his own to perform, Olsen sets off a series of explosions in the sea. Glauben notices that Olsen never seems to require sustenance, and his only tool is a copper-colored metal box he carries with him. The sequence around the underground sea is, as in the novel, the centerpiece, and the island, the dinosaurs, and the storm are treated as Verne described. In a choice more impressive than the blue of the sea in the 1959 version, *Where Time Began* uses filters to turn the ocean a deep shade of greenish-blue aqua, contrasting with the orange of the land; the striking color combinations make the setting all the more convincing.[5]

Washed ashore with the wreckage of their raft and their equipment after the storm, Axel and Glauben go in search of Olsen, passing through a field of fossils and into a forest. Only at this point does *Where Time Began* become increasingly far-fetched. Axel and Glauben are suddenly attacked, not by the ten-foot prehistoric man of Verne's imagination, but by a giant ape that appeared as a matter of production expedience but failed to connect with Verne's evolutionary link.[6] Olsen comes to the rescue, escorting Axel and Glauben through a cave, where they see in the distance a whole city of men who resemble Olsen, each carrying an identical metal box and dressed in a similar Russian tunic and hat. Passing more dinosaurs on their return to the shore, they eagerly rejoin Lidenbrock and Hans aboard the reconstructed raft.

Olsen sets off an explosion that will open an escape for Lidenbrock, Axel, Glauben, and Hans, saying he will find his own way to safety. The scene comes rather suddenly and is confusing in its brevity and lack of explanatory dialogue. *Where Time Began* avoids saying whether the explorers actually reached their destination or not, so there is no sense of the downward distance they have traveled.

In a coda, Axel and Glauben have married, Hans is once more a prosperous sheepherder, and Lidenbrock still haunts the old bookshop.

Prehistoric creatures were the promised attraction in a fresh live-action return to Verne's center of the earth in *Where Time Began* (1978).

One day he learns that a parcel has been left for him, and, unwrapped, it proves to be Olsen's metal box. Looking toward the shop window, Lidenbrock sees an aged man, the same one who had brought in Saknussemm's journal, and recognizes that he is "Olsen." This parallel closure brings the film back to where it began and in supplying another clue hints at greater mysteries still to be discovered.

In the original Spanish version, Olsen is named "Amutsen," hinting at the name of the polar explorer Roald Amundsen, but Piquer Simón intended him to be a Martian who would serve as another science fiction appeal to young audiences. However, as adapted in *Where Time Began,* the character is far less defined and more open to interpretation. Is Olsen perhaps meant to be Arne Saknussemm himself or a representative of his pioneering spirit? Either or both could be true; Olsen stands in for the absent predecessor whose journey the explorers are re-creating. Significantly, Olsen appears after Lidenbrock loses Saknussemm's original book and will rescue the travelers at the point where Saknussemm's last carving of his initials appears. He is less of a full-fledged character than a symbol, a vivid reminder of the theme of time that in the form of evolution is such a motif in the novel.

The cast credibly enact their roles, and Kenneth More better captures the eccentricity and mannerisms of Lidenbrock than had James Mason. However, at age sixty-three, More too often reveals his age and seems to find the role—never mind the expedition—too demanding physically; he was at the time suffering the first symptoms of Parkinson's disease.[7] The cut-rate special effects (by Emilio Ruiz) are variable; the dinosaurs are far less convincing than those of the 1959 version, but *Where Time Began* also attempts to do far more with them than the previous film, which did not even stage the battle at sea. The picture's most consistent virtue is the impressive photography by Andres Berenguer, especially the volcanic surfaces, the caves, and the underground ocean. Judged by its own standards and scale, *Where Time Began* must be rated a very satisfactory although uneven effort.

Subsequent films during the 1970s were less rewarding. When Verne's first published novel was presented in animated form, it was disserved just as it had been in the live-action *Flight of the Lost Balloon* and *Five Weeks in a Balloon.* Hanna-Barbera's "5 Weeks in a Balloon," with a forty-five-minute running time, premiered on *CBS/Family Classic Tales* on November 24, 1977. Even the Verne name was nowhere mentioned explicitly, perhaps because an entirely new premise was provided. Instead of the scientific mission of exploration, Queen Victoria assigns Dr. Samuel Ferguson (voiced by Laurie Main) to fetch a gift from King Umtali, the "Eye of the Cat." According to tradition, it may be removed from the altar on only one day every century without incurring the wrath of the volcano known as the Devil's Peak—and that day is only seven weeks away.

Victoria rebuffs the offer of the obviously villainous duke of Salisbury (Main's voice once more), who then does everything possible to foil Ferguson. With the setting in London 1862, Salisbury determines to proceed by boat, but Ferguson wants to travel by balloon. When Ferguson initially ascends in England, Salisbury's confederates shoot down the *Victoria* with arrows, whereupon Ferguson decides to use two balloons, one inside the other. Ferguson's scientific genius is repeatedly helped by his traveling companions, including not only Umtali's representative, the courageous and practical Irumu (voiced by Brooker Bradshaw), but also Ferguson's American nephew, Oliver (voiced by Loren Lester), who has been reared as a cowboy and nicknamed "Buck." He becomes the essential figure of identification for young viewers, along with Irumu's pet monkey, Coco, who adds reaction shots but little more.

Within this new narrative, more is to be found resembling Verne than might be expected. The balloon ascends and descends through Ferguson's device to heat the gas, and the water required becomes a prime motivation for actions in the plot. The balloon briefly escapes control when Salisbury cuts the anchor rope; as the *Victoria* passes over the Congo and Victoria Falls, some sense of the spectacular landscape below appears. Tribesmen believe the travelers are gods from the moon, and when the full moon arises, Ferguson wins redemption by putting his medical skills to use for the chief. Not only Irumu, but also later Oliver, briefly saves the descending *Victoria* by jumping overboard, the latter to be picked up again as soon as the balloon has ascended over a mountain pass. Even the character patterns, although diverging from those Verne outlined, are still closer to the original than they are in live-action versions of the novel.

Buck, Irumu, and Ferguson in promotional art for the animated "5 Weeks in a Balloon" on *CBS/Family Classic Tales* in 1977.

Salisbury arrives in advance of the *Victoria*, trying to impersonate Ferguson. However, it is the Devil's Peak that renders final judgment, erupting when a thief tries to take the Eye of the Cat. Irumu, whom Salisbury had taken captive, explains the truth to King Umtali just as the heroes arrive. Ironically, this particular denouement has the effect of undercutting science in two ways: because Salisbury, traveling by land, arrives first, the *Victoria* is rendered less impressive, and superstition in the form of the eruption trumps Ferguson as well.

At the close, Ferguson suggests to Oliver they might take a balloon to his home in Texas, crossing the Atlantic on the way. There are environmental references; during a storm, Irumu leads the *Victoria* to safety in a rain forest. He also predicts that one day, when Europeans have exhausted their own natural resources, they will turn to the wilds of Africa; the big-game hunters are already coming.

For all of the valid criticism of "5 Weeks in a Balloon" from the standpoint of adaptation, it probably succeeded in holding the attention of its intended viewers with its fast pacing and sense of the exotic. The style is in accord, with minimalist animation so ill concealed as to repeat shots and sound effects back to back. There is little character expression, and both Ferguson and Salisbury have white rather than flesh-colored faces. (This lackluster character design was by Marija Miletic Dail and Jerry Eisenberg.) The only surprise comes in the castle scenes with Queen Victoria, suffused with a background expressionist flavor. The color design is dominated by green, no matter the logic, even in such unlikely places as the sky or Salisbury's hair and moustache. Only the score by Australian Screen Music is satisfactory.

"5 Weeks in a Balloon" was a distinct letdown after the success of the Walter Hucker productions to date, and it was undistinguished by the standards of the other Hanna-Barbera adaptations of Verne. Most of the blame can be laid on the clichéd script by Kimmer Ringwald, but production directors Chris Cuddington and Doug Paterson earned little additional credit, nor did Neil Balnaves as executive producer. The film was made in Sydney, Australia, in conjunction with the aptly named, for Verne, Southern Star Productions.

The metaphorical dive in quality continued. The cartoon series *The Undersea Adventures of Captain Nemo* (1974) had little in common with the purported Verne source or hero. The character who had last been featured in the movie *Captain Nemo and the Underwater City* was revived literally but much less satisfactorily eight years later by sixty-six-year-old Jose Ferrer. His portrayal was seen in the United States in the 1978 television miniseries *The Return of Captain Nemo.* The three one-hour episodes were entitled "Deadly Blackmail," aired on March 8; "Duel in the Deep," March 15; and "Atlantis Dead Ahead," March 22. In England, the entire series was re-edited into a 103-minute feature for release to theaters, which now appears on American television. This version was given the overstated title *The Amazing Captain Nemo,* although both the miniseries and the feature offer Nemo's most disappointing screen outing. By eliminating the miniseries' padding with superfluous, episodic action of a non-Vernian nature, the feature version is stronger, while still covering all the principal incidents.

This latest Vernian presentation by producer Irwin Allen could only make one long for his *Five Weeks in a Balloon,* disappointing as that had been. Unlike his earlier effort, Allen's *Captain Nemo* abandoned Verne entirely in favor of a take-off that turned the venerable mariner into a comic book hero that had more in common with Allen's 1960s movie and television series *Voyage to the Bottom of the Sea.* The content of Allen's *Captain Nemo* also ran the same gamut as the television version of *Voyage to the Bottom of the Sea,* from thinly veiled Cold War parables to outrageous science fiction.

During the 1978 war games in the South Pacific, two unctuous navy divers happen across the *Nautilus,* which has been set free by the underwater explosions. Boarding through an airlock, they find Captain Nemo, preserved in a dormant state inside a smoky glass cylinder. Waking instantly, Nemo announces that he is not a fictional character and overcomes disbelief by remarking that Jules Verne was a biographer as well as a novelist. Exactly 101 years ago, the *Nautilus* was trapped by a seismic tidal wave; Nemo sent his crew to the surface while he hibernated. The *Nautilus* is still in advance of modern navy submarines, Nemo having built a fission reactor 127 years earlier. However, his ship now needs refitting, and Nemo accepts the hospitality of dry docks in San Francisco. With a new crew supplied by the navy, Nemo is readily diverted from his search for Atlantis by a request to stop a nuclear

Jose Ferrer as Nemo looking out over Atlantis in *The Amazing Captain Nemo* (1978).

missile aimed at Washington, D.C., by the mad Professor Cunningham (Burgess Meredith) of the submarine *Raven*. Cunningham wants to rule humankind as he does his robot crew, and his intermittent struggle with Nemo climaxes in the sunken city of Atlantis, where a race of humans inhabit a Romanesque undersea grotto beneath the city's ruins.

Ferrer's portrayal of Nemo is passable only with respect to the plot's convolutions. Beyond a white beard, he is scarcely the Nemo Verne imagined. He is entirely beneficent, if stuffy and abrupt, obeying navy commands with alacrity. Unlike Robert Ryan's Nemo in *Captain Nemo and the Underwater City*, Ferrer's Nemo is docile, without a hint of anger or misanthropy. Despite Nemo's transformation into a simple hero here, he is constantly backed up by the original two navy divers, intended as the ideal role models for the preteen audience at which this version was aimed.

The concern with Atlantis is the only element of plot or character taken from Verne's *Twenty Thousand Leagues under the Seas*. The only other faithful ingredient is the imaginative and colorful art direction by Eugène Lourié and Duane Alt, which combines much of the proper *Nautilus* decor, including drapery and a brief shot of Nemo's library, along with the required futuristic tinge. The model of the *Nautilus* appears unusual and interesting from the few exterior shots, but the cut-rate special effects keeps such views to a minimum. Alex March directed the series; Norman Kratkov and Preston Wood wrote the first episode, and other screenwriters credited on the feature include Robert C. Dennis, William Keys, Mann Rubin, Robert Bloch, and Larry Alexander.

Additional animation from Walter Hucker and Air Programs International in 1979 failed to equal their work in *Mysterious Island, Master of the World,* and *A Journey to the Center of the Earth.* In bringing to the screen two of Verne's outer space stories, already proven highly problematic for live-action filmmakers, animators found themselves largely overcome by the same challenges. However, the first outing, *Off on a Comet,* a fifty-minute version of *Hector Servadac,* created the only reasonably faithful animated adaptation, unlike either *Valley of the Dragons* or *On the Comet* with their addition of dinosaurs and more.

*Off on a Comet* opens as Count Timascheff's steamer, the *Dobryna,* captained by Lieutenant Procope, suddenly finds itself in shallow water. The story shifts to Captain Sevadec (instead of "Servadac"), who notes that he and his orderly, Ben Zoof, are suddenly alone on an island, the force of gravity is much diminished, days are six hours long, and the planet is hurtling toward Venus. Sevadec and Zoof are rescued by Timascheff, whose ship was strangely refloated when the sea waters return. Yet this sea is no more than five fathoms deep, there are no fish, and scraping the ocean floor yields an unknown metal. The film eliminates the romantic rivalry between the two heroes, leaving them only as Russians and Frenchmen who quickly put aside nationalism in the face of the calamity. Zoof is even more a comic relief than in the novel, but all of the characters, although presented much as Verne imagined, remain vague, especially Sevadec, and the voices are not appropriately matched.

A storm carries the *Dobryna* toward Gibraltar, where they find, just as Verne had described, a garrison paying little attention to the changes outside, absorbed in their games of chess. The environment is much more geologically unstable than in Verne's description; a series of sudden uplifts at sea endanger the *Dobryna,* until a snowstorm of ash sets the ship afire. The survivors are picked up by a Mediterranean trading ship run by Honest Hakkabut, who has already found the children Nina and Pedro in his travels in this strange world.[8]

Sevadec realizes the meaning of a cryptic message in a bottle that Zoof plucked from the sea, warning of Jupiter's passing. The sea is freezing around them, and to survive they take shelter in the caverns of a volcano, until a pigeon's note signals another survivor, Sevadec's old astronomy professor. After they make a hazardous sled trip to save him, Professor Rosette is finally able to explain that there has not been any change to Earth and that they are instead on Gallia, a comet he discovered. It will return to Earth but miss it by a mile, and so Sevadec comes up with the idea of a balloon to take them from the comet's atmosphere to Earth's. Amusingly, another balloon carries the men from Gibraltar, still playing chess, as the film ends.

Although the return to Earth is shown as pulling Gallia apart, both collisions are overall far less convincing than they should be. An animated film, of all forms, offers the greatest range of possibility in depicting sights almost impossible to imagine, as had been the case with Hucker's *A Journey to the Center of the Earth,* yet *Off on a Comet* fails in what should be its most unique aspect. It includes colorful and intriguing landscapes and vistas, but it obviously skimps in the visualization under Richard Slapczynski's direction. Nor does *Off on a Comet* capture the excitement of the other adaptations in the Hucker series, possibly because it was one of the last productions in the series. Despite these shortcomings, *Off on a Comet* retains far more of *Hector Servadac* and its characters than any other screen adaptation of the novel.

The same could not be said of the 1979 animated film *From the Earth to the Moon,* which goes even further than the 1958 movie in liberally interpreting both lunar novels within the expectations of modern science fiction, so the results are similarly dismal. The central characters Nicholl and Barbicane here are portrayed as the quarrelsome secretary and president of the Baltimore Gun Club. Barbicane realizes that, six months after the Civil War, the club is doomed without a great challenge and looking up at the moon gives him a plan. In France, Michel Ardan is determined to travel to the moon, and he adores the "crazy people" of the United States. The novel is followed as the details of the cannon, the shell, and use of guncotton are determined, and Ardan insists that Barbicane and Nicholl travel with him to the swamps of Florida to select the launch site, convincing them to join him on the journey.

With the construction of the cannon at Tampa, Ardan's background as a circus performer who is fired out of a cannon serves as a parallel to the journey. Shortly after the firing of the lunar shell, Ardan discovers it is losing air and uses a hardhat diving suit to make the repair outside the ship. Simultaneously, the meteor approaches, as seen by the observatory at Earth when the cloud cover has finally dissipated. As a result, the entire climax is altered, piling absurdity on top of absurdity rather than follow the plot of the novel *Around the Moon*. The meteor's gravitational pull does not send the moonship into orbit, but rather to the moon's dark side. Active volcanoes are observed before the shell crashlands, somehow ending upright on its rocket engines. In such a context, it should be hardly surprising that the trio find breathable air and the remains of a city where humans once lived centuries earlier. A dangerous robot force is activated with their arrival, compelling the travelers to blast off back to Earth. After the splashdown, Barbicane tells the Baltimore Gun Club that men will return to the moon even if it takes more than a hundred years, but Ardan wants to return before then, and an end title reminds viewers that Verne's novel was written a century before the Apollo 11 mission was launched.

Direction by Richard Slapczynski reveals a distinct lack of imagination in both the earth-bound portions and the moon shot itself; only the lunar surface is visually arresting, although seemingly using ideas left over from another production, more redolent of H. G. Wells's *The First Men in the Moon*. Again, a film of *From the Earth to the Moon* not only failed to reach the level of Méliès's original 1902 short but also altered Verne's orbit of the moon to a landing on it instead. The concluding weighty pronouncement recalls the pretentiousness of the 1958 movie *From the Earth to the Moon,* lacking the light touch that rendered *Those Fantastic Flying Fools* a pleasant variation. Despite an otherwise sterling record of scripts for Air Programs International, John Palmer in this instance failed to deliver Verne's story, bringing a disappointing end to the Hucker series.

As Hollywood's Jules Verne cinema cycle faded, so would the frequency of imports to the United States. Three years passed after *The Light at the Edge of the World* before the arrival in 1974 of *The Mysterious Island of Captain Nemo*, edited from a six-hour miniseries on European television and starring Omar Sharif as Nemo. Although the 1975 Mexican version of *Five Weeks in a Balloon*, entitled *Fantastic Balloon Voyage*, was an exemplary and faithful rendering of the novel, superior to any of the Hollywood versions, it was far less widely seen.

By the 1970s, such live-action theatrical movies as *From the Earth to the Moon* (1958), *Journey to the Center of the Earth* (1959), *Master of the World* (1961), *Mysterious Island* (1961), *Flight of the Lost Balloon*, *Valley of the Dragons*, *Five Weeks in a Balloon* (1962), *The Three Stooges Go around the World in a Daze*, *Those Fantastic Flying Fools*, *The Southern Star*, and *Captain Nemo and the Underwater City* had all become staples of the small screen. Joining their broadcast niche were the imports *Michael Strogoff* (1956) and *The Fabulous World of Jules Verne*. The two movies that inaugurated the cycle, *20,000 Leagues under the Sea* (1954) and *Around the World in 80 Days* (1956), after their final theatrical re-release in 1970 and 1971, respectively, were network events upon their television premieres. Hence, collectively as well as individually much of the cinema activity celebrating Verne in the previous two decades echoed endlessly on the small screen. There were times in Los Angeles and doubtless in other cities when two and even three different Verne films were coincidentally shown in a single evening. A canon had been created that kept the author's name before television viewers, an even more powerful reinforcement of the idea of the man and his writing than a cycle of theatrical releases. The frequent reshowing of these films also served to make sequels and pastiches all the more natural.

In becoming the dominant aesthetic for new productions, animation had utilized all the trends already evident—whether straightforward adaptations, narrative continuations of a feature version (as occurred with the 1959 version of *Journey to the Center of the Earth* taken up by the 1967 Filmation series), or pastiche, as in *Around the World in 79 Days*. Animation could distinguish new product from reruns of live-action movies that were increasingly familiar to television viewers and allowed experimentation in style and approach to Verne precluded by the necessary investments for live-action, big-screen movies—a trend that continues to the present. The animated versions have offered almost as rich a range of narrative and visual interpretations of the author's stories and themes, and Verne's presence in forms suited to young viewers is essential to his status as an author uniquely accessible to children. Studies of literary adaptations have usually concentrated on live-action rather than animated telling, but in Verne's case doing so would mean overlooking a vital vein. Thanks to animation's innovations, the Verne screen cycle that had commenced in the 1950s endured for another decade. However, by the 1980s a rapid decline was about to begin.

## 8

# The Wandering Trail, 1981–1993

If the explosion of science fiction filmmaking in the wake of *Star Wars* (1977) impacted Verne filmmaking, it was only in a deleterious way. Seldom would Verne productions rise above the level of mediocrity, as remakes often paled in contrast to their predecessors in the Verne cycle of the 1950s and 1960s. The various possibilities of adaptation, pastiche, and animation having been explored, further innovation was absent from the next dozen years of Verne filmmaking.

The one exception began the 1980s, attempting a story that offered modernist opportunities; Verne had debunked his own fascination with the desert island myth by mocking the formula in *The School for Robinsons*. A rich and wily American, in order to curb his day-dreaming nephew's wanderlust, buys an island and endows it with all the accoutrements of a Robinson—spurious animals and actors to play savage natives, even a man Friday. A shipwreck is staged, stranding the lad, and for companionship he is given the burden of T. Artelett, his hapless tutor of dancing and deportment. All get more than they expected, however, when the island is invaded by fierce wild animals, and *The School for Robinsons* is one of the wittiest of Verne's Robinsonades.

When *The School for Robinsons* was filmed as *Mystery on Monster Island* (also known simply as *Monster Island*, 1981), a rousing, promising beginning was added. Several treacherous pirates kill one another over a cache of gold, heightening the motivations and allowing the brief participation of cult star Paul Naschy. Taskinar (Terence Stamp), in league with the pirates, learns of the gold but is outbid for Spencer Island by the

191

wealthiest man in America, Kolderup (Peter Cushing, in a part originally slated for Jimmy Stewart before a Screen Actors Guild strike intervened).

Kolderup realizes his nephew, young Jefferson Morgan (Ian Serra), hungers for adventure before settling down to marriage and his inheritance, so he provides him with a year-long world cruise accompanied by Artelet (David Hatton). Only the name of his yacht, the *Dream,* and a wink between its captain and Kolderup foreshadow what is to come. As the voyage commences, initially the only surprise is the discovery of a Chinese stowaway, Sehng Wu (Ioshio Murakami). Then one night finned monsters carrying flares kill several crewmen, and Jeff and Artelet dive overboard, the vessel exploding behind them.

Ashore, Jeff and Artelet explore their island refuge, finding the ruins of a cabin guarded by a friendly chimp and rescuing a native, Carefinotu (Gasphar Ipua), from cannibalism. As in the book, Artelet is wholly dependent, a constant comic presence who will simultaneously instruct both the chimp and Jeff in teatime social graces. Scenic and music interludes serve to bridge the work of building living space on the island.

Giant dinosaur-style monsters suddenly appear, and the castaways' launching of a small boat is interrupted by kelp creatures. (These creatures had their antecedents in real wild animals that Kolderup and Taskinar had let loose in the novel.) A French female castaway, Dominique (Blanca Estrada), whose coiffure looks like she has just returned from a stylist, leads Jeff, Artelet, and Carefinotu to her cave. She has salvaged ragtime cylinders from her own shipwreck, to which they dance in a decidedly modern fashion; she is especially interested in a fragment of the gold they have found.

The parade of clichés continues until the volcanic activity impels Carefinotu to reveal, as in the book, that he speaks perfect English and is a San Francisco actor. Explaining Kolderup's trick, he tells Jeff and Artelet that the eruption was the rescue signal for the *Dream* to reappear, and on shore Jeff is reunited with his sweetheart, Meg (Ana Obregon). Kolderup reveals that the creatures were made by a toy manufacturer, an apt description considering their rubbery look. However, at that point all are surrounded by hooded men after the gold, led by Taskinar; Dominique is an imposter, too, and part of Taskinar's plans.

Yet a third twist occurs with a cascade of fireworks courtesy of Wu,

A German lobby card showing, from right, Carefinotu (Gasphar Ipua), Artelet (David Hatton), and Morgan (Ian Serra) as castaways in *Mystery on Monster Island* (1981).

who was of course only playing a stowaway, and in the ensuing melee the crew of the *Dream* captures Taskinar. Wu had arranged for the *Dream* only to appear to go down in an explosion; in the book, the ship had used tanks to appear to be sinking, an explanation only slightly more believable. The succession of creatures ensures a series of thrills for very young viewers but loses Verne's farcical intent, as already indicated by the shift in title. The series of twists, turns, and unexpected developments in the script by J. Grau, J. Piquer, and R. Gantman strains credibility, adding absurdities to Verne's expected improbabilities.

The performances are agreeable, with Cushing and Stamp adding dignity and Hatton not quite becoming an irritant. With a few less strange beasts, *Mystery on Monster Island* would doubtless have been more successful, less evidently juvenile in its approach. The plastic quality of the creatures was of course intentional, so to criticize them as unconvincing misses the point, and the island visuals are capably produced and directed by Verne enthusiast Juan Piquer Simón, who had previously made the worthy *Where Time Began*.

Piquer Simón believed that *Mystery on Monster Island* offered several advantages as a story that could be filmed on a reasonable budget and as one of the author's narratives not already familiar to audiences.[1] He hoped that the Spanish film industry, emerging in the post-Franco era, could participate in the family adventure genre. The locations in the Asturias, Zarago, the Canary Islands in Spain, and Puerto Rico create a setting both idyllic and Edenic, sufficiently primitive to make believable all the incredible events that occur there. Shooting (in English) spanned fifteen weeks with special effects on a budget of $2 million. The joint production of Almena Films (Spain) and Fort Films, a New York company providing 30 percent of the financing, *Mystery on Monster Island* was eventually released internationally in theaters and domestically on television in the United States by 20th Century-Fox.[2]

A return to surprisingly adult, sophisticated retellings occurred with a 1985 animated *20,000 Leagues under the Sea*.[3] This adaptation opens at the novel's close, when Ned, Aronnax, and Conseil are tossed ashore in a small boat, where Conseil transcribes Aronnax's words. The only concession to young viewers is the figure of burly, ever-hungry Ned (Tom Burlinson, the sole vocal performer credited). From the outset, Ned's physique contrasts with the squat, bearded Nemo, clothed in an unfortunate officer-style uniform. To heighten the contrast but also explain why Nemo tolerates Ned's insults, the encounter with the squid becomes the initial incident in the story, with Ned saving Nemo. However, the two remain at odds, whereas Aronnax and Conseil are satisfied with their studies of the deep. The artistic conception of the *Nautilus* is fresh, as elegant as Verne imagined it, and the animation (directed by Warwick Gilbert) is lively within formulaic limits.

By placing the key action scene at the opening, the narrative tends to be more introspective, revealing scenes about Nemo's life. Nemo tells Aronnax that no nation has funded the *Nautilus* and that his treasure comes from the deep. Fear turns to wonder as they go pearl diving, this time saving a young female diver. In response to Nemo's question as to why she hunts in shark-infested waters, she explains that despite the danger she needs to support her people. Nemo gives her an enormous pearl, meanwhile preventing Ned from harpooning a dugong. Any men-

A typical animated rendition of a burly Ned Land in the 1985 version of *20,000 Leagues under the Sea.*

ace, Nemo notes, comes from sharks and men, merging his social and ecological concerns.

Ned's hope for escape when he is able to go ashore for Christmas is frustrated by his encounter with savages, and for Nemo the electrification of the vessel's hull demonstrates his ability to keep the world at bay. He confines his captives and drugs their food, but Aronnax glimpses a ship through a porthole before losing consciousness. The *Nautilus*'s ram slices through the hull of the vessel, destroying it. Nemo must awaken Aronnax to ask if he can assist one of his crew who has been injured, but the man is dying.

As the *Nautilus* descends deeper than ever, the sounds of the pipe organ music nearly deafen Conseil, revealing the captain's distraught mood. Nemo responds to Aronnax's demand for freedom by replying that there is only one way to leave the *Nautilus*. Outside, the ritual of an underwater burial is observed amid the ruins of Atlantis—eliminating any spiritual aspects that are sometimes suggested in such burial scenes.

Planning an escape, Ned learns from Nemo's charts that the captain intends to meet a ship, the *Conqueror,* near the ruins of the *Avenger.* Nemo explains that he is consumed with a hatred no man can comprehend, from the loss of family and country, and he ties himself to the periscope of the *Nautilus* as the submarine and the *Conqueror* shell one another amid a storm's fury. Unable to convince the captain to relent, Aronnax joins Conseil and Ned in escaping in the submarine's small boat.

Ashore, they wonder what has become of the *Nautilus* and Nemo and whether his torment will ever be resolved. The screenplay by Stephen MacLean fails to cohere entirely but explores many of the darker aspects of the novel, despite the mere forty-five-minute running time. Tim Brooke-Hunt produced, with Tom Stacey as executive producer for Australia's Burbank Films.

Three years later, in 1988, another Burbank Films production approached Verne in a different way but with equally laudable results. A unique animated approach to *Around the World in Eighty Days* is found in a version produced by Roz Phillips, with Tom Stacey as executive producer. All of the characters are played by animals, with their various facial and vocal expressions serving as a way to convey their nature— for instance, Scotland Yard is incarnated by British bulldogs. Among the rare exceptions are Passepartout as a mouse and the Indian heroine as a cat, while the American railroad conductors are porcine.

This approach had first been tried in the 1981 Spanish-produced series of twenty-six half-hour episodes, *Around the World with Willy Fogg;* although widely seen in England, it was not distributed in the United States. All the characters were literally anthropomorphized, and the same treatment subsequently appeared in "Willy Fogg" serials of *Journey to the Center of the Earth* and *Twenty Thousand Leagues under the Seas,* with feature-length versions of all three having video release in the United States.

In turning the characters into animals, the Burbank Films version of *Around the World in Eighty Days* begins atypically. After the bank rob-

Fogg, Passepartout, and the other characters all become animals in the 1988 animated film of *Around the World in Eighty Days.*

bery, the thief sheds his disguise, apparently becoming the man who will shortly be introduced as Phileas Fogg (drawn as a suave fox). Yet little tension arises because it would be difficult for the viewer to believe the individual so evidently the hero could be so guilty. This plot device does, however, make more credible Fix's assiduous trailing of the suspect.

After making his fifty-thousand-pound bet, Fogg surprises the members of the Reform Club by ascending from the club roof in a balloon; such effective touches as passing Big Ben underline Fogg's obsession with punctuality. Landing at Suez, Fix steals the balloon, forcing Fogg to catch a ship, but the balloon crashes aboard, a motif that reappears throughout, keeping Fix close to Fogg but never alongside him as a recognized passenger. The actor voicing Fix imitates Robert Newton's vocal intonations from the 1956 version, and local accents and various ethnic touches enhance the sense of the different countries on the journey.[4]

The elephant pulls down the temple of Kali as Fogg rescues Jasmine (in place of Aouda), and Passepartout impersonates the goddess to distract the priests. Showing the sequence from many angles serves to enhance the eeriness beyond what is typically found in such animated depictions. However, Jasmine does not continue the journey with Fogg, instead remaining in India.

Outside of visiting the pyramids, Fogg has little interest in his surroundings; as he tells Passepartout, one arrives in Bombay only in order to leave it. Quick 360-degree swish pans serve as punctuation between scenes, and Passepartout is repeatedly dismayed at the sums his master spends on the travels. Fogg must take a ship to Bordeaux and commandeer it, purchasing the vessel and taking it directly into London with hours to spare—whereupon stowaway Fix arrests him. By the time Fix finally comes to Fogg with word that the real thief has been arrested, it is too late, and Fogg can only respond with a punch to Fix's nose. Nonetheless, the thief is identical to the gentleman Fogg, and the resemblance even had the members of the Reform Club doubting him.

Fortunately, a newspaper boy alerts Fogg and Passepartout to the real date, allowing Fogg to win the wager. The minor changes to the plot create little harm; mostly it is the necessary condensation to a forty-five-minute running time that causes the elimination of nuances in the synopsis by Alex Nicholas and the screenplay by Leonard Lee. Nonetheless, the artistic expression through animals as the characters is both original and effective.

On April 16–18, 1989, the three-part, six-hour, live-action miniseries *Around the World in 80 Days* was televised, written by John Gay and directed by Buzz Kulik for Harmony Gold; Renee Valente (who oversaw the production) and Paul Baerwald were executive producers for ReteEuropa's Berlusconi Group. The miniseries was above the commercial average for the time, with neither the humor nor the romance overdone, and the longer format allowed for a credible version that still had a few nagging deficiencies. The beginning and concluding hours are nearly equal to the 1956 version, and unlike its predecessor's explanation of the eighty-first day by mentioning the International Date Line, the miniseries more effectively follows Verne's scientific explanation, which is more appropriate to Fogg, his nature, and his era.

There is frequent name-dropping of nineteenth-century figures whom Fogg encounters on his travels, such as Sarah Bernhardt, Louis Pasteur, the empress of China, Jesse James, and Cornelius Vanderbilt, but the encounters are far less cleverly handled than they could have been. The viewer can only wonder why balloonist Félix Nadar (or perhaps even Verne himself) was not included among them, especially since there was a balloon ride. Instead, the miniseries' anachronistic balloon, called the *Purple Cloud,* is credited to Jean Joseph Etienne Lenoir, developer of an 1860s combustion engine.

Employing 151 actors and 4,300 extras, the miniseries does follow Todd's example in the casting of 19 cameo stars, although here so often made up as to be unrecognizable. Among them, the best portrayals are supplied by Christopher Lee as a member of the Reform Club, Henry Gibson as a train conductor, and John Hillerman, who easily outshone Sir Cedric Hardwicke as the companion in India. Two veterans of the 1956 production's cameos return in different roles: Robert Morley, formerly a club member, now plays the bank president; and John Mills, previously a cabby, is an aide to Queen Victoria (Anna Massey). Eric Idle as Passepartout and Julia Nickson as Aouda are capable, in many respects etching their roles more appropriately than had Cantinflas and especially Shirley MacLaine twenty-three years earlier. Aouda becomes a temperamental and realistic woman, acquiring an edge of feminism and anti-imperialism compatible with her background.

The series was six years in development, with 400,000 feet of film exposed during shooting on an $18 million budget over seventy days. Although television admittedly lacks the resources of the big screen spectacle, the 25,499 miles of travel and locations in England, Macao, Hong Kong, Thailand, and Yugoslavia conveyed no more spectacle than could be gleaned from a cheap backlot. For instance, Thailand never remotely resembles India, and even the *Henrietta* seems rather small, proceeding on an unrealistically smooth and glassy Atlantic.

Other advantages and disadvantages of this television miniseries are evident: there is time for the relationships among the characters to be admirably handled, but the narrative is arranged in the episodic style necessary for the periodic interruptions of commercials. The worst fault of the miniseries is the decision to avoid many of Verne's most delightful incidents simply because they had already been memorably filmed in 1956. The perfect symmetry of Verne's narrative, with the rhythm of events appropriate to each country building throughout the story, is completely lost, every area or means of transportation turning predictably into a disaster. Although lacking the 1956 movie's hiatus in Spain, the miniseries made up for it with extended episodes in Burma and especially China, probably inspired by the recent hit movie *The Last Emperor* (1987). As a result, *Around the World in 80 Days* seems stretched and overlong, emphasizing moments more reminiscent of television conventions than of Verne, concealing rather than displaying the degree to which the novel lends itself to the miniseries format. Indeed, the production could easily have been cut to five hours or even two parts. Critical reaction was fair to negative, with constant unfavorable comparisons to the 1956 version; the Nielsen ratings declined for each night it was shown.[5]

Peter Ustinov, as Detective Fix, a role he claimed Michael Todd had originally intended for him rather than for Robert Newton, at age sixty-seven was clearly well past the appropriate age. He often plays the role in a hammy, maudlin manner, although made more sympathetic with the provision of a motive for the reward money—to marry. Finally, in a betrayal not only of the source but also of the narrative logic of the miniseries, Fix is recouped from villainy back into the group, rejoining them in accompanying Fogg to London.

The miniseries places more emphasis on probing Fogg's character, and in this respect Pierce Brosnan is ideal in the role, preserving the integrity of Verne's eccentric and ambiguous character as well as the gradual metamorphosis he undergoes. Brosnan's youth, accent, and straight-laced appearance convey Fogg as a lonely introvert, distant and

Pierce Brosnan as Fogg, Julia Nickson as Aouda, and Eric Idle as Passepartout in the television miniseries *Around the World in 80 Days* (1989).

incredibly shy; his personality is ably contrasted with the innately flirtatious Passepartout. Wrapped in the security provided by his schedule, punctuality is Fogg's defense against the world around him, yet he desperately breaks the routine. The changes his character undergoes and his love for Aouda are more difficult trials for Fogg than the various adventures. As Brosnan told an interviewer, "In the beginning, [Fogg is] a man who's very starchy and polished and reserved and private. For him, the unforeseen does not exist—he lives his life by the book. Then he takes this wager—and there's this slow kind of crumbling of the man's interior. You see him reborn, as it were."[6]

Although the return to *Around the World in Eighty Days* as a source of inspiration to filmmakers had positive results, just the opposite occurred when attention was turned to *Journey to the Center of the Earth*. In 1986, Cannon Films began a new live-action movie, directed by novice Rusty Lemorande and written by Debra Ricci, Regina Davis, Kitty Chalmers, and Lemorande. The picture was so worthless that some of the main shooting as well as postproduction and special effects were never completed, and it was shelved for several years. However, in 1989, after Cannon had gone defunct, Viacom released an apparently finished film as an original for home video and eventual television distribution. The release was only an attempt to salvage some profit from a clear loss, and no commercial theatrical release ever occurred—little wonder.

The resulting product was as bad as could be expected, with the only elements reminiscent of Verne being that it remains light inside the underground caverns and that the explorers nearly run out of water. The filmmakers' familiarity seems to have been with the 1959 movie, not the book; for instance, Lemorande steals the precise three-pronged design of Saknussemm's markers used in the previous version, without explaining their derivation or meaning. The script has disconnected dialogue and a senseless plot, beginning with a young English nanny in Hawaii who follows a dog and several boys, and they all become lost underground.

The 1989 *Journey to the Center of the Earth* becomes utterly incoherent as the focus shifts to an Atlantis in the center of the earth, presented as a big-brother metropolis reminiscent of George Orwell's novel *1984* (1949). The cause of this disconnected quality is the fact that the edited *Journey to the Center of the Earth* is actually the patchwork of two films. The project began with director Albert Pyun, who intended it as a modern serial-style satire on the Vernian journey wherein a traveler from the surface is caught in an underground Atlantean police state. However, the film was given to Lemorande on the basis of his script, although he had never directed before. When his efforts fumbled, Pyun was called back, although he and Lemorande had clashing styles and ideas for the story. Lemorande intended the underground storyline to concern the search by Saknussemm, an eccentric, comical scientist, for his grandmother, to have been played by the ailing Hermione Gingold, who died while filming was under way.

Pyun eventually offered to complete the movie for free if he were also allowed to make another science fiction film for less than $1 million. This second movie became *Alien from L.A.* (1988), made in South Africa and based on Pyun's original intentions for *Journey to the Center of the Earth*. Kathy Ireland stars as a girl named Wanda, this time the daughter of a modern Professor Saknussemm. When he disappears, she goes to his African excavation. In Saknussemm's journal, she reads that humankind's ancestors were alien colonists known as Atlanteans, whose giant spaceship served as a floating city, sinking into the earth, where they may still survive. Falling into the pit where Saknussemm had been working, she begins to make her way through the caverns toward Atlantis, whose residents refuse to believe that a surface world exists. Wanda finds her father, and together they escape home. Subsequently, to save on effects shots, sets, and production cost, a new second half to *Journey to the Center of the Earth* was shot, rehashing ideas, effects, sets, and the cast from *Alien from L.A.,* which was also coscripted by Debra Ricci and Regina Davis. At least *Alien from L.A.* secured a normal theatrical release. Chaotic, troubled productions could sometimes have favorable outcomes, as with *The Mysterious Island* (1929), but Cannon's *Journey to the Center of the Earth* was abysmal in every respect, and no salvage job could redeem it.

Heedless of the Cannon disaster, several other studios considered making movies of the novel, but the only result was further mishandling. In 1991, Fuji Eight Co. created two direct-to-video entries in Saban's animated *Funky Fables* series, each lasting twenty-five minutes. "An Excellent Journey to the Center of the Earth" was written by Mark Ryan-Martin and produced by Eric S. Rollman. It has Navan, a nine-year-old boy in Holland, help his uncle Burt (replacing Axel and Lidenbrock, respectively) decipher a lost Bwonalingo manuscript from his grandfather's trunk. Fortunately, they gain practical assistance from the strong One-Eyed Dan the Mountain Man (taking the place of Hans) and his one-eyed pink horse, Sparky. Resolving to follow the directions given and explore the center of the earth for themselves, they discover a hidden opening and with the help of dynamite are soon heading downward through caves.

Despite the character shifts, the cartoon still follows much of Verne's narrative and the standard incidents. Strange signs, first evident in the manuscript, appear in the rocks at various points along the way, indicating the explorers are on the right track. They discover hot springs where minerals give off light, and Navan becomes lost, falling down watery tunnels. He lands at Burt's camp beside a mushroom forest and the underground sea, where Dan has converted one of the mushrooms into a raft. Leaving Sparky behind, they set off across the sea; three days out they are attacked by a sea monster but are saved when it starts to battle another of its species. They encounter a place where there is no gravity, water floats, and their compass goes wild; it is the core of the planet (and the only visually imaginative scene). However, struck by lightning, their raft is wrecked, and they wash ashore to where they originally set sail—Sparky waiting there for them. When a giant walks by, they hide and find a rock carving that indicates the way back as well as the bones and diary of an earlier explorer. Taking refuge in a giant's skull, they set off their dynamite, which has a larger impact than anticipated, starting a volcanic eruption that sends them to the surface. Turning their tent into a hot-air balloon saves them from the lava when they reach the surface, thereby inserting the balloon sequence that has become so frequent in Verne adaptations since *Around the World in 80 Days* in 1956.

As the series title, *Funky Fables,* indicates, "An Excellent Journey to the Center of the Earth" is filled with silly touches and pitiful attempts at tongue-in-cheek satire that fail throughout. The day on which Scartaris's shadow will point out the passage the explorers are to follow is linked to Elvis Presley's birthday. The shore of bones on the underground sea is described as filled with deceased cartoons, destroyed by critics, and a narrator provides a postmodern-style commentary, ruminating on the characters and events as well as explaining the action. Nearly every line is intended as a joke of some sort, relying on slang, pathetic puns, and references that in many cases are already badly dated. The low level of humor, combined with primitive minimalist animation based on simple circular outlines drawn in a caricature style, leads to a tiresome viewing experience.

The next Verne entry in the *Funky Fables* series was almost inevitably an improvement; "20,000 Leagues under the Sea," made the same year, had Jerald E. Bergh as executive producer. The (attempted) humor remains, but this time it succeeds in serving more as an entry point to the Verne story for the very young. An opening tune by Haim Saban and Shuki Levy announces the tone, "going deep, deep, deep," and a narrator has as much a role in shaping the events as the dialogue by the characters.

When a ship is struck by an apparent sea monster, three boys, Ned (voiced by Matt Hill), Allen (Venus Terco), and fearful Joey (Tony Ach), the youngest, speculate that it could have been caused by a dinosaur or even Godzilla. They convince Joey to stow away with them on the navy vessel that is sent to find the monster. Unfortunately, the gunners on board were taking other night classes and didn't learn how to hit a target, so when they sight the *Nautilus,* their shells fail to strike it. Captain Nemo (Richard Newman, who also voices the narrator in different intonations) sinks the vessel, saving only Ned, Allen, and Joey, telling them they must remain onboard to keep his secret, and they acknowledge that he was fired upon first.

Although children as protagonists alter the point of view, many of the character traits of Verne's Ned, Aronnax, and Conseil remain. The casting of Nemo as an adult, even if blustery and bewhiskered, secures him some of the authority given in the novel. Unlike many adaptations, this one returns to the book for a number of seldom-dramatized incidents, from Nemo's giant pearl to a rather surprisingly realistic depiction of near-asphyxiation on the subpolar journey.

However, when a giant octopus attacks the *Nautilus,* the battle is leavened with farce, the narrator explaining that the octopus doesn't crush the *Nautilus* because it has a crush on Nemo. When another ship attacks the *Nautilus* and is rammed, the reason for Nemo's exile is finally revealed—he bet his fortune on the army–navy game, and navy lost. The most transparently silly explanation ever offered on screen is even acknowledged as a "petty reason for revenge."

"20,000 Leagues under the Sea" for the 1991 *Funky Fables* series was the most juvenile animated adaptation of Verne's novel.

Ned, Allen, and Joey escape in Nemo's previously unmentioned minisub as the *Nautilus* is caught in an undersea tornado. They compare this escape to what happens in *The Wizard of Oz* and wonder if they have simply dreamed the entire story. This conclusion is consonant with the rather dismal, cheap animation style used throughout, which gives the film an almost pixilated appearance; only the rather organic design of the *Nautilus* is unexpectedly intriguing.

In 1993, for the first time in a dozen years, Hollywood dramatized a novel not previously filmed rather than offering another remake. *The Jangada* (1881) is another Verne novel featuring an unusual mode of travel and utilizing the "floating island" theme. A *jangada* is a large Brazilian raft used on the Amazon, hence one of the translation titles, *The Giant Raft*. Joam Garral's family, in order to take daughter Minha to the far end of the Amazon to be married, decides to tour the region by building an enormous, self-contained raft large enough to serve as a complete home with all the comforts during the months-long journey. The form allows not only an exciting travel narrative but also the unfolding of a typical Vernian geographical and scientific canvass of the region as the travelers pause at various villages and locales along the way. The second motif dominating *The Jangada* is Verne's fascination with cryptograms; Verne explicitly reveals his debt for the idea to Edgar Allan Poe and cites "The Gold Bug" (1843) for comparison.[7] When Joam is accused of murder, the evidence that would prove his innocence has been set down in a cipher, and it is up to an eccentric judge to find the key to the puzzle.

*The Jangada* also includes a third Verne motif, a diving sequence as a corpse must be brought to the surface from the bottom of the Amazon, a scene clearly reminiscent of *Twenty Thousand Leagues under the Seas*. Probably *The Jangada* was filmed because the book's subtitle, *Eight Hundred Leagues on the Amazon*, with its use of the word *leagues*, is so closely associated with *Twenty Thousand Leagues under the Seas*. Like the American television release of the 1960 Mexican movie of the novel, *800 Leagues over the Amazon*, this new Hollywood version utilized the novel's more descriptive subtitle.

The new movie could best be described as cheap and was the result of a new trend in feature production: movies produced directly for release in the video market and subsequent cable and television broadcast. They could be made for as little as a million dollars and therefore lacked the budget of those intended for showing in theaters or even of made-for-television movies. In fact, although the original running time of *800 Leagues down the Amazon* was eighty-eight minutes, it was released for video in a considerably shortened version, seventy-five minutes. For this production, with joint Peruvian backing, Roger Corman was executive producer, and Luis Llosa the producer and director.

There is no introduction to establish the setting, the year, or the country, and *800 Leagues down the Amazon* has no feeling for the locale or time of the story in such basics as costumes and decor. In one embarrassing scene, when the villain Torres places his foot on a table, he reveals that he is wearing a boot with a modern sole. Lighting and photography are only passable at best, failing to fully exploit the story's pictorial possibilities.

Despite this fact, the picture has an unusually good cast for such a budget. Barry Bostwick adds a touch of class as a dignified, understated Joam Garral. (The picture suffers accordingly once he is jailed and largely off-screen.) Daphne Zuniga is fairly credible as his daughter, Minha, transformed into a courageous heroine and modern-style woman. A devotee of horseback riding, she easily outshines her rather impractical fiancé, Manoel, played by Tom Verica. The plot is changed so that it is Minha, not Manoel, who pursues and kills Torres—overacted by Adam Baldwin. The story has been pared down to its essentials and five principal individuals, eliminating the novel's supporting characters save for the comic relief provided by Fragoso (E. E. Ross).

The raft design roughly follows the Verne concept, although vaguely resembling a converted boat (as was also true of the 1960 version). The trip itself is portrayed as an almost semiannual, prosaic event rather than as a unique tour of the Amazon. The picture's best portion is the middle third, showing the adventurers traveling down the Amazon after a dynamic fight with alligators, but the screenplay by Laura Schiff and Jackson Barr contains the most simplistic dialogue. The beginning rearranges Verne's chronology so that Torres joins Joam and his family in a manner that would have aroused anyone's suspicions. Other changes from the book are also harmful, including some distasteful, gratuitous violence, such as a scene showing Torres as a bounty hunter who brings

*From left:* Tom Verica as Manoel, Daphne Zuniga as Minha, and Barry Bostwick as Joam Garral in Russian advertising art for *800 Leagues down the Amazon* (1993).

in his victims' severed heads and the dangerous attacks by ferocious natives. The judges lose all the humane traits Verne had given them, and the deciphering of the confession, so key to the book, is not re-created in a credible manner. Sadly, this undeserving Hollywood treatment was more widely distributed in the United States than the exemplary 1960 Mexican film of *The Jangada*.

Just as the attempts by Hollywood to tackle novels for the first time—*Mystery of Monster Island* and *800 Leagues down the Amazon*—would mark the last attempt to look beyond the standard titles, most of the other Verne products of this period were remakes, some of them the most second-rate ever produced, especially repeated attempts to tackle *Journey to the Center of the Earth*. Only the television miniseries *Around the World in 80 Days* and the two animated Burbank Films productions offer renditions that matched those of earlier years.

There is little doubt as to the reason for this extended low point. Unlike the numerous different Verne titles published in the 1950s and 1960s, many of which were still in print into the 1970s, by the end of that decade and into the 1990s the range of Verne books published was in steady decline. The volumes on which *Mystery of Monster Island* and *800 Leagues down the Amazon* were based had last been reprinted in the Fitzroy edition in the 1960s but otherwise had been out of print in English for decades. Filmmakers echoed publishers as editions of *Around the World in Eighty Days, Journey to the Center of the Earth,* and *Twenty Thousand Leagues under the Seas* were republished again and again, the three books forming an exclusive and excluding triumvirate. Further familiarity with these three tales was provided by numerous children's retellings. Publishers pointlessly competed against one another by issuing the same titles, satiating the market in a way that sabotaged Verne's sales potential.[8] *The Mysterious Island* and *From the Earth to the Moon* were no longer appearing as often, the latter having lost the fashion it enjoyed in the Apollo era. Such potentially commercial titles as *Master of the World* were nearly entirely forgotten. The poorest translations were reprinted, the existence of variant, preferable versions having also been seemingly forgotten.

Other eras of Verne filmmaking had always offered a much wider range of newly published books; never before was the pool of offerings so stagnant for such a long time. However, renewed, fresh public attention was about to be given to the author, which would in turn spark beneficial changes in screen treatment.

# 9

# The Revival, 1993–1996

Even as an overall decline in the quality of Hollywood's Verne film-making began in the 1980s, a renaissance in scholarship had been gaining momentum. The 150th anniversary of Verne's birth in 1828 led to such original biographies as Peter Costello's *Jules Verne: Inventor of Science Fiction* (1978) and Peter Haining's lavishly illustrated *The Jules Verne Companion* (1979), both building on the translation of the second familial biography by grandson Jean Jules-Verne in 1976 and the 1972 translation of Jean Chesneaux's *The Political and Social Ideas of Jules Verne*. A bibliography of English-language Verne criticism published by G. K. Hall in 1979 was followed by critical studies of Verne's oeuvre: *Jules Verne Rediscovered: Didacticism and the Scientific Novel* (1988) by Arthur B. Evans (no relation to I. O. Evans), *The Mask of the Prophet: The Extraordinary Fictions of Jules Verne* (1990) by Andrew Martin, and *Verne's Journey to the Centre of the Self: Space and Time in the "Voyages Extraordinaires"* (1990) by William Butcher.[1]

It was at this point that I began writing *The Jules Verne Encyclopedia* with Stephen Michaluk Jr., emphasizing Anglophone cultural reception of Verne's work.[2] In researching the various translations and discovering precisely which Verne stories had not yet appeared in English, we noted that among them was *Adventures of the Rat Family* (1891), which was placed with Oxford as a separate book in 1993. My afterword explored why it and other Verne stories had not previously appeared in English; not since I. O. Evans, nearly three decades earlier, had a never-before translated story been published.

Several Verne books that had been published in France for the first time since the mid-1980s began to be published in English as well. British interest in Verne's depiction of their country facilitated the 1992 translation of *Journey to England and Scotland* (written in 1860 but not published in France until 1989). In 1994, numerous articles appeared in newspapers and periodicals touting the discovery of the manuscript of *Paris in the 20th Century* and its prophetic anticipations. *Paris in the 20th Century* was soon appearing in the languages of the globe with as much alacrity as the books of Verne's heyday, but when the English version commissioned by Random House was finally published in December 1996, readers had largely forgotten the publicity, with the result that sales did not meet expectations.[3]

New biographies were published, beginning in 1992 with two throwbacks—another volume for children, *Jules Verne: The Man Who Invented Tomorrow* by Peggy Teeters, and a slim adult volume, *Jules Verne* by Lawrence Lynch. They were followed by Herbert R. Lottman's detailed *Jules Verne: An Exploratory Biography* (1996), the first book on Verne that originated in English to be also published in French.

In 1993, the North American Jules Verne Society formed and has steadily grown with annual meetings, a newsletter, *Extraordinary Voyages*, and book publications. The launching in 1996 of the Jules Verne Forum, a listserv devoted to international discussion of the author, was followed by a website that set the standard for the most accurate and comprehensive information about the author.[4]

The growing audio book industry provided readings of Verne volumes, continuing to this day. First on cassette tape and then on CD, these readings were usually unabridged, although largely from the poorly rendered, often censored public-domain texts.[5] The audio book industry also relied on the same three titles as publishers and filmmakers generally: *Journey to the Center of the Earth*, *Twenty Thousand Leagues under the Seas*, and *Around the World in Eighty Days*.

These varied developments were about to be reflected in a range of contrasting screen efforts that spanned a widening range of genres and forms of screen media, from documentary to pastiches, animation, and children's shows. Inventiveness and originality were evident once more as filmmakers approached all of these genres simultaneously, informed by the wave of new scholarship.

Sadly, only a fraction of these many advances were evident when "The Extraordinary Voyages of Jules Verne" episode appeared on the Arts and Entertainment (A&E) television cable channel's *Biography* series. Premiering April 17, 1995, this one-hour documentary was produced by Martin Kent for Greystone Productions and was subsequently dubbed and distributed in many other countries. A program on Verne had been desired for *Biography* over several years, but despite a nine-week shooting schedule the result is lacking even by the modest standards of the series and is noticeably worse than the episodes devoted to such other literary phenomena as Edgar Allan Poe and Sir Arthur Conan Doyle.

After the briefest possible overview of Verne's importance, "The Extraordinary Voyages of Jules Verne" follows a pedantic and strictly chronological organization, although Kent's original intention had been to concentrate on *Paris in the 20th Century,* examining Verne's literature and reputation through this novel. "The Extraordinary Voyages of Jules Verne" intends to convey Verne's significance in literature, his pioneering role in the science fiction genre, and his struggle against constraining family influences, but it fails in all of these aspects. Kent highlights Verne's romantic and familial failures as a device to hold audience attention, and Jules's son, Michel, is described in clichés as "a juvenile delinquent and then an adult who would have difficulty 'finding himself.'" There is inadequate linkage between Jules's life and stories, and the extent of the literary analysis is the identification of Verne "trademarks" as "a voyage at sea, good versus evil, a struggle with nature, and technical details."

Throughout the program, images are disappointing and usually only vaguely relevant to the narration. "The Extraordinary Voyages of Jules Verne" opens in an unpromising manner: a poorly reproduced excerpt of a movie trailer from *Around the World in 80 Days* (1956) shows the film's balloon flight. Old engravings are heavily used, although relatively few are from Verne novels. Shots of the locations of the European areas where Verne once lived, with views of streets and buildings, are seldom adequately identified, leaving the viewer disoriented. Despite photographing many of the unique items from the Verne collection then held by Count Piero Gondollo della Riva in Turin and the collections in the museums in Amiens and Nantes, the program did not exploit these resources to achieve the maximum impact.

With the narration providing only dry facts, the interpretation is left to six interviewees, and their remarks are the highlight, in particular the comments by Walter James Miller. Biographical insights and background and brief discussion of *Paris in the 20th Century* are provided by della Riva. The author's great-grandson, Jean Verne, offers the perspective of a family member, and screenwriter Gavin Scott seeks to explain the mythological aspects of the Verne oeuvre.

A&E presented a modified version of "The Extraordinary Voyages of Jules Verne" on its Saturday-morning series *Biography for Kids* on March 7, 1998. Most of the original work remains intact, slightly re-edited and corrected by writer-director Kathy Kinsner. A simplified version of the original narration is read by child actress Tara Carnes, who also appears in opening, middle, and closing segments surrounded by Vernian movie posters and library books, along with such items as a diving helmet and a Zeppelin model. The interview segments are, for the most part, retained. Ironically, because of some changes to the visuals, this *Biography for Kids* version may actually be slightly more accurate than the original show, although most of the primary flaws remain.[6]

During this period, even with new scholarship about the author, the same Verne characters and narratives were repeated on screen again and again. Following two new mass-market paperback translations of *Journey to the Center of the Earth* in 1991 (by Lowell Bair) and 1992 (by William Butcher), the novel was finally situated to benefit from screen treatment, as opposed to the dreadful Cannon live-action films and the *Funky Fables* cartoon. A vastly different approach to introducing children to the Verne novel, one in a much more modernist vein, was the segment "Hot Diggety Dawg" (1995) of the highly popular Public Broadcasting Service children's series *Wishbone,* a Big Feats!Entertainment production. Wishbone is a Jack Russell terrier (whose thoughts are voiced by Larry Brantley) who enlivens his mundane life by imagining himself cast in a succession of famous stories. *Wishbone* is essentially a beginner's version of the old Classics Illustrated comic books and seeks to serve as a stepping-stone in luring young audiences toward literature.

As created and executive produced by Rick Duffield, each *Wishbone* episode presents two parallel tales. In the framing story, Wishbone is an ordinary family pet, full of the sort of "cute" remarks expected of a pet's unspoken thoughts. However, in the inset story, his telling of a classic tale, he is appropriately costumed, enacting one of the story's lead roles. The fact that in his dreams Wishbone retains the body of a dog does not stop him from behaving in an entirely human manner and interacting with people as if he were one of them. This device, in turn, echoes small children's desire to be treated as "grown-ups" and to be able to live the seemingly glamorous and freer possibilities of adult experience, thus allowing literature to offer this potential through the example of Wishbone's wish-fulfillment.

"Hot Diggety Dawg," directed by Fred Holmes, begins with a neighbor who has bought a tree in honor of Arbor Day for Wishbone's family, a mother and her child and his friends. Wishbone begins to assist them in digging a hole for the tree, and, with the framing story established, Wishbone begins to narrate the Verne story, imagining himself as Professor Lidenbrock. It is the summer of 1863, and Lidenbrock's nephew, Axel (Jonathan Brent), who prefers reading adventures to living them, does not share his uncle's enthusiasm for repeating the trip Arne Saknussemm claimed to have made three hundred years earlier. Hans (Matthew Thompkins) follows quietly, eager to please Lidenbrock. Soon they are hot, tired, and thirsty as Lidenbrock gives his last water to Axel.

At this point, the story cuts back to the surface, where the children are fascinated with a gold medallion that Wishbone has dug up. Underground, the discovery of gold leads to finding a river inside the rocks, which relieves the explorers' thirst. Meanwhile, aboveground the mother helps the children to translate the Latin inscriptions on the medallion. Beneath the earth, Lidenbrock, Axel, and Hans escape a sea monster threatening their raft in the underground ocean. Going ashore, they discover the jawbone of a mastodon. The explorers know they are on the right path, for Arne Saknussemm's initials appear on a rock, but beyond it their route has been blocked by an avalanche. The unstoppable Lidenbrock is at last discouraged, but Axel suggests guncotton to blast their way through. A miscalculation instead sets off a volcanic eruption.

Aboveground, the family realizes the medallion is incomplete, and

# The Adventures of WISHBONE™

# DIGGING TO THE CENTER OF THE EARTH

By Michael Anthony Steele

Inspired by *A Journey to the Center of the Earth* by Jules Verne

A novelization of Wishbone's 1995 trip to the center of the earth.

only half has been found. Continuing the search with an excess of enthusiasm, they break open a water pipe. A cut back to the explorers shows them being thrown out of a volcano in Italy. On the surface, the children discover the other half of the medallion, which belonged to the founder of their town, Oakdale, and is an important historic relic. Meanwhile, Wishbone is eager to resume his own digging to reach the center of the earth.

At the conclusion, Wishbone narrates several minutes showing how the special effects were achieved, an unusually direct acknowledgment of the fictional nature of the story portrayed. This lack of any pretense provides both charm and referentiality as the episode manages to tell two separate but complementary stories simultaneously. The episodes selected from *Journey to the Center of the Earth* accurately convey the novel's tone and plot despite their brevity. The transitions between the two storylines are effective, fading in between similar visuals in each realm, such as the broken pipe spewing water and the volcanic eruption. However, the difference between the persuasive belowground portions and the annoyingly simplistic family proceedings aboveground is jarring. The only drawback of *Wishbone* is that so much of the running time is spent on the framing story, which remains invariably prosaic and dull, relieved only by Wishbone's whimsical thoughts; it is no wonder, given his surroundings, that Wishbone has such lively dreams.[7]

A more traditional children's version is the 1996 Canadian animated version *Journey to the Center of the Earth,* clearly indebted to the 1959 movie of the novel, even as new permutations were added. Directed by Laura Shepherd, it runs forty minutes and was produced by Phoenix Animation Studios for Blye Mijicovsky Productions but had only very limited showings through Catalyst Distribution, Inc.

As written by Mark Shekter and Robert Sandler, with Shekter supplying original songs and lyrics, the story is set in London in 1897. Professor Otto Lidenbrock believes that a network of passageways exists beneath the surface, as Arne Saknussemm had proposed centuries ago. An Icelandic rock expelled from an Italian volcano reveals an engraved message from Saknussemm explaining the route. Lidenbrock refuses to allow his daughter, Alexa, or her articulate and verbose pet mouse Hercules to accompany him. Doctor Greed, who mocked Lidenbrock's beliefs, decides to follow him and ultimately to destroy him to secure his own fortune and fame. Greed orders Gower, an orphan boy living in terror under Greed's supposed protection, to spy on Alexa. Instead, Gower joins her as a stowaway on the steamer carrying Lidenbrock to Iceland.

When the adventurers reach the center of the earth and finally arrive at the shore of the underground sea, their raft is carried along by a giant turtle. Drawn into a whirlpool, they awaken on a distant shore, where Hercules finds a key with Saknussemm's initials on it. It opens a temple containing a lodestone that is the true center of the earth, along with a bounty of gems that dazzle Greed. He refuses to join Lidenbrock, Alexa, and Gower in an altar stone that safely conveys them up to the surface during a volcanic eruption.

Logic is openly defied; Alexa and Gower forget to bring water when they begin their descent, and Gower brings the lodestone to the surface without any harm to the earth's central balance. The other changes are largely innocuous; Lidenbrock as parent instead of uncle is negligible, and shifting "Alex" to "Alexa" brings in the necessary female participation without adding an unnecessary character. The orphan Gower's finding of a true family and love is a typical plot device of children's stories. Interspersing the narrative at frequent intervals are effective fades from a scene to a similar picture on the page in a book, which then turns over to reveal a new picture as narration helps to bridge one plot development to the next and provides a momentary respite from the action. The songs serve to advance the plot and are presented with montages of imaginary scenes. Only in the fact that Hercules far more clearly resembles a chipmunk than a mouse is the animation at fault; the style is simple but sufficient, in a lifelike vein.

Animation was next used to create a new, original sequel to the adventures of Verne's Captain Nemo in 1995. *Space Strikers* (also known as *20,000 Leagues in Outer Space*) is an animated series of forty half-hour television shows directed by Bruno Bianchi and distributed by Saban Entertainment, with Dana Booton in charge of production. This multinational production made in Europe, the United States, and South Korea combines conventional line drawing with computer animation to achieve a three-dimensional effect in selected sequences, labeled "Strikervision 3-D."

Ned, at left, standing next to Nemo for the intergalactic exploits of the *Nautilus* in the animated 3D series *Space Strikers* (1995).

*Space Strikers* relates the outer space exploits of a descendant of Verne's Captain Nemo. This new Nemo captains a heavily armed super-spacecraft, the *Nautilus,* which in appearance more closely resembles a submarine than a rocket ship. His two principal mates are Ned Land, a fellow human, and Dakkar, a man from another planet who has been transformed to resemble a wolf. A robot is named Aronnax, and a blond crew member, Dana, supplies feminine interest for Nemo.

Nemo and his crew battle "the Master Phantom," who believes he is destined to rule the galaxy. Before adopting this identity, he was once human and Nemo's close friend when the two were youths at the Space Academy. However, "the Master Phantom" believes Nemo deliberately abandoned him on an asteroid during a meteor shower. Wounded, he was saved by the evil Metallic, who turned him into a figure part man, part machine, now seeking vengeance. Nemo, by contrast, is in the forefront of the fight for freedom as he and "the Master Phantom" engage in what is described in the narration as the "ultimate battle" across the galaxy.

Despite distinct echoes of the *Star Wars* saga, *Space Strikers* is an unexpectedly exciting, imaginative series, well written and produced, ably taking a place among the original media sequels to the adventures of Verne's undersea hero.[8] Each episode depicts an encounter between the two adversaries on distant planets and abandoned space stations. Whereas "the Master Phantom" has the resources of fleets of spacecraft to hurl at the *Nautilus,* Nemo must rely on clever tactics and a magical talisman, "the stone of Solara," to outwit his adversary.

In contrast to the animated, futuristic reimagining of Captain Nemo in *Space Strikers,* Verne's hero was adapted to a live-action television series that same year. *Mysterious Island* is a far less derivative, more original conception of the novel and the character of Captain Nemo, presented over twenty-two one-hour-long episodes in syndication. The series was a coproduction of Atlantis Films Ltd. and Tasman Film & TV Ltd., and series producer Sean Ryerson wrote or coauthored a number of the episodes.

The first eight episodes adhere as closely to the novel as is possible for a series; from the escape by balloon to finding refuge in the cave of Granite House and the building of the kiln, the various plot strands are intertwined with increasing success. Only one major character alteration was introduced, Pencroft's wife, Joanna (Colette Stevenson), cast as the stepmother of his son, Herbert (Gordon Michael Woolvett). With a television budget, as might be expected, there are some unconvincing portions, such as the balloon journey, although New Zealand coastline photography adds to the visual appeal.

Generally the acting is passable to good, with Stevenson and Alan Scarfe as Cyrus Harding the strongest. The makeup and costumes, save only for Jack Pencroft's (C. David Johnson) coiffure, are commensurate with what would be expected of the time, and the speech patterns are

The crash of the balloon in the 1995 television series *Mysterious Island.*

far more redolent of the 1860s than are most television programs with a period setting. As the series progresses, the performers show the wear of their sojourn as their personal appearance, hair, and clothes become unkempt, adding a sense of realism.

There is some initial emphasis on Neb (Andy Marshall), who is portrayed as a former slave freed when Cyrus inherited his father's plantation. Gideon Spilett (Stephen Lovatt) is shown as a writer, often putting pen to paper and providing rather naive reflections on all that has occurred. He is physically the least resourceful; in an opening episode, he is pinned under a rockslide caused by Nemo and nearly loses his life until Cyrus realizes how to free him with an explosion using gunpowder created from the island's resources.

Expectations are constantly raised and dashed. By a third of the way through the series, no less than two regular characters, Neb and Pencroft, and two reappearing guest performers, Ayrton (Frank Whitten) and Captain Cutler (Kevin Wilson), have been killed off. This is doubly unusual because the names of the cast members playing both Neb and Pencroft continue to appear in the opening credits. The weak performances by Marshall and Johnson might have been one reason for their elimination, although Whitten offers fine support. The diminished range of characterizations is subsequently a disadvantage, particularly in the case of Neb, and in his absence visits by various local native tribes to the island allow a continuance of the emphasis on issues of race and colonialism.

Most surprising about the series is that, although ostensibly aimed at a family audience, it has little action, ranging past the point of a thinking man's adventure to explore the characters in depth. There is initial tension when Pencroft resists the natural authority of Cyrus, whose later unspoken attraction to Joanna becomes overt. Cyrus experiences anguish over the separation from his own wife and daughter, amplified by the presence of the Pencroft family on the island. Further, Cyrus blames himself for having instigated the balloon journey that took them to the island in the first place.

To the castaways, the mysterious other presence gradually becomes known as "the phantom." When Nemo in diving gear appears to Cyrus, Cyrus believes that he is losing his mind, although the truth is readily apparent to the audience. The green lights and bubbles from Nemo's suit and the *Nautilus* become a motif, signaling the phantom's presence and strange events to come. Through cameras located around the island, Nemo is able to see, from inside the *Nautilus,* all that occurs. He can even hear everything, depending on the location—especially in Granite House. It turns out, in the ninth episode, that he is even recording all of it. However, beyond Nemo's electronic spying on the castaways, there is no real use of science fiction.

After the first third of the series was filmed, the decision was apparently made that the theme of survival had run its course, and with the elimination of Neb, Pencroft, and Ayrton a new, less successful path was chosen. As Nemo proceeds from virtual deity to über-Freud, he recites with clinical detachment the plans and reactions to an endless series of "modification in human behavior" experiments. The use of Nemo's omniscience in his self-imposed isolation is reminiscent of Omar Sharif as Nemo running a film of his background in India in *The Mysterious Island of Captain Nemo* (1974)—as in the novel *The Castle in the Carpathians*—but the television series' creation of a frequently malevolent Nemo distinguishes it from other adaptations.

John Bach has a nearly impossible role, Nemo's actions lacking consistency and motivation. Although at times saving the castaways, he does so less from compassion than from the desire to use them as human guinea pigs, often placing their lives in peril or sowing seeds of distrust. He is determined to subject those on the island to his will; rather than the scientist inventor, he is more of a psychoanalyzing predator, an interlocutor manipulating events. He wants to learn how the castaways will respond, apparently using Ayrton for this same purpose before they came to the island. An entire episode is consumed by Nemo capturing Cyrus and tormenting him over slavery and his emotions for Joanna, which are deeper than they should be but also far more innocent than Nemo implies. Gideon, like Cyrus, is subjected to Nemo's cross-examination, discovering secrets of a troubled British childhood that led him to resent authority and seek a living by his pen in America.

The island is not a place of isolation, but a frequent if inadvertent gathering place for castaways, pirates, and natives—all liable to Nemo's experiments. The series is often too much at pains to reverse expectations, thus becoming predictable in its determination to be on the modern side of every stereotype. There is a labored, inverse treatment of colonialism when Polynesians descend on the island to enact a competition among the men for a bride, which Joanna finds dismaying. When Cyrus befriends them in the hope they will assist the castaways in getting off the island, the Polynesians consign them to a reservation as the more numerous new residents take over Granite House and become dominant. The Polynesians even overturn Nemo's godlike position when the tribal medicine woman's intuition allows her to recognize his observation of them. She ultimately saves his life after he steps on poisoned lichen. Like the series as a whole, the perspectives highlighted are neither original nor active enough to make them entertaining or enlightening, and sometimes they are even tiresome and stale.

In the final episodes, the castaways turn the tables on Nemo, pretending to be under attack to compel him to emerge from his fortress. Cyrus penetrates the cavern concealing the *Nautilus* and at last confronts Nemo. Nemo is, as Verne described, the enemy of Britain, but he is not, as in the book, marooned or exiled. The *Nautilus* has no crew but is operated by Nemo himself, and he had traveled to the United States to learn about

Cyrus and his companions. However, the biggest surprise is that Neb is being kept alive in the submarine.

Nemo reasserts control because it is his science on which Neb's life depends. Nemo tells Cyrus that a ship is near the island, but he will sink it and Neb will die if Cyrus informs the others. Only Cyrus knows why they must not depart on the vessel, and in this way Nemo plots to drive the castaways apart, with Cyrus finally about to take his own life. Nemo at last reveals himself to all, promising that his experiments are over and he will take them back to civilization. Instead, he returns Neb (now played by a different actor) and abandons the castaways once more, intending to ascertain if his absence has made them stronger or weaker in six months.

It is an odd climax to the series, one that offered multiple possibilities for future episodes if the series had been renewed for a second season—which predictably it was not. In fact, *Mysterious Island* received minimal publicity and had limited showings, appearing in the United States only through a Canadian cable channel. The twenty-two episodes were also halved into thirty-minute form, and ultimately the original had a DVD release. Nonetheless, for all its shortcomings, the series is unique and because of its variations on the original offers a much more absorbing version than *Space Strikers* or many other adaptations and pastiches that have been less experimental. Other television adaptations were shortly about to present Verne in more mainstream, commercially successful versions.

# 10

# Telefilms and Miniseries Reign, 1997–1999

Although in 1995 the animated series *Space Strikers* and the live-action series *Mysterious Island* offered largely new conceptions of Captain Nemo, *Twenty Thousand Leagues under the Seas* was about to appear in several major live-action television films and miniseries. The time was ripe; of all Verne's books, none had so received repeated literary validation in translation. Since the Walt Disney film in 1954, three mass-market paperbacks had appeared and remained in print: translations in 1962 by Anthony Bonner, in 1965 by Walter James Miller, and in 1969 by Miller's New York University colleague Mendor T. Brunetti. Miller's annotated trade edition in 1976 was followed by a similar version in 1992 by Emanuel Mickel, and Miller himself, in conjunction with Frederick Paul Walter, rounded out his project with a completely fresh edition in 1993.

A critical mass had been reached, and Hollywood was confident that collective memory had faded sufficiently to try the first live-action adaptation since Walt Disney, and so for the 1996–1997 season not one but three new such television productions were made of *Twenty Thousand Leagues under the Seas,* a phenomenon *TV Guide* labeled "submarine warfare, network style."[1] First arriving was a Hallmark telefilm on CBS, then an ABC miniseries, and finally a separate CBS children's series episode with a different cast but using much of the telefilm's footage. Between them was as much difference as could be imagined, but all three had one prominent element in common: the belief that a female presence was necessary—although each introduced her in different ways. Computer-generated special effects suggested a new production could be considerably cheaper than it would have been in the past.

Most notable was the miniseries *20,000 Leagues under the Sea,* first broadcast on ABC on May 11–12, 1997, which marked a vigorous, fresh interpretation. The filmmakers had respect for the Disney version, and director Rod Hardy, proud owner of a first edition of the novel, explained his rationale for the remake. "The industry is always searching for new material. . . . Sometimes there is no reason why stories that have been told before couldn't be updated. I loved the Disney version, but when you set it up in the '90s it seems very cute. There was another side to Jules Verne. You know Jules Verne had a fairly dark side to him. This version is certainly a little more edgy than the '50s version."[2]

Michael Caine was cast as Nemo because Hardy felt he had the "stature" to follow in a role so closely identified with James Mason.[3] Fortunately, executive producer Richard Pierce realized the period flavor had to be preserved without any attempt to update the situations, characters, or dialogue. "You can't make it seem hokey or old-fashioned, because to the characters in that time and that place, it wasn't. That was their reality. You just have to commit to that, and that's how classics become classics," Pierce commented.[4]

Scriptwriter Brian Nelson utilized many incidents, dialogue, and situations directly from the book but also offered embellishments. There is not one but two professors Aronnax. The miniseries opens with Pierre Aronnax experiencing a nightmare as he is almost drowned, caught in a net, threatened by a sea monster, and denigrated by his father, Thierry, as a "little man." Pierre then is seen offering his explanation of the sea monster of 1867, believing it to be a giant narwhal, although others suspect a man-made vehicle. The Cunard Line offers him the opportunity to leave his father's shadow and join the search by the *Abraham Lincoln,* but once aboard Pierre learns that his father has already besmirched his reputation with Admiral William McCutcheon. However, McCutcheon's own nature is foreshadowed by his pet hawk.

Encountering Cabe Attucks, a free black who experiences virulent prejudice, Pierre hires him as a servant. However, Cabe displays ill-directed anger on many occasions; for instance, he pointlessly quarrels with Ned Land over the harpooner's desire to hunt whales. The trio fall overboard during the attack of the *Nautilus* on the *Abraham Lincoln* and eerily discover the "monster" submerged just a few feet below them, limned by a greenish hue.

Taken aboard the *Nautilus*, they are confronted by Nemo, initially seen only in silhouette in perhaps the best enactment of this pivotal scene in the novel. As Caine explained, "Nemo is on his way to his paradise, and he sinks a ship and picks up survivors from the hated surface world. He takes aboard different characters. . . . [Except for Pierre, the] others he brought on board are either evil or violent representatives of the surface world. He tried to get away from everything on the surface, and he ends up taking them with him."[5] The sequence winds up with the first view of the sea floor from inside the *Nautilus,* entirely computer generated and evoking a supernatural feel rather than the realism strived for in the 1916 and 1954 versions and shown in the 1997 Hallmark telefilm. Nemo gives his speech on freedom and the sea; the entire opening sequence aboard the *Nautilus* has closely followed the novel's dialogue.

Nemo explains that he kills only when necessary and was careful merely to disable the *Abraham Lincoln* despite its firing upon him. He swears, "No one will ever use the *Nautilus* as a weapon of conquest." To make this possible, Nemo has a partly artificial hand containing a device that can instantly destroy the *Nautilus,* which Hardy described as a "'90s touch,"[6] but which instead suggests a resemblance between Nemo and the half-machine, half-human Darth Vader of the *Star Wars* series.

Unlike other adaptations, the miniseries then returns to the *Abraham Lincoln* and the surface world as the narrative subsequently alternates between the surface and undersea realms. Aboard the deck of the *Abraham Lincoln,* amid those wounded by the ramming from the *Nautilus,* McCutcheon swears a personal vendetta in his duel against what he now knows to be a submarine and so mounts a second expedition. This time he is joined by Thierry Aronnax, ostensibly to avenge his son; in fact, the two men are competing over who will first take possession of the submarine once it is captured. The craven nature of Nemo's adversaries makes whatever revenge Nemo seeks far more understandable.

When Nemo and his captives visit the island of Crespo and encounter sharks, Ned shoots an electric bullet from his rifle at Nemo, but Nemo fires a bullet that saves Ned from a shark. The sequence is amplified when a Malaysian pearl harvester accidentally triggers a strange underwater device, and behind her the *Nautilus* looms as one of the ship's divers tries to prevent an explosion but is killed. Cabe helps rescue the apparently drowned Malay, but it is Nemo who is able to revive her. He explains that, like her, he is from the land of the oppressed, but he will not tell what caused the explosion.

The late crewman is buried at sea, dropped through the diving hold, a far more effective device than a trip to the coral cemetery, one that avoids the Christian implications of placing a cross in the cemetery, as in the Disney rendering. Cabe, angry that the Malay is now a prisoner like himself, challenges Nemo to a fistfight, which Nemo accepts. Cabe fights only with physical violence, like a man of the surface world, Nemo tells him, not with intelligence. This sequence is the least motivated and weakest dramatically in the entire film, simply defying believability, especially given that Nemo is obviously twice Cabe's age.

While the fight is happening, Ned convinces Pierre to help him literally put a wrench into the engine, not realizing that it will place the *Nautilus* in peril of crashing onto reefs. Trying to remedy the mistake, Pierre gets his hand crushed and falls down a passageway, where he sees a woman (here the first part of the two-night miniseries ends) but then wakes up with Nemo caring for him. His hand has been rebuilt, metallic like Nemo's own; Ned sees this prosthetic as one further sign that Pierre is becoming more like Nemo daily.

Nemo tells Pierre that the woman was a figment of his imagination, like a mermaid, but Pierre soon learns that she is Nemo's daughter, Mara, who lives in isolation on the *Nautilus*. Introducing Nemo's daughter had already been part of such versions as the *Twenty Thousand Leagues under the Sea* in 1916, the *Tales of Tomorrow* episode in 1952 (in which Farragut turns her against her father), and the imported anime series from Japan, *Nadia of the Mysterious Seas* (1990). Although in the miniseries, Nemo's actual background is never made clear (or the fact that his name means "no one"), he does say that his wife was tortured to death before his eyes. He wished to spare his daughter any knowledge of the cruelty of the world; Pierre tells him he now has an ally in protecting her.

Hardy noted that "network requirements" dictated including women in the story despite their absence from the novel, but Nelson noted, "I like the fact that the fantasy is not just a boys club. I like to bring women and girls into that same fantasy world."[7] Mara (credibly enacted by Mia Sara) now emerges; she had already read Pierre's book, and the two young scientists are soon in love. Nemo recognizes that his daughter is a genius in her own right, and she openly assists him—a relationship so opposite to that of the Aronnaxes or to other versions of her character.

Mara explains that the explosive device found by the pearl diver was one of a series; by setting them off simultaneously, Nemo hopes to ease pressure on the tectonic plates and put an end to earthquakes, making it safe to live on the ocean floor.[8] However, Mara realizes that her father's plan tampers with nature and that one of the explosives near Antarctica has triggered a new volcano, its heat nearly destroying the submarine. This addition resembles an aerial episode in Verne's *Robur the Conqueror* in which the *Albatross* is imperiled. The *Nautilus* emerges afterward into the icy waters of the pole, the first live-action treatment of this portion of *Twenty Thousand Leagues under the Seas*. Short on air, asphyxiation is close when Nemo finds a clearing in the ice to surface. That night Pierre and Mara watch the northern lights together, although Pierre finds greater interest in gazing at her.

Cabe has been caring for the pearl diver for weeks, and upon her recovery she reveals that her name is Imei (Cecily Chun). Ned, examining the stars, realizes they are sufficiently near to shore to swim there, and he escapes briefly, only to be retaken by Nemo's crew. Back aboard the *Nautilus,* Ned pulls a knife on Mara, and Pierre quickly saves her. The angry Nemo has Ned once more placed behind bars, and when Cabe offers sympathy for Ned, he is forced to join him.

Nemo leaves gold for rebels off the coast of India, explaining that "until God seems to care about these people, I will intervene," but with more screen time given to looting a pirate ship than to delivering the riches, the impact of the scene is minimized. Nemo's crew look like ordinary sailors, although they are evidently of various nationalities, with

An advertisement promoting the cast of the 1997 miniseries *20,000 Leagues under the Sea,* with Patrick Dempsey as Aronnax, Mia Sara as Nemo's daughter, Bryan Brown as Ned, and Michael Caine as Captain Nemo.

first mate Shimoda (Ken Senga) a Japanese; the captain remarks that he is tied to all by bonds deeper than blood.

Asking Pierre one day why he mumbles "little man" in his sleep, Nemo realizes Thierry's abuse of his son, allowing the development of Nemo's relation as a second father to Pierre. As Caine explained, Pierre is different from the other two prisoners: he "is basically our leading hero. . . . The relationship with him is something that [Nemo] never had with a son."[9] Nemo's forbearance toward Cabe and especially toward Ned is astonishing, and with the comparison to Thierry, Nemo need no longer take the antagonistic screen role usually assigned him. Rather, it is Nemo's opponents who are ambiguous (Cabe) or obsessed (Ned), while McCutcheon and Thierry are driven by jealousy over their desire to capture the submarine. When Cabe reminds Nemo that Nemo had said he was on the side of the oppressed, and Pierre is unimpressed by his gallery of portraits of liberators, Nemo rethinks his position. Making an effort at reconciliation, the captain places in Ned's hands the device to end geological upheavals and thus the decision whether to continue his plan; the harpooner predictably smashes it.

The ongoing danger on the ocean floor serves as a bridge to the introduction of Nemo's destination, Atlantis, the filmmakers perceiving a need to give Nemo's voyage a greater purpose than Verne's life of exploration of the deep. Nemo has domed the ruins of ancient Atlantis to make it live again as an underwater refuge (making this film a virtual prequel to *Captain Nemo and the Underwater City*). Life, Nemo says, will return to the sea from whence it began. Here he hopes his captives will willingly settle, and he believes his life's work is nearly done.

However, the miniseries is about to conclude on a crescendo of violence, cross-cutting between three different settings. Ned, left in chains aboard the *Nautilus,* escapes and smashes the library window, although such an action drowns him. It also symbolically destroys the best of civilization—books, music, and art. The crew surfaces the crippled *Nautilus,* unfortunately within cannon range of McCutcheon's ship. When the *Nautilus*'s torpedoes jam, and a small one-man sub attaches explosives to its hull, the crew emerges on deck to surrender—only to be massacred by a machine gun operated by McCutcheon's crew. Seeing the distress aboard the *Nautilus* but unaware of what is happening, Nemo and Pierre return from Atlantis to the *Nautilus,* leaving Cabe, Imei, and Mara in the other diving bell. A giant squid that had hidden itself in a crevasse under the city seizes their bell; the cetacean is undoubtedly the least convincing special effect in the film, a true disappointment, not much better than J. E. Williamson's hand-operated squid of 1916.

The action now concentrates on McCutcheon's vessel and the *Nautilus.* To escape the squid, the diving bell with Mara in it surfaces and is hoisted aboard by McCutcheon's crew. Mara now meets the hated Thierry, determined to claim the *Nautilus.* Nemo, back aboard his own vessel, short-circuits wires to fire the torpedoes, sinking McCutcheon's ship, as he now wishes he had done long ago. Climbing to the deck, Nemo and Pierre find the dead crew—and Thierry armed. He claims that the Aronnaxes together now control the *Nautilus*, but Pierre disowns him, telling him that men like Ned and McCutcheon are his true offspring. Thierry reveals that Mara was aboard McCutcheon's ship, leaving Nemo heartbroken, and Thierry shoots both the captain and his own son. Realizing that Thierry is about to use the *Nautilus* for his own wicked purposes, Pierre accepts the imminence of death to help Nemo trigger the device in his mechanized hand that explodes the *Nautilus*—and so kills his father. However, Pierre survives when he is thrown clear, near where the diving bell is floating with Cabe and Imei, but not Mara. In the final shot, Pierre is re-reading his notes in 1900, and a final voice-over from Nemo exhorts living in the freedom and the embrace of the sea.

All are killed save those who are completely innocent and not of the *Nautilus:* Cabe, Imei, and Pierre. This ending defies patriarchy and science in a true hecatomb that dwarfs even the one Verne described. This denouement is the most memorable version of the novel since Disney's, although neither is faithful to the book. In that predecessor and in the 1929 version of *The Mysterious Island,* humankind is saved from misuse of the science that Nemo created, ensured by his death. Although this ending is less true to Verne, it does allow a fulfilling dramatic arc in accord with Hollywood's preference for closure.

Caine is an offbeat choice for the role of Nemo but brings an apt intensity and dignity in portraying the exile from civilization as well as the inventor and visionary who recognizes in time his own errors. He uses a clipped speech but makes no change in his traditional Cockney accent, and Mara, too, speaks with a British accent. Caine described the role as one that you don't turn down: "It's like a classical actor getting the chance to play Hamlet; you just have to do it, because you can pull out all the stops with him. It doesn't matter what you do, because there's no going too far over the top."[10] He had read the novel as a lad and seen the Disney version, but in order to approach the characterization in a fresh and different manner he did not undertake any further study.[11]

With Nemo's ethnicity adjusted to fit the casting of Caine, however, some scenes lack credibility, as when he claims kinship with the pearl diver. In replacing Conseil, the addition of the African American Cabe suggests the two divergent effects of social injustice, but, unlike Nemo,

Cabe (sulkily enacted by Adewale Akinnouye-Agbaje) is never able to go beyond anger. He is different from Ned only in lavishing affection on another victim, Imei. However, the parallel couples—Mara and Pierre, Cabe and Imei, the former separated forever and the other surviving—provide symmetry.

Although Nelson's screenplay goes well beyond what Verne had described, this approach enriches some of the characters. From the wellsprings of the death of his wife and his own alienation from the surface world, Nemo has created an alternative society of his own that promises to extend the peace he has found under the sea. Although Pierre's own traumas are vastly different from either Nemo's or Cabe's, he is able to empathize with Cabe, the victim of racism, and understand Nemo, emerging with a productive resolution; Patrick Dempsey performs the role of Pierre with understated skill.

Just as the miniseries offers two love stories, it contrasts the examples of parenting in Nemo's bond with Mara and Pierre, on the one hand, and Thierry's mistreatment of Pierre, on the other. Thierry is a man who has belittled his son from childhood to bolster his own ego and as a perverse homage to the memory of the wife who died giving birth. The portrayal of the abuse from childhood into adulthood is highly realistic, and even on those rare occasions when Hollywood tackles antipatriarchal themes, as in the Luke Skywalker–Darth Vader relationship in the *Star Wars* saga, the necessary outcome is usually homogenized to restore familial relationships and offer paternal redemption. None is possible for Thierry; he is pure psychological cruelty, no less injurious than the social evils Cabe and Nemo have battled. This new approach to Aronnax vitalizes his relationship with Nemo in a fresh manner, enhancing this aspect of the novel.

The script and casting are rife with intertextuality. Caine would later appear as the discoverer of Nemo's isle in the 2012 movie *Journey 2: The Mysterious Island,* and Bryan Brown would take a pivotal role in the 1999 miniseries *Journey to the Center of the Earth.* Other actors in the 1997 miniseries brought a Vernian background with them: John Bach, as Thierry, had played Nemo in the 1995 television series *Mysterious Island,* and Peter McCauley as McCutcheon had played Gideon Spilett's father in a flashback episode of that same series. In taking the place of Captain Farrugut, Admiral McCutcheon is an homage to Wallace McCutcheon, who may have directed and starred in the purported first film of *Twenty Thousand Leagues under the Seas* in 1905.[12] Most important are the references to Verne. For instance, McCutcheon shows the engraving of the crew battling the squid when asking Pierre about sea monsters; Pierre finds a copy of *Journey to the Center of the Earth* in Nemo's library, realizing it means that Nemo has only recently left the land; and Thierry's former mistress, Lydia, is told to look up a Frenchman named Verne. At the end, Pierre says no one believed his account, accepting only Verne's novelized rendition.

The executive producer of the Hallmark telefilm, Robert Halmi Sr., thought his two-hour time slot was perfect for dramatizing the novel rather than the four commercial hours used for the miniseries.[13] Michael Anderson, who had directed *Around the World in 80 Days* for producer Michael Todd almost four decades earlier, directed the telefilm, and his most recent efforts had been high-quality 1990s television remakes of such other classic sea novels as *The Sea Wolf* (1993) and *Captains Courageous* (1996).

Anderson joined *20,000 Leagues under the Sea* in March 1996, after scriptwriter Joe Wiesenfeld had authored a first draft. Together, they dramatized the narrative and characterizations, deciding scenes from the novel that should be included and those they felt could be safely dropped while still retaining the feel of Verne's story. Budget was a constant limiting factor; for instance, unlike in the miniseries, the episode at the South Pole with the *Nautilus* trapped beneath the ice was abandoned as too expensive. Nemo explains that the art gallery and treasures are salvaged from shipwrecks, but they unfortunately resemble mass-produced reproductions. A brig large enough to contain the entire crew suggests the use of inappropriate standing sets.

While shooting of the Hallmark version took place from July 22 to August 30, 1996, in London's Pinewood studios, for the miniseries the brothers Richard and Keith Pierce had found a production partner in Australian-based Village Road Show Pictures, which already had the necessary studio facilities. Working in England, Anderson learned about the Australian version. "I heard about it a little while after I started on the project. . . . It didn't affect my film at all. Once you're engaged in a project you do *your* project. You can't worry about what somebody else is doing. . . . It's the same book, and I'm sure somebody else will have a different point of view. You could place these characters and the way they're portrayed in almost any time. I tried to make them as real as anyone."[14] The production of the miniseries began during September 1996 on a fifty-day schedule, twice the time of its Hallmark predecessor, and with a $15 million budget, high for a television production; all of these aspects provided the miniseries an epic quality Hallmark could not match.

There are also suggestions of not only haste but also sloppy production in the Hallmark telefilm: Nemo plays the pipe organ without apparently moving his fingers; the shots of the Nautilus ramming vessels are unconvincing; and a chest full of gold supposedly destined for rebels is simply tossed into the sea, where no one save Nemo's divers could possibly retrieve such a heavy object. The same sort of thoughtlessness is evident in the major change to the plot, solving the need for a female character outside of the traditional manner used by the miniseries. Replacing Conseil is Sophie (Julie Cox), the daughter of Henry Aronnax (Richard Crenna), who has followed the paternal lead to become an expert in marine biology. Her presence varies the perspective, the story unfolding through her experience; for instance, she, not her father, is shown exploring the *Nautilus*. However, the approach quickly reverts to formula: she spurns overtures from intellectual men but is smitten at first sight with the man of brawn, not brains—harpooner Ned Land (Paul Gross).

Previous Verne films that added a love triangle, such as *Master of the World* (1961), had wisely left the inventor figure outside of such emotions. The Disney version had placed these emotions at the metaphorical level with the affections of the captain's pet seal, Esmeralda, and with Conseil shifting his loyalty from Aronnax to Ned. In the Hallmark version, Wiesenfeld offered an unabashed explanation for the changes made. "In order to reach a wide audience in prime time, you have to make the story of interest to a female audience. . . . Essentially we are dealing with four main characters in a tin can. Relationships become paramount in a story like that, and the conflict within relationships. Nothing adds that ability to create conflict in a story more than sexual relationships."[15]

In other respects, Halmi, Anderson, and Wiesenfeld said they sought to return to the source.[16] Halmi explained, "What I wanted to do was to rid ourselves of the kind of 20th century irony and perspective that we have and make it all absolutely fresh, the way the book was for [Verne's] audience."[17] The portions that do so are the Hallmark version's greatest virtue, with a number of scenes and lines taken directly from the book. Wiesenfeld said he strived to remain closer to the novel's seriousness than Disney and integrated elements of Nemo's background in a manner compatible with the portrait Verne offered in *The Mysterious Island*.[18] Wiesenfeld has Nemo reveal that he was educated to be a king and lead his country into the modern scientific age, but the armies of the West had interfered, killing his parents, wife, and children.

Ben Cross as Nemo does what can be done with the role as written. He lacks any strong racial or ethnic identity and speaks with a slight and modulated accent. Although more appropriate to the role than most who have played it, he is also more menacing than tortured or vengeful. The *Nautilus* intends to secure a stranglehold on the shipping of the world so Nemo can demand his country back; he claims he has never deliberately sunk a ship. The crew of the *Nautilus* are simultaneously more and less interesting than in other versions: as in the book, they are of vague ethnicity, but for the first time they are made up of members of both genders. Nonetheless, they never speak, and there is no sense of familial relationships; unlike in *Captain Nemo and the Underwater City,* the Hallmark Nemo regards the crew as followers, not friends.

The lonely Nemo initially regards Sophie as a gift of the sea and a perfect match; he has been looking for someone to understand him and share his passion for science. He unsuccessfully tries to flatter her with beautiful dresses that have been salvaged from wrecks, asking her to be the queen of the *Nautilus* rather than his subject. She asks why he doesn't marry one of the female crew, and he expresses disdain for the idea (although later, given his noble blood, an unwillingness to marry one of his own subjects becomes understandable). When she accuses him of selfishness and lack of caring for humanity, he reveals the chests of gold he is leaving at designated spots for other rebels committed to kindred political causes. Her reluctance changes to repulsion upon learning that Ned has been chained in the brig. By contrast, Aronnax establishes

Ben Cross as Captain Nemo and Julie Cox as Sophie Aronnax in the 1997 Hallmark telefilm *20,000 Leagues under the Sea.*

an amicable relationship with the captain and is fascinated when the *Nautilus* passes over the remains of Atlantis, where a volcano is still active after nine thousand years. Aronnax urges Sophie to consider Nemo's marriage proposal and the scientific opportunity it offers, but she responds by telling her father that he, not she, has been seduced by Nemo. Romantic melodrama and jealousy simply do not mix well into the Verne context; as one critic remarked, "it's the attempt to turn *20,000 Leagues under the Sea* into *Sophie's Choice* [1982] that sinks the *Nautilus*."[19]

A gray color motif predominates among the crew's uniforms and the submarine itself, while the bright shot-on-video colors are saved for the exterior scenes above and below the sea. The only lengthy visit to the sea floor is the sole diving expedition to Crespo, vividly shot in the Red Sea. The divers, including Ned, are imperiled by marauding sharks, which they shoot with electric bullets, and Nemo gladly leaves Ned behind when Ned apparently falls over a ledge to his death. Inside the *Nautilus,*

Sophie is tearful at the outcome until she sees Ned making his way back to the window of the *Nautilus* with his last air.

As in the miniseries, the Hallmark telefilm enacts the hecatomb of the Verne novel. Ned waves at the attacking vessel, and Nemo dares its shells to strike him or the *Nautilus,* but the book's essential dialogue to explain his emotions is not included. The *Nautilus* rams the ship, and Nemo opens the undersea window to demonstrate that he can sink any vessel at will and now feels great joy (not the torment Mason showed in the Disney version). Aronnax is disillusioned when he learns that 650 sailors have drowned.

Nemo reveals a plan to release Ned on the surface with surrender terms to the world and Aronnax to testify to Nemo's character, while Sophie will remain aboard. On a journey to a trench to prove Aronnax's theory of deep-water evolution, however, they are interrupted by the very creature he initially thought had caused the sinkings, a "proto-leviathan," but instead of attacking a surface vessel, it tries to devour the *Nautilus.* This sequence replaces the novel's squid and polar episodes; as the *Nautilus* runs out of air, the electric guns fail, and several of Nemo's divers are killed. Nemo finally becomes fearful for the first time as he loses mastery of his domain. Only Aronnax offers a plan to place a harpoon with a delayed electric charge in the beast, but Ned's skill is needed to do this, allowing him to bargain for freedom. In contrast with the miniseries, here Ned emerges once more as the ultimate hero, echoing the Disney version.

Nemo realizes that his dream is over and that the *Nautilus* is nothing more than his refuge. The motto "Mobilis in Mobile" (translated in the telefilm as "Free in a free world"), prominently featured in the *Nautilus*'s décor, had exemplified Nemo's belief that he has found liberation and not exile, but by the conclusion Ned undercuts and belittles that motto. Ned, Aronnax, and Sophie are set free in a large inflatable raft—which, shaped like a picnic basket, sadly epitomizes the weaknesses of the Hallmark version—and Aronnax wonders whether anyone will believe their experiences and if Nemo has yet found peace. Anderson's *20,000 Leagues under the Sea* is ultimately a modest, flawed addition to the Verne film oeuvre; without the love triangle, it would have been vastly more satisfactory. Its more contemplative approach to the story and the open-endedness of Nemo's fate are more compatible with the novel, but they simultaneously serve to highlight the vicissitudes of the intrusive love story. Hardy had directed the miniseries with much more movement of the camera and actors than had Anderson and thus effectively obscured the weaknesses of his own version through a lightning pace.

Some elements of the Hallmark telefilm were drawn from the novel; Nemo explains that the *Nautilus* has an endless supply of energy from sodium batteries, and the costumes with boots and cummerbund, colors suggesting rank, resemble those of the 1916 film *Twenty Thousand Leagues under the Sea,* echoing the book's original French engravings. By contrast, the miniseries clothes Nemo and the crew in sharkskin-style costumes, which truly look as if they are from the sea; only occasionally does Nemo appear in the clothing Verne described. Anderson noted that production designer Brian Ackland-Snow designed a *Nautilus* that was "functional in terms of Jules Verne's story, and could resemble either a sea monster, a whale, or could be mistaken for such things by other people. It doesn't look like a submarine as we know it, and yet I wanted something that you believed could go underwater and do the things it did, such as spouting like a whale to discharge waste."[20] The spouting was shown for the first time in the telefilm among all the adaptations of the novel, and there are matching small towers for the light and navigation. In these exteriors and in such shots as the divers approaching the *Nautilus* in the distance, the telefilm achieves a majestic quality, amplified by an exemplary score by John Scott.

The miniseries goes in an entirely different direction, with a *Nautilus* that resembles the elongated, flat, manta-ray shape created for *Captain Nemo and the Underwater City.* Director Rod Hardy had asked production designer Stewart Burnside to avoid a futuristic look: "I wanted to have sets that you can feel, with rusty metal and the clanking of the engine under the water."[21] For instance, in the miniseries the *Nautilus* rams the *Abraham Lincoln* at a slow, lumbering, but believable pace, far from the speed of Disney's version. The interior is elaborate, shown in circular shots, including a three-story library and salon with organ, a spiral staircase and giant portals offering a vista of the sea—the most original and effective design in any film, closest to Verne's luxury ideas for the *Nautilus.* By contrast, the interior in the Hallmark telefilm, with its lower budget, echoes the cramped quarters of the Disney version and modern conceptions derived from today's submarines, and its *Nautilus* lacks even a helm.

Of the three television efforts in 1997, the Hallmark telefilm was the first to be shown, broadcast on CBS on March 23, but it was also the least successful critically and commercially, failing to be rated among the Nielsen top 20 and receiving many unfavorable reviews in newspapers and magazines. It was also poorly publicized and broadcast at one of the worst possible times, the day before the Academy Awards, when entertainment programming was geared almost entirely toward the following day's event. The ABC miniseries was better publicized and broadcast during a "sweeps" month, indicative of greater network confidence in the product. It received better reviews, although still with many reservations, but favorable comparisons were made with the CBS telefilm effort. Unfortunately, the ABC version was broadcast opposite a gangster miniseries by the author of *The Godfather* saga, and this more typical generic offering won the largest share of attention.

Effects, models, and underwater scenes from the Hallmark version were used to create a third version of the story for the *Crayola Kids Adventures* series, originally broadcast on CBS on August 15, 1997. (Robert Halmi Sr. was the executive producer for Binney & Smith and Hallmark Entertainment, Inc.) Making maximum usage of the existing footage provided a sense of expense that would otherwise have been prohibitive for a show aimed at this demographic. The *Crayola Kids* structure cast children in all the roles in classic stories (for instance, Professor Pierre Aronnax's age is given as eleven years old), the young characters behaving as adults without ever losing the child in their nature. Such a tactic inevitably governs the narrative arrangement, but nonetheless a surprisingly fresh and effective telling of *Twenty Thousand Leagues under the Seas* emerged in this adaptation.

Writer-director-producer Michael Kruzan dispensed with all of the superfluous conflict and relationships that had otherwise plagued the adult Hallmark version, improving on aspects of his footage source, considering the intended audience. For instance, Conseil is again replaced with a female character, but this time she is related to Pierre (Justin Jon Ross) as sister and assistant and is named Beth (Molly Orr). Ned Land

As the three adventurers waited for rescue in Nemo's lifeboat, the *Nautilus* returned to the depths of the ocean. They could only wonder if they would ever see Captain Nemo again . . . and no one ever did.

The Crayola Kids aboard the *Nautilus* in their own version of *20,000 Leagues under the Sea* (1997), with the model designed for the Hallmark telefilm the same year.

(Phillip Van Dyke) clashes with Nemo, but only in the manner Verne had described rather than as a romantic rival. After Pierre, Beth, and Ned fall overboard when the *Nautilus* rams the *Abraham Lincoln,* they soon spot the surfacing beast and recognize that it is actually man-made. A hatch opens, and they enter to see Captain Nemo (Adam Wylie) and two of his crew. Nemo offers them the opportunity to immediately leave his ship, but with the *Abraham Lincoln* firing in their direction, going back on deck seems more ominous than descending with Nemo.

Pierre, Beth, and Ned discover that Nemo has developed an apparatus to recycle oxygen and has harnessed "the power of the sun." Nemo briefly plays the pipe organ, then opens an amazing undersea window to reveal the colorful world of the deep and tells them his motto, "Mobilis in Mobile." At dinner, predictably, what seem to be chicken, spaghetti, and a hamburger turn out to be actually made from sea delicacies. Nemo explains that he only damages ships as a warning to leave him alone; he does not sink them. The riches from under the sea are salvaged from sunken ships; "I'm a collector, not a pirate," Nemo adds. Yet in addition to his desire for isolation, he clearly is consumed by a muted anger, and surprisingly nothing in the adaptation for youth changes the basic Vernian conception or attempts to reintegrate Nemo into social norms.

Nemo shows Pierre, Beth, and Ned something far more dangerous than sharks as they pass over the sunken city of Atlantis. Now Nemo explains the price that Pierre, Beth, and Ned must pay for having sought refuge on his submarine: they will be his guests permanently because he cannot take the risk that they might reveal his secrets. The *Nautilus* is attacked by a giant, thought-to-be extinct prehistoric sea monster (the "proto-leviathan" of the Hallmark version). The ten million volts of electricity from the *Nautilus* and the guns fired by the divers prove futile; Pierre recognizes that they have failed because the creature lacks a central nervous system, and so he bargains with Nemo for freedom in exchange for a plan to kill the beast. Nemo agrees, with the same results as in the Hallmark version and a final shot of the trio being picked up by a passing fishing boat.

One element was truly unique to the *Crayola Kids* version—songs, less disruptive than might be expected.[22] The combining of new and previously shot footage mix seamlessly. Even the mismatch of divers with adult bodies and children's faces superimposed over their helmets is less irksome than would seem likely. The interior sets and props for the most part appear fresh, but less than half of the forty-five-minute running time was new footage. The acting is commendable, considering the players' tender years, and *Crayola Kids* again demonstrates the ready capability of Verne's work to be adapted for a younger audience without sacrificing the essential story or characterizations, this time in live action rather than in the more typical vehicle for youth, animation.

Ironically as well, it was *Crayola Kids* that offered a Ned Land closest to the natural dignity of Verne's creation. As demonstrated by the childish hero etched by Kirk Douglas for Disney and the standard muscular romantic lead played by Paul Gross in the Hallmark telefilm, the relatively simple harpooner has seemed more difficult for live-action filmmakers to portray than the more complex Captain Nemo. This is particularly true of the miniseries, in which Ned's unrelenting hunger for personal freedom transforms him into a caged animal, heedless of others' well-being, and Bryan Brown's performance offers no insight into a largely undeveloped character.

The *20,000 Leagues under the Sea* miniseries had originally been written by screenwriter Brian Nelson as a 115-page script for feature production in 1992 before the success of the miniseries *Gulliver's Travels* in 1996 prompted ABC executives to decide that Nelson's new interpretation would be viable in similar form, and it was rewritten as a 205-page script. Much the same happened with a new *Journey to the Center of the Earth;* even as Robert Halmi Sr.'s Hallmark Entertainment was planning their two-hour telefilm, *20,000 Leagues under the Sea,* he also announced a new version of *Journey to the Center of the Earth* for the Sci-Fi Channel from a script by John Ireland. In the wake of the commercial success of the USA Network's four-hour miniseries of *Moby Dick* (1998), the project was switched to USA, the Sci-Fi Channel's parent company, and the two-hour telefilm was expanded to four hours, with Thomas Baum enlarging Ireland's script.[23] Director George Miller, already attached to Halmi's new *Journey to the Center of the Earth,* was eager for the miniseries length, adding new episodes, such as an encounter with Maori tribesmen. Miller produced the miniseries with Connie Collins, and shooting began in April 1999 in Australia and New Zealand on a $12 million budget; the series premiered five months later on September 14 and 15, 1999.[24]

This version of *Journey to the Center of the Earth* retains the period setting of the Verne novel—given as 1868 this time—and adapts the protagonists' nationalities and names to suit the cast. Instead of the German professor Otto Lidenbrock, the hero is the American name-alike Theodore Lytton. As portrayed by forty-seven-year-old Treat Williams, Lytton is as much an action hero as a man of science. He is initially shown boxing to raise money for his work and escaping a police raid to find refuge in the university. There, he lectures on continental drift and evolution, having studied with Darwin in the Galapagos. Like Verne's characters in the novel, Lytton is a rather dominating father figure to his initially fearful young nephew, Jonas (Jeremy London), who is in love with the profoundly unsympathetic homebody Helen (Tessa Wells). They take the place of the novel's Axel and Graüben.

Alice Hastings (Tushka Bergen), a wealthy American mountaineer, hires Lytton to search for her husband, Casper, who disappeared on a hunt for gold seven years ago. Casper had gone down in a remote part of New Zealand, the Ruapehu caverns, rumored to be an area of monsters and mystery that descends deep inside the earth. Because of the scientific possibilities of such an expedition, Lytton agrees, convincing Jonas to go with him, although it means postponing his marriage. To Lytton and Jonas's surprise, Alice is determined to be part of the search—fulfilling the screen convention of such an added character and providing an opportunity for a love interest to develop between Lytton and Alice.

This new narrative strand is only one of several changes that incorporate aspects of Verne's 1868 novel *The Children of Captain Grant* (and probably also the filmmakers' memories of the Disney version, *In Search of the Castaways*). In a manner similar to Alice in the miniseries, Mary Grant is looking for her father, and for both the trek will end in marriage. Moreover, roughly one-third of *The Children of Captain Grant* is set in New Zealand, and the shift in the setting for the miniseries *Journey to the Center of the Earth* utilizes the desired filmmaking locations without harming the storyline.[25]

Further borrowing from *The Children of Captain Grant* is apparent in the replacement of the phlegmatic Icelander Hans with a new character who is no less loyal, hardy, and strong but who speaks English. The burly, kilt-wearing MacNiff (Hugh Keays-Byrne) integrates aspects of the Scotsman MacNabbs and the underhanded Ayrton from *The Children of Captain Grant;* he is a crack shot and a hard-drinking exconvict, wily enough to steer the Lytton party through the dangers of a colonial rebellion and hostile Maoris.

The descent as depicted in this miniseries, unlike in previous films of *Journey to the Center of the Earth,* is in a tropical climate filled with vegetation, and once the explorers are underground, the sets are relatively sparse and shot from different angles. The Lytton party experiences the usual episodes —using Ruhmkorff lamps, searching for water, and getting lost. The filmmakers acknowledged familiarity with the 1959 movie of the novel, and a shot of the group descending a rock bridge that crumbles behind them, the truncated raft voyage, and unconvincing land dinosaurs rather than ones at sea all emulate this predecessor.[26] However, there are other influences and changes; following the precedent of *Where Time Began*, a shift of natural colors gives an otherworldly impression of the explorers' arrival at the underground shore, this time with a yellow sky and blue plants, the cavern roof supported by columns of rocks. Jonas had already discovered prehistoric insect life, so the explorers are hardly surprised when they see a flock of pterodactyls.

Jonas glimpses a remarkably agile, tattooed, redheaded female, Ralna, whom they follow into a jungle where two species have evolved on a parallel path: a primitive but more physically developed humankind and a reptile race, Saurians, with their own language, science, and urban centers in a world where human and dinosaur coexist. The Saurians abduct Alice, while in the human village Lytton, Jonas, and Mac-Niff find Casper living as their ruler in a manner reminiscent of Kurtz in Joseph Conrad's *Heart of Darkness* (1899). Verne himself had used a similar plot device in *The Aerial Village*, involving a trek into Africa in search of a man who turns out to have become a false high priest to a "missing link" ancestor of humankind. Bryan Brown as Casper portrays another destructive character in a Verne film, no less than his Ned Land in the *20,000 Leagues under the Sea* miniseries two years earlier.

As star Williams noted, "Another whole plot line develops once [they] reach the center of the Earth."[27] Miller's version further demonstrates how Verne's novel and Sir Arthur Conan Doyle's *The Lost World*, so closely related from the time the latter was published, have become a source of shared inspiration for filmmakers, in much the same way that H. G. Wells's *The First Men in the Moon* has often inflected adaptations of Verne's lunar novels since Georges Méliès's *A Trip to the Moon*.[28] Whereas the first half of the new *Journey to the Center of the Earth* is for the most part clearly indebted to that novel and to *The Children of Captain Grant*, the second half abandons Verne altogether to portray the conflicts among intelligent, humanlike prehistoric life that had fired Conan Doyle's imagination.[29]

Hugh Keays-Byrne as MacNiff, Treat Williams as Lytton, Jeremy London as Jonas, and Tushka Bergen as Hastings, with a Saurian looming behind them, in art for the 1999 miniseries *Journey to the Center of the Earth*.

Casper's greed for the gold he has found leads to his death on his return to the surface, and MacNiff decides to remain behind with the tribe, who idolize him. The explorers cross the underground sea again but land on a different part of the shore, and Lytton's dynamite blast opens a fresh passage that proves unstable. Jonas, Lytton, and Alice are abruptly sent to the surface by a vortex phenomenon that Saknussemm (the only context in which he is mentioned) is said to have predicted: underground storms that turn into giant waterspouts that feed surface lakes. One of these waterspouts funnels the travelers to the Maori tribe near where they began their journey in New Zealand. Lytton and Alice decide to honeymoon in Iceland and explore fresh caverns that may offer a more direct route to the center of the earth (which has the curious effect of making the Verne novel seem like a sequel to this miniseries).

However, Jonas must recover from an unknown virus transmitted by Ralna, with whom he has fallen in love. It leaves him with dreams of her and causes him to leave Helen behind and return to New Zealand and a life of adventure—clearly providing an opening for a sequel. The theme of Jonas's initiatory trajectory and his gradual emergence as a hero remains from the novel, despite the miniseries' deviation from Verne's conclusion (the Lytton–Alice nuptials have rendered Jonas's own wedding superfluous).[30] The journey has been narrated through the diary entries Jonas has made for Helen, which abruptly cease when he meets Ralna and resume after she is left behind, ingeniously revealing in more subtle terms his change of heart.

Evolutionary themes are incorporated from the outset in an attempt to provide sufficient dramatic motivation for veering into *Lost World* territory, but the use of the theme of warring tribes in the second half fails to generate memorable results. The subterranean world is offered as an example of a different outcome of Darwin's theories, but the theme is insufficiently explored; nor is any connection made between the underground tribes and the Maoris on the surface. Although avoiding the pitfalls of "caveman" movies and remaining entertaining, these scenes are one more echo of the visits that Lindenbrook, Axel, Cindy, and Lars make to cities inhabited by various creatures in the 1960s Filmation animated series *Journey to the Center of the Earth*.

Ultimately, the second half of the miniseries disappoints in contrast to a strong first half, with the filmmakers unable to come up with an adequate destination and refusing to allow the trek itself to serve as the goal. One reason for this alternate plotline was economic, with sets for the Saurian and tribes people already existing from the Sheep Pavilion at the Royal Melbourne Showgrounds. The Saurians are obviously actors in masks in close shots but computer generated in long shots, so that their overall movement remains convincingly alien and nonhuman. Their speech is birdlike, and their eyesight recognizes heat, as revealed in point-of-view shots. Nonetheless, the miniseries is not effects driven but remains low key, with measured pacing and emphasis on character.

Despite drawbacks, this sequence of four telefilms and miniseries in rapid succession brought Verne back to screen prominence; the author was again the subject of big-budget, star-laden productions, many of which offered fresh interpretations of their sources, not simply rehashes. For the first time in decades, a number of book tie-ins were issued: for *Twenty Thousand Leagues under the Seas,* the tie-ins were in conjunction with the *Crayola Kids* adaptation, with a video game from IBM and several books emphasizing the pedagogical side of the voyage aboard the *Nautilus;* Hallmark Entertainment Books republished *Journey to the Center of the Earth* with a dust jacket and plates using scenes from the miniseries.[31] New productions were to follow, born amid a renaissance in Verne publishing, yet the quality that these telefilms and miniseries seemed to foreshadow was only sporadically fulfilled.

11

# Biography or Pastiche, 2000–2003

Even as the canon of Jules Verne stories adapted for the screen diminished to retellings of *Twenty Thousand Leagues under the Seas, Journey to the Center of the Earth*, and *Around the World in Eighty Days*, Hollywood would build on the growing number of pastiches involving Verne's literary characters. In *Return to the Center of the Earth* (1999), Rick Wakeman's rock opera and album followed his similar musical treatment of the original novel a quarter-century earlier, but in a modern version that retained fidelity to the author's conception of the journey.[1] Sequels to Verne tales appeared in the 2005 anthology edited by Mike Ashley and Eric Brown, *The Mammoth Book of New Jules Verne Adventures;* Adam Roberts's novel *Splinter* (2007) was a sequel to *Hector Servadac*.[2] More innovative were the fictionalized treatments of Verne himself in the wake of the discovery and publication in 2001 of Mark Twain's novelette *A Murder, a Mystery, and a Marriage*, written in 1876, in which Twain invoked Verne as a character to mock the 1870s vogue for all things Vernian. Twain's views were already known in his day; *Tom Sawyer Abroad* (1894) had been a pastiche of *Five Weeks in a Balloon* and *The Mysterious Island*. For the centennial of Verne's death in 2005, such novels as *The Extraordinary Voyage of Jules Verne* by Eric Brown and *Flaming London* by Joseph Lansdale, featuring Verne as a character, were published.

Imaginary versions of Jules Verne the man offered the most filmic possibilities, and it was Disney theme park offerings that best realized the possibilities. Beginning in 1992, an attraction featured an Audio-

Animatronic "Timekeeper" who has overcome science's last challenge, time travel. He sends his robot sidekick, 9-Eye (for the number of screens shown in 360-degree Circle-vision), on a journey through the ages. After pauses in prehistoric times and a glimpse of Leonardo da Vinci and Mozart, Timekeeper wants to view his heroes, Jules Verne and H. G. Wells, at the Paris Exposition of 1900.

As the two men meet hurriedly, discussing their divergent approaches to writing, Verne (played by Michel Piccolini) emphasizes the possible and Wells (Jeremy Irons) the impossible. The Englishman must hasten away to give a speech, but Verne sights 9-Eye and grabs on. Taken on a trip through time, the white-bearded writer rides a high-speed train, causes a traffic jam at the Arc de Triomphe, drives a racing car, descends in a submarine, and rides in a helicopter, enjoying the sort of scenic views for which Circle-vision had previously been used in Disney travelogues. The adventure ends with Verne taking a space walk.

Back at the exposition, Verne and Wells meet again, and in a glimpse of Paris in the times to come 9-Eye observes the writers flying together, for, as Verne exclaims as he waves good-bye, in the future anything is possible. Although purely imaginary (no such meeting between the two writers ever took place, but they did write and speak about one another), this glimpse of Verne associated with the wonders to come was absorbed by millions, especially children, far more than ever saw a more factual presentation. The title varied according to location and whether it was the film itself or the attraction: it was Le Visionarium and *Un Voyage à travers le temps* in France, Visionarium and ビジョナリアム— in Tokyo, and *The Timekeeper* and *From Time to Time* in the United States. As directed by Jeff Blyth, this first Disney Circle-vision film in narrative form rather than travelogue reveals its shortcomings in that the story foregrounds an individual who can be on only one screen at a time in the theater, while the surroundings cover the horizon. The film was finally replaced with new attractions in the first decade of the twenty-first century, and although its closing marked the fading of Verne from Disney theme parks in America, the author continued to have a major presence in Paris and especially Tokyo.

Lacking the imaginative success of the Disney presentation and even less related to Verne the author was *The Secret Adventures of Jules*

Chris Dematral as the young Verne in *The Secret Adventures of Jules Verne* (2000), the older Verne looking down in this art from the series.

*Verne,* an independent, Canadian-produced television series that lasted one season upon syndicated release in 2000. The potentially rewarding premise remained unfulfilled, with Verne (Chris Dematral) introduced as a young, aspiring writer and inventor in the 1860s (when in fact by that time he was older than thirty, married, a father, and becoming a literary success). Meeting the actual Phileas Fogg and Passepartout, Verne shares travels with them around the world, transported aboard the giant balloon *Aurora*—again saddling Verne with a technology he thought less promising than a heavier-than-air vehicle. They are accompanied by the added character of Fogg's cousin Rebecca (Francesca Hunt), the first female Secret Service agent—who is unfortunately too derivative of Emma Peel (1965–1968) in the British television series *The Avengers*. In a somewhat uneven but appropriate performance by Michael Praed, Fogg remains much as Verne imagined him, with an already mysterious past, intrepid but phlegmatic and reserved—without going to the degree imagined by Philip José Farmer in his 1973 novel *The Other Log of Phileas Fogg*. In an odd combination, Passepartout (Michel Courtemanche) continues as comic relief but is also an inventor.

*The Secret Adventures of Jules Verne* was created in an unusually low-key style and freely mixes fantasy, horror, and science fiction. Despite the claims made in publicity and by series creator Gavin Scott that Verne was placed in his own stories, these laudable intentions proved impossible to realize, and the series ultimately did just the opposite: Verne's purported exploits are consonant more with modern science fiction. The characters are first united in stopping an underground mole operated by a "League of Darkness" determined to preserve the aristocracy and curtail the advance of democracy in Europe—goals that Fogg and Verne the character naturally oppose (in fact, Verne the man had royalist sympathies). Verne journeys to the Wild West, where he meets Thomas Edison, Jesse James, and Mark Twain, and then encounters a mummy, a castle full of vampires, and a golem.

Only one episode of *The Secret Adventures of Jules Verne* evokes the author's oeuvre, but it yet again manifests the series' shortcomings. "Rocket to the Moon" should logically celebrate Verne's moon shot, yet it fails to achieve the standard satire or suspense of Méliès's *A Trip to the Moon* and *Those Fantastic Flying Fools*, which seems to have been its inspiration. Fogg's wealthy friend has built a giant cannon, with a base resembling the one designed by Herr Schultze in *The 500 Millions of the Begum*, to fire a shell that will destroy St. Petersburg in a manner akin to Schultze's plan for Franceville. Instead, Phileas, Rebecca, Jules, and Passepartout storm the well-guarded fortress with an ease that would be the envy of James Bond. The cannon's builder falls into the shell, which automatically loads and fires, so that the episode ends with him as the first astronaut. However, it is unclear if the shell is orbiting the earth, heading to the moon, or simply tumbling in space. The episode epitomizes the tone of the whole series, disregarding what Verne considered essential while emphasizing all those elements he eschewed.

Alan Moore's graphic novel series *The League of Extraordinary Gentlemen,* which began in 1999, was based on his fascination with the characters and situations of nineteenth-century popular literature, including Nemo. Sadly, when it came to filming the first volume in 2003, in James Dale Robertson's screenplay the cliché that "the more things change, the more they remain the same" proved true. The title was typically abbreviated as *LXG,* and for the first time a Verne film has cast an Indian actor in the role of Captain Nemo, the nationality Verne chose for him.

Unfortunately, *LXG* deserves no more than an asterisk; nowhere is it explicitly stated on screen that Nemo is an Indian, and it is only to be inferred from his costume and that of most (but not all) of his crew—for instance, Nemo is given a first mate who announces, "Call Me Ishmael," in this way failing to mesh with the provided ethnic background. Most egregiously, Nemo is shown not as the Hindu he would have been, but as a worshipper of Kali, goddess of death. As portrayed by Naseruddin Shah, Nemo seems initially to offer some dignity, but that characteristic soon dissolves as he is shown fighting in a style that might make a kung fu expert envious. As the movie progresses and no insight is offered into Nemo's character (unlike the other league members), Shah becomes steadily more stiff, and Nemo's last line is that he now wants to see the world from which he has been too long isolated.

*LXG* proves that more than an actor's nationality matters. Other films, although ostensibly miscast, still offered an explanation of background and motives that, if not parallel with Verne's in *The Mysterious Island,* at least elucidated the protagonist's actions in a manner compatible with *Twenty Thousand Leagues under the Seas.* Michael Caine in the 1997 miniseries *20,000 Leagues under the Sea* and Robert Ryan in *Captain Nemo and the Underwater City* captured the mix of Nemo's moods, the dark vengeance that drove him, as well as his

Captain Nemo (Naseeruddin Shah, right) in *LXG* (2003) is transformed into an expert in hand-to-hand fighting.

visionary side. In contrast with Verne's imagining, *LXG* makes Nemo the inventor of guided missiles and superpowered automobiles as well as the eager supporter of the British just as Irwin Allen made him the tool of the American navy in *The Amazing Captain Nemo*. The *Nautilus* of *LXG*, decorated with curved archways, is more emblematic of Orientalist archetypes than representative of any specific background, yet it also resembles a modern naval submarine and is described as "the sword of the ocean," shallow and narrow enough to ply the canals of Venice or Siberian rivers.

Perhaps some expository material ended on the cutting-room floor; *LXG* was apparently the victim of overshooting and conflicts between director Stephen Norrington and star-producer Sean Connery (playing Allan Quatermain). "It was a nightmare," Connery told the *Times* regarding the filming. "The director should never have been given $185 million. On the first day I realized he was insane."[3] K. J. Anderson, in the wake of his own original 2002 novel *Captain Nemo: The Fantastic History of a Dark Genius,* provided a novelization of the movie with a bit more characterization of Nemo. The *LXG* website offered a rich tapestry of Nemo's background and motivation; too bad it was not utilized on screen.

A documentary treatment of Verne's original story offered little more than *LXG. Great Books* was a series of separately produced documentaries churned out by Atlantic Productions for the Learning Channel in 2001 and highly variable in quality. The "20,000 Leagues under the Sea" episode, broadcast August 10, 2001, sadly ranks near the bottom. It uses the typical approach of such product for cable outlets, beginning afresh after each commercial break rather than attempting to build in a coherent manner. The mistakes range from the minor (claiming undersea photography was invented for the 1916 film adaptation of the novel rather than for *Thirty Leagues under the Sea* two years earlier) to the major, basic interpretive flaws—most notably, Nemo is labeled at the outset as a "rebel without a cause" driven by "an insane desire for revenge." *Twenty Thousand Leagues under the Seas* is examined almost entirely as an example of prophecy, with the documentary's fifty-minute running time structured along a series of comparisons with scientific facts known today in order to mix in inexpensive or free footage often pulled from other Discovery network documentaries. Background footage provides visual motifs, actors mutely portray the story's protagonists, and a constrained view of Nemo's library and cabin is given, along with exterior views, for once following Verne's original design.

By contrast, in 2002 DIC Entertainment offered a new animated version of the novel, unheralded but arguably the most faithful version to yet reach the screen. Only in a framing device, to open the film's narrative for the intended youthful audience, was there a significant divergence. Two modern boys and a girl, scuba diving from a motor boat, must hide from a shark in a grotto. Finding an old chest, they take it to the surface and open it, discovering a bottle with a 130-year-old manuscript.

The manuscript was written by Bernadette, a girl of seventeen who was accompanying her father, captain of the *Scotia,* when his vessel was struck. With the telling of the story from her teenage perspective, other shifts in narrative become unnecessary—from adding a daughter for Nemo to making Conseil female. Verne's novel also becomes part of her life: coming of age, gaining knowledge of the world—and of several divergent men within it—falling in love, and even, by the conclusion, dying. Outside of her added participation, in every case where the adaptation faced narrative choices, the script adheres to the novel, successfully dramatizing the original's incidents instead of creating new episodes.

Bernadette was studying a narwhal in a museum when Pierre Aronnax, concluding a lecture on the mysteries of the deep, introduces himself. When he is invited to join the search for the monster, she begs to join the expedition and is refused according to the gender dictates of the time, so she pretends to be her twin brother, Bernard. Also aboard is Ned Land, harpooner and former slave. As the rudder of the *Abraham Lincoln* is struck, Bernadette falls into the sea despite Pierre's attempt to save her, and the two swim until nightfall, when out of the fog they glimpse a strange hull, on which Ned and Conseil (pronounced "Konseal" throughout) have found refuge. Ned, wisely recognizing the nature of the vessel under their feet, swiftly uses his knife to shorten Bernadette's hair, lest they fall into the hands of pirates. During most of the story, Bernadette has adopted the guise of a man, even as her relationship with Pierre changes from flirtation to a committed romance.

When Nemo introduces himself, Pierre knows his name is Latin for "no one," just as Nemo recognizes his visitor by reputation. Saying he was attacked and would have been so whether the *Abraham Lincoln* knew it was a monster or a submarine, Nemo also tells them he wants no part of other people save his devoted crew and offers the foursome a choice: return to the sea or accept life permanently on board the *Nautilus.* The first meal of course proves to come entirely from the sea, and Nemo explains that the "N" in his banner stands for both "Nemo" and "*Nautilus.*" The vessel is powered by electricity from the sea, and the interior has a striking, bold design far more imaginative than other animated tellings of the novel. Touring through the library and salon filled with undersea specimens, Nemo opens the window of the *Nautilus* to offer a view of the sea. Only Ned refuses to join the first undersea trek; outside the vessel, they are struck by what Bernadette describes as the full magnificence of the *Nautilus*—although its exterior design is sadly no match for the interior in originality.

Ned, planning an escape and embittered at now again being in what he perceives as the sort of servitude he was only freed from recently, wonders if the crew numbers more than a dozen. Nemo tells Bernadette (as Bernard) that he has no anger toward her country and made sure that the *Scotia* was only damaged. The next day, however, she sees a different side of what Pierre calls Nemo's evil genius as the *Nautilus* sinks a ship from another nation.

To satisfy Ned's craving for a steak, Nemo allows his captives ashore in New Guinea, launching the dinghy from a hatch inside the *Nautilus,* as described in the book. However, when the natives attack the landing party, Nemo repels them with a shower of water; this film reserves electricity as a weapon against the denizens of the deep. Later, Ned joins another underwater stroll as Nemo shows his prize pearl; when a shark menaces a diver, Nemo attacks with a knife and is assisted by Ned with an electrically charged harpoon. Laying the diver safely ashore, Nemo gives him gold coins, saying he is the victim of a tyrannical government.

Although to Pierre three months at sea is nothing, Bernadette begins to agree with Ned's restlessness, realizing her father by now believes her dead, but she also tells Pierre she will not leave without him. Nemo braves the tunnel from the Red Sea to the Mediterranean and offers to show Pierre and Bernadette an underwater volcano and the remnants of a vast underground civilization. As Nemo writes a word in chalk, it is first glimpsed in reverse in Bernadette's visor, before it is seen from her viewpoint: Atlantis. However, a fresh eruption begins, and the three divers barely escape, Pierre and Bernadette saving Nemo. Even as Nemo lauds the freedom of the deep, it is constantly perilous to all.

The *Nautilus* turns south. Ramming the ice and emerging at the pole, Nemo claims the continent with his flag, which Ned regards as arrogant. However, Conseil points out that the harpooner is in a foul mood because Nemo refused to allow him to hunt the polar creatures who have never seen humankind and thus have no fear. The opportunity

Captain Nemo in danger in the 2002 animated film *20,000 Leagues under the Sea.*

is taken for an interlude amid the adaptation's otherwise unrelentingly serious tone: Conseil tries to harvest penguin eggs until an army of them force him to stop, while Pierre and Bernadette engage in a snow fight ending in their first kiss. Although ostensibly a film aimed at children, these scenes are the only moments of levity.

Returning northward, the *Nautilus* is assaulted by the giant squids of legend. When Nemo and Ned fight them on the surface with electrically charged harpoons, Nemo saves Ned from one creature's "beak." Bernadette becomes feverish; a lingering cough has worsened. She begins to hallucinate—a startling sequence combining ocean monsters, undersea ruins, a mysterious whirlpool (foreshadowing the voyage's end), and her father mourning at her grave. Nemo gives Pierre the last of an elixir he made from plants near Atlantis, and it returns Bernadette from the brink of death.

Nemo braves an Atlantic gale on the surface as Pierre accedes to Bernadette's wish to go home. Soon, however, a warship's attack against the *Nautilus* reveals that the world is aware that the previously unknown "monster" is a submarine, and Nemo's captives are as much in danger from the navies of the world as he and his crew. With cannonballs aimed at him, Nemo proclaims the ship an enemy of freedom and himself the law and then rams and sinks the attacking vessel. Below deck, he responds to the mute accusation revealed in his captives' eyes by explaining that those he fights are the monsters who took from him his country and family, unveiling their portrait. Although Ned, as a former slave, had been skeptical of whether Nemo can comprehend oppression, by the conclusion both he and the viewer are brought to an awareness that the captain has indeed suffered, creating sympathy for his troubled character.

Nemo then reveals to Bernadette that he had known her gender from the first moment she spoke but had kept the secret and tells her she reminds him of his own daughter. She begs him to give up his revenge, but Nemo tells her to leave him in peace. The captives prepare an escape, and as they walk past the salon, they see him break down in tears before his family's portrait, crying, "Enough, enough." As the *Nautilus* is swept into the maelstrom's depths, the captives enter the dinghy and are flung out of its reach. Bernadette's father picks them up in Norway and marries her and Pierre at sea. Conseil becomes a museum curator, and Ned is the most changed by his time with Nemo—giving up hunting to care for the seals in a zoo. Years later, the Aronnaxes receive a single package: the giant pearl, a mute message from Nemo they can easily decode, hoping he has found peace. In turn, when all the others have passed away, the aged Bernadette returns the pearl to the chest and drops it back into the sea from whence it came, along with her story.

The children in the opening believe her account will live forever and now see that the chest includes the pearl—wrapped in Nemo's flag. Other than Bernadette's hallucination, the animation style is rather simple and thus not really adding further to the sophisticated, dense script. The seventy-four-minute running time is crowded with conflicts and occurrences, challenging the youthful audience in a manner beyond the most serious and considerably shorter other animated versions.

In the 1960s through the 1980s, Verne books, especially otherwise repetitious editions of standard titles, had become regarded as a vehicle for modern illustrators, who were often as highly touted as the author himself. A change in visual philosophy began with Oxford's publication of the first translation of *Adventures of the Rat Family* in 1993, using the original engravings from *Le Figaro illustré* in 1891—the first time they all were reproduced in color in any language. Such artwork, embodying the visualization of Verne in his own time, was a graphic equivalent to the new translations, part of the larger process of returning to the original text. This element began to be echoed in other Verne critical editions aimed at adult readers, especially two series in the twenty-first century, six books from Wesleyan University Press and nine volumes in an ongoing series copublished by the North American Jules Verne Society.[4]

This new visual orientation was evident in the most rewarding Anglophone television biography, which appeared in 2003 and was again titled *The Extraordinary Voyages of Jules Verne*. As a BBC–Atlantic Productions joint venture, this biography originated outside the American documentary industry and reflected the influence of the more intellectual Verne documentaries from France. It was written and directed by Shaun Trevisick and produced by Sarah Strupinski; great-grandson Jean Verne addresses specific topics, and Verne scholar Timothy Unwin was a co-consultant on the script. This version is full of interesting images, and, although not always related to the author, they are presented at a rapid clip and without the repetitions found in other documentaries. By all appearances, including the listing of a special-effects crew, an unusually large budget seemed to have been allocated for this part of the production. And even as a variety of Verne vehicles are shown in inconsistent images and a number of actors depict Verne in reenactments in which he either gains or loses a beard, these discordances have minimal impact. Perhaps as a result, this program is the most referential of the English-language screen biographies, with more mention and usage of Verne movies.

The central topics are Verne's boyhood and his early attempts at writing, with *Propeller Island* and *The Castle in the Carpathians* depicted as showing a shift away from technology toward social concerns and an obsession with death. In a departure from the usual "prophet" motif, the conclusion describes Verne as a science fiction writer who did not so much foresee elements of the modern age as place them in an adventurous formula with emphasis on the human community's behavior. Such Verne documentary regulars as Ron Miller and Gavin Scott are on hand, and science fiction writers Gregory Benford and Bruce Sterling enhance the commentary.

There are lapses, however. Perhaps most amazingly, *Around the World in Eighty Days* is hailed as having been made famous by Michael Todd's film, ignoring its 1870s status as best seller and stage hit. Robur is presented as a megalomaniac presaging Adolf Hitler, a leap in logic considering that despite Robur's proclamations of world supremacy he never takes a life and indeed saves shipwreck victims and slaves about to be executed. Nonetheless, *The Extraordinary Voyages of Jules Verne* has fewer flaws than other television documentaries about the author and lacks the narrative interruptions caused by the necessity of commercial breaks in similar American products.

Seldom had Verne the man and writer appeared on the screen until the 1990s. Then, with new information about the author, he increasingly became not only a subject in documentary form but also a character in fiction. This shift was possible due to the proliferation of cable informational networks hungry for subject material able to appeal to more specialized audiences; *The Secret Adventures of Jules Verne* aimed at a mass audience, and the Timekeeper presented Verne to the largest spectatorship imaginable at Disney theme parks globally. Verne himself as well as his books were now part of Vernian filmmaking; a simple adaptation of a story was no longer the only option.

# 12

# Dismal Reiterations, 2004–2008

Despite the achievements in developing new ways to present Vernian ideas, from pastiche to television, in both adult and children's versions of his novels and plays, an astonishing slide was about to occur early in the twenty-first century. From documentary to telefilm to big-budget theatrical adaptation, the urge to remake according to the latest notions led to a quick succession of weak rehashes.

Of Verne's most famous novels, from its first translation *Around the World in Eighty Days* had been the least problematic in English. Both *Journey to the Center of the Earth* and *Twenty Thousand Leagues under the Seas* had appeared in English several years after their first French publication, but *Around the World in Eighty Days* had been an instant global sensation from its first publication in 1873, a success echoed almost immediately on the stage.[1] In 2004, a new, more accurate translation of this volume became the first to appear as a Verne movie book tie-in: the rendering by Michael Glencross for Penguin. Otherwise, that year's new screen version proved to have little interest in its source, and its main marketing promotion would be a video game by Game Boy Advance. Just as Nemo had become a martial arts champ in the 2003 film *LXG*, the sidekick Passepartout karate-chops his way to the spotlight in the 2004 version of *Around the World in 80 Days,* reconceived as a star vehicle for Jackie Chan. Chan had not read the book, incorrectly believing it had not been translated into Chinese.[2] Perhaps he saw Cantinflas in the 1956 movie and imagined he could undertake a similar ethnically tinged performance, but he neglected to note that the previous movie was not built around the supporting character.

Moving the plot to the end of the nineteenth century, the film inverts the Verne source from the opening shot: the man masquerading as Passepartout is the robber of the bank of England and accepts the dangerous job of Fogg's valet to hide from the police. Some politically sensitive critics labeled the movie racist for casting Chan (the executive producer) ostensibly as Fogg's servant, when in truth Fogg has been made imbecilic and Passepartout the hero. The racism instead comes in through the use of Chan's martial arts stunt teams to invoke all the most hoary Asian villainy to justify his casting. The filmmakers of the Chan version would have been well advised instead to consult Verne's own 1874 adaptation of his play for the stage, which enhanced the Far Eastern incidents and characters; Verne's stage variation would have also solved the desire for fresh incidents that had faced the 1989 miniseries, while still retaining the author as a source.[3]

Whereas in 1956 Cantinflas simply played a Frenchman as Latin, in 2004 Chan's accent and appearance are explained as the result of a French father and Chinese mother. Adding Chan also tilted the novel's ethnic makeup; with one of the three central characters already Asian, Aouda was replaced by a new love interest, Monique (Cécile De France), encountered at the first stop in France. As a result, instead of colonial opposites attracting, a man of England and a woman of India, the traditional British and French enemies are united.

The filmmakers regarded their wholesale changes as updates and improvements—simultaneously closer to Verne, despite the obvious contradiction. Director Frank Coraci said that he had only fleeting memories of the 1956 movie before he went back to research the material for his update. "I went to the book first and re-read it, since I read it as a kid, and I remembered some of the scenes."[4] He wanted to change the main character to make him more accessible to viewers today. In the book and the 1956 "movie, Phileas Fogg was a very secure, confident person, and he . . . didn't really change enough for me to make the story worth telling for now."[5] So, Coraci explained, "in this version he's an inventor. That was inspired by the idea that Jules Verne was way ahead of his time, and so our Phileas Fogg is a man way ahead of his time, living in a Victorian era when people didn't want to accept big change. They were very stodgy and trying to hold onto their old ways, and the bet stems out of him trying to prove to them that the world is a much more progressive place and that anything is possible. In that sense, I think it's the modern day version of a Jules Verne theme. Think ahead."[6]

Just as the 1972 Australian animated series changed Fogg's motive for the journey, to marry Belinda Maze, the 2004 film offers a new reason for the trip—his status at the Royal Academy of Science. If he wins, he will become minister of science, but if he loses, he must cease inventing. The skullduggery is shifted from an errant, obsessed police detective to the aristocrat Lord Kelvin (a flamboyant Jim Broadbent), who uses the Royal Academy of Science to impede progress and is also selling arms to Chinese warlords. Fix, in a manic performance by Ewen Bremner, becomes a very minor, even more incompetent character who finally redeems himself by exposing Kelvin.

The serious aspects of Fogg's nature become awkward intrusions rather than insights. He explains that he has no family while sitting in a tub with Passepartout in a scene that, like his later mention of learning to wear women's clothes, adds a dimension to his sexuality beyond the supposed intention to appeal to the family audience. Steve Coogan, as Fogg, was trying to shift the role away from the characterization in the 1956 movie. "David Niven's rendition of the character is very close to the way it's written in the book," Coogan commented. "He's kind of passive, inscrutable, undemonstrative about emotion and utterly confident of his ability to win this bet. Even though [Niven] did it very well in the original one, that doesn't appeal as a performance. I like the idea to have somebody who on the outside is very confident, on the inside is slightly vulnerable and nervous about his ability."[7] Coogan's interpretation ultimately adds up to little more than a man who is socially inept and unsophisticated, unable to discern Passepartout's obvious subterfuges, as awkward in his dealings with other people as he is in producing workable scientific results.

The introduction of a balloon is not the only cursory homage to the 1956 version; there are also guest stars. A hokey stop in Turkey replaces the previous version's unnecessary pause in Spain, with Arnold Schwar-

Jackie Chan and Cécile De France's attempt to switch Passepartout's and the love interest's ethnic backgrounds, in conjunction with Steve Coogan's interpretation of Fogg *(center)*, had erratic results in the 2004 movie *Around the World in 80 Days*, as shown on a German lobby card.

zenegger as a much-married Turkish prince who lusts for Monique. Whereas the 1989 miniseries effectively recaptured the 1956 idea of cameos, in 2004 they are sometimes so obscure as to be unrecognizable (Rob Schneider as a San Francisco bum), wasted and unnecessary (John Cleese as a bobby), or quite simply inexplicable (Owen and Luke Wilson appearing as the Wright Brothers in the American desert).

The 1989 miniseries had added a stop in mainland China, and *The Three Stooges Go around the World in a Daze* took Fogg's grandson through the nation's Communist bureaucracies in 1963. In 2004, it is revealed that Passepartout is named Lau Xing in his homeland. He visits his idyllic village as he returns the idol stolen from the bank in England and carried halfway around the world. At this point, the movie comes to its logical end; that it continues is almost an afterthought, having so thoroughly supplanted Verne's plot in primary importance.

The book episode in which Passepartout becomes lost in Yokohama and finds employment in a circus should have been a natural for Chan. Instead, Fogg angrily leaves his companions, is quickly robbed in San Francisco, and then is found a homeless beggar. The movie never explains how the remainder of the trip is financed; a scene in which Lau was to fight John L. Sullivan for their fare was cut (as were, probably, other scenes in a choppy and disconnected narrative that at 125 minutes is already too long).

Symbolizing the fact that the revisions have removed all the tension from the novel is the substitution of the transcontinental railroad with a stagecoach trip, nonsensical given the necessity for speed. The transatlantic voyage becomes a base to create, in six hours, a flying machine catapulted into the air, powered solely by Lau Xing's pedaling, to travel the final leg of the trip. When the machine crash-lands at the Academy of Science, among those waiting to applaud is Queen Victoria (Kathy Bates)—a character who had also seen crackpot science in the 1967 Verne film *Those Fantastic Flying Fools.*

The new plot might have suited an animated version (perhaps in Chan's cartoon series *Jackie Chan Adventures* [2000–2005]), but here, weak as the script by David Titcher, David Benullo, and David Goldstein is, Coraci's unimaginative direction is far worse. Scarcely a joke is not muffed or an opportunity for wit not missed. The only commendable innovation is animated transitions between locales that try to replace absent connective scenes and give some pace to an otherwise leaden experience.

Budgeted at $110 million, shot in Thailand and Germany's Babelsberg Studios, *Around the World in 80 Days* was bought in November 2003 by Disney to be one of the company's key family releases for summer 2004.[8] Given the filmmakers' confident assertions, the movie ironically debuted in ninth place, and by the second week it had already begun to disappear from theaters. This result suggested that a better investment might have been the comparatively small sum necessary for a theatrical restoration of the 65 mm. version of the 1956 movie rather than the simultaneous DVD release that occurred. William Arnold, critic for the *Seattle Post Intelligencer,* best summed up the impression this new version made: "We seem to have entered a brave new millennium of filmmaking in which our entire collective cinematic past is being remade and reinterpreted as moronic farce. . . . [In this case] it's been turned into a stupid kung fu movie."[9]

For 125 years, English-speaking readers could find only one translation of *The Mysterious Island* in print, by W. H. G. Kingston, who had changed the name of Verne's hero from the symbolic "Cyrus Smith" to "Cyrus Harding" and, more importantly, transformed Captain Nemo into a supplicant rather than a rebel against British rule.[10] Finally, two new, quality translations of *The Mysterious Island* were published simultaneously in 2002, and they immediately set in motion a fresh adaptation, but with minimal benefit.[11] The new telefilm would premier on September 10, 2005, after Adam Armus and Kay Foster developed an entirely new, three-hour script for Hallmark, produced over sixty-one days in Krabi, Thailand.

Although *Mysterious Island* uses the correct name for Verne's hero, "Smith," other corrections in the new English renditions of the novel did not survive the transition to the screen. While in 2002, *LXG* had used its basis in the graphic series *The League of Extraordinary Gentlemen* to finally cast an Indian as Nemo but changed his motivation to pirating, three years later the new *Mysterious Island* returns to the James Mason–Herbert Lom European performance style, putting Patrick Stewart in the role and Roy Marsden as his assistant, with whom Nemo has almost a brotherly relationship; their performances are professional and enacted with conviction. Nemo's motivations and loyalties are as Verne presented, although he is now an Englishman who has adopted India, given Stewart's casting.

Overall, the Armus–Foster concept was entirely too derivative of the 1961 movie of *Mysterious Island* and too full of clichés from the 1990s. The screenwriters, noting the novel's vast scope and the fact that Nemo appeared only briefly in the end, decided to provide continuous interaction between him and the castaways, eliding Verne's more mundane episodes of survival. The story is enacted in an entirely perfunctory manner, with minimal characterization, led by Kyle MacLachlan as Smith, and the balloon escape brings together a slightly different group than Verne imagined. Pencroff, played by Jason Durr, becomes a Confederate colonel desirous of pirate gold. Spillet is transformed from a war correspondent to a female nurse in the Confederate prison, here given

Patrick Stewart as Captain Nemo in the 2005 telefilm *Mysterious Island*.

the first name "Jane" (Gabrielle Anwar), and Harbart is replaced by her daughter, Helen (Danielle Calvert). She is saved from a giant bird (à la *The Children of Captain Grant*) by Atherton (Chris Larkin) in place of Ayrton. Marooned on the island eight years, Atherton in this film is the brother of buccaneer Bob Harvey (Vinnie Jones). Omar Gooding is Neb, which he plays rather in a more modern and assertive vein than the novel's characterization.

The tale itself is like a movie serial, depending on repetitious thrills to fill the running time. The island is inhabited with more of the giant beasts that were the highlight of the 1961 version. Instead of a sporadic threat, the giant bug, rat, and bird appear at such a relentless pace under Russell Mulcahy's direction as to destroy any novelty or surprise. The principal subplot, occupying more of the film than Nemo, focuses on the pirates; one such group provides the opening scene, before cutting to Smith and the others at the Confederate prison in Virginia.

Further clichés are presented as Nemo inhabits an island compound, surrounded by an electrified fence to keep out the creatures, an unimaginative device redolent of *Jurassic Park* (1993) and, to a lesser degree, H. G. Wells's *The Island of Dr. Moreau* (1896). Only in the Indian design and architecture of Nemo's home in the caves is there some originality, but this version's *Nautilus* design also replicates that of the 1961 movie. A new element is added with Nemo seeking to end war by building a weapon so powerful that it can destroy a city. He hopes that the existence of this weapon will dissuade humanity from armed struggle, but Cyrus refuses to assist him, saying that every nation will instead want one. The secret ingredient of his bomb, found only on the island, is what makes the animals so abnormally large. Reprising the conclusion of the 1961 version, Nemo warns the castaways of the volcanic eruption, and they escape in a small boat while he is trapped in the grotto as the *Nautilus* is crushed by the rocks and lava. It is a familiar ending that attempts an elaboration on the Verne story but remains too evocative of what was better accomplished decades earlier.[12]

A deeper dive to the depths of quality was achieved with *30,000 Leagues under the Sea,* a 2007 direct-to-video release also broadcast on the Syfy Channel and produced by the aptly named company The Asylum. The results of trying to cross Verne with Tom Clancy were even more unpromising than the updating of Nemo in *The Amazing Captain Nemo.* As in that film, *30,000 Leagues under the Sea* is predicated on Nemo interacting with modern naval technology. Some characters remain; there is the scientist Aronnax, but Conceil is now his ex-wife (hence the new spelling) and military superior. However, none of the individuals have any resonance with the novel, nor do any of the other supporting characters. Indeed, the name "Conceil" is pronounced not as a French name, but as if it were a type of seal. The director of *30,000 Leagues under the Sea,* Gabriel Bologna, claimed to be a fan of Verne, even saying that he named his son after the author; however, the screenplay he coauthored with Eric Forsberg has more reverses and nonsensical twists than a movie serial but none of that form's charm.[13]

Aronnax and his crew are dispatched by Commander Farragut from the U.S.S. *Abraham Lincoln* in a special deep-sea diving sub into the Marianas Trench, where another, larger submarine was lost, apparently in the grip of a giant squid. The rescuers somehow wake up aboard the *Nautilus,* and Nemo introduces himself as a jolly eccentric billionaire who plans to release his captives shortly and is on the friendliest of terms

Advertising art for a dismal reimagining in 2007, this time entitled *30,000 Leagues under the Sea.*

with Farragut. Sean Lawlor's Irish brogue and the naval tour-of-duty pins on the tunic that serves as his costume are entirely out of place.

The contrasts with the archetypal Verne plot only grow as the movie progresses. Nemo regards himself as an idealist, determined to save the deep and create an undersea utopia because humankind is despoiling the surface world. His crew seems to contain all types, and the *Nautilus* is more of a city than a submarine, including a nightclub on board, where prostitutes openly ply their trade.

Only two ideas beyond character and vessel names are to be found from the book: the sunken Atlantis and the giant squid (several of them, but this time under Nemo's control). *30,000 Leagues under the Sea* constantly returns to plot points to recycle shots and sets. Nemo proves steadily more monomaniacal in trying to capture the escaping Aronnax and his crew, needing their "oxygenator" to resurrect Atlantis. A trap destroys the *Nautilus;* as Nemo's followers haplessly abandon ship, their captain weeps, crashing the submarine into the remains of Atlantis. Surely no film has ever offered so pitiable an etching of Verne's hero.

Not that Lorenzo Lamas offers more as Aronnax or Natalie Stone as Conceil. The actors have little opportunity to shine, given the script and Bologna's direction, which basically alternates between close-ups and extreme close-ups. The economics and narrative of direct-to-video releases and ultimate television showings had declined precipitously even since 1993 and the release of *800 Leagues down the Amazon,* itself a minor work but at least a recognizable adaptation. On the heels of the remakes of *Around the World in 80 Days* and *Mysterious Island, 30,000 Leagues under the Sea* made the future of Verne adaptations looked irremediably bleak.

Upon the centennial of Verne's death in 2005, new books appeared. The long-standing need for an anthology of modern international Vernian criticism began to be filled by Edmund Smyth's *Jules Verne: Narratives of Modernity* in 2000, while full-length studies continued with Timothy Unwin's *Jules Verne: Journeys in Writing* in 2005 and William Butcher's *Jules Verne: The Definitive Biography* in 2006. Only one of the myriad new books that appeared in France for the centennial, Gonzague Saint Bris's *The World of Jules Verne,* was translated into English, but there were original children's books afresh, including

Tom Streissguth's *Science Fiction Pioneer: A Story of Jules Verne* (2001) and William Schoell's *Remarkable Journeys: The Story of Jules Verne* (2002). However, little of this knowledge of Verne was evident in the next biographical film, and documentaries followed the downward turn of adaptations.

*Prophets of Science Fiction* (2006), running forty minutes, chronicled both Verne and H. G. Wells but returned to the familiar pattern, describing the French author as having uncanny, eerie gifts as a sort of nineteenth-century Nostradamus, albeit one based in the science of his age. Rather than undertaking a more challenging comparison between Verne and Wells, the program is essentially composed of two separate biographies, only briefly linking the two at the opening and close. The treatment of Wells is considerably more comprehensive; Verne is described only for his lunar novels and *Twenty Thousand Leagues under the Seas*. Given the broadcast of *Prophets of Science Fiction* on the Discovery Science channel, there is little surprise in the emphasis on Verne's consultation with experts to verify his prognostications. Rather than on the literary aspects of his work, the emphasis is on the credibility of the books' scientific details—their modern equivalents ranging from the Apollo missions to modern experiments with a space gun and nuclear-powered naval submarines.

As written and directed by Dan Levitt for Veriscope Pictures, *Prophets of Science Fiction* has the expected breaks and repetitions resulting from the circular structure required to accommodate commercials. Most strikingly, the inventiveness of visuals in the BBC's 2003 version of *The Extraordinary Voyages of Jules Verne* is abandoned in favor of the more typical, slow-paced style. There is abundant use of stock footage, and, to make up for the paucity of still images, *Prophets of Science Fiction* follows the standard Discovery practice of focusing toward or away from an item rather than cutting to a fresh one. For instance, three engravings and a Scholastic paperback suffice to illustrate *From the Earth to the Moon*, demonstrating the minimal research. The conclusion was equally facile, consisting of the remark, "You can love or fear the future—that's Verne versus Wells."

The next documentary was derived not from scholarship but from Michel Lamy's 1984 volume *Jules Verne, initié et initiateur*, translated into English in 2007 as *The Secret Message of Jules Verne: Decoding His Masonic, Rosicrucian, and Occult Writings.*[14] Lamy's lead is followed in the 2008 production *The Extraordinary Voyages of Jules Verne: An Odyssey from the Sea to the Air, from the Earth to the Moon* to offer an interpretive approach in which screenwriter Philip Gardiner explores Verne, his writing, his relationship with publisher Pierre-Jules Hetzel, and his supposed esoteric inclinations.

The structural analysis of Verne in *The Extraordinary Voyages of Jules Verne: An Odyssey from the Sea to the Air, from the Earth to the Moon* is less facile than most English-language biographical films and videos about the author, with their standard, ostensibly factual approach. Several of Verne's books are discussed in the search for secret symbols and codes, discovering hidden significance in *Twenty Thousand Leagues under the Seas* and *Journey to the Center of the Earth.* Used as the servant's name in *Around the World in Eighty Days,* the term *passe-partout,* "skeleton key," is to be found in the initiatory language used to inscribe multiple layers of encrypted, symbolic meaning in narratives sometimes misread as fables for children. Verne's books are deconstructed for Rosicrucian secrets, with some providing an account related to Masonic initiation. Axel's prototypical initiatory trek is explicated, and the derivation of the names "Axel," "Robur," and others offer fresh insights. Further details undermine the program's credibility: a balloon becomes the icon for *Around the World in Eighty Days,* and Hetzel's interest in fostering Verne's career is credited to mutual Masonic membership, with the publisher teaching his author protégé how to insert secret symbols into popular stories.

Visuals provide the feel of a video game and are almost entirely computer generated and one dimensional. A number of image sequences are repeated; for instance, a tracking shot of a harbor with a lighthouse on a distant breakwater, ostensibly Nantes, doubles as a motif for the exploration of Verne's consciousness. Some visuals simply do not match the narration or are inappropriate, such as Apollo capsules and modern rockets for *From the Earth to the Moon,* and appear to have been lifted from other productions. This seventy-minute Reality Entertainment and Rea12Can video was produced by Michael pralin (as spelled),

Paul Huges, and O. H. Krill, had DVD release in the United States, and was broadcast in England on the channel "Controversial TV."

Sadly, this pseudo-documentary was a fitting end to a period that placed so many misinterpretations of Verne and his characters on screen in disastrous contexts that ranged from a kung fu movie to a pale imitation of an earlier success. It need not have been so; in 2006, connoisseurs could locate the American DVD release of Venezuela's Academy Award entry of the year before, *1888—The Extraordinary Voyage of Jules Verne*. This ingenious interpretation retold Verne's *The Mighty Orinoco* (1898) as the author's actual experience, not in the faux manner of *The Secret Adventures of Jules Verne* but as a meditation on the novel, persuasively involving Verne in the creation of his own narrative.[15] Hollywood's foreign counterparts had emerged from the bleak thicket of retreads with a fresh conception, and a fortuitous, unexpected shift was likewise about to emerge domestically.

# 13

# A New Formulation, 2008–Present

By the end of the first decade of the twenty-first century, two conflicting trends were apparent. Along with the renewed scholarship and the appearance of some titles for the first time in English, many lesser-known Verne books were also translated anew.[1] For all the progress, however, a fresh peril emerged, threatening to extend indefinitely the life of the worst nineteenth-century Verne translators: public-domain texts from such Internet sources as Project Gutenberg could be reissued with minimal investment, and so the market was flooded.[2]

Both of these approaches would resonate on the screen. For every film having any originality, there was another reiteration. Experimentation foreshadowed by biography and pastiche was about to enrich the adaptation vein, combining all three in 2008 in a new theatrical version: *Journey to the Center of the Earth 3D*. Immediately before this version was released, however, two lower-budgeted exercises were made to cash in on the Verne interest, one by Robert Halmi Sr. and Robert Halmi Jr. and the other a direct-to-video production by the same firm that had created *30,000 Leagues under the Sea*.

The latter company, The Asylum, has a reputation for producing films from public-domain stories and titles reminiscent of big-budget productions concurrently offered by major studios, so it was not surprising for it to continue riding on the Verne bandwagon. As weak as The Asylum's *Journey to the Center of the Earth* is, however, it is vastly superior simply as entertainment to *30,000 Leagues under the Sea*. Although the latter actually has more in common with Verne, it is such a distortion that the company's *Journey to the Center of the Earth,* which simply abandons the author's plot save to credit his name, deserves less opprobrium. The retelling written and directed by Scott Wheeler and Davey Jones has a greater similarity with the pattern established in Edgar Rice Burroughs's Pellucidar saga, and locating dinosaurs is as close as the movie gets to Verne.

Halmi's *Journey to the Center of the Earth* appeared first, followed by The Asylum version on July 1, 2008. As with Halmi's 2005 adaptation of *Mysterious Island,* the filmmakers did not return to the novel but chose instead to take inspiration from an earlier film, in this case with a rewrite of Halmi's 1999 miniseries of *Journey to the Center of the Earth,* compressing it into a ninety-minute telefilm for RHI Entertainment that appeared on the ION network on January 27, 2008. William Bray adapted the 1999 Tom Baum teleplay, this time helmed by T. J. Scott; the principal characterizations and motives remained the same but were more tightly paced.

The setting remains around the 1870s but is transplanted to Alaska, still known as "Seward's Folly" and with vestiges of Russian influence. This locale and a decidedly similar center of the earth were a result of Vancouver location shooting, which determined production design. The switch to an American background, with Western-style towns, however, gives the adaptation more of a familiar, natural feel rather than an exotic one, but the fact that the center of the earth looks almost exactly like the world above makes the narrative less convincing. Even as the underground visuals of the 1999 miniseries are lost, the basic characters and situation remain; anthropologist Jonathan Brock, like Theodore Lytton, is engaging in boxing bouts while his nephew Abel handles the betting to earn the money for an expedition to the Dutch East Indies. Neither Rick Schroeder nor Steven Grayhm is as appropriate for his respective role as were Treat Williams and Jeremy London in 1999, Schroeder lacking the physical strength and Grayhm unable to reflect the transformation the journey exerted on London.

By contrast, the wealthy Martha Dennison, who hires the pair to search for her husband, is this time incarnated by Victoria Pratt, who had a decade of female action roles to her credit. There is no mention of Saknussemm; instead, Martha's husband Edward Dennison has a map

German art advertising the 2008 television version of *Journey to the Center of the Earth.*

supposedly pointing to a mine shaft leading to the center of the earth, which he had followed four years earlier. Martha is presented as the daughter of a mine owner, who had grown up surrounded by men and is consequently unconcerned about the perils, discomfort, and male companionship of the expedition.

Most intriguing is the change in the Hans character. Rather than use a storyline from *The Children of Captain Grant,* as the 1999 miniseries did, the new version offers a Russian outlaw, Sergei (Mike Dopud), whose brother had descended with Edward. This change provides an appropriate shift of character that merges with the new locale and, unlike all previous versions, a compelling reason for the "guide" to descend. Sergei is also vital in helping the expedition reach the lake where, according to the map, on a single July day of the year the sunlight will point out the location of the mine that leads to the underground lake.

By the lake's shore, trees freshly felled with an axe indicate an earlier traveler, and here Brock's group decides to make a journey by raft. Attacking prehistoric birds and a plesiosaur are described as extinct, but the use of special effects is brief and has little impact. A subterranean people resemble, predictably given the budget, Native Americans, who made the journey beneath the surface and resettled there eons ago. Edward (Peter Fonda, a modest improvement over the 1999 film's Bryan Brown as Caspar) has taken advantage of the people's superstition and made himself king. He remains possessed of the same egotism that disrupted his marriage to Martha, and when he heartlessly shoots a youth, she slaps him so hard that he bleeds—undercutting his divinity in a moment reminiscent of a scene in the Rudyard Kipling film *The Man Who Would Be King* (1975). Edward leads the way to a cave reputed to be the way out; in a change from the 1999 version, he is allowed redemption by sacrificing himself to save Martha, Brock, and Abel. They are sent to the surface of a lake in a waterspout, a theory that Martha had proposed earlier and Brock had dismissed. To save the tribe from further exploitation by the aboveground world, Abel proclaims his diary to be merely a piece of fiction. Meanwhile, Brock and Martha have realized their attraction for each other.

The hokeyness that was so apparent in the subplot of the 1999 miniseries is rendered less evident by the new version's more rapid pacing, and the resemblance to Conan Doyle's *The Lost World* is less pronounced. This time there are, mercifully, no Saurians, no love affair with one of the underground girls, and no one remaining behind as king. However, the evolutionary theme that bound the various plot points is also lost. Ultimately, nothing is accomplished by the new version to suggest any reason for a remake beyond cashing in on the increased commercial viability of the title.

Four years earlier Walden Media had perpetrated the Jackie Chan *Around the World in 80 Days* catastrophe, but now its new theatrical version, *Journey to the Center of the Earth 3D*, broke the hex on Hollywood Verne. The filmmakers overcame several complications. *Journey to the Center of the Earth 3D* was a summer movie, a time when the purest escapism is expected from the widest audience—a difficulty that the Chan *80 Days* and *LXG* had already found insurmountable. During the height of Verne theatrical filmmaking, 1950 to 1971, each new movie presented a story idea afresh to cinemagoers, but subsequently these movies began to show on television ever more often and to be increasingly available in video formats. In the years since, new versions, even animated renderings, were of Verne stories already presented on screen. The 1959 movie *Journey to the Center of the Earth* is a case in point; once occasionally appearing on network television, today it is broadcast sometimes more than once a month on cable channels and has been available on home video since the birth of the medium.

With that movie so readily available and so capably achieved, there was little need to remake it on its own terms, thus impelling new ways to tell the story. In most cases, the latter imperative has been handled with dreadful license: *Alien from L.A.* and Cannon's abortive *Journey to the Center of the Earth,* "An Excellent Journey to the Center of the Earth" for the *Funky Fables* series, and now The Asylum's version. Director Eric Brevig himself changed the setting of the script of *Journey to the Center of the Earth 3D* from the nineteenth century to the present to appeal to modern audiences, but because Verne had set his novel in the period in which it was published, there were no "period" elements central to the narrative.[3] As well as avoiding the feel of a remake, Brevig hoped to get away from some of the elements that made the book unlikely from a scientific standpoint and to avoid the intrusion of modern technology.⁴ *Journey to the Center of the Earth 3D* is a movie of taste and intelligence, with reverence for the author. Fidelity to Verne's conception as well as a referential dimension were achieved with the conceit that Verne's book is in fact nonfiction, based on the account of someone else who made the trip. Following the book, the trek may (and will) be duplicated, a notion at once making *Journey to the Center of the Earth 3D* as much sequel and pastiche as adaptation yet also erasing the difference between them.⁵ The homage to the source is warm, never campy, and steadily leavened with humor.

In the planning, leading man and first-time executive producer Brendan Fraser had arrived with his own copy of the Verne book and mentioned its importance in many interviews.⁶ He prevailed upon studio executives to revise the script's proposed father–son relationship back to the novel's uncle and nephew.⁷ "'Let's go back to the book,' he stated. 'Take the relationships there, let the lead character be an uncle to a nephew, and let the guide create the boy–girl friction, all on top of the backdrop of these big set pieces, all the [computer-generated imagery] and 3-D elements.'"⁸ The result is deceptively simple but also very tightly plotted.⁹

A fresh filmmaking technology, computer-generated 3D (already used with Verne in the *Space Strikers* television series) further governed the adaptation, and considering how Verne himself was involved in successfully adapting several of his novels to the requirements of nineteenth-century stage spectacles, he would likely have understood the necessities imposed. As the fifteenth film of the book made around the world since 1909, *Journey to the Center of the Earth 3D* achieves the best results possible while experimenting with the respective form. In 1909, it had been Segundo de Chomon displaying the effects possible with trick films; in 1959, it had been CinemaScope; and in the case of the 1976 version the challenge was animation. In each case, the new possibilities on the screen served Verne's premise.

Indeed, the suitability of CinemaScope to the subject matter was one of the reasons for the 1959 version's appearance as the first feature movie of the novel. In the case of the 2008 theatrical version, producer Charlotte Huggins had been making 3D films for IMAX and theme park attractions and had sought a property that could use the technology for a traditional theatrical feature. The 3D format becomes an essential part of the visual design, from the opening-title sequence of a fossil trilobite to a living one. Its antenna wiggle directly at the audience, hinting at the trip to come—into a strange realm where time has little meaning.[10] An extensive array of book tie-ins and a video game were offered, all aimed at youth rather than adults, demonstrating the primary intended appeal.[11]

The basic troika of characters remains, and there are no melodramatic additions or villains to provide tension beyond the conflict with nature. In place of Professor Lidenbrock, seismologist Trevor Anderson (Fraser) is unappreciated at his university. His sister-in-law leaves nephew Sean (Josh Hutcherson), age thirteen, with him for a visit, and although younger than Verne's first-person narrator Axel, Sean undergoes a similar trajectory, his age allowing youthful filmgoers to relate more easily. (Indeed, Hutcherson's casting was less bothersome than that of pop idol Pat Boone in the 1959 movie.) Sean's father, Max, is seen in the opening precredits scene, pursued over a volcanic cliff by prehistoric creatures, with the story proper beginning a decade later as successive revelations are made about Max and his discoveries. The added incentive of finding Max, although not in the novel, adds to the book's intended maturation process. Initially there is no love lost between uncle and nephew, but subsequent events allow the two to bond and become willing to endanger their own lives for each other.

Arriving with Sean are some of Max's possessions, including his carefully studied copy of Verne's novel, full of notes and even a cipher that, as in Verne's telling, the nephew decodes. Here is a clear displacement: in the new narrative, Verne's novel takes the position of Saknussemm's relic. The book itself becomes the document that leads travelers to follow in the footsteps of those who went before, using the novel itself as their guide.

One of Max's cryptograms leads to the Asgeirsson Institute of Volcanology in Iceland, where Trevor and Sean meet the late Asgeirsson's daughter, Hannah (Anita Briem). She explains that her father was a Vernian—one of a small group who believed that what the author wrote was indeed fact. Here is a neat twist on both Verne studies and Sherlockiana, which has long treated Sir Arthur Conan Doyle as Dr. John Watson's literary agent. Indeed, the "Vernian lore blogspot," a fictive blog by Max and Asgeirsson on the *Journey to the Center of the Earth 3D* website, was a referential echo as well as an extended practical joke.[12]

Hannah believes her father's Vernian convictions were foolish, but as a mountaineer herself she agrees to guide Trevor and Sean to Mount Snaefells. She thus assumes Hans's purpose in the novel, proving no less resourceful. She also provides the easiest way of including female participation and romantic tension, necessary in a modern movie, without other versions' tendency to add an additional participant. As Briem commented, "It was a great joy for me to develop a strong female character in the spirit of an Icelandic woman. . . . I think that came in very handy because as Hannah the mountain guide I often found myself in these very dangerous situations, and I have on one hand a geeky scientist and the other a small child, and they are both going to get us killed, so I have to intervene and save the day, regularly."[13] The two males, Trevor and Sean, are initially dependent on her, and it is only later that Trevor's scientific knowledge becomes an asset and Sean learns self-reliance.

After some initial location views of the ascent of Snaefells, the interior of the earth is created entirely through computer-generated backgrounds rather than with any actual caves. A rockslide traps the trio, and a flare ignites magnesium-encrusted cavern walls, so that the movie starts to emulate Verne's own habit of concealing pedagogical purpose (in this case geology) in the guise of an exciting narrative. A deposit of emeralds, rubies, and diamonds is found, evidence of a volcanic tube ascribed to Verne. However, the thin sheet of muscovite on which Trevor, Hannah, and Sean stand shatters when Sean greedily snatches a diamond. They fall an incalculable distance before finally reaching waterslides and a grotto, where bioluminescent birds extinct on the surface lead them to the center of the earth and a sea lit by an underground sun.

Here is the world Verne described but visualized in an entirely fresh manner, lush and verdant, full of vibrant colors, and teeming with life. Trevor reads aloud from Verne as they walk past the mushroom forest described in the novel. The doubts that both Hannah and Sean had in their fathers and in the unorthodox belief these men had shared in Verne has been wiped away, transforming the two characters' perspectives and making them eager participants in the expedition. Trevor's faith in his

Japanese advertising emphasizing the 3D for the 2008 movie *Journey to the Center of the Earth 3D*.

brother is validated, and Sean regrets that he had not read the book for
the understanding it would have given him. The trek becomes one of
redemption for not only Asgeirsson and Max, but also for Verne and his
literary wonders.

A tree house, first thought to have belonged to Lidenbrock, is recognized as Max's, and Hannah discovers his remains nearby.[14] They build
a cairn for Max near the underground sea, stunningly designed in a sun-
set view, as Trevor reads from his brother's diary ten years earlier. However, there can be no lingering, for the rising temperature indicates the
presence of volcanic magma; in this way, the narrative provides a concession to modern knowledge of the earth's core to enhance credibility.
The only exit is the path of Verne's travelers, so the new explorers must
build a raft to cross the sea and find the vent on the other side.

Only *Where Time Began* had previously attempted a live-action
depiction of the underground ocean's prehistoric creatures described in
the novel, but *Journey to the Center of the Earth 3D* stages this scene
in a way possible for the first time with computer-generated effects. A
storm breaks out, and the raft is overrun with flying, fanged fish, which
the explorers fight off with sticks used like baseball bats, but these fish
are chased by larger fish. As the wind's velocity increases, Sean tries to
rescue the kite they use as a sail and finds himself lifted aloft into the elements in a manner reminiscent of the boy ascending in a kite in Verne's
novel *Two Year Holiday.*

Sean wakes alone, ashore, as Trevor and Hannah search for him
from the spot where their raft wrecks. Their respective treks are cross-
cut as they hope to meet by following the predetermined plan to search
for Verne's vent to the surface. Here is a perfect approximation of the
novel's episode in which Axel is separated and lost. When Trevor decides
to go in search of Sean and thus potentially miss his own opportunity
to escape, Hannah realizes her attraction to him. Guided only by one
of the bioluminescent birds, Sean discovers that the compass goes wild,
and he enters a region where rocks float in the air. Back on solid land is
a live *Tyrannosaurus rex,* which traps Sean until Trevor leads it toward
another layer of muscovite that collapses under its weight.

In the volcano's chimney, water cushions the rising magma as Hannah, Trevor, and Sean take refuge in the jawbone of another *Tyran-*

*nosaurus rex,* which replaces the novel's raft. In this way, the escape, through an eruption of Mount Vesuvius, is made more credible than the explanation Verne gave or those shown in any of the other screen versions. Back at the surface, the explorers slide in the jawbone downhill through a vineyard, bringing to closure the journey that had begun with the mine ride. Sean has brought back with him diamonds to provide for his uncle's new lab, but also another prehistoric relic—one of the bioluminescent birds, which had become a good-luck companion, especially when Sean was alone. Not only does the bird fill the familiar R2D2 function from the *Star Wars* saga, but it also recalls another inspiration in filming *Journey to the Center of the Earth*—Sir Arthur Conan Doyle's *The Lost World,* in which a baby pterodactyl is brought back to London, an idea already used in the animated *A Journey to the Center of the Earth* (1976).

All the vital motifs, characters, and themes of Verne's novel are retained as far as possible in the format of a summer "thrill ride" movie. The 3D effects themselves serve to enrich the visual presentation of a story in which the otherworldly dimension is so key. Only a few scenes were unsuccessful, such as an encounter with carnivorous plants too reminiscent of "B" jungle movies. The major change is having the journey take place over days rather than weeks to accommodate a running time of ninety-two minutes. Although certainly this version lacks the nineteenth-century period and the epic quality allowed by the 1959 version's 132-minute running time, *Journey to the Center of the Earth 3D* replaces its predecessor's deliberate pace with a series of accidents— the rockslide, the mine, and the shattered muscovite—that enable the descent. Similarly, the camerawork is quick and fragmented, unlike its predecessor's more classical CinemaScope framing. The script by Michael Weiss, Jennifer Flackett, and Mark Levin evidences clever duality of structure: muscovite and magnesium both imperil and save, just as Max's copy of the novel *Journey to the Center of the Earth* is originally unearthed alongside a baseball mitt and baseball-type athletics save the raft from the flying fish.

At the last minute, *Journey to the Center of the Earth 3D* had to drop *3D* from the title in many screenings owing to a lack of theaters ready for the new 3D films. It had already been held back for a full year precisely because not enough theaters were equipped with the technology. Having been made on a relatively modest budget of $54 million (with ten weeks of principal photography in Montreal), *Journey to the Center of the Earth 3D* required a simultaneous release of "flat" prints in many theaters lacking the 3D technology. Fortunately, the movie did astonishingly well at the box office, considering it received little advertising because of the lack of preparation for 3D. Although Verne may not have been in the same league as summer 2008 competitors Batman (*The Dark Knight*) or Pixar (*Wall-E*), *Journey to the Center of the Earth 3D* was already in the black by its third week, long before overseas revenues, cable, and video.

In the wake of *Journey to the Center of the Earth 3D,* three separate films were also made, all of them reaching screens in February 2012. One was a biography. With the Science Channel offering a series of hour-long episodes on writers and filmmakers in the genre, entitled *Prophets of Science Fiction* (unrelated to the 2006 production of the same title), an episode entitled "Jules Verne" was inevitable. However, as directed by Declan Whitebloom and written by Kevin Tavolaro, the program was plagued by poor editing and ultimately doomed by its form and contradictions. Innovations include color renderings from the engravings in the Hetzel books and licensed high-definition footage of the *Nautilus* from *LXG* and Disney's *20,000 Leagues under the Sea.* In contrast are unrelated visuals, most dismally the use of futuristic cartoon-style images to illustrate *Paris in the 20th Century,* incorrectly proclaimed as Verne's only novel published after his death. Reenacted sequences are poorly staged, and Verne abruptly ages to an old man in 1874 after being depicted by a youthful actor for scenes set only a few years earlier. Interviews of familiar faces are excerpted, adding George Slusser as the senior Verne scholar.

What renders this *Prophets of Science Fiction* episode distinctly beneath such endeavors as the A&E *Biography* show on Verne and closer to the *Great Books* segment on the Learning Channel (which, like Science Channel, is part of the Discovery Network) is the determination to constantly relate Verne to contemporary developments. These links, in five segments, shift the *Prophets of Science Fiction* segment away from any biographical or critical perspective. Although mention of the proposed space gun in connection with *From the Earth to the Moon* is a natural, other comparisons are far more tenuous, most egregiously the Taser as a descendant of Nemo's undersea electronic rifle. At three to five minutes in length each, these digressions become so significant as to resemble embedded infomercials (in addition to the expected commercial breaks).

A fresh television adaptation, the eponymous *Jules Verne's Mysterious Island,* appeared in February 2012. Shifts from the novel mount from the beginning. During the balloon escape, Confederate Pencroft shoots Spillett—eliminating one top-billed cast member at the outset—the remainder flying through a storm into a wormhole. Sadly, when they awaken on a shore, what should be contrasting scenery looks exactly like the Richmond they supposedly just left (and is the same Louisiana shooting location; not even a filter is used to distinguish it). However, night marauders carry off one of the group, Confederate deserter Tom Ayrton, and his companions find his half-devoured remains the next day.

An apparently abandoned plantation-style home seems to offer refuge even as the volcano erupts and an airplane flies out of another wormhole. From it, Harding (Lochlyn Munro) rescues two sisters with the surname "Fogg," characters billed in advance advertising to suggest an element of pastiche but ultimately left at the level of an "in-joke." Julia Fogg (called "Miss Jules" and played by Gina Holden) and the irritating Abby Fogg (Susie Abromeit) have to explain their "flying locomotive" to Harding and dismay Pencroft by telling of an African American president, but these challenges to the castaways' Civil War mindset only become annoyingly repetitive rather than serving the time-travel idea.

As Herbert (Caleb Michaelson) tends the wounded Abby in the house, they must conceal themselves from pirates, while outside the nocturnal creatures continue to threaten. Pencroft, unable to adjust either to a "union" on the island or to the future foretold by the Foggs, tries to escape to sea in a small boat, only to be consumed by a giant squid. Harding and Julia meet Captain Nemo when he kills the pirates with a laser gun and explains that the home was built by his crew, with a door leading to a hatch into the *Nautilus.* He and his submarine have been land-locked on the island for twenty years; after the British Empire took his family and kingdom, he realized that vengeance only brings

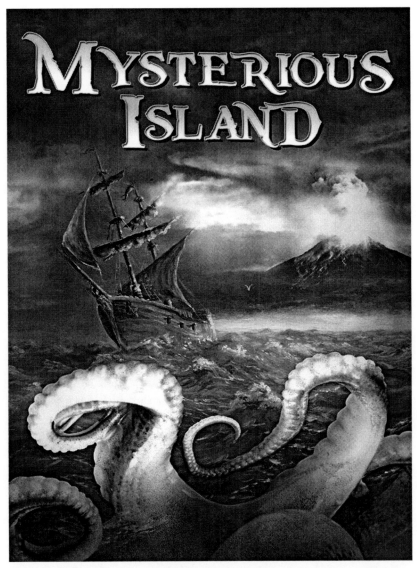

Conceptual art for the 2012 television adaptation *Jules Verne's Mysterious Island*.

pain. Then (amid dismal interior *Nautilus* décor) Nemo made a new discovery, that time functions differently at sea, but an experiment to use nuclear fusion to accelerate the *Nautilus* went awry when the vessel was seized by the giant squid. (William Morgan Sheppard plays Nemo, and his son, Mark Sheppard, plays the captain in his younger years in the retrospective scenes; Mark Sheppard also directed *Jules Verne's Mysterious Island*.)

Unlike the 2005 telefilm, which had used the appropriate name "Cyrus Smith" from the fresh, more accurate translation, the new filmmakers returned to the name "Harding" used in the flawed older English edition. More damaging is the exposition; accelerating volcanic eruptions start to destroy the island but also drive the creatures out by day, and the attempt to transform Nemo's previous technical mumbo-jumbo into a way off the island through a new portal leads to a preposterous denouement. Initially suggesting a tiny steam engine, Harding's invention to guide the balloon must be tossed overboard to ascend. First, however, Herbert is killed by the monsters—who turn out to be Nemo's men gone insane, dressing in furs and turning cannibal. Nemo, dying (apparently of consumption), is left behind aboard the *Nautilus*. As the balloon ascends thanks to the volcano's vapors, carrying Nemo's time machine into a vortex, a voice asks, "That which is far off and exceeding deep, who can find it?"—echoing Ecclesiastes 7:24, the final sentence of *Twenty Thousand Leagues under the Seas* but without the purpose for which it is used in the novel.

Such an open-ended resolution suggests the possibility that *Jules Verne's Mysterious Island* was serving as a television pilot.[15] Its grab bag of clichés seemed to fulfill the expectations and demographics of Saturday night Syfy Channel viewers, garnering a successful 2.4 million.[16] The second-rate, sometimes transparent special effects are the least of its faults; given the fast shooting schedule, the acting provided by Munro, Holden, and the elder Sheppard is commendable. Although the filmmakers pleaded the impossibility of adapting such an epic novel for their two-hour time slot and budget limitation ($1.1 million), the fault is not in such limitations; there have been, of course, many acceptable low-budget Verne movies.[17] To cast a certain number of Louisiana actors, to use local scenery, and to satisfy Syfy Channel demands for monsters are understandable—but not to draw the monsters from the people who once accompanied an otherwise respectable Nemo and with so little rationale. This version will be most remembered for this crass indignity, with Cameron Larson's script spiraling into absurdity.

The most fortuitous follow-up to *Journey to the Center of the Earth 3D* reunited four of the producers (Beau Flynn, Charlotte Huggins, Evan Turner, and Tripp Vinson), composer Andrew Lockington, and 3D for the descriptively titled *Journey 2: The Mysterious Island*. With costar Michael Caine having once played Nemo in 1997, his casting cleverly opened the question of what role Nemo would have in this version of the story, and the answer remained deliberately concealed from trailers until the opening weekend. Like its predecessor, *Journey 2* is based, from the movie's opening words of Caine's narration, in the belief that Vernians know that the author's nineteenth-century writing is not science fiction, but fact. (This assertion is clearly meant facetiously, not factually in the more facile manner of documentaries such as *Prophets of Science Fiction* that literally connect the author to modern science.)

*Journey 2: The Mysterious Island* also reflected for the first time how video games based on Verne's works had begun to influence the films. Dreamcatcher, having several other Verne stories in video game form to its credit, had offered the game *Return to Mysterious Island* (produced with the Adventure Company) in 2005. Mina, a girl sailing around the world, is stranded on an uninhabited island, where she interacts with the ghost of Captain Nemo, finds the remnants of the settlement of Verne's castaways, and is able to use the solutions they found as she too struggles to survive. A 2009 video game sequel, *Return to Mysterious Island 2: Mina's Fate,* continues her story as the helicopter sent to rescue her crashes; she remains trapped on the island and must save the plants and animals from outside pollution.[18] Aspects of the *Return to Mysterious Island* video games were incorporated into *Journey 2,* no less than *Journey to the Center of the Earth 3D* used elements of the ride based on Verne's novel at Tokyo DisneySea. There, traveling aboard a mine trolley allows an excursion into the amazing underground world of colors and monsters conceived by Verne.[19] The center of Tokyo Disney-Sea is the live volcano of Mysterious Island, from which the participant can also take the 20,000 Leagues under the Sea submarine ride in search of Atlantis. For both *Journey to the Center of the Earth 3D* and *Journey 2,* the filmmakers were wisely aware that many audiences were almost as likely to have experienced theme park attractions or video games as the author's original novels.[20] The possible intertextuality influencing the creation of Verne movies had increased; no longer were video games or theme park evocations based solely on movies already produced—as had been the case with Disney attractions derived from *20,000 Leagues under the Sea.* The four influences—the novels, previous screen versions, theme park rides, and video games—now combined in the creation of a new film.

In *Journey 2,* Sean Anderson, again played by Josh Hutcherson, visibly older than in the first installment, still facilitates the sense of commonality with the target youthful audience. His new companion is not his uncle, but his stepfather, Hank (Dwayne "The Rock" Johnson). Sean is a typical rebellious teenager, but one steeped in Verniana, his room cluttered with mementoes of the author, just as Hannah Asgeirsson still had her father's Hetzel volumes of Verne on the bookshelves. Sean receives a radio cryptogram using the names of Verne characters, which proves to be from Sean's grandfather Alexander. Sean and Hank decipher the cryptogram as indicating that Jonathan Swift's *Gulliver's Travels* (1726), Robert Louis Stevenson's *Treasure Island* (1883), and Verne's *The Mysterious Island* all refer to the same supposedly fictional lost island in the South Pacific, located near Palau.

This time, rather than a modern soft cover of the novel *Journey to the Center of the Earth,* accompanying Sean is the 1875 edition published by Henry L. Shepard of Boston, *The Mysterious Island: Shipwrecked in the Air,* and the subtitle proves prescient. Only a battered helicopter, piloted by Gabato (Luis Guzmán) with his daughter, Kailani (Vanessa Hudgens), will convey Sean and Hank to the island when other pilots insist superstitiously that no such body of land exists. Rather than the balloon of Verne's novel, it is the helicopter that crashes in the storm in spectacular 3D.

Ashore, the survivors, like Verne's travelers, are almost bereft of supplies, with only a backpack between them. Inland proves a sight no less amazing than the center of the earth: the Mysterious Island, verdant, filled with waterfalls, surmounted by a volcano from which wisps of smoke emerge. They find both adorable Lilliputian elephants and a terrifying giant lizard, from which they are saved by a trap engineered by Alexander (Caine), who has built an elaborate Swiss Robinson–style tree house. This tree house confirms the emphasis on family: Sean with his stepfather and grandfather, Gabato with his daughter. However, there is tension between Alexander and Hank, insider and outsider, as the two meet for the first time. Whereas in *Journey to the Center of the Earth 3D,* Sean and Uncle Trevor were almost equally inspired to undertake the search for Sean's father in the center of the earth, in *Journey 2* Sean is initiating Hank; as Alexander tells Hank at first, he is clearly not an Anderson. By the conclusion of *Journey 2,* the family tensions are resolved as Hank demonstrates his own adventurous skill, he and Sean matching one another as nephew and uncle had previously. Only in some attempts at humor by coproducer and star Johnson does *Journey 2* veer into too jocular a tone.

Despite the brief early allusions to Swift and Stevenson, the evocation of Verne dominates the script by Brian Gunn and Mark Gunn from their story (written with Richard Outten) and directed by Brad Peyton. Alexander takes them to a lost city: the Grecian-style Atlantis (which Nemo had shown to Aronnax undersea in the novel *Twenty Thousand Leagues under the Seas*). However, Hank realizes what Alexander has not, that saltwater is again about to submerge the island ahead of schedule, and they need a quick escape, one that will allow them to depart in a matter of hours—reminiscent of the seismic peril that impels the travelers in *Journey to the Center of the Earth 3D.* Of course, there is only one way off the island: the *Nautilus,* conveniently left behind by Verne, and *Journey 2* charts a new course in screen treatments revitalizing the submarine.

The question of the *Nautilus*'s location, however, as Alexander declares, can be solved only by Captain Nemo, and at once the invocation of his name brings uncertainty and wonder. Nemo is not immortal, although his reach extends beyond the grave; for the first time, a film depicts his tomb, built by his crew adjacent to Atlantis. Only Kailani is sufficiently petite to enter a shaft and secure Nemo's journal clutched by his corpse; a headband and white tufts of beard distinguish the great man's skull. In a throwaway line that is wholly unnecessary for most audiences but reveals the filmmakers' immersion in all matters Vernian, Nemo is identified as an Indian, whose writing is naturally in Hindi.

The *Nautilus* proves to be on the other side of the island, and Sean and Hank must dive into the grotto where the *Nautilus* has remained

*Journey 2: The Mysterious Island* (2012) offered a cinematic first—Captain Nemo's tomb and remains.

submerged for 140 years. With an eel emitting sparks threatening them, they manage to open the diving hatch just in time and are able to operate the *Nautilus*. Whereas most filmmakers would have explained this ability to operate the submarine through the characters' naval experience (as in *The Amazing Captain Nemo*), in *Journey 2* it is credited to their reading the Verne novel, a visual motif in the film; for instance, Hank is engrossed in the book even during the trek across the island. The *Nautilus*'s dormant batteries (a prop that, in contrast to the conventional substitution of nuclear power, remains faithful to Verne) are jumpstarted when Hank dives and throws the familiar harpoon at the eel, allowing another allusion to *Twenty Thousand Leagues under the Seas*: this time the harpoon, once hurled vainly at the vessel by Ned Land, now brings the *Nautilus* to life.

Although Verne had casually foreclosed the possibility of a second voyage of the *Nautilus* by placing it in a grotto that becomes blocked by a landslide, *Journey 2* renders the grotto's reopening just as possible, bringing the *Nautilus* vibrantly back to life in 3D, allowing Nemo's science to live on. The *Nautilus* itself, both inside and outside, is an original design, the interior resembling a nineteenth-century vessel, not a modern equivalent. Its exterior is closest to the "manta ray"–style depiction

Hank takes on a role similar to Ned Land's to harpoon an electric eel and revitalize the dormant batteries of the *Nautilus* in *Journey 2: The Mysterious Island* (2012).

of the 1997 miniseries *20,000 Leagues under the Sea* as well as that of *Captain Nemo and the Underwater City*. It even navigates like a flying wing, with Gabato able to guide it, so that everyone is saved by the vessel even as the island crumbles into the sea around them. This *Nautilus,* like that of other screen versions back to 1916, is fortunately equipped with torpedoes able to destroy boulders blocking its way.

Six months after this escape from the Mysterious Island, Kailani visits Sean's family to celebrate his birthday; the earlier tension between them has had the expected cinematic resolution as she comes to respect his heroism. Kailani's father is now prospering by using the *Nautilus* to guide tourists on views to appreciate the marvels of the deep, so that in a way it serves much of Nemo's original purpose; it does not seem a sad fate for his vessel. Alexander's birthday gift to his grandson is a nineteenth-century copy of *From the Earth to the Moon;* as the camera goes out into space to end the film on a view of the moon in the foreground, Earth at a distance, a further sequel is hinted at, one that would tell of a journey even more incredible than those that came before it.

In traversing the island, the castaways are showered with volcanic ash of gold. In 2008, the original text of Verne's novel *The Golden Volcano* had first appeared in English, part of a series from several publishers between 2002 to 2014 of works hitherto translated only from revisions by Michel Verne, Jules's son.²¹ The expanding Anglophone corpus facilitated extending the degree of referentiality in Vernian filmmaking; interjecting *The Golden Volcano* as one of the inspirations of *Journey 2* added a disquisition compatible with Verne's novel on the deceptive worth of gold.²²

As proved with *Journey to the Center of the Earth 3D*, successful Verne filmmaking in the twenty-first century requires a consciousness of the author, his work, and the long history of adaptations of that work. Unlike the jumbled mishmash of *Jules Verne's Mysterious Island*, *Journey 2* is a coherent, original confection, one that lives in Verne's world despite the changes it makes to the primary source novel. At ninety-four minutes, its running time is almost the same as *Jules Verne's Mysterious Island,* and the benefits from a bigger budget simply added gloss. Watching *Journey 2* is an exhilarating experience, beyond an adaptation, as the audience is surprised by the many allusions to Verne's novels and their interpretations, manipulating knowledge of the outline of the narratives and previous screen adaptations. By this point in Verne filmmaking, Ray Harryhausen's 1961 additions to *The Mysterious Island* narrative have become a part of the collective memory of audiences, and *Journey 2* includes an inspired homage to Harryhausen's giant bees, with Sean and his companions riding bees like aerial horses, pursued by even larger birds in an elaborate, breathtaking computer-generated race across the island—a far more able tribute than the blatant Harryhausen imitation in the 2005 telefilm *Mysterious Island*. Both *Journey to the Center of the Earth 3D* and *Journey 2* succeed in setting Verne in a modern world rather than in the nineteenth century, which appeals to its intended youthful audience yet brings to life Vernian tropes—aerial castaways, a mysterious island, the golden volcano, and the *Nautilus*. No less than *Journey to the Center of the Earth 3D*, *Journey 2* opens a portal to Verne's world in an entertaining manner far more likely to entice the viewer than a documentary and offers narrative experiences akin to those a reader might experience. While building on the elements of *Journey to the Center of the Earth 3D* to make a transition to *The Mysterious Island* and incorporating *Twenty Thousand Leagues under the Seas* and even *The Golden Volcano*, *Journey 2* also offers a variety of fresh interpretations of the Vernian world, which render it, just like *Journey to the Center of the Earth 3D,* simultaneously an adaptation and a pastiche.[23] It similarly resonated with its intended audience, earning its $80 million budget back after a few weeks, and was for a month the number-one picture at the foreign box office, by March 2012 outgrossing the first installment of the *Journey* cycle.[24] Together, the brilliant combination of Vernian elements offered by the two *Journey* movies in 2008 and 2012 demonstrated the original big-screen possibilities for the author in the twenty-first century.

# Epilogue

The elements of pastiche and homage to the author in the *Journey* 3D series were the result of the widespread availability of Verne to small-screen viewers. Narratives could be integrated in fresh ways, and newly published stories that appeared in English for the first time could be tapped into. So, too, novels retranslated, often complete for the first time in English, would inspire filmmakers from the 1997 telefilm and miniseries of *Twenty Thousand Leagues under the Seas* to the 2005 version of *The Mysterious Island*. In 1914, Verne films had been affected by their stage versions; in the 1970s animated adaptations had been influenced by comic books; and by 2012 Verne films would be impacted by video game adaptations as the range of intertextuality steadily increased.

During the twentieth century, a canon of Verne films has served to introduce the author to new audiences, not only English speakers but also non-English speakers around the globe, creating a benchmark by which subsequent films were constantly compared. *20,000 Leagues under the Sea* (1954), *Around the World in 80 Days* (1956), *Journey to the Center of the Earth* (1959), *Master of the World* (1961), *Mysterious Island* (1961), *Five Weeks in a Balloon* (1962), *In Search of the Castaways* (1962), the 1989 miniseries *Around the World in 80 Days*, and the 1997 telefilm *20,000 Leagues under the Sea* had become staples of television broadcasts and video releases. *Journey to the Center of the Earth 3D* and *Journey 2: The Mysterious Island* demonstrated how the canon need not stultify but might suggest new approaches.

In many cases, foreign productions have equaled or bested Hollywood efforts, as in adaptations of *Five Weeks in a Balloon* and *The Jangada*. Others have a surprising amount of commonality with their

American counterparts, making similar narrative choices, as in several European versions of *Master Zacharius,* but some cinematic stories have yet to be adequately brought to the screen in any nation, such as *Hector Servadac.* In other countries, filmmakers have successfully adapted stories that would seem promising for Hollywood but have been overlooked, from the chronicle of invisibility *The Secret of Wilhelm Storitz* to the tale of an underground city in *The Black Indies.*

Formula has often twisted adaptations into avenues for which they are not suited. Robert Halmi Sr. inflicted major love subplots on his Hallmark renditions of Verne—the 1997 telefilm *20,000 Leagues under the Sea,* the 1999 miniseries *Journey to the Center of the Earth,* and its 2008 telefilm remake. His view was that such a romance was essential, saying that Verne "was far less interested in telling a dramatic story than he was in just exemplifying science. The stories were never really strong dramatically."[1] His remarks almost precisely echo those of Alfred Zimbalist, producer of *Valley of the Dragons* (1961), who said, "One thing about Verne . . . whatever you say about his imagination and his genius, he just did not have a good story line."[2] Yet as frequently as such logic is found, it is far from dominant, whether in feature filmmaking, television, or animation.

Verne stories continue to offer a fertile field for the film industry. Many exciting Verne adventures, such as *Mistress Branican* and *Wonderful Adventures of Master Antifer* (1895), remain completely untapped, and there are more. *The Will of an Eccentric,* featuring a race in the style of *Around the World in Eighty Days,* except across America rather than the globe, would seem an obvious television miniseries, a natural in this country. So would *The Hunt for the Meteor,* with its American protagonists and science fiction theme, so much more probable and original than other recent cinematic treatments of objects from space endangering the earth. *Family without a Name* (1889) dramatizes the roots of the struggle for Quebec nationalism.

With all the publicity that surrounded its discovery and its deep cynicism commensurate with modern dystopias, *Paris in the 20th Century* remains unfilmed. So does the futuristic *Propeller Island,* with its portrayal of how a potential technological paradise for the superrich is destroyed by the reemergence of national, ethnic, and religious hatreds.

*The Steam House,* with its historical setting and automated elephant, would be the ultimate steampunk adventure and could now be brought to the screen with convincing special effects or through animation. In a time when creationism and evolution remain at the focus of debates, *The Aerial Village* would seem a natural, and *Adventures of the Rat Family* is an ideal candidate for the trend toward animated Verne adaptations. Nor should we forget the powerful combination of modern race relations in the developing world in Jules and Michel Verne's *The Astonishing Adventure of the Barsac Mission* (1914), depicting the crumbling of a superscientific, white-ruled city in the Sahara.

The process of adapting Jules Verne's works to movies and television is hardly at an end after more than a century. The peak years of Verne film production and importation in the United States, the 1950s through the early 1970s, are receding into the distance, but the product of that cycle is more widely viewed than ever as television replays these many movies almost endlessly, amplifying their impact.

Enough time has passed for three generations, of which I count myself a member, to have received their initial impression and knowledge of Verne from these media renderings. Such an introduction implies the formation of preconceptions and expectations that will inevitably shape how Verne books are subsequently read and received. Verne has become an author whose reputation has to a large degree been shaped by filmmakers to create a legend not always related to the concerns of his books. This is why many of the films discussed here are so important beyond their inherent cultural and artistic significance or their impact on the science fiction genre. Verne films demonstrate the reverse relationship that the process of adaptation has on literature, movies forming the way an author is understood. As such, they are a vital part of the worldwide Verne phenomenon and have become one with the larger Vernian text known everywhere.

# Acknowledgments

My interest in Jules Verne in film goes back to the time when as a ten-year-old I happened to see *Master of the World* on television. I had already begun to read Verne's books and soon was seeking more, including biographies and critical studies, writing term papers and boring my *Star Trek*–minded classmates with presentations on this nineteenth-century author. My interest continued during my studies in film at the University of Southern California, where I found much encouragement.

This book owes a very special debt to three individuals in particular, one of whom is noted in the dedication. Another is director Robert Florey, a Verne aficionado himself. As a boy, Florey had lived near the Georges Méliès studio and watched him film his Vernian creations, and he unfolded to me the dynamic exchange between Verne and the cinema that had existed from the beginning of the twentieth century. Florey's guidance of my youthful hobby ensured that it would flower, and his gift of 1870s Hetzel editions for my twelfth birthday allowed me to perceive the breadth involved in understanding Verne.

No book of mine on Verne could also fail to mention the third mentor in my life, Walter James Miller, whose Verne translations I first read at age eleven and guaranteed a proper grasp of the author. When I finally met Walter in 1990, a twenty-year friendship ensued, and my Verne scholarship will always be indebted to his lead and personal kindness.

By the late 1980s, Stephen Michaluk Jr. and I began compiling *The Jules Verne Encyclopedia,* published by Scarecrow in 1996. Partly as a result of this research, we delineated the many Verne stories that remained untranslated into English, and although it had been twenty-five years since any had appeared in English for the first time, in 1993 I was able to persuade Oxford University Press to issue a translation of

Verne's only fairy tale, *Adventures of the Rat Family* (1891). For this edition, I wrote an afterword on the Verne stories not yet available in English, and in the wake of *The Jules Verne Encyclopedia* and *Adventures of the Rat Family,* other first-time Verne translations began to appear. In 2010, the North American Jules Verne Society asked me to edit its Palik series, stories and plays by Verne that had never before been published in English; as this book goes to press, nine Palik volumes have appeared, all illustrated critical editions.

I am grateful for the encouragement offered by other Vernians around the world. The filmographies by Hervé Dumont and Daniel Compère were an international foundation. Jean-Michel Margot and Philippe Burgaud provided invaluable information and videos accessible only in Europe. Ross Bagby rigorously read this manuscript and gave helpful suggestions. Dennis Kytasaari's mutual interest in film resulted in sharing data and videos. Bert Grollman secured a VHS of *The Day before Tomorrow,* and Garmt de Vries-Uiterweerd assisted with material from the Nederlands Filmmuseum. Jan Rychlík contributed his thoughts on European Verne filmmaking, and John Goodwin allowed me to read his script of *The Steam House.* Arnie Davis scanned Verne covers from his incomparable movie tie-in book collection. Larry Brooks, the leading expert on Disney's *20,000 Leagues under the Sea,* generously shared his knowledge.

I am especially thankful to my Library of Congress colleagues Zoran Sinobad, George Willeman, Colleen Cahill, Carol Armbruster, and Clark Evans. Ned Comstock of the University of Southern California Cinema Library went the extra mile in assisting my research. James Layton and Crystal Kui of George Eastman House provided images and data on the 1929 version of *The Mysterious Island.* At the Centre d'études verniennes de Nantes, Agnès Marcetteau and Jean-Michel Margot facilitated my study of the Verne family's film-related papers.

Kevin Brownlow, Marc Sandberg, Lenny Borger, and Francis Lacassin kindly supplied information from their historical knowledge. Karen Lund taped programs from obscure cable channels. The Margaret Herrick Library of the Academy of Motion Picture Arts & Sciences provided information on various films. Over the years, such dealers as Movie Poster Service and Eddie Brandt's Saturday Matinee sympathetically bolstered my collection of Verne movie memorabilia, and I benefitted from scans preserved by Ed Poole at learnaboutmovieposters.com. Elvira Berkowitsch and Pachara Yongvongpaibul furnished help in preparing the illustrations.

Filmmakers Edward Bernds, Michael Anderson, Ken Adam, Juan Piquer Simón, George MacDonald Fraser, Nicholas Meyer, Richard Matheson, William Witney, and Robert Florey generously shared their experiences of Verne filmmaking. I had the pleasure of the company of Ray Harryhausen for several days during a panel and screenings at the Cinema Retrospective Jules Verne, which I organized at the Utopiales, Festival International de Science-Fiction de Nantes, November 10–13, 2005. Maria Towers kindly responded to questions about the Verne work by her late husband, Harry Alan Towers. Sylvia Munro, the daughter of undersea film pioneer John Ernest Williamson, facilitated my examination of her father's papers at the Bahamas Archive and of the relics and records of the locales of his filmmaking in the islands.

This book is the outcome of decades of viewing and reflecting on these films, writing articles, curating festivals, reading Verne, discovering more films, learning about productions that nearly came to fruition, and experiencing decades of shifts as new Verne films have been produced for the large and small screen.

My love goes to my mother, who has always supported my interests, and to my wife, Pachara, who always understands—no man has been more fortunate.

# Notes

## Introduction

1. Quoted in Gregory Benford, "Introduction: The Exact Dreamer," in Jules Verne, *From the Earth to the Moon,* translated by Lowell Bair (New York: Bantam, 2008), xvii. Asimov more formally labeled the author as "Father Jules" in his foreword to the combination volume *20,000 Leagues under the Sea and Around the Moon* (New York: Platt & Munk, 1965).

2. Marc Angenot, "Jules Verne: The Last Happy Utopianist," in Patrick Parrinder, ed., *Science Fiction: A Critical Guide* (London: Longman, 1979), 29; Walter James Miller, "Jules Verne," in Jane M. Bingham, ed., *Writers for Children* (New York: Scribner's, 1988), 596.

3. Walter James Miller, foreword to *The Annotated Jules Verne: Twenty Thousand Leagues under the Sea* (New York: Thomas Y. Crowell, 1976), xiii, xviii.

4. Jean Chesneaux, *The Political and Social Ideas of Jules Verne,* translated by Thomas Wikely (London: Thames and Hudson, 1972), passim.

5. Miller, foreword to *The Annotated Jules Verne: Twenty Thousand Leagues under the Sea,* xvii–xix, xiii.

6. Chesneaux, *The Political and Social Ideas of Jules Verne,* 198; Jean Jules-Verne, *Jules Verne: A Biography,* translated and adapted by Roger Greaves (New York: Taplinger, 1976).

7. Alberto Savinio, *Operatic Lives,* translated by John Shepley (Marlboro, VT: Marlboro Press, 1989), 101.

8. Throughout this book, I give literal English translations of the original French titles and the date of their publication in France. This is the only possible consistent method because Verne's sixty-eight novels, dozens of short stories, works of nonfiction, and plays have appeared in more than a century of different translations, retitlings, and abridgements, sufficiently baffling for Anglo-American readers but utterly incomprehensible to those approaching Verne from other cultural contexts. For instance, if a reader attempts to find the novel that inspired the 1962 Walt Disney film *In Search of the Castaways,* he or she would find no original work in French matching that title. However, Verne's long novel *Les Enfants du Capitaine Grant* (1868) became in various translations not only *The Children of Captain Grant* and *Captain Grant's Chil-*

*dren* but also *In Search of the Castaways, The Castaways, A Voyage around the World,* and, depending on the translation, two separate trilogies known as *The Mysterious Document, On the Track,* and *Among the Cannibals* and *South America, Australia,* and *New Zealand.*

9. *The Hunt for the Meteor* is the title of the version of this novel extensively rewritten by the author's son, Michel Verne; Jules had concentrated entirely on American characters, but Michel had added a major French character, skewing Jules's intended exclusively American focus.

Michel also authored a story of the next millennium, "In the Year 2889," first published in the United States under his father's name and subsequently often reprinted as the work of the father, not the son.

For the most extensive analysis of *The Will of an Eccentric,* see the afterword to the first American edition, published in 2009 by Choptank Press.

10. Miller, foreword to *The Annotated Jules Verne: Twenty Thousand Leagues under the Sea,* vii.

11. As a result, Verne became a sort of cultural icon, in France especially. Verne's regular yearly output had become so expected in his day that André Maurois wrote, "I well remember the impression his death made upon the young Frenchmen of the time; his annual book had seemed to us to be a part of the laws of the universe, like the changing seasons" ("Jules Verne Sets the Pace for Modern Adventure," *New York Times Magazine,* March 23, 1930, 22).

12. Not even the title as it was given accurately reflects what Verne wrote; he had entitled his 1893 Dickensian novel *P'tit Bonhomme* (Little boy). For details on the abridgements, see the critical material by Walter James Miller in *The Annotated Jules Verne: Twenty Thousand Leagues under the Sea* and by Kieran O'Driscoll in Jules Verne, *The Extraordinary Adventures of Foundling Mick* (Dublin: Royal Irish Academy, 2008).

13. Edward Roth, preface to Jules Verne, *From the Earth to the Moon and All around the Moon* (New York: Dover, 1962), 5. For more on Roth, see Brian Taves and Stephen Michaluk Jr., *The Jules Verne Encyclopedia* (Lanham, MD: Scarecrow Press, 1996), 113–114; I. O. Evans, *Jules Verne and His Work* (London: Arco, 1966), 144–145. The contacts with Dover regarding its 2009 reprint of the Roth edition are revealed in Walter James Miller and Brian Taves, "The Tribulations of Responding to a Publisher," *Extraordinary Voyages* 15 (March 2009): 9–10.

Inaccurate translations reached their nadir when *The Invasion of the Sea* was "translated from the original French and edited by Oswald Mathew" for the American-Journal-Examiner newspapers as *Captain Hardizan,* serialized in late summer 1905. Instead of Verne's clash between indigenous customs and colonial opportunism as plans are made to irrigate the Sahara for the French navy, Mathew departed from the original plot after a few chapters to substitute a story of a European heroine who is taken hostage by Arab bandits, in turn led by a woman with apparent supernatural powers in situations reminiscent of H. Rider Haggard's *King Solomon's Mines* (1885) and *She* (1887).

14. Jules Verne, *The Demon of Cawnpore,* translated by A. D. Kingston (New York: Scribner's, 1881), 44 n. 1.

15. Jules Verne, *The Demon of Cawnpore*, edited by I. O. Evans (Westport, CT: Associated Booksellers, 1959).

16. To use this idea in a movie, filmmakers had to develop one of the most complex renderings of Verne. The original book, *Les Chateau des Carpathes*, revealed the combined influences of Jacques Offenbach, E. T. A. Hoffman, Edgar Allan Poe, and the gothic and has since been turned into Georges Aphergis's opera *Pandemonium* as well as a French television production in 1976. In 1981, a Romanian adaptation was filmed, *Castelul din Carpati* (Castle in the Carpathians), but the most widely seen version also appeared in 1981, the Czechoslovakian production *Tajemstvi hradu v Karpatech* (The mysterious castle in the Carpathians). See Brian Taves, "Reviews: *The Mysterious Castle in the Carpathians*," *Film Quarterly* 38 (Winter 1984–1985): 48–50. Details from *Le Chateau des Carpathes* have also been used in other Verne films, such as *Le Secret de Wilhelm Storitz* (Czechoslovakia/France, 1967) and *L'Ile mysterieuse* (a 1973 television miniseries also released as a theatrical feature film), in which Captain Nemo uses a sort of motion picture to reveal his autobiography to the castaways.

17. At present, the only truly global, multiform survey of Verne on film is to be found in Pierre Gires and Hervé Dumont, "Jules Verne et le cinéma," *L'Ecran fantastique*, no. 9 (1979): 58–109. A note on counting the number of adaptations: Each individual work (or a sequel to it) has been counted separately, although an entire serial, series, or miniseries (such as one devoted to *Around the World in Eighty Days* or the series *The Secret Adventures of Jules Verne*) has been counted as a single work. This seems closest to the consensus view per a discussion on the H-film listserve on March 15–16, 2011 (https://networks .h-net.org/h-film), which, however, also revealed the lack of an established pattern, largely a result of the tendency for adaptation studies to be concerned with a specific feature film, not taking television and series into account.

18. Among my articles on Verne on screen outside the Hollywood context are "Appendix: The Play on Screen," in Jules Verne and Adolphe D'Ennery, *Around the World in Eighty Days—The 1874 Play* (Albany, GA: BearManor Fiction, 2013); "En pantalla: El maestro relojero en versión libre—Maestro Zacarías," translated into Spanish by Sergio O. Manancero, *Mundo Verne*, nos. 9–10 (2009): 21–24; "Expedition into a Novel," *Verniana* 1 (2008–2009): 23–29, reprinted by Jules Verne Genootschap in *De Verniaan*, no. 47 (2010): 23–26; "Adapting Jules Verne's *Journey to the Center of the Earth*," *Extraordinary Voyages* 12 (September 2005): 1–13, with an updated version posted online at the North American Jules Verne Society website, http://najvs.org/articles/ JCErev.shtml, in September 2008; "The Novels and Rediscovered Films of Michel (Jules) Verne," *Journal of Film Preservation*, no. 62 (April 2001): 25–39, translated into German by Volker Dehs as "Die Romane und wieder entdeckten Filme von Michel (Jules) Verne," in Volker Dehs and Ralf Junkerjurgen, eds., *Jules Verne—Stimmen und Deutungen zu seinem Werk*, 295–314 (Wetzlar, Germany: Phantastische Bibliothek, 2005), and shortened as "Michel Verne, de l'ecrivain au realisateur," *Revue Jules Verne* 19–20 (2005): 190–195; "Les

Récentes émissions documentaires sur Jules Verne à la television," translated into French by Jean-Michel Margot, *Bulletin de la Société Jules Verne,* no. 125 (1998): 44–52; "Jules Verne et Walt Disney," translated into French by Philippe Burgaud, *Bulletin de la Société Jules Verne,* no. 113 (1995): 8–11; and "Reviews: *The Mysterious Castle in the Carpathians.*" In organizing the Cinema Retrospective Jules Verne at the Utopiales, Festival International de Science-Fiction de Nantes, November 10–13, 2005, I ensured the emphasis was on European films and telefilms of Verne's work, not on the usual Hollywood versions; see Brian Taves, "Cinema at the Utopiales in Nantes, November 10–13, 2005," *Extraordinary Voyages* 12 (December 2005): 9.

19. Thomas Renzi has fully explored this approach in attempting to identify possible derivations that do not credit the author in *Jules Verne on Film: A Filmography of the Cinematic Adaptations of His Works, 1902 through 1997* (Jefferson, NC: McFarland, 1998). However, problems inevitably result; for instance, Renzi lists *The People That Time Forgot* (1977) as inspired by Verne's *Journeys and Adventures of Captain Hatteras,* but there is no lost race in Verne's novel, and the film is based on an Edgar Rice Burroughs source and was produced as a sequel to *The Land That Time Forgot* (1975). Renzi took a different, more successful tack in *H. G. Wells: Six Scientific Romances Adapted for Film,* 2nd ed. (Lanham, MD: Scarecrow, 2004).

20. Françoise Schiltz's *The Future Revisited: Jules Verne on Screen in 1950s America* (London: Chaplin, 2011) samples for cultural themes of the time five of the most renowned 1950s and early 1960s live-action Verne films (renowned by today's standard, not according to their success at the time of release).

21. For an examination of all the adaptations of a single book, see Taves, "Adapting Jules Verne's *Journey to the Center of the Earth.*"

## 1. The Silents

1. Although the influence and spirit of his fellow countryman is seen throughout his oeuvre, Méliès produced four unmistakable Verne adaptations: *A Trip to the Moon* (1902), based on *From the Earth to the Moon* and *Around the Moon* as well as the 1874 operetta *Voyage dans la lune* by Jacques Offenbach and H. G. Wells's *The First Men in the Moon* (1901); *The Impossible Journey / Whirling the Worlds* (1904), from the play *Journey through the Impossible; Two Hundred Thousand Leagues under the Sea* or *A Fisherman's Nightmare / Under the Sea* (1907), from the novel resembling the former title; and *The Conquest of the Pole* (1912), from several Verne works dealing with the poles, most notably *The Sphinx of Ice* (1897).

2. See Taves, "The Novels and Rediscovered Films of Michel (Jules) Verne," and two volumes, translated and with notes by Kieran O'Driscoll, in the Palik Series published by BearManor Fiction in conjunction with the North American Jules Verne Society: Jules Verne and Michel Verne, *Vice, Redemption, and the Distant Colony* (2012), and Jules Verne, *Golden Danube* (2014).

3. The North American Jules Verne Society has brought to print the first

critical editions of Verne's plays translated into English. The first was Jules Verne and Adolphe d'Ennery, *Journey through the Impossible*, translated by Edward Baxter, introduction and notes by Jean-Michel Margot (Amherst, NY: Prometheus, 2003). Subsequent volumes have appeared in the society's Palik Series, published in Albany, Georgia, by BearManor Fiction. They have included, to date (with more to appear), Jules Verne with Michel Carré, Charles Wallut, and Victorien Sardou, *Mr. Chimp and Other Plays*, translated by Frank Morlock, introduction by Jean-Michel Margot (2011); Jules Verne and Adolphe d'Ennery, *Around the World in 80 Days—the 1874 Play*, with the original translation commissioned by the Kiralfy Brothers, published for the first time since 1874, with critical material by Philippe Burgaud, Jean-Michel Margot, Brian Taves, and Jean-Louis Trudel (2013).

4. "Michael Strogoff," *Variety*, December 8, 1926, 16 (no volume number available).

5. Advertisement in *New York Clipper* 58 (March 19, 1910): 152.

6. The only surviving print is held at the Library of Congress, Motion Picture/Broadcasting/Recorded Sound Division.

7. A decade later the studio remade *After Five*, this time under the title *The Night Club*, but changed the story completely, in part to accommodate star comedian Raymond Griffith. Verne's notion of the arranged suicide, which had still been central to *After Five*, instead becomes fodder for a mere subplot that occupies a fifth of *The Night Club*.

8. Jules Verne, "Future of the Submarine," *Popular Mechanics*, June 1904. Both "San Carlos" and "Future of the Submarine," along with critical and historical background by Daniel Compère on "San Carlos," are included in the first book publication in English of both: Jules Verne, *Bandits & Rebels* (Albany, GA: BearManor Fiction, 2013).

9. The title refers to the total distance traveled while underwater rather than to an impossible depth. The plural form *seas* more accurately reflects the original French title, *Vingt mille sous les mers*, but *mers* has been typically translated as "sea" in the singular, *Twenty Thousand Leagues under the Sea*.

10. The persistence of these themes' impact was demonstrated when Wyss's novel became one of the two books to which Verne wrote a sequel, *Second Homeland* (1900).

11. *The Mysterious Island* actually evolved from a book Verne had begun in 1861 but had never completed because of his publisher's negative reaction. *Uncle Robinson* concentrates on family characters and was finally published in France in 1991. It was first published in English in 2011 in the Palik Series by the North American Jules Verne Society and BearManor Fiction under the title *Shipwrecked Family: Marooned with Uncle Robinson*. The title was changed because Verne had used "Robinson" in the title of his 1882 novel, *The School for Robinsons*.

12. Anthony Boucher, "Introduction," in Jules Verne, *The Mysterious Island* (New York: Dodd, Mead, 1958), n.p.

13. Readers should avoid the incomplete and inaccurate older translations

that christen Cyrus Smith as "Cyrus Harding," a name used in Hollywood film versions of the twentieth century.

14. S. J. Perelman, "Cloudland Revisited," *New Yorker* 28 (August 16, 1952): 24–27. This amusing piece is unfortunately an all too accurate account of *Twenty Thousand Leagues under the Sea* (1916).

15. The India set on the Universal lot would be utilized again shortly afterward in the studio's melodrama *The Gates of Doom* (1917).

16. Not until 2009 was Robida's book translated by Brian Stableford as *The Adventures of Saturnin Farandoul.*

Sequels have been an important part of the Vernian canon from the beginning, since the author himself made use of this concept when at the outset of his career he created sequels to his own work. He began with *Around the Moon* (1869), the almost inescapable conclusion to his open-ended novel *From the Earth to the Moon,* written four years earlier. Although the lunar saga was thereby brought to closure, Verne would recall his heroes of the Baltimore Gun Club for a third and last time nineteen years later in *Topsy-turvy* (1889). In the same way, eighteen years after the glories of *Robur the Conqueror* (1886), the aerial hero would be brought back as the menace of *Master of the World.* Although *The Children of Captain Grant* and *Twenty Thousand Leagues under the Seas* were complete novels, Verne provided an ultimate sense of finality by incorporating the fate of Ayrton and Captain Nemo in *The Mysterious Island.* Verne's play *Journey through the Impossible* lampooned situations from many of his novels and provided further exploits. He would also author original sequels to two novels by writers who had influenced him. *Second Homeland* offered another adventure of Johann Wyss's family of the Swiss Robinson in the spirit of the original, but Verne believed Edgar Allan Poe's *The Narrative of Arthur Gordon Pym of Nantucket* (1838) was incomplete, and so in *The Sphinx of Ice* he wound up the mystery that Poe had been content to leave open-ended. In Verne's sequels to his own work and to that of others, there is sometimes little thematic resemblance between them and the original, and he changed motivations and characterizations.

17. "Round in Fifty Scores," *New York Clipper,* April 5, 1922, 14. The play was written by Sax Rohmer, Julian Wylie, and Lauri Wylie.

## 2. Searching for a Popular Approach, 1925–1945

1. For more on the career of J. Ernest Williamson, who filmed these underwater portions, see Brian Taves, "With Williamson beneath the Sea," *Journal of Film Preservation,* no. 52 (April 1996): 54–61, and "A Pioneer under the Sea," *Library of Congress Information Bulletin* 55 (September 16, 1996): 314–318. A French version of the *Library of Congress Information Bulletin* article appeared in the *Bulletin de la Société Jules Verne,* no. 124 (1997): 46–52. For Williamson's own account, see his 1936 autobiography *Twenty Years under the Sea* (Boston: Hale, Cushman & Flint, 1936), and for his daughter's perspective see Frances Jenkins Olcott and John E. Williamson, *Child of the Deep* (Bos-

ton: Houghton Mifflin, 1938). For other perspectives, see Victor E. Allemandy, *Wonders of the Deep: The Story of the Williamson Submarine Expedition* (London: Jarrold & Sons, [1915]), and Thomas Burgess, *Take Me under the Sea: The Dream Merchants of the Deep* (Salem, OR: Ocean Archives, 1994), which focuses on George Williamson, who, unlike J. E., did not continue with filmmaking after the initial ventures. See also "20,000 Leagues under the Sea," *The Electrical Experimenter* 47 (March 1917): 791, 831.

2. Another version was issued as the "Boy Scout edition" (suggesting its intended audience), and J. S. Ogilvie issued a paperback version illustrating the film.

3. Lucien Hubbard, unpublished interview with Kevin Brownlow and David Bradley, June 1969, copy provided to me by Brownlow. See also "The Mysterious Island: 7th Wonder of the Sea," *Famous Monsters of Filmland*, no. 68 (August 1970): 7–14, reprinted in *Famous Monsters of Filmland*, no. 137 (September 1977): 43–50.

4. This 1929 film is likely to reemerge even more after the 2013 discovery of an extant color print.

5. For years, the 1926 version of *Michel Strogoff* was believed to be nearly lost, with only a three-reel 9.5 mm. Pathescope version for home distribution surviving. However, in 1988 the Cinématheque Français restored the entire full-length original French version in all of its colors and tints, and I arranged its premiere in the United States in 1997.

6. For the 1926 release, Grosset & Dunlap had mass-produced an illustrated photoplay edition of the novel, and in England a Readers Library version was issued in conjunction with the film.

7. See Stanford L. Luce Jr., "Jules Verne: Moralist, Writer, Scientist," PhD diss., Columbia University, 1953. Luce himself was influenced by his grandfather, who had collected Verne as he was first published, and more than forty years after writing his dissertation, Luce was to emerge as a major Verne translator.

8. Two years later, in 1942, Allott's biography inspired a similarly intelligent episode of the BBC radio program *The Children's Hour* by Rupert T. Gould, who was popularly known as "The Stargazer"; for a transcript, see Rupert T. Gould, *The Stargazer Talks* (London: Geoffrey Bles, 1944), 114–120.

## 3. Creating a Style, 1946–1955

1. Patrick Moore, *Science and Fiction* (London: George G. Harrap, 1957), 45; Marc Angenot, "Jules Verne and French Literary Criticism," *Science-Fiction Studies* 1 (Spring 1973): 34. Letters and manuscripts published recently reveal that this constraint had been largely compelled by Verne's publisher, who insisted on a pedagogical background that loaded the narratives with information that often bore modern readers but also serve to make the scientific portions seem more credible. Verne's publisher compelled rewrites of *Hector Servadac* and *The Black Indies* (both 1877) to diminish the science fiction elements and rejected

outright *Paris in the 20th Century*. The stories signed by Verne that do have a futuristic quality, such as "In the Year 2889" (1889), *The Eternal Adam* (1910), and *The Astonishing Adventure of the Barsac Mission* (1914), were largely written by Jules's son, Michel, using his father's name.

2. From an interview reprinted in Brian Taves, ed., "Jules Verne's Autobiography: A Collage of Interviews," in Taves and Michaluk, *The Jules Verne Encyclopedia*, 48–49. Wells's *The First Men in the Moon* was not his only novel related to Verne; his book *The Food of the Gods* (1904) has similarities to Verne's *A Fancy of Doctor Ox* (1872), both dealing with the alterations in humankind and its environment due to changes in the chemicals the species is supplied. Most educative is the single reverse influence, Verne's *The Secret of Wilhelm Storitz*, which is partly a response to H. G. Wells's *The Invisible Man* (1897). For Verne, invisibility was impossible, and so he transformed the key concept into a gothic tale of alchemy rather than following Wells's psychological concern with how invisibility's effects lead its inventor to madness. Because of these contradictory approaches, a comparison of Wells and Verne on screen, although perhaps tempting, is ultimately impractical; moreover, Wells authored many nonscientific social dramas for which there is no counterpart in Verne.

3. *Serial Quarterly*, no. 6 (April–June 1967).

4. John S. Hamilton and Eddie Hyans play two of Nemo's crew, "Swede" and "Slay," respectively.

5. Jack Gould, "Radio and Television: A.B.C. Presents Verne's '20,000 Leagues under the Sea' on TV as 'Boy-Meets-Girl' Story," *New York Times*, February 4, 1952, 24.

6. Eric Clavering, Colin Eaton, Earl Grey, William Holland, Murray Kash, Ed McNamara, Al Pearce, and Warren Wilson were in the cast.

7. "An Interview with Harper Goff," *The "E" Ticket*, no. 14 (Winter 1992–1993): 5; Bill Warren, *Keep Watching the Skies!* vol. 1 (Jefferson, NC: McFarland, 1982), 203. See also David Hutchison, "Undersea with Harper Goff," *Starlog*, no. 31 (February 1980): 36–38, 60–61; Joel Frazer and Harry Hathorne, "20,000 Leagues under the Sea—the Filming of Jules Verne's Classic Science Fiction Novel," *Cinefantastique* 14 (May 1984): 32–53, reprinted in *Cult Movies*, nos. 34–36; David Hutchison, "Aboard the Nautilus," *Starlog Spectacular*, no. 4 (March 1992): 39–46. For the definitive history of the making of the film, see Lawrence Brooks, "The Squid That Got Away!" serialized in *Filmfax*, no. 111 (July–September 2006): 64–73; no. 112 (October–December 2006): 54–61, 102–104; and no. 113 (January–March 2007): 50–59, 100–102.

8. For an examination of the movie within this context, see J. P. Telotte, "Science Fiction as 'True-Life Adventure': Disney and the Case of *20,000 Leagues under the Sea*," *Film & History* 40 (Fall 2010): 66–79.

9. James W. Maertens, "Between Jules Verne and Walt Disney: Brains, Brawn, and Masculine Desire in *20,000 Leagues under the Sea*," *Science-Fiction Studies* 22 (July 1995): 209–225.

10. Quoted in Clive Hirschhorn, *The Films of James Mason* (Secaucus, NJ: Citadel, 1975), 27.

11. Leonard Maltin, *The Disney Films* (New York: Crown, 1973), 121.

12. Warren, *Keep Watching the Skies!* vol. 1, 199.

13. Jack Moffit, review of *20,000 Leagues under the Sea*, *Hollywood Reporter*, December 15, 1954, 3.

14. Before *20,000 Leagues under the Sea*, Disney had produced four live-action features: *Treasure Island* (1950), *The Story of Robin Hood and His Merrie Men* (1952), *Rob Roy—the Highland Rogue* (1953), and *The Sword and the Rose* (1953).

15. Tom Tumbusch, "Disney Merchandising Part 42: *20,000 Leagues under the Sea*," *Tomart's Disneyana Update*, no. 42 (Summer 2001): 42–43.

16. These publications included a novelization in the January 1955 issue of *Screen Stories* magazine, a Whitman storybook novel, and a Giant Golden Book from Simon & Schuster. Most of these volumes were reprinted for the film's 1963 re-release. Unlike the Simon & Schuster volume, which had drawings adapted from the film, in England the Dean & Son, Ltd., volume *Walt Disney's 20,000 Leagues under the Sea* included color stills from the film on nearly every page. In 1978, in the United Kingdom, Australia, Canada, and New Zealand, the New English Library/Times Mirror issued an original illustrated softcover novelization of the movie by Ann Spano. The tie-ins continue to the present: see Jeff Bond, "Toybox: Captain's Treasures," *Cinefantastique* 36 (February–March 2004): 12–13; and material related to the film is considered avidly collectible: see Justin Bilow, "Blazing through the Depths," *Autograph Collector* 16 (August 2006): 38–43.

17. For more details on the 20,000 Leagues exhibit at Disneyland, see *The "E" Ticket* 1991, 10–29.

## 4. Establishing a Mythos as the Verne Cycle Begins, 1956–1959

1. Budding filmmakers were also inspired, including twelve-year-old Nicholas Meyer, who over several years shot his own feature-length home movie version on 8 mm. He later became a successful novelist, screenwriter, and director.

2. Michael Todd Jr. and Susan McCarthy Todd, *A Valuable Property—the Life Story of Michael Todd* (New York: Arbor House, 1983), 320.

3. Ibid., 342, 346, 348.

4. For the 1968 re-release of *Around the World in 80 Days*, Michael Todd Jr. produced a fifty-minute documentary on his father's life, *Around the World of Michael Todd*, that includes abundant behind-the-scenes footage in telling the story of the making of the movie. Todd's widow, Elizabeth Taylor, provides a gracious portrait of her late husband in extensive interviews. Martin Balsam reads from Todd's own recollections, telling, for instance, how Todd had taken over the directing on the first day after John Farrow had not shot a single frame after three hours as well as how he decided to drop the initial preface to the film and create an entirely new one at considerable expense. In addition to interviews with many Todd associates, Orson Welles appropriately (considering Todd's role in Welles's own stage production) provides narration.

For a traditional account of the making of the movie, see Frederick C. Szebin, "The World on a Shoestring," *American Cinematographer* 78 (February 1997): 109–113.

5. Todd and Todd, *A Valuable Property*, 134–135, 267–268. In mid-1954, Todd bought for $100,000 the screen rights to *Around the World in 80 Days* from British producer Alexander Korda, who had negotiated detailed film rights with the Verne estate and for two decades hoped to film the novel. For Korda, a native of Hungary, Verne was his favorite author as a youth, and into adulthood he would still recall the details of the author's description of the *Nautilus* (Michael Korda, *Charmed Lives* [New York: Random House, 1979], 40–41). Korda had shot a portion of an animated feature version, *Indian Fantasy* (1939), which is now held by the National Film Archive in London.

6. Todd and Todd, *A Valuable Property*, 281.

7. A final cost of $6.3 million (Todd owning 88.2 percent of the film, which netted $25 million) is given in ibid., 319. A 1958 biography, *The Nine Lives of Michael Todd* by Art Cohn (New York: Random House), tells of the producer's exploits. Production designer Ken Adam provided further details in my interview of him, June 1991, Los Angeles.

8. Ward Morehouse, "Mike Todd, Broadway's Man in Motion," *Theatre Arts* 40 (October 1956): 19; Charlotte Bilkey Speicher, "New Films from Books," *Library Journal* 81 (November 15, 1956): 2676.

9. Todd and Todd, *A Valuable Property*, 287.

10. Ibid., 274–275.

11. For information on new discoveries about *Around the World in 80 Days* (1956), learned as a result of the cataloging of 426 reels of film on the movie donated to the Library of Congress by Elizabeth Taylor, see Brian Taves, "*80 Days:* Discoveries from a Unique Collection," *Library of Congress Information Bulletin* 55 (October 21, 1996): 388–390, which was expanded as "La Collection E. Taylor à la Bibliothèque du Congrès ou 'Le Tour du monde en 80 jours' à Washington," translated into French and annotated by Pierre Antifer, *Bulletin de la Société Jules Verne,* no. 123 (1997): 45–49; the definitive version of this essay appeared as "*80 Days:* Discoveries from a Unique Collection," *Journal of Film Preservation,* no. 56 (June 1998): 18–22.

12. Such satire was not unique, but it was a prominent element in other Verne stories, whether in the treatment of evolution in "The Humbug" and *Adventures of the Rat Family* or in the desert island formula in *The School for Robinsons.* In *A Fancy of Doctor Ox,* Verne cleverly mocks his own literary genre, with a mad scientist who fills a small town's atmosphere with more oxygen, speeding the pace of living to a frenzy, and Verne subjects Ox and many of the heroes of his more serious novels to a farcical humiliation in the play *Journey through the Impossible.*

13. Todd and Todd, *A Valuable Property*, 277. Tests for the role were shot in late September 1955, including Jacqueline Park, a former Miss Ceylon inexperienced in acting, and two actresses who had brief careers, Suzanne Alexander and Marla English. Only after deciding against all of these women did Todd

bring Shirley MacLaine in to portray Aouda; at that time she had appeared in only two movies. See Taves, "*80 Days*," *Journal of Film Preservation*, 21.

14. Miller, "Jules Verne," 596.

15. Todd and Todd, *A Valuable Property*, 319.

16. Ibid., 320.

17. Norman Carlisle and Madelyn Carlisle, "Jules Verne: Uncanny Prophet," *Coronet Magazine*, January 1950, reprinted in Jules Verne, *Five Weeks in a Balloon* (New York: Didier, 1950), n.p. Although *From the Earth to the Moon* and *Around the Moon* foresee with uncanny accuracy the motivations for the space race of the 1950s and 1960s, there are also striking technical parallels. Verne's capsule was nearly the same size, weight, and cylindroconical shape as the *Apollo* command module. His launch site, Tampa, Florida, is west of Cape Canaveral, and his space shot ends with a splashdown in the Pacific Ocean. Verne's estimate of the initial velocity necessary to escape Earth's atmosphere is almost exactly correct. His flight time is ninety-seven hours, and that of the Apollo 8 mission was only a few hours longer. Verne's astronauts experience weightlessness; they orbit at the same distance above the moon. Everything that Verne could calculate with the science of the time was correct; only the necessary guesswork revealed flaws.

18. Unidentified clipping, review file on *From the Earth to the Moon*, Warner Bros. Collection, Special Collections Library, University of Southern California, Los Angeles.

19. Tom Weaver, "First Maid in the Moon," *Starlog*, no. 249 (April 1998): 64.

20. Quoted in Joe Adamson, *Byron Haskin* (Metuchen, NJ: Scarecrow, 1984), 233.

21. A fictionalized view of Verne in a different context is given in *The Day before Tomorrow*, subtitled *The Story of the United States Army Ordnance Ballistic Research Laboratories;* I have not included a discussion of this film in the text because its date of release, by Warner Bros. in association with Filmways, has been impossible to ascertain, but it was during the late 1950s.

A typical dry narrator, Jim Thorne, begins to unfold what promises to be a dreary documentary until he mentions *From the Earth to the Moon*. Promptly interrupting is the novel's author (played by Leslie Daniels), perched on a scientific apparatus; he tells Thorne that he defies the laws of gravity. Jumping to Thorne's side, Verne denies that he wrote merely a prophetic novel. "It was no dream. Everything I have written you have accomplished—almost everything. So you see I did not dream it, merely told you how to do it! Your atomic submarine, for instance, you even named it after my *Nautilus*. Did I not foresee world travel by air?" Verne reminds Thorne that his Baltimore Gun Club was located in the same state where they now are, at the Aberdeen Proving Ground in Maryland. They make a wager—Thorne to prove there is more than Verne foresaw and Verne to provide an expenses-paid trip to the moon if anything Thorne mentions is not in his book.

DeWitt Copp's script sets up a lively exchange between the two, serving to make palatable what would otherwise be simply a propagandistic demonstration of increasingly technical weapons and means for testing them. *The Day before Tomorrow,* like other Verne films of the late 1950s, offers atomic power as making war obsolete, yet for its military purpose *The Day before Tomorrow* must argue that strength through defense is necessary to ensure there will be no war in the future. Although the direction by Nicholas Webster is otherwise routine, Daniels's heavy accent, costume, Vandyke beard, and facetious tone in his portrayal of Verne keep the pedantic portions from becoming excessively heavy-handed.

A duality is achieved between Thorne as the scientific authority and Verne as an "everyman" figure who is learning. Yet the exchange is ultimately more sophisticated, for Verne proves to be an authority in his own right, denying Thorne's belief in the inherent sophistication of modern science and reminding him of the nineteenth-century background, both scientific and fictional, of today's achievements. Verne consistently recognizes and offers variant interpretations on the usefulness and purpose of the devices shown him. There is no diminishing of the author in *The Day before Tomorrow;* through performance and scripting, it is the figure of Verne rather than the confident, didactic Thorne who is the most memorable.

By the end, Verne is encouraged by what he has seen, but it also provides further inspiration. "I have no doubt now that someday, and very soon, man will finally realize his dream, victory in the conquest of space. In fact, based on what you show me, I'll write a book, on where man will be, one hundred years from now." Verne and Thorne call their wager a draw, walking off into the distance together, uniting past and present in the future. As a rocket fires into the sky, Verne's voice offers a prophecy of his own dreams moving far beyond the present, in an echo of Captain Nemo's concluding voice-over of a hope for the future in Disney's *20,000 Leagues under the Sea.*

Because of the charismatic enactment by Daniels and the musical score that allowed Joseph D. Lamneck's production to have distribution beyond the classroom, the twenty-nine-minute color film has the largesse that is lacking in most Verne educational films. Like the Carl Esmond characterization of Verne in *From the Earth to the Moon,* Daniels's portrayal in *The Day before Tomorrow* offers a place for the author and his vision in the years to come. In *The Day before Tomorrow,* Verne has a portrayal more richly humorous and central to the unfolding diegesis, validating the timelessness of historical importance, creativity, and his literature.

22. Beyond shorter works, Verne's pure fantasy was limited to his play *Journey through the Impossible* and short stories and novelettes such as *Adventures of the Rat Family* and "Mr. Ray Sharp and Miss Me Flat" (1893) as well as to two works that crossed over the border into horror, *Master Zacharius* and "Frritt-Flacc." In novels, he only undertook to describe what were obviously impossible feats, with an extinct volcano revealing the path to the center of the earth, a comet providing interplanetary travel in *Hector Servadac,* a sea serpent emerging from the seas in *The Yarns of Jean-Marie Cabidoulin* (1901), and

an alchemist discovering invisibility in *The Secret of Wilhelm Storitz*. Even in such books, Verne cloaked these exploits with modern scientific thinking and methods, providing seemingly rational explanations with a basis in geography or science. For instance, in *The Sphinx of Ice*, Verne's sequel to Edgar Allan Poe's *Arthur Gordon Pym*, Poe's climactic white figure is explained as a gigantic sphinx-shaped lodestone at the southern magnetic pole. The strange behavior of the townspeople subject to Dr. Ox's experiment in *A Fancy of Doctor Ox* is revealed to be the product of a superoxygenated atmosphere.

23. The basic concept of journeys to the earth's interior and the discovery there of parallel worlds inspired many other imaginations in different ways, and many subsequent stories and films have told their own tales of subterranean worlds unrelated to Verne's. Indeed, this has become a recognizable theme in science fiction, but outside of the adaptations of Verne's novel it has seldom led to memorable filmmaking. Among the titles that use this concept are the serial *The Phantom Empire* (1934) and the features *The Mole People* (1956), *The Incredible Petrified World* (1960), *Journey beneath the Desert* (1961), *The Slime People* (1963), *Battle beneath the Earth* (1968), *What Waits Below* (1983), and *Tremors* (1989). Only one, *Unknown World* (1951), has some similarities to Verne's story. These films are concerned primarily with monstrous creatures or the effects of underground atomic explosions and thus have little in common with the trek Verne imagined.

24. Although the journey and the underworld discovered in *Journey to the Center of the Earth* seem distant from scientific possibility, Verne's description of the underworld was based on the latest knowledge and theories of his time, and the novel caused a stir not only for its literary properties but also for its informed scientific speculation. In the 1860s, an underground connection was proposed between Mediterranean volcanoes; another was said to stretch from Iceland to the Canary Islands, and the existence of an abyss from the North Pole all the way to the center of the earth was seriously debated. Verne would reject the idea in his own Arctic novel, *Journeys and Adventures of Captain Hatteras*, and while exploring subterranean passages in *Journey to the Center of the Earth*, he opted to fill the center with the same geography found on the surface, including volcanoes, caves, oceans, and forests.

25. For a detailed analysis and production history of the 1959 version of *Journey to the Center of the Earth*, see William Schoell, "The Making of Jules Verne's *Journey to the Center of the Earth*," *Filmfax*, no. 55 (March–April 1996): 51–57, 74. See also the film's pressbook.

26. Patrick McGilligan, ed., *Backstory 2* (Berkeley: University of California Press, 1991), 242–244.

27. Lawrence Knight, "The Journeys to the Center of the Earth," *Dakkar*, no. 1 (1968): 22.

28. Bob Rusk, "Pat Boone's *Journey to the Center of the Earth*," *The Big Reel*, May 15, 1996.

29. See also Bill Warren, *Keep Watching the Skies!* vol. 2 (Jefferson, NC: McFarland, 1986), 299.

30. L. B. Abbott, *Special Effects: Wire, Tape, and Rubber Band Style* (Hollywood: ASC Press, 1984), 74–78.

31. Evans, *Jules Verne and His Work*, 146–147.

32. Between and within each scene there are bright contrasts in colors, and distinct hues dominate different scenes. As John Goodwin pointed out in a letter to the August–September 1996 issue of *Filmfax* (no. 57, p. 76), the printing of the original theatrical release copies was carefully controlled scene by scene in the lab, whereas modern copies are printed uniformly in a manner that excessively darkens some scenes and lightens others, losing the color variations that 1959 audiences enjoyed. For instance, a viewing of an original print on the big screen reveals that the caves are filled with fireflylike lights flashing on the rocks, a nuance that vanishes in a television viewing and is only partially visible in laserdisc versions.

33. Quoted in liner notes to the album titled *The Fantasy Film World of Bernard Herrmann*, first released on vinyl in 1974 and as a CD in 1995.

34. These reissues of *Journey to the Center of the Earth* are commercial not print-on-demand editions. See Taves and Michaluk, *The Jules Verne Encyclopedia*, 106–110, and subsequent bibliographic updates.

35. The reissued novels were *Five Weeks in a Balloon, Journey to the Center of the Earth, From the Earth to the Moon and Around the Moon, In Search of the Castaways, Twenty Thousand Leagues under the Sea, Around the World in Eighty Days, Dr. Ox's Experiment, The Mysterious Island, Hector Servadac, Michael Strogoff, The Clipper of the Clouds, A Long Vacation, The Purchase of the North Pole,* and *Master of the World.*

36. These titles were perpetuated purely due to the Fitzroy edition: *A Floating City, The Blockade Runners, Measuring a Meridian, The Fur Country, The Chancellor, Black Diamonds, The Begum's Fortune, The Tribulations of a Chinese Gentleman, The Steam House, The Green Ray, The School for Crusoes, The Flight to France, Salvage from the Cynthia, North against South, Family without a Name, Carpathian Castle, For the Flag, The Mystery of Arthur Gordon Pym,* and *The Hunt for the Meteor.* Nine appeared for the first time in English: *The Village in the Treetops, The Sea Serpent, A Drama in Livonia, The Golden Volcano, The Thompson Travel Agency, The Danube Pilot, The Survivors of the Jonathan, The Secret of Wilhelm Storitz,* and *The Astonishing Adventure of the Barsac Mission.*

Unfortunately, for uniform books to be issued in the Fitzroy edition, many of Verne's longer works were divided into two volumes, which is confusing to readers and collectors, and in other cases I. O. Evans literally slashed longer novels into single-volume length. And there was more: as a man who proudly touted the initials of the Royal Geographical Society after his name, Evans brought his own nationalistic and religious sentiments to his task. He usually cut descriptive passages and deleted sections he found personally unappealing or offensive. For further analysis, see Brian Taves, "'Verne's Best Friend and His Worst Enemy': I. O. Evans and the Fitzroy Edition of Jules Verne," *Verniana* 4 (2011–2012): 25–54.

37. Dick Williams, "New Film Vogue Is Jules Verne," *Los Angeles Mirror View*, May 27, 1961, part 3, pp. 1, 4. See also P. Schuyler Miller, "The Reference Library: Verne on Wide Screen," *Astounding/Analog Science Fact and Fiction* 68 (November 1961): 160–164.

## 5. The Height of the Verne Cycle, 1960–1962

1. Verne's grandson Jean Jules-Verne wrote an original novelization of *Le Triomphe de Michel Strogoff*, adapted from the scenario by Marc-Gilbert Sauvajon; the book was published in Paris by Hachette in 1967 in the Bibliothèque Verte series, which at the time reprinted most of Verne's novels in newly illustrated and often condensed form.

2. Don Keefer, Jesslyn Fax, Vito Scotti, and Henry Beckman guest-starred on "Death Is a Red Rose."

3. The episode "Red Rose" was first heard on the March 2, 1951, broadcast of *Richard Diamond—Private Detective*, starring Dick Powell.

4. *Master Zacharius*, among Verne's earliest published works, had gone beyond fantasy to be one of his relatively few stories crossing over into horror, along with such mature efforts as "Frritt-Flacc," *The Castle in the Carpathians*, and *The Secret of Wilhelm Storitz*, all of which have been filmed in Europe.

5. Quoted in "Further Comment," in William Johnson, ed., *Focus on the Science Fiction Film* (Englewood Cliffs, NJ: Prentice-Hall, 1972), 160. See also Jeff Rovin, *From the Land beyond Beyond* (New York: Berkley, 1977); John Brunas, "*Mysterious Island*," *Scarlet Street*, no. 23 (1996): 43–44; Howard Roller, "The Films of Ray Harryhausen," *The Perfect Vision* (Winter 1992): 118–123; Ted Bohus, "An Interview with Effects Wizard Ray Harryhausen," *SPFX*, no. 3 (1995): 5–11; Ted Newsom, "When Harryhausen Ruled the Earth," *Imagi-Movies* 2 (Spring 1995): 14–28, 61; Matthew R. Bradley, "Ray Harryhausen: Now and Then," *Filmfax*, no. 52 (September–October 1995): 50–57, 74; Ray Harryhausen and Tony Dalton, *Ray Harryhausen—an Animated Life* (New York: Billboard, 2003); Ray Harryhausen and Tony Dalton, *The Art of Ray Harryhausen* (New York: Billboard, 2006); Ray Harryhausen and Tony Dalton, *Ray Harryhausen's Fantasy Scrapbook* (London: Aurum, 2011). Further background is provided in Harryhausen's commentary in supplements on video releases of *Mysterious Island*.

6. In publicity, Jackson pointed out that *Mysterious Island* was unique for treating Neb no differently from the other castaways, never mentioning race or color in the script, which was usually considered essential at the time to justify the presence of an African American in the cast.

7. Andre Winandy, "The Twilight Zone: Imagination and Reality in Jules Verne's 'Strange Journeys,'" *Yale French Studies* 43 (November 1969): 99.

8. Verne's comments on Poe's story appear in his 1864 article "Edgard [*sic*] Poe et ses œuvres" (Edgar Poe and his work), which has been excerpted several times but only fully translated by I. O. Evans in *The Edgar Allan Poe Scrapbook*, edited by Peter Haining for Schocken Books in 1978.

Verne had intended to provide a more natural explanation and climax for Gallia's journey, with the comet slamming directly into the Caspian Sea, the consequences of which are not environmental but monetary—the comet proves to be made largely of gold—rendering the mineral plentiful forever. Verne's publisher compelled a rewrite of the climax to give dreamlike overtones reminiscent of Cyrano's voyage to the moon. The characters' joint experiences—all apparently susceptible to confirmation and proof—were explained as a vague dream. Yet the absurdity of this new ending is obvious because all the castaways had the same dream, and their friends back on Earth have noted their long absence. This dissonant ending mystified generations of readers until the discovery of Verne's original manuscript in 1986.

As a result of the interference, when Verne decided to write another fanciful story of travel in outer space, he evaded his publisher's constraints by writing it as a stage play, *Journey through the Impossible.* After his editor's death, Verne would expand the premise of the suppressed conclusion of *Hector Servadac* in one of his last novels, *The Hunt for the Meteor,* published posthumously in 1908. Here, Verne sought to explore the international ramifications of what might happen if an extraterrestrial object composed of the very metal most valued were to collide with Earth.

9. Zimbalist sold the concept to New York executives by promising that any cost overruns on the deal would come out of the producer's fees (Edward Bernds to Brian Taves, letter, June 30, 1994).

10. Ibid.

11. This Zeman film was *Cesta do praveku* (variously translated as: A journey into the primeval ages / A trip into primeval times / Journey into prehistory), made in 1955. The film, loosely inspired by *Journey to the Center of the Earth,* was released in the United States as *Journey to the Beginning of Time* and in England as *Voyage to Prehistory* in a version partially reshot to provide an American setting and child actors.

Despite a more lavish budget, Zeman's third Verne film, *Ukradena vzducholod / I Ragazzi del Capitano Nemo / The Stolen Airship / Captain Nemo's Children* (Czechoslovakia/Italy, 1967), was not released in the United States; it was based on *The Mysterious Island* and *Two Year Holiday.*

12. "Valley of the Dragons," *Variety* 224 (November 22, 1961): 6.

13. Warren, *Keep Watching the Skies!* vol. 2, 592–595. Warren offers the conventional disparaging interpretation of *Valley of the Dragons.*

14. Jules Verne, *Robur-le-conquérant* (Paris: Librairie Hachette, 1966), 246–247. This passage provides a typical example of the problems with existing Verne translations; neither of the two that have been published provide a complete or accurate translation, so this crucial passage as given here was specially translated by Evelyn Copeland. See *The Clipper of the Clouds* (London: Sampson Low, Marston & Co., n.d.), 176, and *A Trip around the World in a Flying Machine* (Chicago: M. A. Donohue, 1887), 180.

15. Jules Verne, *The Master of the World* (Philadelphia: J. B. Lippincott, n.d.), 158–159.

16. The status of *In the Year 2889* always was murky; at times it was announced as derived not from Verne but from H. G. Wells's *When the Sleeper Wakes* (1910). Roger Corman was to film *In the Year 2889* in Japan in early 1959, but it was not until the middle of that year that George Worthing Yates was signed to script it. In 1967, when deciding to remake an earlier AIP film and release it direct to television, a new title was needed. Since AIP had already registered *In the Year 2889,* this title was given to the new film, although it had nothing in common with the Verne story.

17. Matthew R. Bradley, *Richard Matheson on Screen: A History of the Filmed Works* (Jefferson, NC: McFarland, 2010), 89; Charles Beaumont, "The Science Screen," *Magazine of Fantasy and Science Fiction,* June 1957, 80.

18. Jim Hollifield, "Fly by Night, David Frankham Interviewed," *Scarlet Street,* no. 48 (2003): 47, 66.

19. William Witney in Tom Weaver, *Monsters, Mutants, and Heavenly Creatures* (Arlington, VA: Midnight Marquee, 1996), 279–281.

20. William Witney, phone interview by Brian Taves, June 1, 1992.

21. Richard Matheson to Brian Taves, letter, May 6, 1989.

22. When Bronson emerged as a superstar in Europe, his casting allowed *Master of the World* to have multiple reissues there, and he was both listed in credits and visually represented as the star over Vincent Price; it was Bronson who in advertising became the "master of the world."

23. Douglas Menville and R. Reginald, *Things to Come* (New York: Times Books, 1977), 120.

24. James Powers, "*Master* Fine Adventure," *Hollywood Reporter,* April 26, 1961, 3.

25. Witney, interviewed by Taves.

26. Ibid.

27. Ibid.

28. Powers, "*Master* Fine Adventure." In 2009, Intrada Signature Editions issued an exemplary CD containing not only the original soundtrack recording, with music played by the 100 Men with Cal Carter conducting for Varese Sarabande, but also the rediscovered original stereo music from Baxter's original sessions. Hearing the two back to back allows an understanding of two very different interpretations of the score. The CD also includes the two songs, the romantic "Master of the World" and the waltz-style "Come Dance with Me," that were ultimately cut from the film but that had been intended for radio play.

29. Warren, *Keep Watching the Skies!* vol. 2, 566.

30. Witney, interviewed by Taves.

31. Vincent Price, "Mean, Moody, and Magnificent," *Films and Filming* 11 (March 1965): 7.

32. Kenneth Allott, *Jules Verne* (New York: Macmillan, 1941), 138.

33. Paul Nathan, "Rights and Permissions," *Publishers' Weekly,* August 7, 1961, 52.

34. The spaceship in Irwin Allen's television series *Lost in Space* (1964–

1967) would be named the *Jupiter II* because it was the second time Allen had given this name to a vehicle in one of his productions.

35. The payment was 350,000 French francs (Société des Gens de Lettres de France, represented by Robert Dupuy, October 10, 1958, Motion Picture and Television file, Centre d'études verniennes de Nantes).

36. Ironically, Pocket Books used the faulty "Hardwigg" translation, and in England a Digit Royal paperback reprinted the Bradley translation—demonstrating the lack of coordination among publisher and movie producer, so that the film used approximations of the names Verne actually gave his character. In 1973, Scholastic Book Services issued *Journey to the Center of the Earth,* an abridged and edited version of the "Hardwigg" translation in conjunction with television showings of the movie.

37. Quoted in Murray Schumach, "Hollywood Mines the Gold in Verne," *New York Times,* February 3, 1961, 15.

## 6. The Cycle Changes, 1963–1971

1. In fact, although *Around the Moon* is dependent on *From the Earth to the Moon,* and the two books are generally discussed jointly, *From the Earth to the Moon* is able to stand on its own from a literary standpoint. It is quite possible to read *From the Earth to the Moon* not as the first part of the story of a lunar journey that it ultimately became, but as an open-ended novel, which it was for the first five years after its publication. By its close, the ambition of humankind has been thwarted, and the Baltimore Gun Club has failed in its aim, instead creating yet another satellite—no less than when Herr Schultz in *The Five Hundred Millions of the Begum* seeks the destruction of Franceville, but his missile instead becomes a satellite, too. In *From the Earth to the Moon,* the Gun Club's reach exceeds its grasp, just as it will again in the ultimate volume of the trilogy, *Topsy-turvy.* In this context, the seemingly sudden "surprise ending" apparently offered in *From the Earth to the Moon* may be sufficient and inevitable. The implied death of all the protagonists (despite the hopes held by Maston, who has been foolish throughout the novel) is Verne's experiment with a downbeat, dystopian ending. Hence, regarding *From the Earth to the Moon* as incomplete without a sequel is an incorrect reading; a sequel was possible but certainly not essential, any more than *The Mysterious Island* was required to resolve the open strands of *Twenty Thousand Leagues under the Seas* and *The Children of Captain Grant.*

2. Christopher Koetting, interview with Don Sharp, "Taste for Excitement," *Filmfax,* no. 65 (February–March 1998): 122. A 364-page novelization by Jim Fagan was published in paperback in 1967 by Horwitz in Australia and New Zealand, entitled *Rocket to the Moon.*

3. Barnum's introduction into an adaptation of the Verne story was not as incompatible with the source as it might seem because Verne himself included a brief passage in *From the Earth to the Moon* in which Barnum tries to enlist Ardan in his traveling show, a prospect the Frenchman quickly declines. Indeed,

the idea for this aspect of the movie may have sprung from the 1960 reprint of the 1874 Edward Roth translation of Verne's moon novels, in which Roth, in a demonstration of the outlandish behavior often exhibited by Verne translators, expanded Verne's two-sentence reference into a whole paragraph. Assuming Verne's authorial voice, Roth suggests an entire new possibility for Barnum, along with a political sentiment: "The Prince of Humbugs was withal so genial, so plausible, so insinuating that Ardan, finding it impossible to get angry with him, promised to accede to his demands on the return of the party from the Moon, if he, Barnum, would only join them in the trip. But the genial showman, knowing what a serious loss even his temporary absence would prove to the progress of the great Temperance movement in the United States, hastily declined the offer with many thanks, and started that very night for New York" (*From the Earth to the Moon, All Around the Moon: Space Novels by Jules Verne, Translated by Edward Roth* [New York: Dover, 1962], 164). Whatever complaints may be made by critics of Hollywood's Verne, the films' changes to Verne's stories cannot rival the liberties taken by the translators.

4. Tom Kelly, "Journey to the Center of the Earth," *Epi-log*, no. 25 (December 1992): 94–98.

5. The Big Little Books volume, adapted by Paul S. Newman and subtitled *The Fiery Foe*, tells how Saknussemm traps the Lindenbrook party in the realm of a strange underground race.

6. Fred MacMurray was initially approached for the role of Captain Nemo, which would have changed Nemo's persona entirely, considering MacMurray's recent work as the comedic scientist in Disney's "Flubber" films in 1961 and 1963 as well as his paterfamilias role in the television series *My Three Sons* (1960–1972).

7. I. O. Evans, "Introduction," in Jules Verne, *The Southern Star Mystery* (Westport, CT: Associated Booksellers, 1966), 8.

8. For *The Wreck of the Cynthia*, Grousset was credited with his pseudonym "André Laurie." Fluent in English, Grousset was often engaged in translations and wrote adventure as well as a series of pioneering science fiction novels. Such topics as interplanetary travel and undersea exploration are included in *The Conquest of the Moon* (1889), *New York to Brest in Seven Hours* (1890), *The Crystal City under the Sea* (1896), and *The Secret of the Magian; or, The Mystery of Ecbatana* (1897).

9. The book had been filmed by Michel Verne as a 1918 feature under its original title, *L'Étoile du sud*. Michel had practical experience of mining and had authored his own novel of Africa, *The Astonishing Adventure of the Barsac Mission*, incorporating his father's ideas and publishing it under the paternal name.

10. "Film Being Shot in Africa," *Chicago Daily Defender*, May 8, 1968, 13.

11. The music for *The Southern Star* was also issued on a soundtrack album and single.

12. "Filmland Events: Hardy Kruger Signs for New Verne Film," *Los Angeles Times*, November 24, 1962, B3; Jan Read, *Young Man in Movieland* (Lan-

ham, MD: Scarecrow, 2004), 135; Kirk Douglas, *The Ragman's Son* (New York: Simon and Schuster, 1988), 409–413.

## 7. Toward a New Aesthetic, 1972–1979

1. Among the vocal talents were Carl Banas, Len Birman, Bernard Cowan, Peg Dixon, Keith Hamshere, Peggi Loder, Donna Mills, Frank Perry, Henry Raymer, Ellie Mae Ricardis, Alfie Scoppk, and Paul Soles.

2. George W. Woolery, *Children's Television: The First Thirty-Five Years, 1946–1981*, part I: *Animated Cartoon Series* (Metuchen, NJ: Scarecrow, 1984), 25, 67–68.

3. H. G. Wells was hardly the only immediate successor to Verne; Sir Arthur Conan Doyle, who learned French through reading Verne, also acquired a reputation for early science fiction directly influenced by Verne. Two of his Professor Challenger stories, *The Lost World* and "When the World Screamed" (1928), resemble portions of *Journey to the Center of the Earth*. Another Challenger novel, *The Poison Belt* (1913), is reminiscent of *A Fancy of Doctor Ox*, and both "Danger!" (1914) and *The Maracot Deep* (1929) recall *Twenty Thousand Leagues under the Seas*. *The Lost World* was also extraordinarily similar to Verne's *The Aerial Village*. Both *The Lost World* and *The Aerial Village* relate expeditions that follow an earlier discovery of the survival of ancient life forms in the globe's remote regions (a South American plateau and a giant forest in Africa, respectively). Although dinosaurs are the most memorable part of *The Lost World*, more of the narrative is actually taken up with the competition between different tribes of early men and ape-men; a "missing link"–type species is also the subject of *The Aerial Village*.

4. Juan Piquer Simón to Brian Taves, letter, December 12, 1998.

5. Andres Berenguer, "The Adventure of Photographing Jules Verne's *Fabulous Journey to the Center of the Earth*," *American Cinematographer* 58 (December 1977): 1294–1295, 1308–1309.

6. Piquer Simón to Taves.

7. Ibid.

8. This rather adept variation preserves Hakkabut's occupation and ethnicity while changing his nature completely; in the book, the character is a miser, written in this way as a result of the author's anger over a widespread rumor at the time claiming he was not French but a Polish Jew. For a discussion of this issue in Verne's writing, particularly in connection to its only other major appearance, see Daniel Compère's introduction to Verne, *Bandits & Rebels*, 12–15.

## 8. The Wandering Trail, 1981–1993

1. Piquer Simón to Taves.

2. Peter Besas, "'Monster Island' Helps Revive Old Spanish Lensing Location," *Variety* 300 (August 8, 1980): 39–40; *Daily Variety* 188 (August 7, 1980): 8; Christopher Gullo, *In All Sincerity, Peter Cushing* (N.p.: Xlibris, 2004), 313.

3. Allusions to the *Nautilus* are also found in the film *Dream One*, also known as *Nemo* (1984), which references Captain Nemo along with Zorro, Alice in Wonderland, and others. A neglected boy named Nemo (also a homage to the comic-strip character Little Nemo) disappears during a dream in which he imagines himself leaving home via an elevator, descending to another planet, where he finds the *Nautilus* rusting and abandoned, half-covered with sand on a beach, a monkey its sole survivor. Only because *Dream One* shows the submarine with the interior dimensions as Verne imagined does it have any relevance to Verne. With its title character portrayed as a child by Seth Kibel and as a teenager by Jason Connery, the fantasy fails to create the intended low-budget, Munchausen-style sense of magic. Producers of the ninety-seven-minute movie, never released in the United States, were John Boorman and Claude Nedjar, with Arnaud Selignac directing a script on which he collaborated with Jean-Pierre Esquenazi and Telshe Boorman.

4. The voices of Colin Borgoron, Wallas Eaton, Ross Higgins, Scott Higgins, Juliette Jordan, and Keith Scott are used.

5. *Around the World in 80 Days* placed twenty-fourth among programs and fourth among specials for the week, with a 15.5 percent share of the audience for the opening; the remaining episodes did worse.

6. Quoted in Pat H. Broeske, "The Brosnan Conundrum," *Los Angeles Times Calendar*, April 16, 1989, 3.

7. Verne had also discussed Poe's ciphers in "Edgard Poe et ses œuvres."

8. For instance, I made this point in a 1991 telephone conversation with an editor for William Morrow, which had just issued a new edition of *Around the World in Eighty Days* using the Towle translation, with illustrations by Barry Moser. The editor did not recognize that one more edition of this book in a market already glutted with the same title would have inherently limited success, nor did he perceive the potential in a Verne title for which there was less competition. Among science fiction specialists, the situation was little different; for instance, TOR books reissued the Lewis Mercier version of *Twenty Thousand Leagues under the Sea* in 1995, a mass-market paperback that remains in print nearly twenty years later. Publisher Donald Wollheim (1914–1990) did express interest in Verne beyond the three main titles, as he indicated in correspondence with me. During this period, authoring *The Jules Verne Encyclopedia* and searching for a publisher for the first translation of *Adventures of the Rat Family* allowed me such firsthand experience of the commercial situation.

## 9. The Revival, 1993–1996

1. Andrew Martin also authored *The Knowledge of Ignorance: From Genesis to Jules Verne* (Cambridge: Cambridge University Press, 1985), devoted in part to Verne.

2. After Stephen Michaluk Jr. and I turned our Verne encyclopedia manuscript in to Scarecrow Press in 1993, publication was delayed for three years, to 1996, because of the company's sale to Rowman & Littlefield.

3. For more on *Paris in the 20th Century* and its publication and translation, see Brian Taves, "Review-Essays: Jules Verne's *Paris and the Twentieth Century*," *Science-Fiction Studies* 24 (March 1997): 133–138, with a definitive, expanded version in the scholarship section of the Jules Verne website at http://jv.gilead.org.il/sfs/taves.71.html.

4. The website is found at http://jv.gilead.org.il.

5. For an examination of the worst (Tantor) and best (Blackstone) audiobooks to be found, see, respectively, my articles in the North American Jules Verne Society's newsletter *Extraordinary Voyages* 16 (September 2009): 12, and 15 (December 2008): 15.

6. For a similar review of this and other recent documentary programs on Verne, together with a complete list of all stage, radio, movie, and television works about Verne from all countries up to that time, see Brian Taves, "Les Récentes émissions documentaires sur Jules Verne à la télévision," translated into French by Jean-Michel Margot, *Bulletin de la Société Jules Verne*, no. 125 (1998): 44–52.

7. The *Wishbone* episode "Hot Diggety Dawg" had echoes in two publications. In November 1996, HarperPaperbacks issued an edition of *A Journey to the Center of the Earth* in the Wishbone Classics series. Although tied in with "Hot Diggety Dawg," the 136-page book (by Billy Aronson) actually retold the original Verne story rather than the *Wishbone* episode. A separate tie-in was published in March 1999 by Big Red Chair Books as *Digging to the Center of the Earth*, no. 17 in the Adventures of Wishbone series. This text was by Michael Anthony Steele (one of the episode's prop men), based on the teleplay by Jack Wesley, which was "inspired by" the Verne novel.

8. For a more extensive analysis of *Space Strikers* in French, see Brian Taves, "Nemo, Héros Galactique?" translated into French by Jean-Michel Margot, *Bulletin de la Société Jules Verne*, no. 119 (1996): 6.

## 10. Telefilms and Miniseries Reign, 1997–1999

1. Cited in Andrew Rogulich to Brian Taves, email, September 11, 1996.

2. Quoted in Dan Scapperotti, "*20,000 Leagues under the Sea:* Director Rod Hardy and ABC Bring Jules Verne's Classic Novel to Life," *Cinefantastique* 28 (May 1997): 50. See also the remarks by the executive producer, Richard Pierce, in James Sterngold, "Television: Down to the Sea—Again and Again," *New York Times*, March 23, 1997, H31.

3. Quoted in Scapperotti, "*20,000 Leagues under the Sea*," 50.

4. Quoted in Jay Bobbin, "Jules Verne's Classic Tale '20,000 Leagues under the Sea' Airs on ABC," *TV Times* (*Washington Times*), May 11–17, 1997, T1.

5. Quoted in publicity on the ABC website at http://abc.com/pp/c03.htm, accessed May 5, 1997.

6. Quoted in Scapperotti, "*20,000 Leagues under the Sea*," 50–51.

7. Quoted in Scott Moore, "'20,000 Leagues': Former Local Teacher Pens Script," *TV Week—District of Columbia* (*Washington Post*), May 11–17, 1997, 56.

8. A plan to sink sensors into the ocean floor as earthquake-warning devices was included in *Around the World under the Sea,* a 1966 feature that had no relation to Verne other than the attempt to evoke him in the title.

9. Quoted in publicity on the ABC website at http://abc.com/pp/c03.htm, accessed May 5, 1997.

10. Quoted in Bobbin, "Jules Verne's Classic Tale," T1.

11. Ian Spelling, "The Man Who Would Be Nemo," *Starlog,* no. 239 (June 1997): 27.

12. No contemporaneous sources have been located to confirm the making of this supposed Biograph production, only listings in modern books.

13. Cited in Susan King, "Jules in the Network's Crowns," *TV Times* (*Los Angeles Times*), March 23–29, 1997, 4.

14. Quoted in Frederick Szebin, "*20,000 Leagues under the Sea:* Verne's Classic Tale Updated for CBS," *Cinefantastique* 28 (March 1997): 9, 62.

15. Quoted in King, "Jules in the Network's Crowns," 4.

16. Halmi quoted in ibid.; Anderson quoted in Szebin, "*20,000 Leagues under the Sea,*" 8.

17. Quoted in King, "Jules in the Network's Crowns," 4.

18. Ibid.

19. Robert P. Laurence, "Cover Story: A P.C. Trip for the *Nautilus,* with Love, Kisses, and Women's Formal Wear," *TV Week* (*San Diego Union-Tribune*), March 23–29, 1997, 6.

20. Quoted in Szebin, "*20,000 Leagues under the Sea,*" 9.

21. Quoted in Scapperotti, "*20,000 Leagues under the Sea,*" 51.

22. The conclusion features a reprise of the song "20,000 Leagues under the Sea" (composed by Tom Harriman) and highlights of the entire voyage in the fashion of a music video. The song had first been sung over the dinner table as Nemo introduced Pierre, Beth, and Ned to the strange dishes derived from the deep. Another, "You Gotta Believe" (composed by Matthias Weber), also shot in music video style, is sung aboard the deck of the *Abraham Lincoln,* featuring the first encounter between Pierre and Ned and their respective devotion to science and imagination. Both songs had lyrics by Pamela Phillips Oland.

23. Further suggesting the change was a recent television movie entitled *Journey to the Center of the Earth,* which had even less relation to the novel than the 1980s Cannon movies, returning to the idea of a vehicle carrying travelers to the destination; it was broadcast on NBC as a possible pilot on February 28, 1993.

24. The background here comes from the publicity and articles on the USA Network's *Journey to the Center of the Earth,* located from Internet searches on September 8, 1999.

25. A German-Russian-US-Canadian film of *The Children of Captain Grant* was made in 1996 but apparently had no American release and in fact was little seen anywhere. Donovan Scott directed, coscripted (with Paul Nicholas), and costarred, with Artur Brauner producing the coproduction for CCC-Filmkunst and Genre Films. The cast also included Cassie Branham, Chris

Browning, Adam Gregor, and Ralph Rieckermann, with a running time of 115 minutes. There were many changes; the setting is 1850, and in the wake of Captain Grant's disappearance Robert and Mary have to work for a cruel farmer. The message they discover in a shark reveals that Grant was taken prisoner of war by the Russians. They find him just in time to save him from the hangman's noose.

26. Michael Helms, "Fighting for Science," *Sci Fi Teen*, no. 8 (November 1999): 18; Tony Wright, "Sentimental Journey," *Sci Fi Entertainment* 6 (October 1999): 57–58.

27. Quoted in Wright, "Sentimental Journey," 58.

28. During the production of the USA *Journey to the Center of the Earth*, two new films of *The Lost World* were made, one a pilot for a television series shot in New Zealand, so certainly the ideas from the Conan Doyle novel were very much "in the air."

29. Although the competition for survival amid different species representing humanity at various stages is the major theme of *The Lost World*—emphasizing primitive men, modern natives, and technological man—it is, ironically, seldom explored in films taken from the novel.

30. Helms, "Fighting for Science," 15.

31. *Journey to the Center of the Earth,* issued for Kensington Publishing, used the translation renaming the professor "Von Hardwigg." Golden Books published at least five *Crayola Kids*–related book items, including an "Explore Oceanography" workbook by Keith J. Suranna; a first-act playbook, also by Suranna; a "first chapter book" (relating the adaptation in detail by Francine Hughes and noted as based on Verne's tale); and a book filled with stills from the film, adapted by Justine Korman. There was also a set of fifty-four "Creatures of the Sea Riddle Me" cards from Golden Books.

## 11. Biography or Pastiche, 2000–2003

1. Greg Douglas, "Journey to the Center of Rick Wakeman's Mind," *Outré,* no. 18 (1889): 62–66, 80.

2. There were less commercially significant works in this vein at the time. Other graphic novels include *Voyage into the Deep: The Saga of Jules Verne and Captain Nemo* (2005), the comic book series *The Remarkable Worlds of Professor Phileas B. Fuddle* (2000), and the manga-style *Captain Nemo* by Jason De Angelis and Aldin Viray (2006). Other novels included *The Nautilus Journal* (2000), *Africa in a Balloon: Encounters with Jules Verne* (2004), *Nautilus: A Sequel to Jules Verne's Twenty Thousand Leagues under the Seas and The Mysterious Island* (2009), *Steampunk Holmes: Legacy of the Nautilus* (2012), and T. E. MacArthur's ongoing series on the Volcano Lady (2011–) and the Gaslight Adventures of Tom Turner (2013–). Verne also appears as a character in two 2013 pastiches involving the Baker Street detective, *Sherlock Holmes and the Crater Lake Adventure* and *Sherlock Holmes and the Knave of Hearts.*

3. Quoted in "LXG: The Extraordinary Truth," *Empire*, no. 225 (March 2008): 122.

4. Wesleyan published *The Invasion of the Sea, The Mysterious Island, The Mighty Orinoco, The Begum's Millions, The Kip Brothers,* and *Travel Scholarships.* After *Journey through the Impossible* in 2003, the North American Jules Verne Society began the Palik Series, which was named for a donor and which I edit. All of the Verne Society's stories and plays are ones that had never before appeared in English and offer scholarly commentary. The titles include *The Marriage of a Marquis, Shipwrecked Family: Marooned with Uncle Robinson, Mr. Chimp, and Other Plays,* and *The Count of Chanteleine: A Tale of the French Revolution* in 2011; *Vice, Redemption, and the Distant Colony* in 2012; *Around the World in 80 Days—the 1874 Play* and *Bandits & Rebels* in 2013; *Golden Danube* in 2014; *A Priest in 1835* in 2015; with *Castles in California* and additional volumes in preparation. All of these books prominently feature the original or vintage nineteenth-century covers and engravings from the French first editions and the actual persons or places depicted.

## 12. Dismal Reiterations, 2004–2008

1. Philippe Burgaud, with Jean-Michel Margot and Brian Taves, "Introduction," in Verne and d'Ennery, *Around the World in 80 Days—the 1874 Play.*

2. Jackie Chan in Todd Gilchrist, "Interview: European Comedy and Asian Action Come Together for an American Adaptation of Jules Verne," SciFi.com, http://www.scifi.com/sfw/issue374/interview2.html, accessed August 23, 2004. In fact, the book has been translated into Chinese on multiple occasions, per "Jules Verne's Work in Many Languages," http://verne.garmtdevries.nl/en/languages/work.cgi, accessed June 2, 2012. *The Tribulations of a Chinese in China* has also appeared in that language, and Chan's talents would certainly have been far better suited to a film of that novel.

3. Although the play has been filmed in Europe, Hollywood has never consulted the stage version, which only came back into print for the first time since the 1870s in the original translation commissioned by the Kiralfy Brothers with the 2013 publication of Verne and d'Ennery, *Around the World in 80 Days—the 1874 Play.* The play apparently has not been performed in the English-speaking world since the late nineteenth century, with adaptations by others taking the place of the Verne–d'Ennery stage version in public memory.

4. Quoted in "Coraci Re-Imagines 80 Days," *Sci Fi Wire,* June 15, 2004, http://www.scifi.com, accessed September 2, 2004.

5. In Gilchrist, "Interview."

6. Quoted in "'World' Updates Verne," *Sci Fi Wire,* October 10, 2002, http://www.scifi.com, accessed October 15, 2002.

7. In Gilchrist, "Interview." See also Bill Florence, "Once More around the World," *Starlog,* no. 324 (July 2004): 52–56.

8. William Arnold, "'Around the World in 80 Days' Is a Bad Trip," *Seattle Post Intelligencer,* June 17, 2004, page number unavailable.

9. Ibid.

10. The name "Cyrus Smith" is a fusion of the first name of Cyrus Field, the American who installed the Atlantic cable using the *Great Eastern*—the vessel on which Verne had traveled across the Atlantic to visit the United States, chronicled in his novel *A Floating City* —and a surname that comes from the word *blacksmith*.

11. A Verne enthusiast, Sidney Kravitz, undertook his own independent translation of *The Mysterious Island* in the early 1990s. Ironically, when it was finally published in a critical edition by Wesleyan University Press, Random House had commissioned its own by Jordan Stump. Kravitz also translated Verne's own first draft of *The Mysterious Island,* titled *Shipwrecked Family: Marooned with Uncle Robinson,* for its publication in 2011 by BearManor Fiction in conjunction with the North American Jules Verne Society.

12. Will Murray, "Life on *Mysterious Island,*" *Starlog,* no. 339 (October 2005): 18–31.

13. Director's audio commentary on DVD release, *30,000 Leagues under the Sea* (The Asylum, 2007).

14. This type of esoteric interpretation goes back to the 1960s and was explored by Alfred Renoux and Robert Chotard in four books and a booklet: *Tel que c'était prévu* (As it was planned), *Le grand test secret de Jules Verne* (The great, secret test of Jules Verne), *Jules Verne le divin magicien* (Jules Verne the holy magician), *De Jules Verne aux extra-terrestres* (From Jules Verne to the aliens), and *Comment Jules Verne vient de tracer dans l'espace et le temps le destin de l'homme avec Apollo 8 et les Soyouz 4 et 5* (How Jules Verne draws in space and time the destiny of mankind with Apollo 8 and Soyuz 4 and 5). Michel Lamy's familiarity with the secondary literature about Verne and his tack of suggesting Verne's active participation in the occult milieu of late-nineteenth-century France appealed to the popular desire to find secret elements in established icons.

15. For more on *The Mighty Orinoco,* see Brian Taves, "Adventures on the Orinoco," *Extraordinary Voyages* 15 (March 2009): 11–12, and *1888—The Extraordinary Voyage of Jules Verne* is examined in Taves, "Expedition into a Novel."

## 13. A New Formulation, 2008–Present

1. Titles beyond the canon given modern treatment have included *The Star of the South* and *A Fancy of Dr. Ox* in 2003, *The Adventures of Captain Hatteras* and *The Begum's Millions* in 2005, *Mathias Sandorf* in 2007, *The Castle in Transylvania* in 2010, *The Sphinx of the Ice Realm* in 2012, *Underground City* in 2005, *The Green Ray* in 2009, and *The Blockade Runners* in 2011 (the latter three from a Scottish publisher).

2. Regrettably, the reviews given on Amazon.com, which ought to be a prime opportunity for heightening public awareness, fail to distinguish between different editions of the same title. To try to make up for this lack of accurate

information, the North American Jules Verne Society created a page with members' reviews of various editions at http://www.najvs.org/works/index.shtml.

3. Joe Nazzaro, "To the Ends of the Earth," *Starlog*, no. 367 (July 2008): 11–13.

4. Resa Nelson, "Caving In," *SciFi* 14 (August 2008): 50–52.

5. The constant mention of Verne in the diegesis of *Journey to the Center of the Earth 3D* and the showing of the book and the original Édouard Riou engravings in the visuals provide ample tribute to the author; a conventional "based on" note would have been redundant.

6. Nelson, "Caving In," 50–52.

7. Michael Odorna, "Brendan Fraser Stands Tall with 'Journey to the Center of the Earth,'" *Los Angeles Times*, July 13, 2008, page number unavailable.

8. Quoted in "Journey to the Center of Brendan Fraser," *Life Story: Movie Magic* 2008, 87.

9. Perhaps the greatest sigh of relief among Anglophone Verne aficionados was when the characters refer to Verne's prescient hero as Professor Lidenbrock; fortunately, no one dragged in the misbegotten but endlessly reprinted translation changing the character's name to "Von Hardwigg" and his nephew Axel's name to "Harry." The names are only the tip-off to the constant changes, highlighted by the addition of more monsters than Verne imagined. Brevig revealed to convention-goers that he was familiar with the translation issues and the problems and had referred to a modern edition.

10. Alasdair Morton and Joseph Rugg, "Viva la Revolución," *SciFiNow*, no. 16 (2008): 20–25.

11. THQ issued a video game version for Nintendo DS, and the book *Journey to the Center of the Earth 3D: Choose Your Own Journey—the Search for Earth's Surface*, adapted by Justine and Ron Fontes, has a similar interactive style. Tracey West adapted a children's novelization, and E. Mason re-created a scrapbook-style *Journal from the Center of the Earth* told from Sean's perspective. There were also movie photo books, including one in 3D form; all were paperbacks published by Price Stern Sloan.

12. See the *Journey to the Center of the Earth 3D* website at http://www.journey3dmovie.com.

13. Quoted in Ian Spelling, "Brendan Fraser and Company Add an Extra Dimension to Jules Verne in *Journey to the Center of the Earth* in 3-D," SciFi.com, http://www.scifi.com/sfw/interviews/sfw19086.html, accessed August 1, 2008.

14. The treehouse is another extratextual homage to a different group of castaways outside of Verne and featured in Johann Wyss's *Swiss Family Robinson*, the 1960 Disney film of that book, and the subsequent Disney theme park attraction—which was then appropriated for a different hero in the wake of Disney's *Tarzan* (1999) adaptation.

15. Erin Willar, "TV Review: Jules Vernes *Mysterious Island*," SciFi.com, February 10, 2012, http://scifimafia.com/2012/02/tv-review-jules-vernes-mysterious-island/, accessed March 11, 2012.

16. "Syfy's 'Jules Verne's Mysterious Island' Becomes Second Straight Saturday Original Movie to Break Two Million Total Viewers Mark," February 14, 2012, http://www.julesvernesmysteriousisland.com/scheduled-air-times, accessed March 11, 2012.

17. Christina Radish, "Mark Sheppard Talks Directing and Starring in Syfy Adaptation of Jules Verne's *Mysterious Island,*" *Collider,* http://collider.com/mark-sheppard-mysterious-island-interview/144519/?awesm=fbshare.me_AgFuY&utm_campaign=&utm_medium=fbshare.me-facebook-post&utm_source=facebook.com&utm_content=fbshare-js-small, accessed March 11, 2012; Facebook postings on February 11–12, 2012, pleaded the budget limitation at http://www.facebook.com/groups/107701753929/?ref=ts#!/groups/107701753929/.

18. For an overview of Verne in video games, see "Jogos baseados na obra de J. Verne," *Blog em Português de Homenagem a J. Verne (1828–1905),* July 7, 2011, http://jvernept.blogspot.pt/2011/07/jogos-baseados-na-obra-de-j-verne.html, accessed March 13, 2013. During this time, there was also an authorized sequel to *Mysterious Island* (1961) in the Ray Harryhausen comic books series, with several installments of *Back to Mysterious Island* in 2007.

19. For the ride at Tokyo DisneySea, see http://www.tokyodisneyresort.co.jp/tds/english/7port/mysterious/atrc_center.html, accessed August 1, 2008.

20. Director Brevig, an award-winning special-effects artist, is also widely experienced in designing Disney theme park attractions. He said, "I wanted the film to be like the best day in an amusement park you've ever had" (quoted in *"Journey to the Center of the Earth* 3-D," *Life Story: Movie Magic* 2008, 47–48). The "ride" element is not new; *Twenty Thousand Leagues under the Seas* has been manifested in the Disney parks in Anaheim, Orlando, Paris, and Tokyo. Disney's *In Search of the Castaways* in 1962 also had a ride aboard a rock sled through ice caves suggestive of an unrealized theme park offshoot. (The Disney company has considered producing a version of *Journey to the Center of the Earth* over the years but has yet to do so.)

21. The other volumes were *Lighthouse at the End of the World, The Meteor Hunt, The Secret of Wilhelm Storitz, Magellania,* and *Golden Danube.*

22. The previous publication of *The Golden Volcano* was in 1962 as a two-volume edition in the Fitzroy series of Michel's rewrite as *The Claim on Forty Mile Creek* and *Flood and Flame,* obscuring the overall title.

23. Because Verne "filled his novels with intertextual allusions to his own stories . . . many of the 'Extraordinary Journeys' share common elements and lend themselves quite well to amalgamation, at least in a cinematographic format" (Volker Dehs, "Introduction," translated by Matthew Brauer, in Jules Verne, *Travel Scholarships* [Middletown, CT: Wesleyan University Press, 2013], xxviii).

24. "Foreign Box Office: 'Journey 2' Limps to Fourth Straight No. 1 Victory Overseas," *Hollywood Reporter,* March 4, 2012, http://www.hollywoodreporter.com/news/foreign-box-office-lorax-journey-2-this-means-war-artist-296747, accessed May 19, 2012.

## Epilogue

1. Quoted in King, "Jules in the Network's Crowns," 4.
2. Quoted in Schumach, "Hollywood Mines the Gold in Verne," 15.

# Selected Bibliography

Allott, Kenneth. *Jules Verne*. New York: Macmillan, 1941.

An American in Paris. "Jules Verne Today." *Boston Transcript,* February 11, 1905, page unavailable.

Apslund, Uno. *Jules Vernes Underbara Resor*. Uddevalla, Sweden: Bohuslän Grafiska, 1973.

Barker, Barbara, ed. *Bolossy Kiralfy, Creator of Great Musical Spectacles—an Autobiography*. Ann Arbor: UMI Research Press, 1988.

Barthes, Roland. *Mythologies*. Selected and translated by Annette Lavers. New York: Hill and Wang, 1972.

Baxter, John. *Science Fiction in the Cinema*. New York: Paperback Library, 1970.

Belloc, Marie A. "Jules Verne at Home." *Strand Magazine* 9 (February 1895): 206–213.

Bennett, Charles. "The Jules Verne Influence on *Voyage to the Bottom of the Sea* and *Five Weeks in a Balloon*." In Danny Peary, ed., *Omni's Screen Flights/Screen Fantasies*, 120–123. Garden City, NY: Doubleday, 1984.

Bingham, Jane M., ed. *Writers for Children*. New York: Scribner's, 1988.

Bleiler, E. F. *Science Fiction Writers*. New York: Scribner's, 1982.

"Books and Plays in Pictures." *The Moving Picture World,* July 17, 1915, 196.

Brisson, Adolphe. *Portraits intimes*. Paris: Armand Colin, 1899. See pp. 111–120.

Burgaud, Phillipe. "Les avatars du *Michel Strogoff* de Joseph N. Ermolieff." *Verniana* 7 (in press).

———. "*Cinq Semaines en ballon* en film." *Bulletin de la Société Jules Verne* 184 (December 2013): 30–37.

Burgess, Thomas. *Take Me under the Sea: The Dream Merchants of the Deep*. Salem, OR: Ocean Archives, 1994.

Butcher, William. *Jules Verne: The Definitive Biography*. New York: Thunder's Mouth Press, 2006.

———. *Verne's Journey to the Centre of the Self*. London: Macmillan, 1990.

Butor, Michel. *Inventory*. Translated and edited by Richard Howard. New York: Simon and Schuster, 1960.

Chesneaux, Jean. *The Political and Social Ideas of Jules Verne*. Translated by Thomas Wikeley. London: Thames and Hudson, 1972.

Cline, William C. *In the Nick of Time: Motion Picture Sound Serials.* Jefferson, NC: McFarland, 1984.

Compère, Daniel. "Filmographie des oeuvres de Jules Verne" and "Compleménts à la filmographie." *Bulletin de la Société Jules Verne* 12 (1969): 82–84; 16 (1970): 177; 21 (1972): 123. Later updated and issued together as the pamphlet *Filmographie de Jules Verne par Daniel Compère.* Amiens, France: Centre du documentation Jules Verne, 1978.

———. *Jules Verne: Parcours d'une oeuvre.* Amiens, France: Encrage, 1996.

Compère, Daniel, and Jean-Michel Margot. *Entretiens avec Jules Verne.* Geneva: Slatkine, 1998.

Costello, Peter. *Jules Verne, Inventor of Science Fiction.* New York: Scribner's, 1978.

Dami, Aldo. "Responsabilité du cinéaste." *Trente Jours,* November 29, 1988, 34.

Dawbarn, Charles. "The Prophecies of Romance." *Pall Mall Magazine* 33 (May 1904): 107–110. Reprinted as "Jules Verne at Amiens." *Review of Reviews* 30 (July 1904): 73.

Dehs, Volker. *Jules Verne.* Reinbeck bei Hamburg, Germany: Rowohlt, 1986.

———. *Jules Verne: Eine kritische Biographie.* Düsseldorf, Germany: Artemis & Winkler, 2005.

Dekiss, Jean-Paul. *Jules Verne: Le Rêve du progrès.* Paris: Gallimard, 1991.

Demerliac, Jean. *L'Odyssée Jules Verne.* Paris: Editions Albin Michel, 2005.

Dumas, Olivier. *Jules Verne.* Lyon: La Manufacture, 1988.

Dumas, Olivier, Volker Dehs, and Piero Gondolo della Riva, eds. *Correspondance inédite de Jules et Michel Verne avec l'éditeur Louis-Jules Hetzel (1886–1914).* Geneva: Slatkine, 2004–2006.

Dumas, Olivier, Piero Gondolo della Riva, and Volker Dehs, eds. *Correspondance inédite de Jules Verne et de Pierre-Jules Hetzel (1863–1886).* Geneva: Slatkine, 1999–2002.

Edelson, Edward. *Visions of Tomorrow.* Garden City, NY: Doubleday, 1975. See pp. 15–21.

Edwards, Phil. "The Films of Jules Verne." *Starburst,* no. 21 (1980): 50–55.

Erickson, Hal. *Television Cartoon Shows.* Jefferson, NC: McFarland, 1995.

Evans, Arthur B. *Jules Verne Rediscovered: Didacticism and the Scientific Novel.* New York: Greenwood Press, 1988.

Evans, I. O. *Jules Verne and His Work.* New York: Twayne, 1966.

———. "Jules Verne et le lecteur Anglais." *Bulletin de la Société Jules Verne,* April–June 1968, 3–6.

———. *Science Fiction through the Ages I.* London: Panther, 1966.

Fisher, Margery. *The Bright Face of Danger.* Boston: Horn Book, 1986.

Frank, Allen. *The Science Fiction and Fantasy Film Handbook.* Gotowa, NJ: Barnes and Noble, 1982. See pp. 174–175, 181.

Fraser, George MacDonald. *The Hollywood History of the World.* New York: Morrow, 1988.

Freedman, Russell. *Jules Verne: Portrait of a Prophet*. New York: Holiday House, 1965.

Fritze, Christoph, Georg Seesslen, and Claudius Weill. *Der Abenteurer: Geschicte und Mythologie des Abenteuer*. Reinbek bei Hamburg: Rowohlt Taschenbuch Verlag GmbH, 1983.

Fuzellier, Etienne. "Une mine de scénarios." *L'Education*, no. 343 (February 9, 1978): 33–34.

Gallagher, Edward J., Judith A. Mistichelli, and John A. Van Eerde. *Jules Verne: A Primary and Secondary Bibliography*. Boston: G. K. Hall, 1980.

Gires, Pierre, and Hervé Dumont. "Jules Verne et le cinéma." *L'Ecran fantastique*, no. 9 (1979): 58–109.

Gove, Philip Babcock. *The Imaginary Voyage in Prose Fiction*. New York: Columbia University Press, 1941.

*Grand Album Jules Verne*. Paris: Hachette, 1982.

Green, Martin. *Dreams of Adventure, Deeds of Empire*. London: Routledge and Kegan Paul, 1979.

———. *The Robinson Crusoe Story*. University Park: Pennsylvania State University Press, 1990.

———. *Seven Types of Adventure Tale*. University Park: Pennsylvania State University Press, 1991.

Guerlac, Othon. "Prolific Jules Verne." *New York*, June 28, 1902, 477.

Hahn, Ronald M., and Hans-Joachim Neumann. "Das Abenteuer auf Leinwand und Bildschirm—Jules Verne in film und Fernsehen" and "Filmographie." In Heinrich Pleticha, ed., *Jules Verne Handbuch*, 279–298. Stuttgart: Bertelsmann Clubb, 1992.

Haining, Peter. *The Edgar Allan Poe Scrapbook*. New York: Schocken, 1978.

———. *The Jules Verne Companion*. New York: Baronet, 1979.

Hardy, Phil, ed. *The Film Encyclopedia—Science Fiction*. New York: William Morrow, 1984.

Helling, Cornelis. "L'oeuvre de Jules Verne." *Bulletin de la Société Jules Verne*, no. 1 (November 1935): 15–21.

Hirschhorn, Clive. *The Films of James Mason*. Secaucus, NJ: Citadel, 1975.

Hobana, Ian. "Ocolul galaxiei intr-o ora si jumatate." *Cinema* (Bucharest) 1985, 94–96.

———. "Un Ve nic tân r cineast." *Cinema* (Bucharest) 1978, 126–129.

"James Mason Interview." *Focus on Film*, no. 2 (March–April 1970): 29–30.

"Jogos baseados na obra de J. Verne." *Blog em Português de Homenagem a J. Verne (1828–1905)*, July 7, 2011, http://jvernept.blogspot.pt/2011/07/jogos-baseados-na-obra-de-j-verne.html. Accessed March 1, 2013.

Johnson, William, ed. *Focus on the Science Fiction Film*. Englewood Cliffs, NJ: Prentice-Hall, 1972.

Jones, Gordon. "Jules Verne at Home." *Temple Bar* 129 (June 1904): 664–671. Reprinted anonymously as "Jules Verne on Himself and Others." *American Monthly Review of Reviews* 30 (July 1904): 112.

Jones, William B., Jr. *Classics Illustrated—a Cultural History*. 2nd ed. Jefferson, NC: McFarland, 2011.

———. "From *Michael Strogoff* to *Tigers and Traitors*—The *Extraordinary Voyages* of Jules Verne in *Classics Illustrated*." *Verniana* 4 (2011–2012): 67–92.

"Jules Verne as His Own Hero." *Variety* 220 (September 28, 1960): 1, 78.

"A Jules Verne Centenary." Special issue of *Science Fiction Studies* 32 (March 2005).

"Jules Verne: Une mine pour les cinéastes." *L'Union,* February 7, 1978, page unknown.

Jules-Verne, Jean. *Jules Verne: A Biography*. Translated and adapted by Roger Greaves. New York: Taplinger, 1976.

Lacassin, Francis, ed. *Jules Verne: Histoires inattendues*. Paris: Union Générale d'Éditions, 1982.

Lahue, Kalton C. *Continued Next Week: A History of the Moving Picture Serial*. Norman: University of Oklahoma Press, 1964.

Lengrand, Claude. *Dictionnaire des "Voyages Extraordinaires" de Jules Verne*. Amiens, France: Encrage, 1997.

Lottman, Herbert R. *Jules Verne: An Exploratory Biography*. New York: St. Martin's, 1996.

Lowndes, Marie Belloc. "Jules Verne: A Reminiscence." *The Academy* 68 (April 1, 1905): 363–364.

Luce, Stanford L., Jr. "Jules Verne: Moralist, Writer, Scientist." PhD diss., Columbia University, 1953.

Lynch, Lawrence. *Jules Verne*. New York: Twayne, 1992.

Macherey, Pierre. *A Theory of Literary Production*. Translated by Geoffrey Wall. London: Routledge and Kegan Paul, 1978.

Maltin, Leonard. *The Disney Films*. New York: Crown, 1973.

Margot, Jean-Michel. *Bibliographie documentaire sur Jules Verne*. Amiens, France: Centre du documentation Jules Verne, 1989. Additional updates supplied by Margot.

———. *Jules Verne en son temps*. Amiens, France: Encrage, 2004.

Martin, Andrew. *The Knowledge of Ignorance: From Genesis to Jules Verne*. Cambridge: Cambridge University Press, 1985.

———. *The Mask of the Prophet: The Extraordinary Fictions of Jules Verne*. Oxford: Clarendon Press, 1990.

Martin, Charles-Noël. *Jules Verne, sa vie et son oeuvre*. Lausanne, Switzerland: Rencontre, 1971.

Marx, Adrien. "Introduction." In Jules Verne, *Around the World in 80 Days*, xi–xvi. Philadelphia: Porter & Coates, 1873.

Mellot, Philippe, and Jean-Marie Embs. *Le Guide Jules Verne*. Paris: L'Amateur, 2005.

Menville, Douglas, and R. Reginald. *Things to Come*. New York: Times Books, 1977.

Miller, Marion Mills. "Jules Verne." In Jules Verne, *The Best Novels of Jules Verne: From the Earth to the Moon*, iii–vii. New York: Collier, 1905.

Miller, P. Schuyler. "The Reference Library: Verne on Wide Screen." *Astounding/Analog Science Fact and Fiction* 68 (November 1961): 160–164.

Miller, Ron. *Extraordinary Voyages: A Reader's Companion to the Works of Jules Verne*. King George, VA: Black Cat Press, 2006.

———. "Jules Verne: The Silent Era." *Filmfax*, no. 50 (May–June 1995): 40–44.

Miller, Walter James. *The Annotated Jules Verne: From the Earth to the Moon*. Updated ed. New York: Gramercy/Random House, 1995.

———. *The Annotated Jules Verne: Twenty Thousand Leagues under the Sea*. New York: Thomas Y. Crowell, 1976.

"M. Jules Verne at Home." *Pall Mall Gazette* 33 (September 17, 1883): 1–2. Excerpted as "How Jules Verne Writes His Books." *Frank Leslie's Illustrated Newspaper* 57 (October 27, 1883): 155.

Moré, Marcel. *Le Très curieux Jules Verne*. Paris: NRF, 1960.

Naha, Ed. "The Films of Jules Verne." *Future*, no. 3 (July 1978): 34–39, 47.

North American Jules Verne Society. "Bibliographic Note to Publishers and Translators on Works by Jules Verne Not Published in the United States." In "Work to Be Done," http://www.najvs.org/work2bdone.htm. Accessed May 25, 2007.

O'Driscoll, Kieran. *Retranslation through the Centuries: Jules Verne in English*. Oxford: Peter Lang, 2011.

Park, A. J. "'Chums' Visits Jules Verne." *Chums* 2 (August 20, 1902): 7.

Parrinder, Patrick, ed. *Science Fiction: A Critical Guide*. London: Longman, 1979.

Pohl, Frederik, and Frederik Pohl IV. *Science Fiction: Studies in Film*. New York: Ace, 1981. See pp. 125–130.

Poivre d'Arvor, Olivier, and Patrick Poivre d'Arvor. *Le monde selon Jules Verne*. Paris: Mengès, 2005.

Pourvoyeur, Robert. "Jules Verne et le théâtre." In Jules Verne, *Clovis Dardentor* (coll. *10/18*, no. 1308, série *Jules Verne inattendu*), 5–30. Paris: Union Générale d'Éditions, 1979.

Prédal, René. *Le Cinema fantastique*. Paris: Editions Seghers, 1970. See pp. 206–208.

Rebierre, Jean-Roger. "Les romans de Jules Verne que vous aimez: Une mine inépuisable de scénarios de films." *Tribune de Genève*, December 11, 1963, 1.

Renzi, Thomas. *H. G. Wells: Six Scientific Romances Adapted for Film*. 2nd ed. Lanham, MD: Scarecrow, 2004.

———. *Jules Verne on Film: A Filmography of the Cinematic Adaptations of His Works, 1902 through 1997*. Jefferson, NC: McFarland, 1998.

Roberdeau, Thomas. *Michael Strogoff—a Screenplay*. With an introduction by Paul Schmidt. Los Angeles: Sun & Moon Press, 1995.

Robida, Albert. *The Adventures of Saturnin Farandoul*. Translated by Brian Stableford. Tarzana, CA: Black Coat Press, 2009.

Roger-Naudin, Gilles. *Jules Verne filmographie Europe*. Paris: privately published, 1996.

Rogers, Tom. "Captain Nemo: 1907–1978." *Space Wars* 2 (August 1978): 28–33, 59–60.

Rovin, Jeff. *The Fabulous Fantasy Films*. New York: A. S. Barnes, 1977. See pp. 172–176.

Ruddick, Nicholas. "Nellie Bly, Jules Verne, and the World on the Threshold of the American Age." *Canadian Review of American Studies* 29, no. 1 (1999): 1–11.

Saariste, Rein. *Jules Verne—Voyages Extraordinaires—Op Film*. N.p.: Jules Verne Genootschap, 2004.

Sadoul, Georges. "Notes sur Jules Verne et le Cinema." *Europe* 33 (April–May 1955): 99–103.

Schiltz, Françoise. *The Future Revisited: Jules Verne on Screen in 1950s America*. London: Chaplin, 2011.

Schumach, Murray. "Hollywood Mines the Gold in Verne." *New York Times*, February 3, 1961, 15.

Sherard, Robert H. [Sherard, R. H.]. "Jules Verne at Home." *Pall Mall Gazette* 49 (December 10, 1889): 3. Reprinted as "Jules Verne's Home Life," *New York Times*, December 22, 1889, 16.

———. "Jules Verne at Home: His Own Account of His Life and Work." *McClure's Magazine*, January 1894. Reprinted anonymously as "How Jules Verne Lives and Works." *Review of Reviews* 9 (February 1894): 217–218.

———. "Jules Verne Re-visited." *T. P.'s Weekly*, October 9, 1903, 589.

Shingler, Joseph. "Horror from the Video Crypt: 'Les Voyages Extraordinaires'—the Fantasy Film World of Jules Verne." *Movie Collector's World*, no. 285 (March 4, 1988): 1, 34–36.

Skotak, Robert. "The Fabulous World of Karel Zeman." *Fantascene*, no. 3 (1977): 24–32.

Slusser, George E., Colin Greenland, and Eric S. Rabkin, eds. *Storm Warnings: Science Fiction Confronts the Future*. Carbondale: Southern Illinois University Press, 1987.

Smith, Don G. *H. G. Wells on Film: The Utopian Nightmare*. Jefferson, NC: McFarland, 2010.

Smyth, Edmund J., ed. *Jules Verne: Narratives of Modernity*. Liverpool: Liverpool University Press, 2000.

Stedman, Raymond William. *The Serials: Suspense and Drama by Installment*. 2d ed. Norman: University of Oklahoma Press, 1977.

Sterngold, James. "Television: Down to the Sea—Again and Again." *New York Times*, March 23, 1997, H31.

Strick, Philip. *Science Fiction Movies*. London: Octopus, 1976.

Sweeney, Kevin. *James Mason: A Bio-bibliography*. Westport, CT: Greenwood, 1999. See pp. 25, 28, 137–138, 146–147, 252–253.

Tarrieu, Alexandre. "Le tour des Etats–unis en 14 romans et 3 nouvelles." *Revue Jules Verne* 15 (2003): 11–22.

Taves, Brian. *The Romance of Adventure: The Genre of Historical Adventure Movies*. Jackson: University of Mississippi Press, 1993.

Taves, Brian, and Stephen Michaluk Jr. *The Jules Verne Encyclopedia*. Lanham, MD: Scarecrow Press, 1996.

Tompkins, Eugene, and Quincy Kilby. *The History of the Boston Theatre, 1854–1901*. Boston: Houghton Mifflin, 1908. See pp. 283–292.

"Topics of the Time: Jules Verne's New Story." *Scribner's Monthly* 7 (April 1874): 755.

"Two Stories by Jules Verne." *Supplement to the Spectator* 79 (November 6, 1897): 624.

Unwin, Timothy. *Jules Verne: Journeys in Writing*. Liverpool: Liverpool University Press, 2005.

Verne, Jules. "The Story of My Boyhood." *Youth's Companion*, April 9, 1891, 221.

Vierne, Simone. *Jules Verne et le roman initiatique*. Paris: Sirac, 1973.

Waltz, George H. *Jules Verne: The Biography of an Imagination*. New York: Henry Holt, 1943.

Warren, Bill. *Keep Watching the Skies!* Vol. 1. Jefferson, NC: McFarland, 1982.

———. *Keep Watching the Skies!* Vol. 2. Jefferson, NC: McFarland, 1986.

Weissenberg, Eric. *Jules Verne: Un Univers fabuleu*. Lausanne: Favre, 2004.

Wells, H. G. Preface to *Seven Famous Novels*, n.p. New York: Knopf, 1934.

Williams, Dick. "New Film Vogue Is Jules Verne." *Los Angeles Mirror View*, May 27, 1961, part 3, pp. 1, 4.

Williamson, J. E. *Twenty Years under the Sea*. Boston: Hale, Cushman & Flint, 1936.

Wilmeth, Don B. *The Cambridge Guide to American Theatre*. New York: Cambridge University Press, 2007.

Woolery, George W. *Children's Television: The First Thirty-Five Years, 1946–1981*. Part I, *Animated Cartoon Series*. Metuchen, NJ: Scarecrow, 1984.

Zvi Har'El's Jules Verne Collection. At http://jv.gilead.org.il/.

Zweig, Paul. *The Adventurer*. Princeton, NJ: Princeton University Press, 1974.

*Rather than include a bibliography of Verne's works here, I point the reader to the critical editions published since 1992 by Oxford University Press, Wesleyan University Press, University of Nebraska Press, and BearManor Fiction (the latter in conjunction with the North American Jules Verne Society), all of which are invaluable both for their translations and for their scholarly material.*

# Index

*Unless otherwise noted, the novels, short stories, and plays listed below are by Jules Verne.*

SCREEN CLASSICS

Screen Classics is a series of critical biographies, film histories, and analytical studies focusing on neglected filmmakers and important screen artists and subjects from the era of silent cinema to the golden age of Hollywood to the international generation of today. Books in the Screen Classics series are intended for scholars and general readers alike. The contributing authors are established figures in their respective fields. This series also serves the purpose of advancing scholarship on film personalities and themes with ties to Kentucky.

SERIES EDITOR
Patrick McGilligan

BOOKS IN THE SERIES

*Mae Murray: The Girl with the Bee-Stung Lips*
    Michael G. Ankerich
*Hedy Lamarr: The Most Beautiful Woman in Film*
    Ruth Barton
*Rex Ingram: Visionary Director of the Silent Screen*
    Ruth Barton
*Von Sternberg*
    John Baxter
*Hitchcock's Partner in Suspense: The Life of Screenwriter Charles Bennett*
    Charles Bennett, edited by John Charles Bennett
*Ziegfeld and His Follies: A Biography of Broadway's Greatest Producer*
    Cynthia Brideson and Sara Brideson
*The Marxist and the Movies: A Biography of Paul Jarrico*
    Larry Ceplair
*Dalton Trumbo: Blacklisted Hollywood Radical*
    Larry Ceplair and Christopher Trumbo
*Warren Oates: A Wild Life*
    Susan Compo
*Crane: Sex, Celebrity, and My Father's Unsolved Murder*
    Robert Crane and Christopher Fryer
*Jack Nicholson: The Early Years*
    Robert Crane and Christopher Fryer
*Being Hal Ashby: Life of a Hollywood Rebel*
    Nick Dawson
*Bruce Dern: An Unrepentant Memoir*
    Bruce Dern with Christopher Fryer and Robert Crane
*Intrepid Laughter: Preston Sturges and the Movies*
    Andrew Dickos

CPSIA information can be obtained at www.ICGtesting.com
Printed in the USA
BVOW03*0747100415

395553BV00002B/2/P